D0914924

READING

for

MY LIFE

READING

for

MY LIFE

WRITINGS, 1958–2008

John Leonard

Edited by Sue Leonard

VIKING

VIKING
Published by the Penguin Group
Penguin Group (USA) Inc., 375 Hudson Street, New York, New York 10014, U.S.A.
Penguin Group (Canada), 90 Eglinton Avenue East, Suite 700, Toronto, Ontario, Canada M4P 2Y3
(a division of Pearson Penguin Canada Inc.)
Penguin Books Ltd, 80 Strand, London WC2R 0RL, England
Penguin Ireland, 25 St Stephen's Green, Dublin 2, Ireland (a division of Penguin Books Ltd)
Penguin Books Australia Ltd, 250 Camberwell Road, Camberwell, Victoria 3124, Australia
(a division of Pearson Australia Group Pty Ltd)
Penguin Books India Pvt Ltd, 11 Community Centre, Panchsheel Park, New Delhi – 110 017, India
Penguin Group (NZ), 67 Apollo Drive, Rosedale, Auckland 0632, New Zealand
(a division of Pearson New Zealand Ltd)
Penguin Books (South Africa) (Pty) Ltd, 24 Sturdee Avenue, Rosebank, Johannesburg 2196,
South Africa

Penguin Books Ltd, Registered Offices: 80 Strand, London WC2R 0RL, England

First published in 2012 by Viking Penguin, a member of Penguin Group (USA) Inc.

1 3 5 7 9 10 8 6 4 2

LIBRARY OF CONGRESS CATALOGING-IN-PUBLICATION DATA
Leonard, John, 1939-2008.
Reading for my life : writings, 1958-2008 / John Leonard ; edited by Sue Leonard.
p. cm.
ISBN 978-0-670-02308-0
I. Leonard, Sue, 1938- II. Title.
PS3562.E56R43 2012
814'.54—dc23   2011039564

Printed in the United States of America
Designed by Nancy Resnick

ALWAYS LEARNING   PEARSON

For Oscar, Eli, and Tiana
to help them remember
the grandest of all grandpas;
he loved you very much

Contents

Introduction

by E. L. Doctorow

John Leonard started out as a novelist but was diverted, presumably under the exigencies of making a living, his brilliance as a freelance writer being quickly recognized by editors and publishers, so that he found himself at a precocious age writing first for the *National Review*, then as daily book reviewer of the *New York Times* and quickly then as editor of the *Times Book Review*. Perhaps he recognized about himself that his creativity was not of the burrowing kind of the novelist, who lives patiently for years with a set of images and torturously realized intentions in the production of a novel. He was from the beginning a quick study, a wunderkind, writing even as a nineteen-year-old sophomore for the *Harvard Crimson* these already typically referential Leonardian lines from a piece he called "The Cambridge Scene": "Did not Eliot return to dead cultures, ancient languages, and the Legend of the Fisher King? Did not Yeats sustain himself on the Irish folklore? Did not Lawrence traipse across continents to Mexico, seeking the meaning of the Aztecs, the wisdom of primitive man? . . . Yours is a motel civilization . . . Your art makes no sense and your music is too loud." No wonder that he abandoned Harvard for the University of California at Berkeley. But in the Cold War fifties, he was to touch down in New York, and his youthful longing for whatever came before, whether the authenticity of folklore or the romantic radicalism of fin de siècle Greenwich Village ("There used to be a time when John Reed and Lincoln Steffens lived at the same Village address . . . No more. The Village today is populated by the smug, the self-conscious, and the literary sycophants"), was, in a sense, the young man's common enough generalized anxiety of influence—his fear that he and his era could never match the grand human proportions of what had been previously conceived. Or was it what he imagined had been conceived—his idealistic sense of a human greatness that he could never attribute to what he found in the world around him? He would all his life be an avowed skeptic but with a religious sensibility that would make of him a celebrant of the moments when he did glimpse something of the full expression of human capacity. And perhaps, in a kind of quest, he was to wade right in, immersing himself totally in what imaginative work his life and times had to offer. He does grow up in the pages of this volume, his idealism reconfigured as a very sharp, keen wit that can with authority assess books and ideas for what they are.

If you consider this collection of John Leonard's essays and reviews as a lifelong accounting, you will have a good idea of what went on of significance in the latter half of the American twentieth century and the first years of the twenty-first. For though this collection is called *Reading for My Life,* and though reviewing literary work was John Leonard's calling, it did not box him in. He was a born freelance, going wherever that tenuous life led him, from the monuments of high culture that he was inspired to celebrate, to the commodities of the low, from which he would take gleanings where most of us would find none. It is difficult to understand how, with his immense reading, and the sustenance his mind sought, he could have sat himself down year after year to examine the products of television. Yet here he is, considering what it meant when sitcom settings moved from the kitchen to the living room, and the family characters sitting on the living room couch, and presumably watching their television, seemed to be watching him. Or here he is, considering what these programs said about fatherhood and motherhood in America. He understood the presumptive sociology in the arrays of sitcoms and to what degree they reflected American domestic reality or in fact helped to shape it.

But the novel was to John Leonard the presiding art—always in its intentions, if only occasionally in its realization, a major act of the culture. He says in the piece that gives title to this volume, "[P]opular culture is where we go to talk to and agree with one another; to simplify ourselves; to find our herd. . . . Whereas books are where we go alone to complicate ourselves." He is an excited first responder when the work is García Márquez's *One Hundred Years of Solitude.* "You emerge from this marvelous novel as if from a dream, the mind on fire. . . . So richly realized are the Buendías that they invite comparison with the Karamazovs and Sartorises. . . ." One book reminding him of another is a Leonardian characteristic, as if books are antiphonal calls and responses. It is in his most exultant reviews that his words tumble forth in catalogues of ascription, as he tries to convey as much of the book as he can short of quoting the thing in its entirety: "Family chronicle, then, and political tour de force, and metaphysical romp, and, intentionally, a cathedral of words, perceptions, and details," he says of the García Márquez, "[amounting] to the declaration of a state of mind: solitude being one's admission of one's own mortality and one's discovery that the terrible apprehension is itself mortal, dies with you, must be rediscovered and forgotten again, endlessly."

The great English critic Frank Kermode has said that every piece of literary criticism rewrites the text that it examines. Less dogmatically expressed, this is the idea that a work is not completed until the reader animates the text, as if the lines of a novel are a printed circuit through which the force of the reader's own life will flow. And so, not just the critic, but every reader rewrites the text, and the rewrite is a measure of the reader's mind. Leonard with his mind of swift moving synaptically fired thoughts, so that his sentences seem to race along and sometimes pile up in their effort to stay abreast, will usually find the expanded possibilities of a text. But it is not only his capacious mind that distinguishes him, it is the wisdom of his critical decency. When he attends to someone's work, there is not only illumination but a beneficence of spirit, as if, even when he doesn't like something and will tell us why, he is still at work championing the literary project.

Of course some writers do arouse his sporting nature, Norman Mailer for one, a writer for whom he has a considerable, if not blind, regard and whose novel *Harlot's Ghost* is examined in the closest thing to a forensic review you ever will read. On another occasion Leonard reviewed a late Mailer work, *The Spooky Art: Some Thoughts on Writing* (not included in this collection), taking it down quietly, gently, and in parentheses.

MAILER: "That is one of the better tests of the acumen of the writer: How subtle, how full of nuance, how original, is his or her sense of the sinister?"

LEONARD: ("George Eliot? Chekhov? Stendhal?")

MAILER: "Few good writers come out of prison. Incarceration, I think, can destroy a man's ability to write."

LEONARD: ("Cervantes, Dostoyevsky, Rimbaud, Koestler, Genet, Havel, Solzhenitsyn.")

MAILER: "It is not only that no other man writes so well about women [as D. H. Lawrence] but indeed is there a woman who can?"

LEONARD: ("If not Doris Lessing, Nadine Gordimer, Grace Paley, Toni Morrison, or Colette, how about Murasaki Shikibu?")

For he can be very funny, his prose skimming along with a breeziness, every page filled with wordplay—cross-cultural allusions, puns, over-reaching metaphors, phrases stolen from German metaphysics, lines from movies, double entendres, political riffs, as if to persuade us that, as serious as the critical enterprise might be, we are not to worry, no solemn self-importance is to be found here, that he is of the street, that if he'd been back in Elizabethan times, watching a Shakespeare play at the Globe, he'd be standing in the pit.

John Leonard was a political animal, and he waded into the social and cultural battles of the day, always pleased to have a forum but never mincing his words by way of holding on to it. He is not kind to the media—*People, Newsweek,* the *Wall Street Journal, Cosmopolitan*—for their buffoon-like coverage of the AIDs epidemic, the racism implicit in their reporting, the prissy misinformation they spread. Speaking of the Iranian *fatwa* or contract out for Salman Rushdie, author of the *The Satanic Verses,* he scorns the book chains that won't sell the book, the Catholic and Jewish religious figures who deplore its publication, and those of Rushdie's fellow writers who demand that it be pulped. Of Richard Nixon's *Six Crises* he says, "Nixon has nothing to offer this nation but the cheap sort of second-rate sainthood he is here busy trying to manufacture." And he functions as a droll chorus to Bob Dylan's tactically cunning ascent to musical stardom in the 1960s, titling his review of books about the singer "Blowing His Nose in the Wind."

Finally what we realize from the intense life in these pages is that John Leonard held back nothing, neither hiding behind a formal diction, nor modulating the demeanor he carried to every piece in deference to the publication running it. In the realm of cultural journalism there was no one quite like him. He gave everything he was, each time out. That is why in this volume we have his mind still thinking, his voice still alive.

There was something of a religious about John Leonard, however much of a principled skeptic he may have been. With his pale complexion, his round eyeglasses, there was a translucence to him such as is given to the spiritually employed. It was as if he had been assigned, somewhere off the earth, to take note of writers and to testify to their value and was, willy-nilly, a patron saint of the writing trade, of the story makers, of the grub street international bunch of us. With his love of language and his faith in its relevance to human salvation, our own inadvertent, secular humanist patron saint.

Reading for My Life

In 1947, a young American and a middle-aged Japanese climbed a tower in Tokyo to look at the bombed temple and the burned-out plain of the Asakusa. The twenty-three-year-old American, in U.S. Army PX jacket, was the critic Donald Richie. The forty-eight-year-old Japanese, wearing a kimono and a fedora, was the novelist Kawabata. Kawabata spoke no English; Richie, no Japanese, and their interpreter stayed home, sick in bed with a cold. And so they talked in writers. That is, Richie said, "André Gide." Kawabata thought about it, then replied, "Thomas Mann." They both grinned. And they'd go on grinning the rest of the afternoon, trading names like Flaubert, Edgar Allan Poe, and Stefan Zweig; Colette and Proust.

It's a lovely story, isn't it? Two men on a tower, after a war, waving the names of writers as if they were signal flags or semaphores . . . I take it personally. It seems to me that my whole life I've been standing on some tower or a pillbox or a trampoline, waving the names of writers, as if we needed rescue. And the first person I had to rescue was myself. Back in 1947, I was in California instead of Japan. I would spend the next ten years of my latchkey boyhood in and out of grammar school, junior high, and high school, in the middle of the toadlike politics of the Joe McCarthy era of American history, growing up on a beach. On this beach, nobody understood me. My scars glowed in the dark, or at least my acne. I couldn't tan, hated cars, refused to surf, and flunked volleyball, grunion-hunting, and puberty rite. Like lonely kids everywhere, I entered into books as if into a conspiracy—for company, of course, and for narrative and romance and advice on how to be decent and brave and sexy. But also for transcendence, a zap to the synaptic cleft; for a slice of the strange, the shock of an Other, a witness not yet heard from, archeologies forgotten, ignored, or despised; that radioactive glow of *genius* in the dark: grace notes, ghosts, and gods. It's an old story, and I won't kid you: I became an intellectual because I couldn't get a date. But we enter the chambered nautilus of metaphor, and suddenly we hear a different music. As the young brat Jean-Paul Sartre observed, on first entering his grandfather's library: "I would draw near to observe those boxes which slit open like oysters, and I would see the nudity of their inner organs, pale, fusty leaves, slightly bloated, covered with black veinlets, which drank ink and smelled of mushrooms." I don't know what he'd make of us today, crouched at our software consoles, slugabed in our romper rooms, tethered to the all-news War Porn channel, flatlined by the adman/music-video consumer grid, home-shopping for friendship in the beer commercials, reading a *Heavy Metal* comic, sampling on a CD carousel a customized sequence of Sonic Youth, Pussy Galore, and Tom Petty's "Jamming Me," online and downlinked to all the other ghosts in our machines, longing for some digitized Xanadu: "Lucy in the Sky with Diamonds."

But from my own childhood I can tell you: First, we possess language, and then we possess ourselves. Alone in literature, we find sanctuary and what John Cheever meant by "simplicity and usefulness," valor, virtue, kindness, beauty, and "the stamina of love, a presence . . . like the beginnings of some stair." We also discover discrepancy. I picked up my plain American style from Mark Twain and Ernest Hemingway, my dreaminess from Greek myths and the King James Bible, my social-justice politics from John Dos Passos and Ralph Ellison, my nose for phonies from J. D. Salinger, and my delusions of grandeur from James Joyce. At first I wanted to *be* Huck Finn and Holden Caulfield, not to mention Prometheus. Later on, I would want to *write The Sun Also Rises* and *Portrait of the Artist As a Young Man*—like God paring His fingernails. Real life has turned out to be less thrilling. After a fast start, I haven't published a novel in twenty years. The public has a way of letting you know that it will pay more for you to discover and to celebrate excellence in other people, and rather less for your own refined feelings. These days, I spend half my day writing about television, and the other half writing about books, and I read instead of sleep. This is innocent enough; I do less damage than a lawyer. In the discovery process, I may even do some good. It sometimes seems that the nonfiction best-seller list in the *New York Times* consists entirely of books by and about war criminals, self-help gurus, and greedheads, and all these books have the same title: *How I Lost Weight, Found God, Smart-Bombed Arabs and Changed My Sexual Preference in the Bermuda Triangle*. But there's always an Eva Hoffman and a Susan Faludi, and so many novels, all of them reinventing the world in words.

And is it really such a big surprise that when we are young and incomplete and curious, we should look for and find ourselves in books, as well as everything we want to be and aren't, might have been and shouldn't? I'm only sorry that as we get older, we stop looking. García Márquez spends half of every year in Havana, in a house mantained for him by Fidel Castro. In exchange, an insomniac Fidel relies on the Nobel Prize winner to supply him with books to read at night as he rumbles the city streets in his chauffeur-driven limousine. One night Gabo gave Fidel a copy of Bram Stoker's *Dracula*. The next breakfast, Fidel slammed down this book: "The bastard!" he cried. "I couldn't sleep!" Nor, of course, should any of them sleep: our pols, those caudillos. They should be looking into books, as if they were mirrors. And they should be seeing Dracula, Hamlet, Kali, Ahab, Frankenstein, Robin Hood, Pinocchio, Oedipus, and Peter Pan.

Anyway, when the alarm bell rang to end the fifties snooze, for many it sounded like Elvis. For me, it was Allen Ginsberg and his "Howl," that elegy for beautiful losers, that closet history of the Other America of Tom Mooney, Sacco and Vanzetti, the Scottsboro boys, and Ginsberg's crazy Communist Jewish mother: "Get married Allen don't take drugs," she told him. I left the beach as soon as I could for Cambridge, Mass., where, for the student paper, I wrote about Kerouac and rock 'n' roll. I also reviewed Nabokov's novel *Lolita*. Amazing that a Russian knew so much about America, especially our motels. But I didn't belong at Harvard, where I read Dostoyevsky when I was supposed to be reading Henry James, any more than I'd belong, decades later, in the Peninsula Hotel in Hong Kong, or the Oriental in Bangkok. You can take the boy out of his class, but you can't take the class out of the boy. I dropped out: for Greenwich Village. In a surplus Army fatigue jacket with pockets full of Baudelaire, I was a cabbage child among the Beats. Like Ginsberg, I wanted to know: "When can I go into the supermarket and buy what I need with my good looks?" I'm not saying that a lot of other stuff wasn't going on besides books. In addition to beer, television, and rock 'n' roll, there were bombs to ban, and Bob Dylan, and Joan Baez. But popular culture is where we go to talk to and agree with one another; to simplify ourselves; to find our herd. It's like going to the Automat to buy an emotion. The thrills are cheap and the payoffs predictable and, after a while, the repetition is a bummer. Whereas books are where we go alone to complicate ourselves. Inside this solitude, we take on contours, textures, perspectives. Heightened language levitates the reader. Great art transfigures. And when we go back to it, it's full of even more surprises. We get older; it gets smarter.

At the end of that decade all the boho boychicks wanted to be Norman Mailer. Back then even Mailer wanted to be Mailer. I'm not sure about now. But after many unpublished manuscripts, I left one Third World country, Greenwich Village, for another, Berkeley Cal. At Pacifica Radio, KPFA in Berkeley, I found that to get free copies of books from New York publishers all you had to do was promise to review them. So, while I worked on my third first novel, I also scheduled myself to talk about brand-new books like *V, Herzog, Hall of Mirrors, Letting Go, Cat's Cradle, Rabbit Run, One Flew Over the Cuckoo's Nest, Catch-22,* and *The Fire Next Time.* And I talked about new novels from abroad like *The Tin Drum, The Golden Notebook,* and *The Mandarins.* On the one hand, Flannery O'Connor and Mary McCarthy; on the other, Julio Cortázar and Chinua Achebe. Loving such books wasn't exactly molecular biology or particle physics; you had merely to trust the tingle in your scalp, a kind of sonar, and their deeper chords possessed you. Looking back at what became of me, I'm sorry I didn't turn out to be Dostoyevsky or Günter Grass or Doris Lessing. I know perfectly well that the relationship between critic and author is more often parasitic than it's symbiotic. "Insects sting," Nietzsche told us, "not in malice, but because they want to live. It is the same with critics: they desire our blood, not our pain."

But when you love these books, they love you back. Having identified with somebody else's heroic imagination; having gone through that shadowy door into realms of feeling never glimpsed before with such luster; having seen centaurs and witches and flying fish and bare ruined choirs and the glowing cores and burning grids and neon clouds and crystal nerves and singing spheres of cyberspace, of thought itself—you are more interesting, and so is the world. Neither of you will ever again be monochromatic. Except for Dos Passos, James Baldwin, and Doris Lessing, I'd never have spent the midsixties in the civil rights and antiwar movements. If I hadn't read Lessing, I'd be just another Mailer—certainly incapable of sending our daughters up like kites, to discover their own lightning.

It was my pleasure and privilege at the *New York Times* to review the very first books by Toni Morrison, Maxine Hong Kingston, Mary Gordon, Cynthia Ozick, and Joan Didion—double-identities doubly *Other*—as if, by the abrasions of sex on race on class on culture, they rubbed up something combustible; as if by these plate tectonics I got the continental drift I need. Since, in Oakland a couple of years ago and up the Hudson just this Christmas, the houses of Kingston and Morrison somehow burned to the ground, my sidekick has suggested that Gordon, Ozick, Didion, and any other woman writer I admire should take out more insurance. But I was partial as well to György Konrad, Milan Kundera, Christa Wolf, and Stanislaw Lem, in whom I found a more compelling politics to construe than dreamt of in the geopolitics of Dr. Kissinger, and just look what happened to Eastern Europe in 1989. I also loved the Latin Americans. Just imagine sitting down to the glorious surprise of *One Hundred Years of Solitude,* before anybody else has told you how to feel. If your passion is cities, as mine has always been, there to explore were the Buenos Aires of Borges, the Lima of Vargas Llosa, the Havana of Cabrera Infante, the Mexico City of Fuentes. Plus, of course, Italo Calvino, Primo Levi, Kobo Abe, Solzhenitsyn, V. S. Naipaul, and Wole Soyinka. Imagine being *paid* to think out loud about *Midnight's Children,* or *The Book of Laughter and Forgetting,* or *The Woman Warrior,* or *Song of Solomon.*

Here, by the way, is what Kingston told a reporter after her house burned down, with all of her manuscripts: "Did you know that when paper burns," she said, "it is very beautiful? It's just amazing to look at a burned book. It looks like feathers, the thin pages, and it's still book-shaped, and you touch it and it disintegrates. It makes you realize that it's all air. It's inspiration and air and it's just returned to that." Talk about your Magic Realism!

It never occurred to me that celebrating Toni Morrison and Maxine Hong Kingston was in any way subversive of the American literary canon, that short shelf of Wonderbread Boys. Nor did it occur to me that García Márquez, Salman Rushdie, Abdelrahman Munif, and Wole Soyinka represented some sinister threat to Eurocentric thralldom. We must live together, and will die alone, and need in the interim all the genius we can get. I *like* the Canon. I just wish there were more of it. After the Great Debate on Great Books at Stanford, they added one woman and one wog. This seems stingy. We don't do these writers any favor by deigning to read them; they've done us the favor by being there to dazzle us into sentience. The novel, after all, was invented a thousand years ago in Japan, by Lady Murasaki. The most important English-language poem of the twentieth century, Eliot's "Wasteland," ends with a Sanskrit quote that's likewise at least a millennium old, and so, too, did the physicist J. Robert Oppenheimer quote Sanskrit in the atomic desert, when he broke light like a pencil. We leave town each summer for Greek light, German sausage, Russian soul, French sauce, Spanish bull, Zen jokes, a Heart of Darkness and the Blood of the Lamb. We will leave the house to deploy in a metropolis of Haitian cabbies, Korean vegetable vendors, Indian newsstands, Greek coffee shops, Arab head shops, and Senegalese street peddlers, hungry for sushi, Mex, falafel, pizza, shishkebob, mousaka, Polish ham, Jerusalem artichokes, Chinese takeout, salsas, and chutney. Why aren't we equally hungry for meaning? It's amazing how avid we are for every goodie in the global-village souk except *books*, how it's somehow all-American to develop a crush on our enemies once we've killed enough of them, to fall in love—after the landgrab and slave auction, the Gatling gun and lynch mob, the atom bomb and napalm—with the very culture we've dispossessed, with the beads, and the blues, and the betelnuts; even to make movies about them. We just won't *read* them: as if their books were some kind of Pearl Harbor sneak attack on Jeffersonian democracy and the Puritan City on the Hill.

But language is guilty of association with rational comment and abstract ideas and magical transcendence. It's subversive of pieties, euphemisms, stereotypes, and agitprop. A book, said Kafka, "must be an ax for the frozen sea in us." Eduardo Galeano, the Latin American historian and Groucho Marxist, reports on a day in the Montevideo slums. He was painting a picture of a pig on the hand of a little boy. "Suddenly," says Galeano, "word got around. I was surrounded by little boys demanding at the top of their lungs that I draw animals on their little hands cracked by dirt and cold, their skin of burnt leather: one wanted a condor, and one a snake, others preferred little parrots and owls, and some asked for a ghost or a dragon. Then in the middle of this racket, a little waif who barely cleared a yard off the ground showed me a watch drawn in black ink on his wrist. 'An uncle of mine who lives in Lima sent it to me,' he said. 'And does it keep good time?' I asked him. 'It's a bit slow,' he admitted."

So are we: a bit slow. There's already an international multiculture. And it isn't a multiculture of bluejeans, gangster movies, and rock music; of bank loans, arms credits, and microchips; of Kentucky Fried Chicken and the CIA and the spider-speak in green decimals of international currency speculation. It's a multiculture of distinctions and connections and the exchange, in the library, in translation, of our highest hopes, darkest chords, and coded meanings. It's Kobo Abe reading García Márquez in Japanese, and Toni Morrison and Salman Rushdie reading him in English; and García Márquez, reading Faulkner and Flaubert in Spanish, not to mention Kafka in a Borges translation. It's Philip Roth, in Czechoslovakia, discovering Jiri Weill. And Maxine Hong Kingston rewriting the classical Chinese *Journey to the West*, to include Abbie Hoffman as the Monkey King. And Naguib Mahfouz organizing forty Arab intellectuals to defend the right of Rushdie to his novels and his life, which teaches us something about courage we'd not otherwise have learned from the cowardly silence on this subject of a John Le Carré and a V. S. Naipaul.

This is what I do for a living. I review this multiculture. And then we leave town—for Paris, Prague, or Johannesburg; for Moscow, Shanghai, or Istanbul; Jerusalem and Bangkok—to see for ourselves what these remarkable men and women have been writing about. As if by magic lantern, we see through these books that we have loved, and those that loved us in return, and it's my opinion that if more of us had read Václav Havel before 1989, the collapse of what my sidekick calls the nonprofit police states of Eastern Europe might not have seemed so astounding. A David Grossman, in Hebrew, and a Jacobo Timerman, in Spanish, prophesy every bit as much as they report, and so has Nadine Gordimer, in novel after novel, from South Africa. Likewise, there were Filipino novelists and playwrights presaging that fairy tale, the Princess Bride in yellow taking charge when the Wicked Frog left town with his Dragon Lady, in an American whirlybird. A close reader of the Chinese *Misties* could have predicted Tiananmen Square. Nor would I be shocked if Milorad Pavič, in his *Dictionary of the Khazars*, proves more reliable than anybody at the U.N. on the worm in the brain of Serbia.

The phone rang a couple of months ago. "Hi," she said: "This is Toni, your Nobelette. Are you ready for Stockholm?" It hadn't really occurred to me to go. It's not as if I put her over the top. The best I could say for myself and Toni Morrison's brilliant literary project—her reimagining of the lost history of her people, their love and work and nightmare passage and redemptive music, a ghostly chorale, a constellation of humming spheres, with its own gravity and so many morning stars—is that, from the very beginning, I'd been there cheering. But who am I *if not a reader she imagined*? And if she wanted me, I'd go. I could always wear a sign around my neck saying in big block letters: I TOLD YOU SO.

Well, look where she is now, after the fanfare and the processional, descending the marble stairs on the arm of the king of Sweden. Our Majesty: I am proud of her. I'm even, a little bit, proud of me. I'm proud, in fact, to be a citizen of whatever country Toni Morrison comes from. In *Beloved*, Denver warns her ghostly sister about their difficult mother: "Watch out for her; she can give you *dreams*." So do they all, these writers I'm waving my arms about, these angels made of words. Watch out for them. They give you dreams.

The Cambridge Scene

H E WORE a fool's cap crowned with tiny bells, and he strummed, of all things, a lyre—probably brass, but it looked gold. And he said:

I am the myth-maker, the symbolist, the seer of truths. I have wandered down the pedestrian centuries, beneath the bright flags, toting a bag of legends and singing the old songs. I have been Homer's eyes. I suggested Mephistopheles. They say—with some salt to be sure—that I pinched Beatrice, and Dante merely followed her flight to comfort. I am the Muse, the Artist, or if you will, the Human Venture. You may think my costume outlandish and my demeanor strange; but that is your fault, not mine. I have endured.

In each age I have found a home: I was swaddled in immortality and time was my play-pen. Men burned candles at my altar—in religion, poetry, the sciences. All the professions engendered their terms, and the terms became symbols, and the symbols grew into myths, and the myths became legends. And the legends were allegories, teaching the racial wisdom.

I was at home in Thebes; I whispered in Cassandra's ear; I felt secure in the shadow of the cross; I rode phantom horses through the Nordic lands and danced on the northern twilight—among the apparitions of the imagination.

In this time only am I alone.

I counseled the children as they spoke, one heart to another. I understand the idiot's smile. I sing of the simple savage.

Know me, and you know why man aspired from the cave to Westchester

County, from the sling to the mushroom cloud. Know me, and you know that primitive man conceived in images, that his images were ideas; that he ascribed words to these ideas. And now, in this technological century, the word has grown further from the idea, until they have separated, and the word is all. The shattered images lie in a pile, along with utopia and dreams.

The dream needs neither time nor mathematics.

Ask me why you have no poets and no epics. Ask me to talk to you of greatness and Art. I will tell you that you are lost. That the Indian with the name of a bird and the hieroglyphic picture-writing and the stone monuments of island cultures have a wisdom which you lack. They have not divided the estate of God into man and nature, into past and present. They have not abandoned the essence of image and the picture-idea.

Civilization, and the apotheosis of abstraction. When words become their own meaning, when Angry Young Men and hipsters plunge into the night and the academicians experiment with style—ask me why there is no literature.

Did not Eliot return to dead cultures, ancient languages, and the Legend of the Fisher King? Did not Yeats sustain himself on the Irish folklore? Did not Lawrence traipse across continents to Mexico, seeking the meaning of the Aztecs, the wisdom of primitive man?

What obsessed scowling Melville to create a new symbolism of the sea? Whence Faulkner's new mythology? Why all the shouting and none of the beauty of literature?

I will tell you, for I know. There are no men who think symbolically. There are no artists who understand the myth. These are no times to sing of the Abstract and the investigating subcommittee.

You come nearest to the ancient rhythms in jazz and rock 'n' roll. Your modern art has lost its meaning. The myth, tongue of the unconscious and language of the race, was sanctioned solely by children, savages, and fools—before Freud. And now only by psychiatrists.

The modern poet comes to symbolism with a consciousness: This is a symbol, meaning such and such. But a symbol means itself, and must be understood for itself, and must be conceived.

Freud discovered mythology and meaning in the dream, explained Hamlet and charted the mind by means of Oedipus. Jung wrote of archetypes, of the recurring myth in art, of the common symbols of man. There is a racial consciousness, a *spiritus mundi*—human history is community property among the family of artists. But the word has supplanted the idea.

I condemn you, who have made me an orphan. You attack the logic of religion and laugh, at cocktail parties, over totem poles and pillars. You dismiss mystics as paranoids and prophets as crackpots. You pride yourselves as Men of Logic when your understanding is mechanical. In your anxiety to reason, you have forgotten how to feel.

Yours is a motel civilization, from gentlemen farmers to university professors. Your literature has standardized the Bible and propitiated the cult of the Word. Your art makes no sense and your music is too loud. You cannot speak to one another and you have forgotten who you are. You have only dictionaries and manuals and wireless sets—tuned in to nothing and listening attentively to babble.

And you give me no home. No home but park benches and gutters and all-night motion picture houses full of sailors. No home but pinball machines and erotica shelves and occasional wine cellars, and a night in jail.

I do not begrudge my loneliness, not my persecution. But you have taken my lyre and broken it, and spit on the dead centuries, and rendered art into pornography. For what it availeth, I can do naught but curse you.

There aren't many soap boxes for men with bells on their heads. (The bells had a tinny sound, anyway.) And, what with his plaid patches and his broken lyre, the myth-maker was only marking time until a vagrancy charge or an asylum.

Besides, only a few of us saw him, and we were drunk at the time.

The Demise of Greenwich Village

THERE USED TO be an old man with a mole on the end of his nose and a paper cup strung around his neck, standing on the corner of Fourteenth Street and Fifth Avenue, playing the violin. Several weeks ago he disappeared. He was subsequently found to have died of indigestion in a hotel room in the South Village.

The fiddler left very little to remember him by—a few sticks of furniture, some pornographic photographs, and a fleeting immortality in several unpublished novels. In a way, he was symbolic of Greenwich Village. As of summer 1958, they were both dead, and nobody could properly recall when they started dying.

A peripatetic observer, traipsing the slow mile of gift shops, bookstores, and bars between Rienzi's (where you take your friend from Chicago) and the White Horse Inn, is bound to get depressed. Bohemia has become a tourist attraction. That careful decadence of dress which used to be the uniform of the *literateur* has become Fifth Avenue fashion. Whether the reason for or the result of this change, Village creativity is at low ebb in everything but drama. The painting is bad and expensive; the poetry is stale and academic; the tablecloths are all checkered; and little magazines litter the streets.

People go to Greenwich Village today to escape from art instead of to it. There are, of course, the visitors. Long-drawn, tweed-beaten, and corn-twanged Idaho sophomores, who couldn't tell flamenco guitar from a Jew's-harp, are shortening the coffeehouse circuit and getting strummed to death. Pre-med Kentucky studhorses come down for a weekend to see what goes on on the other side of the Baptist church. But the permanent residents fall readily into ready-made categories.

First of all, there are my friends (they used to be my friends). They are a splintered group. The guy who flunked out of Harvard at the end of his sophomore year because he sat up all night writing dirty poetry; Bennington girls who left college to do something earthy; NYU poets who need haircuts; college newspaper editors who couldn't land a job with the *Times*; *magnas* in English literature who don't want to teach and can't quite see returning to Des Moines to work for the water company.

Besides my friends, there are other people in Greenwich Village. Walk into any bar, and the first thing you notice are the homosexuals. The Village has become the place to go if you want to rub knees with local expatriates in the Age of Aberration. The classified ad for apartment-sharing "with a congenial young man" (Village address) is a classic form of journalistic pimping. Barroom and street-corner solicitation is commonplace, partly because there are a number of such people who hang out in the Village, and partly because there are a number of people who go to see them—to see what happens to their libido when confronted by something more substantial than that man's hand on your knee in the New Haven bus station.

The Village is one of the few publicized habitats of the lesbian. Red-faced lumberjack women with straight hair, men's ties, and a business suit, buying drinks for their sweet young things, peer with a weary omniscience at the coeds and pickups plying their trade. Pickups, too, have a way of gravitating toward the Great White Arch, although the game is more dignified today as free love and physical self-expression. As one of the former psychology majors explained it: "A community of total tolerance tends to the pornographic. You have to have standards or you engender the obscene."

Real estate values in the Village have skyrocketed. Studio apartments which used to go for ten dollars a week can't be bought for ninety a month. Many a genuine *avant gardiste* has had to content himself with a New Jersey boarding house or a West Side basement.

Patrons today are paying their bills. Mama Gagliano, a grocery store proprietress in the shadow of the marquee, had this to say: "I used to have to carry some of the boys. They couldn't pay for groceries. They'd always ask me to wait awhile, and I would wait. Today, everybody pays. I carry nobody. And they buy more food."

Village shops have tripled their prices for handcraft and chinaware and clothes. On biweekly Thursday nights Manhattan secretaries rush with their paychecks to purchase ninety-dollar coats and twenty-dollar sweaters—for Friday's evening at the theater.

All of which has created a new kind of Village citizen. We are all familiar with the old stereotypes, and they still abound. The wistful Dadaists, the Serious Young Men, who regard Art as a craft, literature as a mental discipline, creativity as a form of calisthenics, and the role of the Artist as a poignant blend of anguished genius and popular messiah. These are the poets living on their parents' allotment checks, waging battle in dozens of little magazines. They are formalist or antiformalist. Their irony has the convolutions of a pretzel. Life is a matter of chamber music, peeled grapes, and a theory of aesthetics. (Almost everybody has either written his own or replied to somebody else's theory of aesthetics.) They prowl the streets, they let their hair grow long, they wear black turtleneck sweaters and dirty white tennis shoes. They scowl frequently, gesticulate elaborately, drink heavily, and live crudely. Their rebellion is in clothes and conduct, not creativity. And it is not long before those clothes— leather-patched, moth-eaten, tawdry, and inexpensive as they may be— become a uniform, a badge by which the manikin inside seeks to say: "I am writing a novel; I think about existentialism; I have read Henry James; I don't have enough money to make it to the Left Bank."

Nobody ever told Morris that needing a haircut, a shave, a bath, and a new suit doesn't make you Rimbaud, or even Thomas Wolfe. The only thing Gladys (who writes sonnets) learned from Radcliffe is not to comb her hair. And she's still wearing the same raincoat. Gladys and Morris never produced anything worthwhile, and they never will. They are the dregs of each college generation for whom bohemianism solves the problem of what to do with themselves.

They live, together, in a cold-water flat with cracked plaster and empty flowerpots (unless they've planted peyote). They've scoured the five boroughs for enough orange crates to hold their books. The floor is strewn with French novels whose pages have been slit but seldom read, trinkets from Chinatown, old college notebooks, and yellow paper. There's a portable typewriter, the *Times* literary supplement, and a half-finished essay on Virginia Woolf. A couple of cockroach colonies maintain the atmosphere of decadence and the myth of suffering. But Gladys and Morris go to bed with full stomachs.

The new citizen is of a different ilk. It's often difficult to distinguish him from the college crowd and the Book-of-the-Month and afternoon bridge brigade that comes to the Village to see what starving Bohemians are all about, and spends most of its time in fashionable restaurants, masqueraded to the earlobes in costumes considered appropriate, looking at each other in simulated excitement and secret disappointment. The new citizen is something different.

Compton is a public relations agency hack or a Madison Avenue adman. He writes thirty-second jingles for a new margarine and depletes the watercooler to lubricate his tranquilizing pills. He graduated with a liberal arts degree, never eats the olive in his martini, and aspires someday to write the suburban or the Organization novel. But he generally returns home from his nine-to-five sojourn too tired for anything but a gin and tonic. Compton lives in the Village (he can afford the rent); his books are hardcover; and his laundry is clean.

What Morris, Gladys, and Compton have in common is their arid little community. In most of the coffeehouses the jazz is so well-modulated that you can't hear it, so far out that it's gone. It serves as a sort of Muzak background for conversational patter and dream interpretation. The imported Italian coffee is forty cents a throw, and usually cold by the time it arrives. You amuse yourself by watching two fellows with beards resolve their existentialist dilemma and despair each evening until midnight, when they probably go to bed together.

The whole Village is one big Hayes-Bick, and it's always two in the morning.

Apathy is the latest religion. Even poetry-and-jazz was a flop in Washington Square.

From the coffeehouses there's no place to go but the bars, where the drinks are about as expensive and as watered as anywhere else. Or spots like Rocky's, with checkered tablecloths, sawdust, cobwebs, bad paintings, and Chianti bottles.

There used to be a time when John Reed and Lincoln Steffens lived at the same Village address, when Mama Gagliano "carried the boys" until that publisher's commission came through. No more. Even Wolfe went to live in Brooklyn. The Village today is populated by the smug, the self-conscious, and the literary sycophants. The bars depend on the tourist trade. The aberrants depend on the college students. The shops depend on the secretaries. The best thing to come out of the Village in a quarter century is Jules Feiffer, and he's certainly the only reason for reading either of the two weekly papers distributed locally. The most absorbing issue of conversation since Jack Kerouac has been the traffic in Washington Square Park.

America's great bohemian subculture still languishes in the corpulent shadow of its European counterpart. We are imitators. We have imitated their knee-socks and their coffeehouses, their existentialism and their morals. We have failed to affirm or deny anything in our own experience. We have failed to realize that the scowl and the furrowed brow and the *hofbrau* philosophizing of the Continent had its roots in a real dilemma, in war and social upheaval. The American Bohemian, Beat, Tired, Brown, or Silent, is a pampered child shaking his rattle, the spoiled spawn of college literary magazines, dissatisfied because America is something more than a whorehouse and something less than a Christmas tree. And all he's creating is noise.

Pasternak's Hero: Man Against the Monoliths

THE CRITICAL HOBBYHORSES have been ridden to hell, and the trumpets are put away. Edmund Wilson and the Nobel Prize Committee and the Soviet Writers Union and the American newspaper editorial pages have had their say on Pasternak—and perhaps now a second reading and some thoughts are in order.

Doctor Zhivago has sold more hardcover editions in the United States than any other book since *Peyton Place*. It was the most popular literary Christmas present of the 1958 holiday season. The proportion of pages read to books bought must be more lopsided than that of the Gideon Bible. And one of the biggest reasons for the disparity is reader fatigue; the busy man must choose between the book itself and the welter of commentary on it.

Zhivago is a novel by a poet, and as such is at once too great and too restricted for its literary form. It is apolitical, and, ironically, a political shillelagh inveighed by both sides in the Cold War. It alternates between axes of profound beauty and profound confusion. It is not quite Dostoyevsky or Tolstoy, but its intellectual vitality and respect for human dignity make it tower above anything else around these days.

The story of Yuri Zhivago is the story of the Russian intellectual—the disintegration of the man of ideas. Zhivago, as a student in the University, welcomes the Revolution; as a professional man displaced, repudiates it; as a degenerate in a one-room Moscow flat, is finally destroyed by it. In the process of that destruction, Pasternak tells the story of Russia in the twentieth century—of the parasites who feed on emergent ideologies, of men serving and struggling against systems and faiths they cannot grasp, of the miasma of bureaucracy, land reform, nobility, and military that was Russia after October 1917.

But the book is much more than an indictment of the Communist system. It is, just as much, an indictment of world-savers and social engineers, the true believer and the legislator of morality; an indictment as much of any political system which seeks to reform the world from the top or bottom, and ignores the basic ingredient and the basic problem, man.

In the process of disintegration, Zhivago devolves from a respected physician and devoted poet to a tired, beaten man who dies of a heart attack on a Moscow trolley-car. And that disintegration cannot be ascribed solely to the disruptive political system which surrounds him, to the "inscrutability of universal chaos."

Zhivago himself is a weak man, a Russian Hamlet to whom reality itself is the greatest antagonist. (The figure of Hamlet dominates Zhivago's conception of himself, culminating in the most notable of his poems collected at the end of the book.) The collection of pygmies in the Soviet Writers Union, besides their fatuous forays against Zhivago's politics, complained that the character lacked a social conscience, that the book itself was devoid of a social meaning. And, in a way, it is legitimate criticism. When a protagonist of great stature fails to come to terms with reality, it is seldom a social novel; but it is often great tragedy, and such is Pasternak's book.

In a sense, Zhivago and the Russian intellectuals he symbolizes are Dostoyevsky's Ivan all over again. Just as the murder of the Father Karamazov was a consequence of Ivan's ideas, so was the Revolution a consequence of the (at once brilliant and naive) Russian intellectual ferment, a century in the coagulating. And just as Ivan was unable to face the practical implications of those ideas, to accept his own involvement in reality, and went insane, so Zhivago and his ilk came out of the October Revolution bewildered and shaken into silence.

Zhivago's tragedy is somewhat confused by Pasternak's limitations as a novelist. This is his first novel. He is a poet, and during the Stalin era of literary frigidity, he devoted himself to Russian translations of Shakespeare. As a poet, he has been schooled to write from a single point of view, a single consciousness ranging on a variety of subjects or focusing on one. Most poetry is characterized by this synthesis of artist and the created personality. For poetry, it is basic; for the novel, it can be disastrous. The fusion of Zhivago and Pasternak admits of no third party and no alternatives. Life is as Zhivago sees it, and the arguments of supplementary characters are given very little stature. Dostoyevsky argued eloquently for all three Karamazovs. Shakespeare's universal vision was splintered into a Lear, and Edmund, and a Fool in just one play. But Zhivago's antagonists are given a few pages of characterization, a few pages of soliloquy, and a few pages of judgment—then back again into the morass of Zhivago's disaffection.

Evgraf, Zhivago's brother, appears once every 150 pages and plays his spasmodic role as a brother's keeper. Pasha, who left his family to become a military commander for the Communists, must explain his love, excuse his motivation, justify his life, and shoot himself in ten pages. These two men offered Zhivago a serious intellectual challenge—service out of love, and service out of duty. But Zhivago fails to come to terms with either concept, and Pasternak abets him. We are told that Lara (for Zhivago, the life-force) symbolizes the oppression of the nineteenth century and the hope of the twentieth; but someone has to say it, for in the characterization of her words and deeds there is no indication of such a symbolic meaning.

The texture of the book itself is often dreamlike. There are no explanations for remarkable coincidences. Useless characters and irrelevant scenes are introduced, languish, and are forgotten. Time sequence and geography and character all blur into a fantastic, exciting, but extremely confusing montage. The Soviet literary critics rightly complained that there was a failure to distinguish between the March and October revolutions. No matter what the color of your party card, there was a difference. Pasternak is not a novelist, and this is not his genre.

So much for the complaints. They have been technical. They have dealt with discipline and character development, the craft and grammar of modern literature. *Doctor Zhivago* is a great book, much greater than the customary valentines and pared prose that usually saturate the book review sections.

Zhivago is great because of its intellectual vitality. Each page brims with ideas. The pages are full of magnificent prose. Pasternak's poetic eye catches the turbulence of mobs and the despair of a nomad class dislocated and displaced by political charades; the disintegration of urban centers, the breakdown of communications and transportation; the ultimate wall between the people and the politicians who legislated for them; the conflicting faces of reality itself. His brilliant intuitive sense re-creates the confusion and the fullness of the times. His feeling for the Russian countryside and his landscape description have few peers in any literature.

It is a book of life—and it makes the distinct contribution of a new dimension, a new aspect, to life. We argue whether literature is written by individuals or incubated by cultures, whether it springs from the lyric spirit or whether it is squeezed out from human misery in terms of protest. We may, indeed, argue whether *Doctor Zhivago* is an affirmation or an epitaph. But it is a book that you profit by having read, an exciting book, a book to the credit of individual man among the monoliths.

Epitaph for the Beat Generation

WELL, IT'S ALL over. Jack Kerouac has gone back to his mother on Long Island. Allen Ginsberg returned to the Village. Gregory Corso was last seen on the Champs-Elysées, bound for the Left Bank. And even that unreluctant radical old dragon of Beat Generation public relations, Kenneth Rexroth, has headed for the warmer waters of the Mediterranean, weary of the bombast.

There was a time, of course, one summer (before the literary critics, in their pursuit of prodigies, discovered San Francisco), when we used to sit up all night in a furnished room on Heavenly Lane, playing chess on an orange crate and guzzling tequila from an old canteen; smearing ourselves with *self* and doing greasy battle over Baudelaire; spending our tortured souls in little midnight coins to buy the body or esteem of world-weary Mardous swathed in dirty serapes. When Sad Sam stood up on a table in Otto's Grotto and blew God from a tiny gold trumpet, and we all read Robinson Jeffers and wrote novels and listened to the wild sad horns of the Pacific.

Then: They published *On the Road*, and "Howl" was banned by the San Francisco police department, and *Harper's* and the *Atlantic*, creaking their dusty kaleidoscopes across the Continent, trained them on North Beach. That was the ball game. Suddenly Ivy League colleges started inviting Ginsberg to read poetry to them, and slick magazines were printing Rexroth again, and Jack Kerouac came down from the mountains strangled by a crucifix, all over the front page of the *New York Times* ("The

New York Times is as Beat as I am," said Kerouac. "Thank God for the *New York Times!*"). Conspicuous consumptives from Boston University's School of Fine Arts read bad poetry to worse jazz downstairs at The Rock, in Lou's Pebble Room; and MacDougal Alley louts in black turtleneck sweaters and white tennis sneakers went running up Sixth Avenue shouting "Buddhism Zens Me!"

Joyfully self-conscious America suddenly discovered its bohemian subculture—in coffeehouses and cold-water flats, congealed in city-slum coagulums reading Ionesco and pretending to be Rimbaud. Maybe America felt guilty about the middle class, about its apartment houses and its antiseptic sex life, about Social Security and the Book-of-the-Month Club. Maybe America was just bored with its suburbs. But whatever it was, America paid more than just attention to its pampered spawn. The Beats made more money than John the Ossified Man.

Colleges threw seminars to discuss them, newspapers sent reporters to interview them, big magazines did photo-features on them, and little magazines published their poetry. America's intellectuals gave up cultural Scrabble and hauled out all the old bogeymen about the Hero-Bum and the Fragmentation of the Modern World and The Failure of Communication and Aspects of the Anti-Social Revolution. Everything from homosexuality to heroin was back in style again.

The Beat Generation was scrutinized to death. America clobbered it into submission with a kleig light. Its writers stopped writing, or tried to pass off narcissistic adolescent novels the publishers had rejected the first time around, e.g., Kerouac's *Doctor Sax* and *Maggie Cassidy.* The perennial college sophomores unbuttoned their button-down collars, strapped on their sandals, and went running down the beach screaming "Moloch!" San Francisco looked more like the Dartmouth Winter Carnival than the American Left Bank.

What did it all prove? Well, every sibling sociologist with a sampler kit could tell you one thing: it was a panicked flight from reality. It was the same thing as Marlon Brando on a motorcycle or Jimmy Dean in a sports car or Norman Mailer in the *Partisan Review.* It was sensation-seeking and anarchic. It was apolitical—the sort of Greta Garbo ideology of "I want to be alone." The world owed us all a living, free wine, easy sex, and folding money. Responsibility had too many syllables and love was a dirty word. But was that all?

It proved at least one thing more. That poetry, painting, music, and fiction are products of the *individual*. That the great American novel will be written by some antisocial SOB who can't stand espresso and never heard of Wilhelm Reich—the guy who sits up all night at a typewriter and brings to his peculiar vision the discipline of form and the love of an educated heart. A generation may be disenchanted, but it takes a man alone to chronicle that disenchantment. Art-by-citadel won't work. It's in league with brainstorming and Groupthink and government-by-committee. Movements, Generations, Subcultures—these are the strewn carcasses of sterile imaginations, conjured up to explain lamely the *why* and *how* of genius. Nobody sees Saul Bellow at Rienzi's or James Gould Cozzens at the Co-Existence Bagel Shop. Robert Frosts don't run in rat-packs. Art is individual, the child of solitary individuals who wed their loneliness to their hope. It is sacrilege to call it by the same name as the sour song of displaced doughboys who stand on street corners strumming banjos, shouting at authority, and passing the tin cup.

You see, we were having fun on North Beach before all this happened. Nobody took himself very seriously. It was a stage in the painful growth to a painful manhood. And the poetry-readings and the beer-drinking and the Baudelaire were all part of our slow trudge into maturity, into a world where men must accept the responsibility for their acts, where, eventually, perhaps, men come to that lonely room and face that typewriter and write that novel. But it couldn't be that way. Nothing is ever slow in America. And that stench you smell from certain quarters is only the burnt wax from wings which ventured too near the sun. *Plus ça change, plus c'est la même chose*—as I always say when I'm sad.

Richard Nixon's *Six Crises*

L ET ME MAKE it clear at the outset that I am not going to be objective. I am one of those people who are called "Nixon-haters"; somewhere along the line we feel that we personally have been somehow soiled by this man, and we become strident on the subject. So several of the propositions of this review are 1) that *Six Crises* establishes conclusively the contention that Richard Nixon has nothing to offer this nation but the cheap sort of second-rate sainthood he is here busy trying to manufacture; 2) that his book might more instructively have been titled *The Death of a Salesman* or *Advertisements for Myself*; and 3) that, in baring his soul, he has shown us just how empty he is inside. That, I think, is fair warning. Switch me off now if you were expecting a few pious remarks about the tragic collapse of Dick Nixon, or a long swoon of meditation on the loneliness of this misunderstood and pitiable man, or a tennis-court slap on the back for the little man who almost made it. I read and I review his book because I am fascinated by the flower of rot, and because I think that more interesting and instructive than Richard Nixon the success is Richard Nixon the failure. I think that more meaningful than the man of tricks is the man of tricks reduced to desperation.

All right. We presume that in a democracy a certain number of hucksters, knaves, cowards, thieves, and assassins will, by virtue of cunning and accident of history, be elevated into high governmental posts and entrusted with responsibilities beyond their grasp. It is only a wonder that more of them don't rise higher, that there is some sort of compensatory mechanism that so often brings them down and discards them, finally, in distaste. I find most interesting in this book those portions in which Richard

Nixon relates his confrontation with that compensatory mechanism, and the absence of his self-knowledge at the time of that confrontation.

In *Six Crises* Nixon triumphantly documents his inability to understand the unfolding of history around him. I refer initially to his conviction that all criticism of him is inspired by his anti-Communism. He quotes himself telling a crowd at a train station in 1952, just after the first reports of the Nixon fund, quote: "You folks know the work that I did investigating Communists in the United States. Ever since I have done that work the Communists and the left-wingers have been fighting me with every possible smear. When I received the nomination for the vice-presidency I was warned that if I continued to attack the Communists in this government they would continue to smear me. And believe me, you can expect they will continue to do so. They started it yesterday." Unquote. Or take his response to the hostile mobs which greeted him in Caracas. It was to bawl out the Venezuelan foreign minister. Nixon told the unfortunate man, quote: "If your government doesn't have the guts and good sense to control a mob like the one at the airport, there will soon be no freedom for anyone in Venezuela. Freedom does not mean the right to engage in mob actions." Unquote. Or after the incident at San Marcos University, where he had been stoned. Nixon asked an aide for a rundown on the reaction to his performance, and was told that almost all reports were favorable, but that Rubottom and Bernbaum, two Foreign Service men, had, and again I quote from the Nixon account: "expressed concern that the episode had embarrassed the Peruvian government and had compromised the goodwill effect of the entire tour. I blew my stack. I told Cushman to have Rubottom and Bernbaum come to my room immediately. He reported back that they were dressing for the state dinner that evening and would come when finished. I told him to have them come at once as they were. A few minutes later the two men appeared before me, half dressed. I ripped into them. I told them it was their right and obligation before a decision was made to advise me against the San Marcos visit. But once I had made my decision in a matter of this importance, it was incumbent upon them, as key members of my staff, to put aside their objections and to support me. . . . No loyal staff member could do otherwise." Unquote. Nixon went on to disparage the Foreign Service in general for too often compromising with the Communists. "We, too," he said, "must play to win. Too often what we try to do is play not to lose. What we must do is to act like Americans and not put our tails between

our legs and run every time some Communist bully tries to bluff us."
Unquote. Well now, what did Rubottom and Bernbaum do to arouse
such wrath? They hadn't gone to the newspapers, or filed an official
report, or complained to a superior; they had merely expressed an opinion. More importantly, we see here that the reduction of international
conflicts to schoolyard tough-guy neighborhood heroics—a reduction
Mr. Nixon often makes in his public addresses to the American people—
that such a reduction is not simply a device he employs for public use, not
simply a little bit of hypocritical legerdemain, but rather an accomplished
simplemindedness he carries with him into the cud-chewing silence of
his lonely thoughts. He really thinks this way. In the Soviet Union, faced
by a belligerent Khrushchev who inveighed against the Captive Nations
resolution just passed by Congress, Nixon notes that Khrushchev used
Russian words which made even his translator blush. Says Nixon, and I
quote: "It was on that 'peasant' note that my courtesy call on the leader
of the world Communist movement came to an end." Unquote. The
word 'peasant' is placed in quotes by Nixon, an especially devastating bit
of prose stylization. These are the things that Richard Nixon notices and
remarks upon: the language of Khrushchev (indeed, the language of
Harry Truman), the brown chewing-tobacco spit which ruins Pat's new
red dress in Caracas, the doubts of a staff member.

Does he really grasp what's going on? Ironically enough, he opens his
book with this reference, I quote: "In April, I visited President Kennedy
for the first time since he had taken office. When I told him I was considering the possibility of joining the 'literary' ranks [Nixon puts "literary" in quotes, like "peasant"], of which he himself is so distinguished a
member, he expressed the thought that every public man should write a
book at some time in his life, both for the mental discipline and because
it tends to elevate him in popular esteem to the respected status of an
'intellectual.' " Unquote, and "intellectual" of course is suspended dan-
gling between another pair of quotation marks. Now, it seems obvious
that Nixon intends here to expose Kennedy's cynicism, and just as obvious, I think, that Kennedy was operating on several levels of irony at
which Nixon has never even guessed. But Nixon wants desperately to be
an intellectual; he takes it seriously. Theodore H. White reports that
Nixon during the campaign turned to reporters with a rather desperate
smile and said he *was* an intellectual, only nobody knew it. But this book
makes it obvious that he isn't an intellectual. It is not only the banality of

style; that might be expected from the predigested prose that issues from ghostwriters. It is the inability to escape from the prison of self, to consider ideas in the abstract, to free himself for even a moment from the terrible demands of a wounded ego. The man has no self-confidence. It is the network of his lacerations which Mr. Nixon here explores—not world events—and all his army of little tin strictures on courage will not rescue him. Courage, anyway, is not the proud gesture, the single act, the glamorous setting-to. It is a quality of the man, a way of life, a grace and a dignity and a meaning which reside in every mood and act of a man. Nixon has dealt with six of the most important events of our postwar history only as they affected his personal fortunes, only as they raised his rating on the Gallup poll, or moved his critics to complaint.

This egoism is all-intrusive, a wall-to-wall carpeting of self it is impossible not to step on. He is obsessively sensitive to the slightest rebuke. His ego, as it emerges from the pages of this book, is a large and delicate blooming flower of tender flesh; it must bask in continual light, it must be watered with regular praise, or it closes in upon itself, onto its inner silence, out of petulance and fear. So all reporters hate him and distort what he says; Communists and left-wingers all smear him; President Eisenhower is callous to his emotional needs; everybody is unfair. Illustrative of this insecurity is his compulsion for seizing upon praise and reporting it in his book. I list a few examples. In his introduction, he reports attending a Washington reception for Congressional Medal of Honor winners, shortly after his return from South America in 1958. Quote: "One of the guests of honor came up to me and, pointing to his ribbon, said: 'You should be wearing this, not I. I could never have done what you did in Caracas.' I answered: 'And I could never have done what you did during the Battle of the Bulge.' Perhaps we were both wrong." Unquote. On p. 118, after the Checkers speech, Nixon reports the TV makeup man who said admiringly: "That ought to fix them. There has never been a broadcast like it before." And he quotes Eisenhower, too, on p. 120: "I happen to be one of those people who, when I get into a fight, would rather have a courageous and honest man by my side than a whole boxcar of pussyfooters. I have seen brave men in tough situations. I have never seen anybody come through in better fashion than Senator Nixon did tonight." On p. 149, after Eisenhower's heart attack, Foster Dulles tells Nixon: "Mr. Vice-President, I realize that you have been under a heavy burden during these past few days, and I know I express the opinion

of everybody here that you have conducted yourself superbly. And I want
you to know we are proud to be on this team and proud to be serving in
this Cabinet under your leadership." On p. 202, after the San Marcos
incident, Nixon reports Tad Szulc of the *New York Times* running alongside his car, shouting: "Good going, Mr. Vice-President, good going."
On p. 205, Nixon's private aide Don Hughes asks: "'Sir, could I say something personal?' 'Sure, go ahead,' I said, still mystified. 'Sir,' he said, 'I have
never been so proud to be an American as I was today. I am honored to
be serving under you.'" On p. 209, still in Peru, Nixon received a tele-
gram from Clare Boothe Luce saying: "Bully." On p. 227 Muñoz Marin
embraces him and says: "You were magnificent in Lima and Caracas." On
p. 258, after the heroic battle with Khrushchev in the model American
kitchen, a United Press reporter tells Nixon: "Good going, Mr.
Vice-President," and Mikoyan himself compliments Nixon—all painstakingly recorded. In the last long section of the book, devoted to the
1960 campaign, there are, of course, innumerable instances of people
apotheosizing Nixon. He reports every one of them.

All I can say is that I am glad such a mass of insecurity is not responsible for the conduct of our government today. Does that sound bitter? It
is. Polite people in polite conversation tend to look at you as if you're telling them a dirty joke when you happen to mention these days the name
of Jerry Voorhis or Helen Gahagan Douglas. Just how far have we come
when Richard Nixon can write: "I had come into this 1952 campaign
well-prepared, I thought, for any political smear that could be directed
against me. After what my opponents had thrown at me in my campaigns
for the House and Senate . . . I thought I had been through the worst."
Unquote. The worm has really turned. Take the preposterous statement
that he feels he should have spent more time "on appearance and less on
substance" in the 1960 presidential campaign. This man has never been
tortured by compunctions; he still isn't. And I have no use for the
pity peddlers who prowl about now dispensing sympathy for him. He
deserves what he gets.

Is his book interesting? Aside from exposing this terrible flower of ego,
and from demonstrating that he isn't equipped for high office, *Six Crises*
isn't a terribly interesting book. It gives us some insight into Eisenhower,
unwittingly. We get a sense of the man's paralyzing lack of decisiveness,
his reluctance to deal with distasteful situations, his tendency, once some
sort of action was forced upon him, to choose rash and wrathful means of

self-expression. Even Nixon wouldn't have been idiotic enough to dispatch two companies of Marines to the Caribbean when the vice-president had his public relations problems in Caracas. Then there are all those terrible Eisenhower platitudes which Nixon quotes with such officious approval, as if they dropped like silver coins from the Old Man's mouth. Here are two examples of what Nixon refers to as Eisenhower's maxims. On p. 177, Ike says: "A politician can always be counted on to have his mouth open and his mind closed," and on p. 235, Ike says: "I have always found that plans are useless, but planning is indispensable." One can imagine what life was like around the White House in those placid bygone days.

Taking the book episode by episode, the Hiss business is most interesting (except for the 1960 campaign), only because it is of such continuing interest. We are still arguing about the typewriter. For myself, I agree with Murray Kempton, whose report on Hiss-Chambers in his book *A Part of Our Time* is the best around. Hiss is probably guilty; the transcript shows he continually lied. But this is both more and less than a "tragedy of history"—it involves two atypical men, both products of the same shabby gentility that produced Nixon, the shabby gentility whose cardinal rule is: you can't be too careful. The worst thing about the Hiss case is that it convinced Richard Nixon he could ride anti-Communism into the Presidency, and he almost did so. To say, as he does, that it cost him that office is balderdash.

But we get bogged down in the chapters devoted to the Fund speech, the heart attack, Caracas, and Khrushchev. The Fund was a nasty little business, a third-rate scandal, really, and rather minor all the way around. But out of it emerged Nixon the cliché machine, the mechanical dispensary: drop in your coins, and out gurgles a wet and sticky sentimentality, a poisonous brew concocted out of mother, America, dogdom, cloth coats, really folks, and all the Technicolored garbage of the boy next door. Caracas demonstrated that he doesn't understand what's going on in the world; the heart attack crisis, that he can be discreet; the trip to the Soviet Union, that he knows a good gimmick when he sees one. But it is the 1960 campaign that really tells us something, and it is there the narrative picks up again. Somewhere along the line the likes of Nixon click off and can't make it. The compensatory mechanism catches up with them, and they haven't the self-knowledge to understand what's happened. All right: Nixon didn't have a chance; he was an outsider; he didn't have time to make himself over into a man. He went too far, too fast, on accidents and cunning, and he never really became a man. He simply didn't exist; he had no style; he was only a Platonic ideal of what he would like himself to be, a cardboard image of what he thought it would take to win. That's what the American voters learned the evening of the first television debate. Substantive questions were not argued, but it was immediately clear that Kennedy had style (the style of the rich, the style of money, the style of Harvard, and the Kennedy style); Kennedy was, as Norman Mailer has observed, a hipster. As such, he existed as a man in his own right, self-assured, with his own private grace and definition and approach. Nixon couldn't compete; he had no such existence. And in his defeat he has only fallen into that flower of bruised ego, and is capable only of this obscure apology and this moral indignation, the sort of indignation H. G. Wells called jealousy with a halo. Therefore this incredible business of Cuba, in which he took a position opposite to that which he says he believed, because Kennedy was saying what he really thought; and now Allen Dulles must strike him down by denying all. Or the humbuggery about Martin Luther King. Or the carpetbagger statement.

These are mistakes, the sort of mistakes which will ensure that he loses even in California, and they are significant mistakes. America is a terrible place in which to live if you fail; it is against the law in America to fail. But Nixon failed. Like a gambler who was always lucky and always won, he was suddenly struck down when the stakes were huge, and he is now reduced to desperation, to wilder and wilder bets, to the flinging of miscellaneous coins upon the table, and the frantic prayer to the great spinning wheel, and he doesn't win. There is something pathetic about it, I will agree; but there are those of us who are unmoved by the pathos of Richard Nixon. He kicked us so often when we were down; we aren't very forgiving. It has been his triumph, the triumph of his assertion and his failure, that we respond to him upon the level on which he first insisted. We are all soiled by his saga, by how long it took the compensatory mechanism to catch up with him, by what he left behind. We all smell of his exploded ego.

Doris Lessing's *The Four-Gated City*

O N FINISHING THIS book, you want to go out and get drunk. *The Four-Gated City* is less a work of art than an act of despair, and its cumulative effect is numbing. It depicts a world—from 1950 until 1997—in which technology and fascism have triumphed; a world in which sex and imagination and intelligence have been brutalized; a world of figurative and literal plague; and a world for which the only hope is drastic biological mutation. What makes Doris Lessing's black vision so compelling is that it is not the product of a literary debauch. It is not a satanic self-indulgence. It is not a tract. It is, instead, a painstaking extrapolation of the present, a sort of elephantiasis of the already obvious and the perfectly ordinary. It is the inevitable terminal point toward which the modern mind is monorailing. Those logical lunatics described by Wallace Stevens in *Esthétique du Mal*—men like Konstantinov, who "would not be aware of the clouds, / Lighting the martyrs of logic with white fire"—have taken over; and our blank uneasiness has turned to terror.

Martha Quest arrives in London in 1950 with an advanced case of blank uneasiness. The intellectual and emotional terrain she has crossed to get there has been exhaustively cartographed by Doris Lessing in the four previous volumes of the *Children of Violence* series. She has gone through a "Zambesian" (Rhodesian) childhood, two husbands, motherhood, racism, the Communist Party, and a war. *The Four-Gated City* will not only finish her off, but will finish off the series and England as well.

After some preliminary skirmishing, Martha settles down as a combination nursemaid-housekeeper-editorial-researcher in the home of Mark Coldridge, a novelist. At first the Coldridge household seems a domestic mirror image of the world outside: private madness taking refuge from public madness. Outside, there are totalitarianism and genocide; spiritual impotence and scientific evil. Inside, there are hallucinations and despair. And Martha Quest, somehow hanging out the window, videotapes it all.

But we become gradually aware that this time Miss Lessing is up to something different. Mark Coldridge has written a fantasy novel, part prophecy and part racial dream, about an ancient city ruled benignly by a clairvoyant priesthood. This "four-gated" golden city was betrayed— a kind of original sin ushering in our modern, postlapsarian civilization —and the clairvoyants went underground. Somehow their psychic powers were dispersed.

Coldridge's novel takes over from Doris Lessing's novel. Suddenly we are no longer living in the world of Doris Lessing's indefatigable realism, but in a nightmare of evil. The city and its destruction and its meaning can only be apprehended fleetingly in dreams; or perceived at the odd angle of madness. We are made to understand that the psychic powers dispersed at the time of the city's betrayal attach now in bits and pieces only to the dislocated and the outcast, the drugged and shocked and suicidal. Our final, chilling realization is that, after the bombs and the nerve gas and the holocaust, the children of these mad believers will be the new clairvoyants, the mutant hope of a new world.

Miss Lessing, in other words, has given up: on politics, on rationalism, on psychoanalysis (except for a dose of R. D. Laing). This most exemplary of modern women, who has moved like a relentless tank over the abstractions, aggressions, and dependencies of the twentieth century, who has noticed and remarked on everything, who has entertained and ultimately refused almost every illusion that tempts the contemporary intelligence, has given up. She seeks now, in prehistoric recesses and unconscious memory, a new sustaining myth, an island of the mind on which to hide.

And what is terrifying about her giving up is the absoluteness of the documentation. She has never been an elegant writer, and she has usually been a humorless one. But her mind is formidable, her integrity monumental, and her operating methods wholly uncompromising. She has not spared herself and she will not spare the reader. So she is not content merely to show us the asylum and the hospital. She grabs us by the lapels and drags us inside. She forces us to touch the slavering idiots and the haunted children, the ideas that fester and the flesh that rots. If hatred is the underbelly of "all this lovely liberalism," then she will take the knife to that belly. And if monsters then climb out of the knife wound, she will introduce them to us. The monsters are our fathers and our children and ourselves, and we can't ask Miss Lessing to dispatch them for us. She has done her job, and what a staggering one it is.

Nabokov's *Ada*

HERE IS VLADIMIR Nabokov's first new novel in seven years, twice as long as any book he has ever written before, and fourteen times as complicated. Naturally, the reviewer approaches it scared to death. Nabokov's prose is always booby-trapped, and if Edmund Wilson can get bombed (the "sapajou" joke in the Pushkin translation), mere mortals want to stay at home with the comic strips. Which is too bad, for there is more pleasure to be derived from a Nabokov novel than from almost anything else available in contemporary literature—or even, for that matter, from any mixed-media group-grope of deracinated starvelings desperate to groove the East Pillage obscene. Why leave the explications to the exegetes? Or the execration to those radical critics who keep trying to put N. down as some sort of recidivistic White Russian ingrate?

He is, as he once wrote about something else, "a goblet of rays of light and pus, / a mixture of toad and swan." He is, as well, our only living literary genius. Nobody else could have written an antideterministic masterpiece, contemptuous of Freud (there is no guilt) and Marx (there are no politics, no economics, not even any history), that is at once a sexual and philosophical romance, a brilliant science fiction, an awesome parody, and a gigantic punundrum.

Let me risk some tentative explications. *Ada* is:

(1) The anthropological description of an alternative world. N., by deciding that certain ancient wars, which were lost, should have been won, has rearranged history to suit himself. There are Russians all over North America, and, because all Russians speak French, they go about obsessively coining trilingual puns. N.'s world is called Antiterra. "Our"

world, Terra, is apprehended only by madmen, philosophers, and science fiction writers. The two worlds are out of technological phase, allowing N. to pump away on his narrative as though it were a slide rule.

(2) A theory of time which makes time a kind of privately owned supermarket of sensations and events, through which the artist strolls to impulse-buy. Time is always present, and the instant becomes eternal insofar as it engages and freezes consciousness into metaphor. (Intense love, for instance, is such a frozen slab of consciousness, always available for a quick fry in the imaginative oven.) Unfortunately, it's a theory of time that only works for geniuses, men of unlimited imaginative capital; the rest of us must live in an empirical funk.

(3) A parody of *Anna Karenina* in particular, the Russian novel in general, and the evolution of The Novel in universal. N. opens *Ada* with a reversal of Tolstoy's opening *Anna* paragraph, and then manages in one book to recapitulate all the various fecundations and despoliations that the great Earth Mother of Prose has had to endure from an army of ravishing innovators for centuries.

(4) A love story. *Ada* is, really, the memoir of a philosopher who, at age fourteen, fell in love with his cousin, age twelve. But the cousin, Ada, turns out to be his sister, and they spend the next seven decades solving the togetherness problem. During those decades, Ada sleeps around and the philosopher, Van, writes the treatises—"catching sight of the lining of time . . . the best informal definition of portents and prophecies"— which account for Explications 1 to 3.

It should be pointed out right here that Ada, as a character, is lovable. There are those critics who—resenting the fact that N. enjoyed a happy childhood—complain of his cerebral chill. They have ignored Pnin, Fyodor, Luzhin, Krug, and even Humbert Humbert in the earlier novels; but if they ignore Ada, there isn't a lyric spark in their gray clay hearts.

It should also be pointed out, before I give the one and only true explication of *Ada*, that the book is full of incidental games: N. makes fun of existentialism, of his own annotators, of Jorge Luis Borges, of Balzac, Kafka, Proust, Joyce, John Updike (very affectionately), and especially himself: "Her spectacular handling of subordinate clauses, her parenthetic asides, her sensual stressing of adjacent monosyllables . . . all this somehow finished by acting upon Van, as artificial excitements and exotic torture-caresses might have done, in an aphrodisiac sinistral direction that he both resented and perversely enjoyed."

Exactly. And what he's done in *Ada* is to write his own artistic auto-biography, a companion piece to *Speak, Memory*, a treatise on his own internal Antiterra. He has constructed an entire shimmering culture out of his exile and wanderings, a language out of his own experience. Combine Van (chess-playing, tone-deaf "old wordman") with Ada (butterfly collector, amateur botanist); superimpose them on a Russian America; add masks, deceit, memory, dreams, conjuring, apostasy, acrobatics, the zoo and the cage; celebrate the crime (which was that of Cincinnatus C.) of being opaque in a transparent world—and you have the elusive N., like "a bifurcated spectre . . . a candle between mirrors sailing off to a sunset."

He has written elsewhere that "the future is but the obsolete in reverse," and that "the only real number is one, the rest are mere repetition." *Ada*, dedicated to his wife, is his jeweled butterfly, singular, timeless, the man himself. If he doesn't win the Nobel Prize, it's only because the Nobel Prize doesn't deserve him.

Gabriel García Márquez's
One Hundred Years of Solitude

Y OU EMERGE FROM this marvelous novel as if from a dream, the mind on fire. A dark, ageless figure at the hearth, part historian, part haruspex, in a voice by turns angelic and maniacal, first lulls to sleep your grip on a manageable reality, then locks you into legend and myth. *One Hundred Years of Solitude* is not only the story of the Buendía family and the Colombian town of Macondo. It is also a recapitulation of our evolutionary and intellectual experience. Macondo is Latin America in microcosm: local autonomy yielding to state authority; anticlericalism; party politics; the coming of the United Fruit Company; aborted revolutions; the rape of innocence by history. And the Buendías (inventors, artisans, soldiers, lovers, mystics) seem doomed to ride a biological tragi-cycle from solitude to magic to poetry to science to politics to violence back again to solitude.

Which isn't to say that the book is grimly programmatic. It is often wildly funny, and superbly translated by Gregory Rabassa. Nor does the specific get buried under the symbolic. Macondo with its rains, ghosts, priests, Indians, Arabs, and gypsies is splendidly evoked. So richly realized are the Buendías that they invite comparison with Karamazovs and Sartorises. Indeed, specificity overwhelms incredulity, setting up the reader for imagist explosions more persuasive than mere data can ever be: Anything goes, and everything comes back.

Would you believe, for instance, men with machetes in search of the sea, hacking their way through "bloody lilies and golden salamanders" to find in a swamp a Spanish galleon? A plague of insomnia? A stream of blood feeling its path across a city from a dying son to a grieving mother?

A mule that eats sheets, rugs, bedspreads, drapes, and "the canopy embroidered with gold thread and silk tassels on the episcopal bed"? A Sanskrit manuscript predicting the hundred years of Macondo, down to the very deciphering of the prediction by the last Buendía? A paterfamilias chained to a tree in the garden, muttering in Latin? Or, when that paterfamilias finally dies, this consequence:

> A short time later, when the carpenter was taking measurements for the coffin, through the window they saw a light rain of tiny yellow flowers falling. They fell on the town all through the night in a silent storm, and they covered the roofs and blocked the doors and smothered the animals who slept outside. So many flowers fell from the sky that in the morning the streets were carpeted with a compact cushion and they had to clear them away with shovels and rakes so that the funeral procession could pass by.

I believe—in the last Buendía infant born as prophesied with the tail of a pig, and eaten alive by ants. In the brothel with alligators. In the three thousand dead strikers against the banana plantation, hauled away by silent train; and Remedios the Beauty, plucked up by the wind and flown to God as she hung up bedsheets to dry; and Melquiades, who introduces Macondo to the miracle of ice. I believe in all the Buendías, from the original José Arcadio and the original Ursula (cousins who marry and by mythic mitosis divide into generations of Arcadios and Aurelianos and Armarantas) down through "the most intricate labyrinths of blood" to the end of the family line in a room full of chamber pots in "the city of mirrors (or mirages)" as the wind comes to sweep away all memory.

Family chronicle, then, and political tour de force, and metaphysical romp, and, intentionally, a cathedral of words, perceptions, and details that amounts to the declaration of a state of mind: solitude being one's admission of one's own mortality and one's discovery that that terrible apprehension is itself mortal, dies with you, must be rediscovered and forgotten again, endlessly. With a single bound. Gabriel García Márquez leaps onto the stage with Günter Grass and Vladimir Nabokov, his appetite as enormous as his imagination, his fatalism greater than either. Don't miss this one.

Arthur Koestler's *Arrow in the Blue* and *The Invisible Writing*

FIRST, LET ME don a penitential sackcloth. Like cowards, reviewers try to kill the thing they love with an apothegm instead of a sword. Thus, commenting some months ago on a collection of essays, I said of Arthur Koestler: "On the twentieth-century grid, he is the ultimate waffle." How fearlessly inadequate! Macmillan's reissuings of the Koestler oeuvre in the handsome, uniform Danube Edition constitutes an enormous reproach. I had managed to forget that Koestler had taught my generation what we needed to know about the century that grilled him. On the evidence of his novels, essays, and four volumes of autobiography, he is the West's preeminent journalist. That he is equally uncomfortable with monogamy and ideology may account for his awe-inspiring vagabondage.

By journalist I mean no slur. If his autobiography lacks the literary elegance of Malraux's *Anti-Memoirs*, it is more specific and engrossing; nor does K. wrap himself in the Gaullist sheet of "I Am a Historical Enigma." If novels like *Darkness at Noon* (the Purge trials), *Thieves in the Night* (Palestinian terrorism), and *Arrival and Departure* (portrait of the revolutionary as a Jung man) are *romans à thèse*, they are still infinitely to be preferred to a bilious *roman à clef* like Simone de Beauvoir's *The Mandarins*, which did a disservice to K., Camus, Sartre, and even Nelson Algren. If *The Ghost in the Machine* and *Drinkers of Infinity* suggest a lamentable lust on K.'s part for material proofs of his metaphysical raptures, at least he seeks proofs, instead of foaming at the mouth about lapwings and absolutes.

A "Case History"

Two of the four autobiographical volumes, *Dialogue with Death* and *Scum of the Earth*, were written immediately after a stint in a Franco prison during the Spanish Civil War and a stint in a French concentration camp two years later. They are timebound. But *Arrow in the Blue* and *The Invisible Writing* deal with K.'s first forty years recollected in as much tranquility as such a man will ever permit himself. They add up, as he says, to "a typical case history of a member of the educated middle classes of Central Europe in the first half of our century," one of those refugees for whom a new word had to be coined: "Stepmotherland." Anger, anomaly, irony, and tragedy abound.

Here is K. as a child in Budapest, precocious and paralyzingly shy; an engineering student in Vienna, torn between political action and contemplative sloth; a twenty-year-old Zionist emigrating to Palestine; a Mideast correspondent for the Ullstein newspaper empire; a science editor turned Communist in Berlin at the moment of Hitler's ascendancy; the only reporter on a marvelous zeppelin expedition to the North Pole. To be followed by K. traveling in the Soviet Union during the famine years of the early thirties; working in Paris as a propagandist for the Willy Münzenberg *apparat*; seeking in Spain evidence of German-Italian collaboration with Franco; finding in Spain "the reality of the third order"; renouncing the Party, settling in England, writing his novels, surviving . . . unlike almost all of his friends, who die throughout these thousand pages at the hands of Hitler or Stalin.

Whether he is brooding about language (he went from writing in Hungarian to German to English, not to mention Hebrew and Russian) or attitudes ("The mystic of the nineteen-thirties yearned, as a sign of Grace, for a look at the Dneiper Dam and a three percent increase in the Soviet pig-iron production") or justice ("a concept of ethical symmetry, and therefore an essentially natural concept—like the design of a crystal") or English prisons ("It was nice to know that you were at a place where putting a man to death was still regarded as a solemn and exceptional event"), K. is superb.

Penchant for Action

His inferiority complex, as Otto Katz told him, may be the size of a cathedral. And, as Orwell said, "The chink in K.'s armor is his hedonism." But he was always where the action was, always scribbling, usually indignant. If his Cassandralike cries embarrassed his friends, they deserved to be embarrassed. (Just this month a magazine whose brows are not quite high enough to let it see much so wholly misses the point of Whittaker Chambers that Chambers, Koestler, Manès Sperber, Gustav Regler, Victor Serge, and André Gide might just as well have recorded their qualms in Quechua.)

As for that rapture, that "reality of the third order," it occurred to him while under a sentence of death in a Spanish prison. Its logic begins with Euclid's demonstration that, in the climb up a numerical series of prime numbers, we shall never discover a "virgin"—the highest prime. Therefore, he concluded, "a meaningful and comprehensive statement about the infinite is arrived at by precise and finite means." Should one object that such statements refer only to a man-made, not an infinite, scheme, one must still cope with K.'s undignified gallivanting after ESP as an anti-materialist proof. Mysticism: The last refuge of an infirm mind?

No. K. rejects any variety of determinism, and had we lived his life, we would, too. But isn't it possible to believe in choice without subscribing to the theistic swoon? Freud, a year before he died, granted K. an interview. Freud had never experienced the "oceanic feeling" nor seen the "invisible writing." Says K.: "I wondered with admiration and compassion, how a man can face his death without it." I submit, with admiration and compassion for the invaluable K., that we must all of us face our deaths without it, learning somehow to swim through what the existentialists have called a "vertigo of possibility." We have to take the rap for our own freedom.

Supergirl Meets the Sociologist

FIRST, LET'S GET rid of the transsexual mash notes. According to Letty Cottin Pogrebin ("an unabashed man fan") most men are "emotionally honest and uncomplicated . . . professionally realistic and straightforward . . . not devious or malicious in their personal relations . . . usually dependable confidants, lavish with praise, fair-minded, and seven and a half times out of ten they have fascinating intellects, interests, or opinions." According to me, without women the world wouldn't be worth living in; seven times out of ten, working women make better wives and mothers than the girl who settles for a tornado in her kitchen; and ten times out of ten, working women are more interesting than any other anybody. So much for the castrating feminist and all those hairy oafs who, never having graduated from the Cub Scouts, want for companionship a combination of Den Motherhood and Tupperwariness.

What's left? One side practicing karate chops, the other fantasizing about the primordial hunting party? Left is a society that wastes half its brains; a culture dividing its sexes according to work objects and play objects; a tax structure pinning women beneath a glass bell that is furnished only by a bed, an oven, and a diaper pail. (The daily $25 business lunch is tax-deductible; the daily $20 child care is not.)

To that society, culture, and tax structure both Letty Cottin Pogrebin and Cynthia Fuchs Epstein address themselves in very different but superbly complementary books. Mrs. Pogrebin—if you read her book you will realize how silly it seems to refer to her so formally—advertises the satisfactions of a career in publishing, advertising, TV, newspapers, motion pictures, and the stock market for women. Mrs. Epstein—who acknowledges her husband as "my most spirited educator in the dynamics of role allocation"—explores why women have a hard time making it as doctors, lawyers, scientists, architects, and engineers.

Presume a "Letty," at nineteen a graduate of Brandeis; at twenty-one director of publicity, advertising, and subsidiary rights for Bernard Geis; at twenty-nine a lawyer's wife, mother of three, happenstantially beautiful, loving every minute of it. Finishing her book, you want to mount a white stallion, gallop off, whisk her up, carry her to your castle where she can write your press releases, throw your parties, stun your friends, improve your mind. (Let's not deceive ourselves: possession is nine-tenths of sexual fantasy.) Alas, she's married. Then bottle her energy and sell it as pep pills; substitute her common sense for Muzak at all midtown business mausolea; feed her wit intravenously to Doctors Spock and Bettelheim; assign her to promote her book to the best-sellerdom it deserves.

She's Supergirl. *How to Make It in a Man's World* is an enchiridion for young women who don't want to deposit their brains in the sugar canister. "Anyone who doesn't like travel, parties, tasteful surroundings, good food, and intelligent people should have her head examined," she says, and then proceeds to spell out how to get paid for it. Whether the chapter is "The Helping Hand and How to Keep It Off Your Body" or "If You Can't Stand the Heat, Get Back to the Kitchen," she has more to say about sexual chauvinism, interoffice envy, the thoughtful boss, lying about your age, how to take a man to lunch—*strategy*—than Norman Podhoretz and Robert Townsend in triplicate. And her account of the time Brendan Behan tried to rape her is . . . mind-expanding.

But what if you aren't a Supergirl? Mrs. Epstein, assistant professor of sociology at Queens College and a project director at Columbia's Bureau of Applied Social Research, weighs in with the grim facts. *Women's Place* is sociology with a vengeance (tables, footnotes, clotted prose), but there is more hard data, perception, cross-cultural comparison, and historical grasp in this book than in any other tome on the Woman Question that I've ever seen. (Mrs. Pogrebin doesn't mention the fact that publishers push bright young women into publicity instead of permitting them to become editors.)

Beyond the Sex Curtain

Mrs. Epstein looks at American child rearing, role conflict, the professions, women's status in radical movements, the psychological consequences of piercing the Sex Curtain, and the ways that other countries cope with the problem. She isn't as breezy as Mrs. Pogrebin—e.g., "To the extent that a status is institutionalized within a body of other statuses and there are definite prescriptions as to the total composition, and to the extent to which one social pattern (social circle and social customs) is integrated with another social pattern (occupation and mode of operation within the occupation), the range of other possible statuses will be limited"—but she cuts deeper.

As of 1960, less than 10 percent of our lawyers, doctors, engineers, and scientists were women. (Eighty-five percent of our librarians, 97 percent of our nurses, were.) Women receive only 11 percent of all the Ph.D.s awarded in this country. Professional women are less than half as likely to be married as professional men. Mrs. Epstein explains why. It is an unsavory story. We should be doing better not only because society needs those female brains, but also because women happen to be people.

In my family, there is one Ph.D. It doesn't belong to me. There are two children. They are better than most. Betty Friedan may be right in interpreting sex bias as a means of preoccupying women with consumership. Mrs. Epstein may be right in deciding that "few middle-class women put the playthings of childhood behind them. . . . Their babies take the place of their dolls." Mrs. Pogrebin may be right in contending that most women are bored and failure-fearful. One thing's sure: Anyone still disposed to laughing off "Women's Liberation" is stupid.

Maxine Hong Kingston's
The Woman Warrior

THOSE RUMBLES YOU hear on the horizon are the big guns of autumn lining up, the howitzers of Vonnegut and Updike and Cheever and Mailer, the books that will be making loud noises for the next several months. But listen: This week a remarkable book has been quietly published; it is one of the best I've read in years.

The Woman Warrior is itself anything but quiet. It is fierce intelligence, all sinew, prowling among the emotions. As a portrait of village life in pre-Mao China, it is about as sentimental as Céline. As an account of growing up female and Chinese American in California, in a laundry of course, it is antinostalgic: It burns the fat right out of the mind. As a dream—of the "female avenger"—it is dizzying, elemental, a poem turned into a sword.

For Maxine Hong Kingston, who was born in Stockton, California, there are two sets of ghosts. One set is Chinese legends, traditions, folklore, and always the unwanted girl child. The other set is Western, American, barbarian, the machine-myths of the Occident. Somewhere in between, like the poet Ts'ai Yen, she is a hostage. And it isn't clear whether there is a place for her to return to, with her songs "from the savage lands."

The Warrior Woman traffics back and forth between sets of ghosts, reimagining the past with such dark beauty, such precision and anger and sadness, that you feel you have saddled the Tao dragon and see all through the fiery eye of God. Then, suddenly, you are dumped into the mundane, into scenes so carefully observed, so balanced on a knife-edge of hope and humiliation, that you don't know whether to laugh or cry. Other writers come to mind—García Márquez, who also knows how to dress myth up in living flesh; or, thinking about warrior women, Monique Wittig, if she had a sense of humor and before she lapsed into balderdash.

But this shuttling, on an electric line of prose, between fantasy and specificity, is wonderfully original. I can't remember when a young writer walked up to and into every important scene in a book and dealt with it outright, as Mrs. Kingston does, without any evasions whatsoever. Or an old writer, for that matter: they have their avoidance tricks. It wearies a writer always having to be in the best form, compromising the least with difficult material, unruly characters. It doesn't weary Mrs. Kingston. And Brave Orchid, the mother to end all mothers in this book, is more real to me than most of the people I see every day.

Who is Maxine Hong Kingston? Nobody at Knopf seems to know. They have never laid eyes on her. She lives in Honolulu, nicely situated between Occident and Orient, with a husband and small son. She teaches English and creative writing. There is no one more qualified to teach English and creative writing.

Edward Said's *Orientalism*

ONE OF THE reasons that Edward W. Said, Parr Professor of English and Comparative Literature at Columbia University, has written this book is that he himself was an "Oriental" child who grew up in the British "colonies" of Palestine and Egypt. His life is on the spindle.

And yet the "Orientalism" of which he speaks is entirely Western. It is a "trope," a "text," and an "archive" compiled by Western scholars, linguists, novelists, social scientists, and colonial administrators from the eighteenth century on. It is "a cumulative and corporate identity" as well as "a *distribution* of geopolitical awareness," a kind of multinational knowledge industry whose secret product is Western self-esteem. The Orient it invents in its laboratories—its museums and libraries—is one that denies the variety and reality of many nations, many peoples, many centuries, and countless individuals, including Mr. Said.

Reviewing the Specialists

Mr. Said, then, proposes to review the Orient of the Western Orientalists as if it were a book with a smarmy subtext, a subliminal anxiety, an anal compulsion to hoard and manipulate. From Antonio Gramsci, he borrows the notion of "hegemony" as "an indispensable concept for any understanding of cultural life in the industrial West." From Michel Foucault, he borrows the notions of "discourse" and "archaeologies," while insisting, against Foucault, on the significance of the imprint of the individual. He seems also to have learned a methodological thing or two from his colleague Steven Marcus, who applied techniques of literary criticism to a fantasy life of Victorians and to the pamphleteering of an Engels. He might also have consulted *The Tangled Bank* of Stanley Edgar Hyman, which treated the works of Darwin, Marx, Freud, and Frazer as imaginative literature.

He argues from the texts that we require such an Orient, hallucinated and nostalgic; that we need, psychologically, a changeless, dependent, and sexy *Other* in an existential equation that will prove the superiority of our science; that "Orientalism," as cataloged and codified and distributed by Westerners, has been essentially racist, imperialist, and "almost totally ethnocentric." It seems to me that his case is not merely persuasive, but conclusive.

Consider, at random, the presumptions of Silvestre de Sacy, Ernest Renan, Schlegel, Fourier, Massinnon, H.A.R. Gibb, Disraeli, and Balfour, or, just metaphorically, the excesses of Goethe, Hugo, Lamartine, Chateaubriand, Nerval, Flaubert, Byron, Richard Burton, and George Eliot. We insist on the mystery, but it must be historical and long gone and inaccessible to contemporary Orientals who require our instruction in their duty. We remove, in fragments, ancient wisdom which we explicate.

Explain, please, our ignorance and resentment of Islam. How long is this medieval hangover, this Constantinople of the fearful imagination, supposed to last? When we decided after the Enlightenment to be scientists instead of Christians, why was it that fledgling philologists decided that the Indo-European language group was superior to the Semitic, that one was "organic" and the other "inorganic"? How come, in the long history of imperialism, our Orientalists invariably condoned and conspired with the colonizers, "us," against the colonized, "them"?

Eden and Babylon

Think of the baggage we take with us as tourists, as "tyrannical observers": the "Arab mind"; the "passive, seminal, feminine, even silent and supine" East; the cluster of images we associate with the "Oriental stage," such as the Sphinx, Cleopatra, Eden, Troy, Sodom and Gomorrah, Astarte, Isis and Osiris, Sheba, Babylon, the Genii, the Magi, Nineveh, Prester John, Mahomet, Hanging Gardens, and cruel Turks and bad hygiene and dangerous sex.

Especially sex, even with boys. To be sure, as Mr. Said observes, "in the Orient one suddenly confronted unimaginable antiquity, inhuman beauty, boundless distance" which confounded "European discreteness and rationality of time, space, and personal identity." But sex, impossibly passive and guilt-free and therefore degenerate, was the coin of this imaginative realm, a displacement of political power, of scavenging. While we generalized about race, mind, culture, and nation, we masturbated.

Mr. Said is partial, inevitably, to Islam and the Levant, and so India and China don't get much notice. He is obsessed, understandably, with the British, the French, and the Americans, and so merely nods at the Germans, most of whom stayed home, anyway, to hallucinate. He scants Marx—see Reza Baraheni's critique of the "Asiatic Mode of Production"— and ignores Freud, who would be easy for him. I wish he had put more of himself onto the spindle. His contempt for us is oddly shy.

Nevertheless, *Orientalism*, in describing a quintessential treason of the clerks, is intellectual history on the high order of Alvin Gouldner's *The Coming Crisis of Western Sociology*, and very exciting. We are surrounded by "Orientalisms" of every sort from "the mind of the South" to childhood and madness and maybe even literary criticism. The ego of the tourist is imperial. No wonder we don't understand what's going on in Vietnam or Cambodia or Lebanon; we've never been there; we've only read about it.

Gay Talese's *Thy Neighbor's Wife*

THINKING ABOUT FICTION in *On the Contrary* (1961), Mary McCarthy explained:

> Making love, we are all more alike than we are when we are talking or acting. In the climax of the sexual act, moreover, we forget ourselves; that is commonly felt to be one of its recommendations. Sex annihilates identity, and the space given to sex in contemporary novels is an avowal of the absence of character. There are no "people" in *Lady Chatterley's Lover*, unless possibly the husband, who is impotent.

Mull that over for a moment while I circle around.

Sizing up the competition in *Advertisements for Myself* (1959), Norman Mailer decided that J. D. Salinger was "no more than the greatest mind ever to stay in prep school."

What have Norman Mailer (inventing a new category of literary criticism) and Mary McCarthy (distinguishing between climax and character) to do with Gay Talese, the gifted parajournalist who managed, in the big-game book hunt, first to bag the *New York Times* and then the Mafia, and who now moves on to shoot at sex in America, from the skin mag to the massage parlor to the commune, new uses for old organs?

Alas, nobody in *Thy Neighbor's Wife* seems ever to have graduated from junior high, not even Mr. Talese; hair grows on every pair of palms. And while the sex is dished up by the oodle—most of it in listless groups and saddened by greed and envy and petulance and bad faith—there is no character. Instead of people, we get recipes, ingredients, tics of personality, and vehement longings—the enigmatic anus!—that are supposed to amount to a person; add sperm and beat vigorously.

These recipes have real-life names, like Anthony Comstock of the New York Society for the Suppression of Vice and John Humphrey Noyes of Oneida and Barney Rosset of Grove Press and Hugh Hefner of *Playboy* and William Hamling of *Rogue* and Samuel Roth of the *Roth* decision and Wilhelm Reich of the orgone box, not to mention Masters and Johnson, Alex Comfort, Max Lerner, Hieronymus Bosch, booksellers, body painters, Supreme Court associate justices, centerfolds, and everybody else who helped make the sexual revolution possible. Since Mr. Talese parajournalizes so promiscuously—reaching into their minds, reading their thoughts, scratching their itches—one would expect to emerge from his book, as if from a novel, with some improved comprehension of what they stand for and a different angle on the culture that produced them. One emerges instead, as if from a mediocre movie in the middle of the afternoon, reproached by sunlight and feeling peripheral to the main business of the universe.

Of course, Maurice Girodias and Ralph Ginzburg and Edward Mishkin and Al Goldstein and Larry Flynt aren't exactly Lenin or Darwin or Bolivar or Daniel Boone or Captain Kangaroo. What they stand for seems no more complicated than the right to cash in on loneliness; what they have achieved is to make America safe for pubic hair; they wave a fellated flag. The First Amendment, in my opinion, protects even the toads in the erotic garden, but it doesn't oblige us to admire them. Still, these men had mothers and, like the rest of us, they will die alone. If Mr. Talese—who wrote the advertisement comparing Larry Flynt to a Soviet dissident, which I signed with the usual misgivings—expects us to take his revolutionaries as seriously as he himself takes them, he has to put them in a social context and make them sound interesting. He doesn't.

I've met Barney Rosset; my appreciation of him is in no way improved by the news that he is descended from "a hapless Russian Jewish patriarch who made corks for champagne bottles." I've met Max Lerner; I would like to know what, if anything, he thought of the Sandstone sex commune run by a part-time engineer who turned himself into a philosopher by reading the novels of Ayn Rand. I haven't met Howard Rubin, the Chicago boy who grew up to run a massage parlor; why should I care that he favored masturbating in front of photographs of Diane Webber in an "art-camera" magazine in 1957? Nor have I met Hugh Hefner, another

Chicago boy who grew up to run the magazine for which I am writing, but I wonder whether I am much the wiser for being told that—

High Hefner remembers being an usher in a movie theater . . . he took long walks through the Chicago night looking up "at the luxurious towering apartment houses," seeing "women standing at the windows," imagining "that they were as unhappy as he was," wanting "to know all of them intimately" . . . he drinks twelve bottles of Pepsi-Cola every day . . . he bought Barbi Benton a red cotton-candy machine . . . there are satin sheets on his rotating bed in Chicago . . . on the other hand, on the round bed in the black DC-9 jet he had to sell, unfortunately, there used to be a Tasmanian opposum fur coverlet . . . whereas, once upon a time at the Acapulco airport, he stomped on his own briefcase, although we aren't sure whether he was wearing white socks that day—

Heavy stuff. Why, Talese asks himself, have so "many Americans accused of scandalous publishing and trading" been born and raised in Chicago—like Hefner and Hamling and Rosset, like Marvin Miller of the X-rated movies and the porno paperbacks, like Ed Lange who snapped all those shots of Diane Webber that Howard Rubin used to ogle? And then why did so many end up in Los Angeles? He replies: "It was as if that strongly Irish-Catholic town was destined to produce sexually obsessed native sons, most of whom would eventually exile themselves into more liberal surroundings. Chicago was America's Dublin."

Which makes Los Angeles America's Paris, crash pad for our homegrown Jimmy Joyces and Sam Becketts? I ask: Why not, instead of Chicago, a strongly Irish-Catholic Boston in Massachusetts, or a strongly Mormon Provo in Utah, or a strongly German Cincinnati in Ohio? I also ask myself why I'm asking. Is *Hustler* in any way to be distinguished from *Playboy* or *Sunshine & Health*? Are the Women Against Pornography merely silly? According to *Thy Neighbor's Wife*, feminism never happened. Norman O. Brown had nothing to say on the tyranny of genital organization. Freud is trivialized. Marx, had he but been mentioned, would probably be chastised, because I'm sure Marx, on taking one long look at the romper room in which we live, would have reminded us that the "fetishism of commodities" applies as much to the anatomy as it does to electrical appliances. Children, conveniently, do not exist, or were a mistake, making group sex—Tinkertoys! Erector Sets!—a hassle.

After everybody else has split for California, where they remove their disposable clothes and go to water bed, I want to have a long talk with the autumnal Freud. Is sublimation really insupportable? If I defer my gratification, will you defer yours? Freud smokes a sad cigar. Did you know, Freud asks me, that Hefner began as a cartoonist, doing obscene parodies of the Dagwood and Blondie comic strip? Freud reminds me that in the motels of California the recipes are discussing "primary relationships." Freud, had he taken one long look, without reading *Screw* magazine, would probably not have written:

> *Four hundred thousand young people, several of them naked and smoking pot, sat listening to a rock concert in Woodstock, New York.*
>
> —Talese

Even Grace Slick knows that everybody at Woodstock was stoned, and it had nothing to do with Moses or monotheism or civilization and its discontents. On the whole, Freud would prefer reading Hunter Thompson on the sort of people who made Altamont possible, or Joan Didion on the Manson gang, or Norman Mailer on J. D. Salinger.

Mary McCarthy, I imagine, is amused to learn that Hefner was disinclined to publish in *Playboy* advertisements referring to such male frailties as baldness, obesity, acne, halitosis, athlete's foot, or hernias. She is, perhaps, alarmed to hear that Hefner's favorite writer was F. Scott Fitzgerald and not Spinoza or St. Augustine.

Mr. Talese is efficient in reporting the history of obscenity prosecutions in this country; Irving Wallace's account of the same in his novel *Seven Minutes* is more fun. Mr. Talese has ambivalent feelings about the sex clubs, like Plato's Retreat, that are now as endemic to a major metropolis as the municipal strike and the air quality that is unacceptable; I prefer the heightened version provided by Jerzy Kosinski in his latest novel, *Passion Play*. Mr. Talese is casual in his précis of D. H. Lawrence; one would do better to consult Mr. Mailer in his *Prisoner of Sex*. Mr. Talese covets Wilhelm Reich; he ought to read Paul Robinson's *The Freudian Left*. Mr. Talese is interesting on the sexual politics of the Oneida colony in the nineteenth century; Nathaniel Hawthorne was more interesting in his novel on Brook Farm. What Mr. Talese has to say about Ayn Rand was said better by Whittaker Chambers, the famous ex-Communist who translated *Bambi*, in his review of *Atlas Shrugged* in the pages of *National Review*, a magazine without pubic hair.

What has possessed Mr. Talese, whom I have met and who has never before been dull? The reporter in him flounders, except for a memorable moment when one of his recipes visits the headquarters of an insurance company in Manhattan:

> Visiting the archives of New York Life during his first week in the building, Bullaro saw in glass cases the famous signatures of entombed policyholders: General Custer, Rogers Hornsby, Franklin D. Roosevelt; and there were also on display the photographs of disasters that had been costly to the company—the Iroquois Theater fire in Chicago in 1903 in which nineteen policyholders burned to death; the San Francisco earthquake of 1904 which included in its devastation a branch office of New York Life; the supposedly indestructible *Titanic* which sank in 1912 with eleven policyholders aboard, and the liner *Lusitania* that was torpedoed in 1915 by German submarines, causing the death of eighteen passengers who had been insured by New York Life.

Neat stuff, although—and I am reading a Xerox of *Thy Neighbor's Wife*, probably unedited, because the lead time for Mr. Hefner's magazine, in which you will never hear about the heartbreak of psoriasis, is many months earlier than books are published or children are born—a professional parajournalist would have known that the San Francisco earth actually quaked in 1906; and that the Free Speech Movement in Berkeley, California, started off in 1964, not 1965 (I met FSM, too: 1964, in particular, was a very good year for revolting in the Bay Area); and that, while he might have wound up as a Los Angeles Ram, the Bernie Casey who cohabited with Max Lerner and Alex Comfort and Daniel Ellsberg at Sandstone in the nude spent most of his professional football career with the San Francisco 49ers.

Quibbles. As *Thy Neighbor's Wife* percolates at Doubleday, these questions may be moot. So, too, may any complaints about style self-destroy: The lazy misuse of "presently" and "hopefully" will disappear; the relentless, almost maniacal splitting of infinitives, four or more to the page, will be corrected; and when a husband calls his wife prior to group sex and a divorce action, most of you will not be required to read, from the husband's point of view, these locutions:

1. Calling Judith to suggest that they have dinner at their favorite restaurant, she refused . . .
2. Still speechless on the phone, Judith asked if he could hear her.

And nobody, anymor, can spelllt.

But what, after his years in massage parlors and *New York* magazine and Hefner's cerebellum and this month's (November) *Esquire*, has Mr. Talese decided is good or bad about our sexual seething? Is the act itself, no-holds-barred, recreational and hygienic, rather like horizontal jogging, healthy and annihilating? Mr. Talese teases. Sometimes the little boy outside the window of the toy-sex shop, he seems to slaver; elsewhere, where his brain-clock is wound up and ticks, he appears to want to punish his Bullaros for their foolish risk and their membership in the John Birch Society. At a nudist colony, one finds oneself without the pockets where one is accustomed to hide one's irony.

Freud, who is considering a Retreat to Plato, just asked me whether, in the postindustrial whatever, we insist on service centers for a baffled eros; if, as cars have filling stations, the rest of us need emptying, on odd and even days. According to Mr. Talese, Arthur Bremer, wearing a tie and a vest, failed to achieve orgasm in a massage parlor only a month before he shot and paralyzed Governor George Wallace. I told Freud to read Thomas Mann and J. D. Salinger.

We all flounder, left in junior high school. According to Tallulah Bankhead:

> I don't know what I am, dahling. I've tried several varieties of sex. The conventional position makes me claustrophobic. And the others either give me a stiff neck or lockjaw.

According to Irving Howe, who does not approve of the Me-First decade, romper room is

> a curious analogue to laissez-faire economics . . . by means of which innumerable units in conflict with one another achieve a resultant of cooperation. Is there, however, much reason to suppose that this will prove more satisfactory in the economy of moral conduct than it has in the morality of economic

relations? . . . Against me, against my ideas, it is possible to argue, but how, according to this new dispensation, can anyone argue against my *need*?

Is anybody happier? According to Mr. Talese, history and stamina and celebration and mystery, along with birth, blood, death, and beauty, not to mention earth, fire, water, work, politics, and everything else that isn't our urgent plumbing, that refuses to swim in our libidinal, all is uncool. Have hormones, lack character, need higher education.

Robert Stone's *A Flag for Sunrise*

HOLD ON TO your tricorn hat, or your cruciform, or your Uzi. In his third novel, after *A Hall of Mirrors* and *Dog Soldiers*, Robert Stone decides to be Dostoyevsky. Perhaps, on conceiving *A Flag for Sunrise*, he was more modest. He would be Graham Greene, sending various quiet, stupid Yanquis to Central America. He would be Joseph Conrad, hyperventilating near a convenient pyramid. He would be Herman Melville, reversing Billy Budd, as if Christ were a black hole or a woman's glove. But he thrashes his way—spaced out on ideas and angry love, possessed by comparative religion, punished by God and history—to Fyodor and a blue eye that turns into a blind sun. He swaggers in evil.

Here are the components of an exalted thriller: courage, dream, sex, compromise, betrayal, blood, ambivalence. Tecan, a serf state somewhere in the "waist" of the two American hemispheres, is on the verge of revolution; this time, the mineral-hungry oligarchs have gone too far. That revolution will be abetted by Atapa Indians so brutal in their simplicity, their "vulgarization," as to prove Marx prescient; by an American nun, "the Queen of Swords"; by a psychopath who has deserted from the United States Coast Guard; by gunrunners who seem to have wandered in from a bad Fellini film, and by the usual Comintern riffraff, including Hungarian Stalinists and Spanish romantics.

Rehearsal for Slaughter

Opposing the revolution are several less-than-charming employees of the Central Intelligence Agency, a remittance man for international capital, a

homicidal Tecan police lieutenant, an albino dwarf, Mafia drug dealers
and chicken hawks, and many jeeps, like taxis to disaster, and many helicopters, like carrion birds. Looking on are an American journalist who
disappears in the mountains, an American priest who drinks his way to
heresy, and an American anthropologist who believes that "Mickey
Mouse will see you dead."

Before the revolution, as if in dress rehearsal for the slaughter of the
innocent, dogs die—and children and young women just passing through.
Anybody in *A Flag for Sunrise* who isn't just passing through—anachronistic
hippies, European apparatchiks, "dilettantes" of apocalypse, tourists of a
South that "reeks of poverty and revenge"—has been "turned around."
Intellectuals have been "turned around" to become intelligence agents; the
Coast Guard deserter is "turned around" any time anyone hurts his feel-
ings; the face of God is "turned around." Turning around requires a "cover."

The anthropologist, Frank Holliwell, falls in love with the Queen of
Swords, Sister Justin: "It would be strange to see people who believed in
things, and acted in the world according to what they believed." Sister
Justin—"shroud weaver," imagining "serenity"—wants to be "used," if
not by God then by history. If we aren't in Holliwell's mind or Justin's,
we are with Pablo, the deserter and psychopath with a diamond in the
pocket of his shirt and a knife strapped in a plastic sheath to his leg.

Holliwell seems to be our best bet. A man of "no blood or folk," from
another planet, "forever inquiring of helpful strangers the nature of their
bonds with one another" and for whom "regret" is "second nature, the
very fluid of his veins," he is nevertheless a husband, father, and teacher,
"capable of honor and sacrifice," disdainful of murder, vampires, phantom
worship, "the gang," positive thinkers with "their eyes awash in their own
juice." He tells us, and Justin, "When I decide what happened, I'll decide
to live with it."

What he can't live with is Vietnam, where he was compromised. For
most of the Americans in *A Flag for Sunrise*, Vietnam is a disease: "Cooking oil, excrement, incense, death. The smell of the world turning."
Another turnaround. For these Americans, Vietnam holds "a kind of
moral fascination." They liked being there, and can't forgive themselves.
They no longer believe in "the just rule of the Lord" that is proposed by
the Roman Catholic revolutionaries. Their Lord was north, and blue-
eyed. The Lord never should have discovered that "each is alone" and
"the rest is fantasy." Holliwell can't rid himself of "the saffron taste" of

Vietnam. "The green places of the world" swarm and bleed and avenge; we experience "existential dread," which is easy.

This thriller has gotten out of hand, hasn't it? We are made to understand why, as a nation, we are hated. The blue eye is blind, sacrificed. Mr. Stone tells us more than we want to know about guilt and strangers. His novel smells of bars and jukeboxes, of boats and ideas, of a Roman Catholicism in the sweat tank of conscience, hoping for a symbol and achieving merely a gesture. That his characters can breathe at all, between the fingers clenched about their dream, is amazing.

But the Church yields to history. The drama is played out among spider monkeys and coconuts, near a pyramid, looking at stelae that aren't quite Mayan—a little Olmec here, with the jaguars; a little Toltec there, with human sacrifice; some Yeats, and Calderon to terrify us—as we sink past that "brain coral" in which we see "the skull of the earth," with which skull we play ball games.

Living in Heresy

The heresy here is Gnostic and Manichaean. There is a "divine spark" and "a library in a jar." Culture and love are both "secret." The demiurge is a tourist. The angels go south and are devoured. The "messenger" reports to a CIA machine. Holliwell is afraid to look at the sun. In the absence of evil—to an anthropologist, nothing is evil, including himself—we have history: snakes, feathers, lizards, jewels, a fanged cat, a wooden cross, a unicorn, and death without mercy.

Mr. Stone kicks the brain around; we live in heresy; Satan prevails; *A Flag for Sunrise* is the best novel of ideas I've read since Dostoyevsky escaped from Omsk.

Tom Wolfe's *The Bonfire of the Vanities* and Jim Sleeper's *In Search of New York*

I. The Way We Are

We live in this imaginary city, a novel that needs a rewrite, where the only politicians not in jail probably ought to be, except for Ruth Messinger, and all of them are Democrats; where the unions don't care, and the schools don't work, and the cops deal drugs, and the mayor has his own foreign policy, and I can't leave home without stepping over the body of a runaway or a derelict. We didn't elect Felix Rohatyn to anything, but the Municipal Assistance Corporation is more important than the City Council. Nor did we vote for Steinbrenner, Trump, or the rest of the bullies and crybabies who bray on our battlements and wave the bloody pennants of their imperial, omaphagous selves—and yet Mort Zuckerman will have his Zuckermandias at Columbus Circle, his finger in the sun, on the same Coliseum site from which Robert Moses before him dispossessed an entire neighborhood; and because none of these heroes ever takes the subway, there's no one to shoot them. Maybe we need Jeremiah more than we need Tom Wolfe or a bunch of disappointed intellectuals.

But Wolfe and *Dissent* have written their New York novels anyway. Wolfe, the parajournalist, looks pretty much the same as always, still grinning at us out of the nimbus of his double-breasted signature white suit, a vanilla-colored Mau Mau. *Dissent*, on the other hand, has had a format face-lift and for the first time in thirty-three years you can read the socialist quarterly without an *OED* magnifying glass. In both their novels, the underclass is the stuff of dreams, the return of the repressed, a kind of historical black magic. They disagree, of course, on whether this is a good thing.

Listen to Wolfe: "You don't think the future knows how to cross a *bridge*? And you, you WASP charity-ballers sitting on your mounds of inherited money up in your co-ops with the twelve-foot ceilings and the two wings, one for you and one for the help, do you really think you're impregnable? And you German-Jewish financiers who have finally made it into the same buildings, the better to insulate yourselves from the shtetl hordes, do you really think you're insulated from the *Third World*?"

Dissent wants this very same Third World—2.5 million "newcomers" since 1965—to be an energizing principle. In diversity we've always found our jumping beans. From the abrasions of culture on culture, we rub up a public philosophy and a civic space. Surely these new immigrants, this ethnic muscle, will rescue us from a mood grown "sullen, as if in contempt of earlier feelings and visions" and "a peculiar kind of social nastiness" (Irving Howe); a "trained incapacity to see the city as a human environment or as anything more than a machine for generating money" (Marshall Berman); "a way of life not much better than jungle warfare" (Ada Louise Huxtable); and "a world devised in its entirety by Dostoyevski's Smerdyakov" (Paula Fox).

It's odd that Wolfe is so much better than *Dissent* on the details of class animus. And he knows exactly where to look for them. Whereas *Dissent* can barely bring itself to mention cops, Wolfe goes underground into the criminal justice system, where the hatred is naked. If *Dissent* is too polite these days to call anybody an out-and-out racist, Wolfe has been to some fancy dinner parties and taken notes, like St. Simon, and bites the hand that scratched his ears, like Truman Capote. It's equally odd that Ed Koch, who certainly deserves it, is all over the pages of *Dissent*, while Wolfe entirely ignores him. A New York novel without Koch is like a court without a Sun King. Even Danny Ortega took time out to rub Crazy Eddie's lucky hump.

But there are many oddities. Neither New York novel has much of anything to say about drugs or organized crime. Both mention Alexander Cockburn.

II. Vanities

Sherman McCoy is a thirty-eight-year-old Yalie who decided to sell bonds on Wall Street instead of going into his father's good-bones law

firm. He made almost a million dollars last year, but when he sits down
on his oxblood Moroccan leather swivel chair in front of the tambour
door of his faux-Sheraton TV cabinet, he's still broke because of his
$2.6-million tenth-floor Park Avenue duplex, a Southampton house on
Old Drover's Mooring Lane, a wife who decorates her interiors with
Thomas Hope chairs, three servants, a handyman, club dues, car insurance for the Mercedes, and private school tuition for cute little Campbell
who, "supremely ladylike in her burgundy Taliaferro jumper and white
blouse with a buttercup collar," bakes bunnyrabbits in the kitchen and
writes short stories about sad koala bears.

Sherman also has a bimbo. Wolfe's no better than Bill Buckley at
heavy-breathing, so he borrows from his betters. Poor-white-Southern-
trashy Maria—faithless wife and merry widow—slinks right out of a
1940s detective novel into Sherman's nerveless arms: "Her medium was
men . . . the way a dolphin's medium is the sea." At the wheel of Sherman's Mercedes, at night on an off-ramp in darkest Bronx, Maria will hit,
run down, and run away from a young, black, fatherless "honor student"
of the nearby bombed-out Projects, and Sherman will be blamed.

This malefaction will excite a black demagogue, the Reverend Reginald Bacon of Harlem; a white, Kunstlerlike attorney, the radically chic
Amos Vogel; an English reporter for a Murdoch-minded tabloid, the
alcoholic Peter Fallow; a Jewish DA up for reelection in a Bronx that's 70
percent black and Hispanic, the publicity-hungry Abe Weiss; a Jewish
assistant DA who'd rather be an Irish cop, the horny and impoverished
Lawrence Kramer; assorted Communists, "the lesbos and the gaybos,"
welfare bums, and fluffy-headed TV nightly-news anchorpeople.

Poor Sherman. In his rent-controlled love nest, he's menaced by the
landlord's hired Hasidic muscle. ("These . . . unbelievable people . . .
could now walk into his life.") When the cops ("insolent . . . Low
Rent . . . *animals*") come to take him to the Bronx for his arraignment,
they are driving ("*the brutes* from the outer boroughs") an Oldsmobile
Cutlass! When he looks down from his tenth-floor co-op, a black mob is
howling for his blueblood. (The *Other* is gaining on *him*!)

Only Tom Wolfe could descend into the sewers of our criminal justice
system and find for his hero a *white* victim in a city where Bernie Goetz
gets six months, John Gotti and Ray Donovan walk, Robert Chambers
blames the victim, and Ellen Bumpurs and Michael Stewart are still dead.
Only Wolfe could want to be our Balzac and yet not notice the real-estate

hucksters and the homeless nor send a single one of his characters to a concert, movie, play, museum, Chinese restaurant, or all-night delicatessen. So the women are Tinkertoys, the blacks corrupt cartoons, the sex silly and the homophobia tedious, the politics a surly whelp of Evelyn Waugh and Joseph de Maistre, and the author less amusing than he was when he trashed modern art. Nobody's perfect.

But on several subjects, all but disdained by *Dissent*, Wolfe can really sweat our socks.

III. The "Delirious Professions" . . . Fear . . . (and) . . . Shoes

By the "delirious professions," Paul Valéry meant "all those trades whose main tool is one's opinion of one's self, and whose raw material is the opinion others have of you." In other words, Creative People, who in New York are not merely artists and writers, actors, dancers, and singers, but journalists, editors, critics, TV and radio producers, anchorpeople and talk-show hosts, noisy professors of uplift or anomie, vagabond experts on this week's Rapture of the Deep at the 92nd Street Y, even (gasp) advertising account execs and swinging bankers and Yuppies in red suspenders on the Stock Exchange. Each is asked every minute of the day to be original: *unique*. Only then will they be lifted up by their epaulets to Steinbrenner's box in the Stadium sky, there to consort with city presbyters the likes of the late Roy Cohn, where you can't tell the pearls from the swine.

Dissent isn't interested in these people, these vanities and their white suits and their bonfires. When *Dissent* nods at the market, it's merely to observe that "a multibillion-dollar, cost-plus, militarized economy virtually guarantees spectacular profits to investors in the West and South" (Berman). When it mentions the media at all, it's only to complain of their role in a "bipartisan incumbent-protection society" and their "'objective' contempt" for politics as anything other than "sport" (Jim Chapin), or to make fun of *Manhattan,inc.* and *Spy* (Brian Morton). Where, for heaven's sake, is an analysis of the *Times*? How come *Newsday* was the only daily to oppose the reelection of Al D'Amato (whom Irving Howe calls "picklehead")? For *Dissent*, the "delirious professions" belong merely and anonymously to a "service sector" as remote from the new Third World as Mars.

Yet these are the people, making images and taste and deals, who write the city's zeitgeist, the heat waves and cold fronts and snow jobs and acid rain of our emotional weather. Without their complicity, there will be no change. Change needs better PR. Dazzle them—mostly male and mostly pale—into a militant sentience. At least take seriously their many failures of intelligence and character.

And Wolfe can't get enough of them: "They were moving about in an agitated manner and sweating early in the morning and shouting, which created the roar. It was the sound of well-educated young white men baying for money on the bond market." Prestaggered cash flows! Convertible asset management! Capital-sensitive liquidity ratios! He's got their number: "He was wearing a covert-cloth Chesterfield topcoat with a golden brown velvet collar and carried one of those burgundy leather attaché cases that came from . . . T. Anthony on Park Avenue and have a buttery smoothness that announces: 'I cost $500.'" He obviously knows his way around the *Post*, where he found that the press are "fruit flies" and the TV types are print-dependent bubblebrains (although demonstrators only appear to protest the latest outrage when they're sure the camera's rolling) and "dancers, novelists, and gigantic fairy opera singers [are] nothing but court jesters" to the bond-selling "Masters of the Universe."

Wolfe knows, too, that his delirious professionals—"frisky young animal[s] . . . of that breed whose natural destiny it was . . . to have what they wanted!"—are scared to death, especially on the subway: "Into the car came three boys, black, fifteen or sixteen years old, wearing big sneakers with enormous laces untied but looped precisely in parallel lines. . . . They walked with the pumping gait known as the Pimp Roll. . . . They drew closer, with the . . . cool blank look. . . . Such stupid self-destructive macho egos."

It's the attitude. Compare Wolfe's to a lovely riff from Wesley Brown in *Dissent*: "A display of bravado by a young, indigo-skinned black male, moving through a crowded subway car like a point guard bringing the ball up court, sporting a haircut that makes the shape of his head resemble a cone of ice cream, and wearing barge-sized sneakers with untied laces thick as egg noodles, is immediately considered a dangerous presence whether he is or not." By whom? By delirious professionals. On the subway, the First World and the Third coincide, at least until the express stop at Columbus Circle.

They are afraid, too, that what they do is make believe; that their luck and charm will run out; that they will look in the mirror one morning and see, if not the other side of the room, then maybe something no longer brand-new and unique, someone *found out*, like Sherman. They will lose their co-op and our good opinion. As cops and press and mob close in on Sherman, his megabucks Paris deal on Giscard bonds is also falling apart, and his panic is palpable. (Nobody writing for *Dissent* seems to be afraid: angry, maybe, or tired, or sad, or contemptuous, but not scared.) Wolfe makes us sweat. As bad as he is on sex, he's terrific on money and hangovers and . . . *shoes*.

There are no shoes in *Dissent*. (There are two references to "shoemakers," but that's just left-wing atavism.) Whereas shoes are Wolfe's big story, from "the Boston Cracked Shoe look" to Maria's "electric-blue lizard pumps with white calf caps on the toes" to Sherman's $650 bench-made half-brogued English New & Lingwoods with the close soles and beveled insteps. Shoes for Wolfe are character. Sherman's dandified defense attorney wears brown suede shoes. Assistant DA Kramer wears Johnston & Murphy clodhoppers. A witness for the prosecution is partial to snow-white Reeboks, but they make him change into leather loafers for the grand jury. Ballet slippers or "go-to-hell sneakers" with Velcro straps, Wolfe's gone that extra mile and worn them.

What does this mean? More than you think. I've consulted Krafft-Ebing's *Psychopathia Sexualis*, Sacher-Masoch's *Venus in Furs*, and Kurella's *Naturgeschichte des Verbrechers*. I know more than I ought to about high-buttoned patent-leather boots, "Hungarian high heels," the legend of Aschenbrodel, the toe-sucking (and later beatified) Marie Alacoque, foot-fetishists East (Junichiro Tanizaki) and West (Rétif de la Bretonne), not to mention vampirism, anthropophagy, and koprolagnia, and not even to think about "shoes of the fisherman" Christian symbolism. On one level, the meaning of shoes in Wolfe is upward mobility—we are what we feet—but there is of course a subtext. Not one, but two Primal Scenes in *Bonfire* make this obvious.

The young men baying for money on the bond market spend most of their time with their mouth on a telephone and their shoes in a stirrup. Felix, the middle-aged black shoeshine man, "was humped over, stropping Sherman's right shoe, a New & Lingwood half-brogue, with his high-shine rag . . . Sherman enjoyed the pressure of the rag on his metatarsal bones. It was a tiny massage of the ego, when you got right down to it—this great strapping brown man, with the bald spot in his crown down there at his feet, stropping, oblivious of the levers with which Sherman could move another nation, another continent, merely by bouncing words off a satellite."

But the Master of the Universe will be punished. Shoes in Wolfe's novel are like guns in Chekhov's plays; they have to go bang. Before Sherman is fingerprinted in the Bronx, he's made to stand outside in the rain and soak his New & Lingwoods. And before he's tossed in the holding pen, where surly men of color want to wrinkle his friskiness, he is made to remove his belt *and his shoelaces,* "like two little dried dead things." His pants fall down and his shoes fall off and he has to *shuffle:* "The shoes made a squishing sound because they were so wet." At the end of *Bonfire* Sherman changes into hiking boots, and we know why. Shoes are sex.

IV. There Are More Than Three Worlds

From Wolfe, you wouldn't know that we've got one big problem with real-estate developers, and another with the homeless. For *Dissent,* these are strophe and antistrophe, as in an old Greek choral ode, with everybody moving right to left and back again. To be sure, Deborah Meier, the heroine of District 4, has important things to say about "teaching for testing" and alternative schools; and Maxine Phillips would like to pay for the care of our sixty thousand children who are abused or neglected each year by taxing cooperative apartments like Sherman McCoy's; and Theresa Funicello is furious at "workfare," wondering why "a black woman hired as a nanny for an upper class white family is a 'worker,' while a mother struggling under adverse conditions to raise her own children on welfare . . . is a parasite on society"; and Anthony Borden points out that 55 percent of all our AIDS victims are black or Latino, and so are 90 percent of our AIDS children, who never had a chance to say no to anything; and Gus Tyler looks at what happened to labor-intensive light manufacturing in this city (it went to Korea and Taiwan); and Michael Oreskes follows the garment industry to nonunion sweatshops in Chinatown or Queens; and Jewel Bellush explains the "room at the top" for black women in organizing hospital, school, and clerical workers; and John Mollenkopf can't find a "good government" reform movement anywhere.

Moreover, *Dissent*'s a lot more cultured than Wolfe. This novel has a chapter by Paul Berman on the sexual confusion and political ambivalence of those "prisoners of culture" who live below Fourteenth Street and therefore have to read Kathy Acker, look at David Salle, listen to Peter Gordon, and go to plays by Albert Innauratto; and a chapter by Juan Flores on the convergence of black and Puerto Rican cultures in "hip-hop," by way of Bo Diddley, Joe Cuba, Frankie Lymon, doo-wop, *capoeira*, break dancing, and rap; and a chapter by Ellen Levy on group theater versus performance art. And then it's Memory Lane: Michael Harrington, who may have less to be ashamed of than any other man of the left I know, admires Ruth Messinger and tries hard to remember when Crazy Eddie was a liberal. Morris Dickstein and Robert Lekachman feel bad and write agreeably about the Upper West Side and our favorite slumlord, hail-Columbia. Rosalyn Drexler and Leonard Kriegel go back to the Bronx (all that Art Deco on the Grand Concourse), and Kriegel finds a whole new *Irish* community Wolfe must have missed while soaking Sherman's shoes. Alfred Kazin has fun spanking such avatars of agitprop as N. Podhoretz, A. Cockburn, H. Kramer, and G. Vidal, and then he gets serious: "When the great Reagan counterrevolution is over, what I shall remember most is the way accommodating intellectuals tried to bring to an end whatever was left among Jewish intellectuals of their old bond with the oppressed, the proscribed, the everlasting victims piled up now in every street."

Which brings us back to the grubby and the brutish. Marshall Berman itemizes everything Tom Wolfe never noticed: "spectacular giveaways to real estate operators; the attacks on the poor, depriving them of industrial work, low-income housing, public hospitals; . . . the casual brutality that has come to permeate our public life, as in the recent wave of mass arrests to drive homeless people out of the railway terminals that the city's own development policies have driven them into; the triumphal march of the city's rejuvenated political machines, whose movers . . . have made the 1980s one long carnival of white-collar crime; the rescue of the city from the clutches of a hostile federal government, by selling it (or giving it away) to rapacious real estate empires that will tear down anything or throw up anything, if it pays; the long-term transformation of New York into a place where capital from anywhere in the world is instantly at home, while everybody without capital is increasingly out of place."

In this corner: the Cross-Bronx Expressway, the Coliseum, Lincoln Center, Westway, Zuckermandias, Trump Television City, Times Square as Alphaville and Disney World. In the opposite corner: the homeless—the usual ghosts, of course, on the brownstone stoop with the little green bottles, and the bag lady who reads *Vogue*, and the portly sociopath with the green beret and the eight-inch pigsticker, as well as the ambassador of this month's designer-zombie mushroom, nodding off on his way to where the action isn't. But they were our "regulars," and they've been overwhelmed by a deindustrialized proletariat, a ragged army of the dispossessed, a supply-side migratory tide of angry beggars and runaway refugee children and almost catatonic nomads. Have you seen the cold-water, crime-ridden, disease-spreading shelters in which we "warehouse" these dropouts and castaways? They are safer on the streets, except for Crazy Eddie and his net. In the parks, of course, we burn them alive.

There are as many as *100,000* homeless in the imperial city today. In the last twenty years—the years of the 2.5 million "newcomers"—housing production has *decreased* from 60,000 new units in 1966 to 7,000 in 1985 (Huxtable). Twenty-five percent of us live below the poverty line. At the end of World War II there were a million jobs in New York light industries; it's down today to 400,000. White unemployment is 7.2 percent, blacks, 11.5, Hispanics, 13.4; the white young, 22.5; black young, 47.9 (Tyler)—*47.9*, all of them Pimp Rolling on Wolfe's subway.

Meanwhile, why do you suppose that real-estate developers, brokerage houses, and their law firms forked out over $4 million in 1985 campaign contributions to Koch and the other seven members of the Board of Estimate? Maybe because Koch and the board have given these same people $11.3 *billion* in property tax breaks and zoning variances since 1978 (Jim Sleeper). Since 1981 we have as much *new* commercial space—45 million square feet—as the total commercial space in Boston and San Francisco *combined* (Sleeper), and yet there's still no room for the homeless. There isn't even any room for a simple idea like San Francisco's: In San Francisco you can't put up new commercial space downtown unless you pay for day care for the children of the people who will work there (Messinger). Of course the Reagan administration won't invest in permanent housing for New York's poor: *that* would be socialism, the dread "S"-word. But Crazy Eddie doesn't want unions or churches or foundations or grassroots community groups or anybody else except his favorite developers in the business of rehabilitating the 100,000 condemned properties the city already *owns*. Nor are a big developer's tax breaks available to these groups. Why not? Maybe because this kind of low-cost community initiative is bad for the Profit Motive and the Power Base. Certainly permanent housing for the poor—the ever-unpopular "free ride"—is bad for the Work Ethic, like aid to dependent children.

It's not just the money. It's a social philosophy which is at the same time greedy and punitive. We might scrounge the money. Messinger reminds us of that mysterious $500 million in unspent revenues—mostly from "Big MAC," World Trade Center, and Battery Park City surpluses—that the city "rolls over" every fiscal year until it disappears whenever anyone wants to spend it on basic decencies. Dan McCarthy can find another half billion in a capital-gains tax on real estate. If we tax cooperative apartments for mortgage-recording and real-property transfer, as Phillips suggests, that's another $60 million. Just suppose we killed off "gratuitous tax abatements to Smith Barney or A.T.&T.," and decided to use the city's zoning clout to insist on social services, and helped low-income communities "establish themselves in properties the marketplace has abandoned" (Sleeper). We aren't talking here about anything so radically Scandinavian as income redistribution. But we *are* talking about more than anybody now in power has the conscience and commitment to attempt. What we need, of course, is a change of philosophy and philosophers.

For this change, *Dissent* looks to those 2.5 million "newcomers," with mixed feelings. We've been a "minority-majority" city since the middle of this decade — blacks and Puerto Ricans joined by Dominicans, Cubans, and other Caribbeans and South Americans, plus Africans and 350,000 Asians. (The indefatigable Sleeper tells us that by 1995, "with revolution in Korea and the defenestration of Hong Kong," our Asian population will have tripled.) To this "Third World" of Tom Wolfe's swamp-fever dreams—Koreans in the fruit and vegetable trade, Indians in the newsstand business, Arabs in neighborhood groceries and head shops, Senegalese street vendors—add 200,000 Russian Jews, Israelis, Poles, Italians, Greeks, and the Irish in Kriegel's Bronx. That's a lot of clout waiting to be mobilized.

But Sleeper, Chapin, and Philip Kasinitz are also cautionary tale-tellers. Blacks and Hispanics haven't got their act together, except in "hip-hop," even in Brooklyn. Many newcomers can't speak English, aren't citizens, aren't registered, or aren't old enough to vote. Why should Korean shopowners in Washington Heights or Cuban doctors in Jackson Heights join a coalition that cares about the interests of welfare mothers in Bedford-Stuyvesant? It isn't Popular Front–romantic when blacks resent

Koreans, the Russians are "rednecks," and the Chinese won't join unions, and the unions are mostly right-wing anyway. Chapin is cold-eyed: "Immigrant insurgencies are generally pluralist rather than radical in nature. Some are even regressive." He asks the left—census figures on this minority have been unavailable since the Molotov-Ribbentrop pact—to "stop mistaking ethnicity for politics; while ethnicity may be more important than class to voting, economics is more important to governing policy than ethnicity."

This doesn't exactly sing, but we'd better learn to hum it. To be sure, even the broadest coalition — of immigrants and intellectuals, teachers and preachers, ethnics who've yet to get their taste, limousine liberals and Republican "good government" types and low-income community organizers and "delirious professionals"—can't save the city all by itself. Even the federal government (another bunch of once and future jailbirds) can't control oil prices or the dollar or the deficit or international drug traffic. No government in the world, says Berman, knows how to regulate "the vastly accelerated mobility of capital, propelled by breakthroughs in information technology," that "is fast bringing about the deindustrialization of America." But if we begin by being ashamed of ourselves and then start working the streets, we might find enough conscience and will to make over again the city Randolph Bourne once called "a federation of cultures."

On the other hand, tourism is up, from 3.3 million in 1975 to 17.5 in 1987. Just like Venice: a theme park. See the pretty Winter Palace.

Don DeLillo's *Libra*

Don delillo's cold and brilliant novel begins with thirteen-year-old Lee Harvey Oswald and his mother—that American Medea, Marguerite—watching television in the Bronx. For "inward-spinning" Oswald, his mother *is* a television. Her voice falls "through a hole in the air." She stays up late to compare test patterns.

Libra ends with a hole in the ground, and Marguerite's apostrophizing. "They will search out environmental factors, that we moved from home to home. Judge, I have lived in many places but never filthy dirty, never not neat, never without the personal living touch, the decorator item. We have moved to be a family. This is the theme of my research."

Between these solitudes, someone else is doing the research. DeLillo, who's shy, has found himself a surrogate: Nicholas Branch, CIA (Retired), sits exactly like an Author-God at a desktop computer in a glove-leather chair in a book-lined fireproof room full of "theories that gleam like jade idols." He follows "bullet trajectories backwards to the lives that occupy the shadows." He feels "a strangeness . . . that is almost holy. There is much here that is holy, an aberration in the heartland of the real." Branch is writing, at the Agency's request, a secret history of Dallas—those "six point nine seconds of heat and light" on November 22, 1963. The Agency has given him more than he needs to know. For instance:

> The Curator sends the results of ballistics tests carried out on
> human skulls and goat carcasses, on blocks of gelatin mixed
> with horsemeat . . . bullet-shattered goat heads in closeup . . .
> a gelatin-tissue model "dressed" like the President. It is pure

modernist sculpture, a block of gelatin layered in suit and shirt material with a strip of undershirt showing, bullet-smoked.

Equally modernist, of course, is the Warren Commission Report, "with its twenty-six accompanying volumes of testimony and exhibits, its millions of words":

> Branch thinks this is the megaton novel James Joyce would have written if he'd moved to Iowa City and lived to be a hundred. . . . Everything belongs, everything adheres, the mutter of obscure witnesses, the photos of illegible documents and odd sad personal debris, things gathered up at a dying— old shoes, pajama tops, letters from Russia. This is the Joycean Book of America.

And what does the historian decide—after his access to goats' heads and pajama tops; psychiatrists and KGB defectors; confidential Agency files and transcripts of the secret hearings of congressional committees; wiretaps, polygraphs, Dictabelt recordings, postoperative X-rays, computer enhancements of the Zapruder film, Jack Ruby's mother's dental chart, microphotographs of strands of Oswald's pubic hair (smooth, not knobby), FBI reports on *dreams* . . . and the long roster of the conveniently dead?

Branch decides "his subject is not politics or violent crime but men in small rooms." To be sure, his own Agency may be "protecting something very much like its identity," but rogue elements of that Agency have conspired in their small rooms to write an enormous fiction. They will mount an attempt on the president's life that's intended to be a "surgical" near miss. They will leave a "paper trail" that leads from this attempt to Castro's Cuba, their "moonlit fixation in the emerald sea." They require someone like an Oswald, a fall-guy *figment*, to point the way.

Libra deconstructs the official story and reimagines the dreary principals whom we know already from the pages of the Warren Report and the fevers of Jim Garrison. But it also peoples the parentheses of this shadow world with monsters of its own—agents disgraced at the Bay of Pigs; cowboy mercenaries shopping for a little war; Kennedy-hating mafiosi, international remittance men, Batista swamp rats; myths (salamanders out of Paracelsus) and freaks (geeks, androgynes). If his surrogate

Branch is a stay-at-home, DeLillo flies by night, and enters, an exorcist, into rooms and dreams. In each room, he finds a secret and a coincidence, a loneliness and a connection, even a kind of theology: "the rapture of the fear of believing."

Win Everett, for instance, is the Agency Author-God of the JFK plot, for whom "secrets are an exalted state," "a way of arresting motion, stopping the world so we can see ourselves in it." In his small room with Elmer's Glue-All and an X-Acto knife, he invents the Oswald-figment out of fake passports, false names, phony address books, doctored photographs; "scripts" him "out of ordinary pocket litter." He has, if not misgivings, at least forebodings:

> There is a tendency of plots to move toward death. He believed that the idea of death is woven into the nature of every plot. A narrative plot no less than a conspiracy of armed men. The tighter the plot of a story, the more likely it will come to death. A plot in fiction, he believed, is the way we localize the force of death outside the book, play it off, contain it. . . . He worried about the deathward logic of his plot.

But the Agency's bound to forgive him: "What's more, they would admire the complexity of his plan. . . . It had art and memory. It had a sense of responsibility, of moral force. And it was a picture in the world of their own guilty wishes."

He sounds like any old modernist at the keyboard of his masterwork, his Terminal Novel, his grand harmonium of randomness. Imagine his surprise on finding that there really *is* an Oswald, sitting there in a Speed Wash Laundromat in Dallas at midnight reading H. G. Wells's *Outline of History*. It's creepy. Dyslexic Lee, who grew up dreaming of Lenin and Trotsky, "men who lived in isolation . . . close to death through long winters in exile or prison, feeling history in the room, waiting for the moment when it would surge through the walls. . . ." Ozzie the Rabbit in Tokyo: "Here the smallness had meaning. The paper windows and boxrooms, these were clear-minded states, forms of well-being." A Marine defector who cuts his wrist to stay in Russia, a wife abuser who gets "secret instructions" from "the whole busy air of transmission . . . through the night into his skin"; a Fair-Play-for-Cuba mail-order assassin whose stated ambition it is "to be a short story writer on contemporary American themes"—he's spent his whole life converging on a plot that is itself just eight months old.

Learning there is a *real* Oswald, Everett feels "displaced": "It produced a sensation of the eeriest panic, gave him a glimpse of the fiction he'd been devising, a fiction living prematurely in the world."

His coconspirator, Parmenter, a member of "the Groton-Yale-OSS network of so-called gentlemen spies," is grateful to the Agency for its understanding and its trust: "The deeper the ambiguity, the more we believe." During the overthrow of Arbenz in 1954, Parmenter's radio station, "supposedly run by rebels from a jungle outpost in Guatemala," was really in Honduras, broadcasting disinformation "rumors, false battle reports, meaningless codes, inflammatory speeches, orders to nonexistent rebels. It was like a class project in the structure of reality. Parmenter wrote some of the broadcasts himself, going for vivid imagery, fields of rotting bodies . . ." A *real* Oswald makes him laugh. "It was all so funny. . . . Everyone was a spook or dupe or asset, a double, courier, cut-out or defector, or was related to one. We were all linked in a vast and rhythmic coincidence. . . ."

But the president dies of coincidence, and so does Oswald. Like Oswald, *everybody* is writing fiction "on contemporary American themes." One conspirator, Mackey, works with a private army of Cuban exiles: "Alpha was run like a dream clinic. The Agency worked up a vision, then got Alpha to make it come true." Another, Wayne, lives on Fourth Street in Miami: "Judo instructors, tugboat captains, homeless Cubans, ex-paratroopers like Wayne, mercenaries from wars nobody heard of, in West Africa or Malay. They were like guys straight out of Wayne's favorite movie *Seven Samurai*, warriors without masters willing to band together to save a village from marauders, to win back a country, only to see themselves betrayed in the end."

So much bad art. This is Joan Didion's territory, isn't it, paranoia and blank uneasiness? Just so, the Mafia boss Carmine Latta, with his wiseguy contempt for social orders not his own, seems to have wandered in from Saul Bellow, Chicago instead of New Orleans. But with Didion, paranoia is personal, and so, for Bellow, is contempt. DeLillo is loftier, in a room that hangs above the world. He's part camera, of course, with a savage eye on, say, pretty Marina with the "breezes in her head," or Ruby, whose desperate jauntiness breaks the heart:

If I don't get there in time, it's decreed I wasn't meant to do it. He drove through Dealey Plaza, slightly out of the way, to look at the wreaths again. He talked to Sheba about was she hungry, did she want her Alpo. He parked in a lot across the street from the Western Union Office. He opened the trunk, got out the dog food and a can opener and fixed the dog her meal, which he left on the front seat. He took two thousand dollars out of the moneybag and stuffed it in his pockets because this is how a club owner walks into a room. He put the gun in his right hip pocket. His name was stamped in gold inside his hat.

But language is DeLillo's plastique. Out of gnarled speech, funny, vulgar, gnomic, he composes stunning cantatas for the damned to sing. *Libra* is as choral as it's cinematic. Marguerite is the scariest mother since *Faust*, and David Ferrie, with his homemade eyebrows, mohair toupee, and the land mines in his kitchen, his expertise on cancer and astrology, seems to speak to us through the cavities in our teeth: "All my fears are primitive. It's the limbic system of the brain. I've got a million years of terror stored up there." For Ferrie, "astrology is the language of the night sky, of starry aspect and position, the truth at the end of human affairs." Oswald is a Libra, which means Scales: "You're a quirk of history," Ferrie says; "you're a coincidence." But we say coincidence when we don't know what to call it: "It goes deeper. . . . There's a hidden principle. Every process contains its own outcome." On learning Kennedy's motorcade route, Ferrie is beside himself. "We didn't arrange your job in that building or set up the motorcade route. We don't have that kind of reach. . . . There's something else that's generating this event. A pattern outside experience. Something that *jerks* you out of the spin of history. I think you've had it backwards all the time. You wanted to enter history. Wrong approach, Leon. What you really want is out."

"*But,*" thinks Ferrie: "*There's more to it. There's always more to it. This is what history consists of. It's the sum total of all the things they aren't telling us.*"

I'm inclined to believe him. I'm not a buff anymore; the assassination hurt my head. Maybe there was a second gunman on the grassy knoll. Maybe Ruby owed money and a favor to the Mob. Certainly the shadow world is full of rogues. We read about the novels they have written every day in the funny papers.

DeLillo, though, is an agnostic about reality itself. With its command of the facts and the fantasies, its slide-rule convergence, its cantatas and its hyperspace, *Libra* is plausible. But it's also art, the peculiar art he's been perfecting since the antihero of *Americana* abandoned the Vietnam War on television in New York for another war in the American interior. Since, in *End Zone*, football became a metaphor for Armageddon. Since, in *Great Jones Street*, a grotesque rock 'n' roll amalgam of Jagger and Dylan hid out in the East Village from the thought police and from the terror he had himself sown in "the erotic dreams of the republic." Since, in *Ratner's Star*, the superstitions of astrophysics were deployed in a galaxy of time running out and space exploding. In *Players*, terrorists want to blow up the Stock Exchange, with some deracinated Yuppie help. In *Running Dog*, secret agents, pornographers, Buddhists, and Hitler all end up in Dallas. In *The Names*, a "risk analyst" for a company insuring multinational corporations against accidents of history goes to Athens, Ankara, and Beirut, to find out that he really works for the CIA, in the service of "new kinds of death." In *White Noise*, Nazis make a comeback in middleamerica in the cognitive dissonance at the heart of the consumer culture, where our universities are indistinguishable from our shopping malls, and we lie to ourselves in euphemisms on the TV set and in our dreams, and one of the ex-wives of a professor of Hitler Studies is a part-time spook: "She reviewed fiction for the CIA, mainly long serious novels with coded structures."

At the end of these DeLillo novels, there was nothing left but relative densities of language. He was limbering up for the big dread.

With the White Knight gone, there's no coherence, no community, no faith, no accountability, merely hum. In a faithless culture, death is the ultimate kick. In a random cosmos (those accidental stars, that coincidental static), we need a new *black* magic, "a theology of secrets." Against anarchism, nihilism, and terrorism, why not an occult of the intelligence agency, the latest in Gnostic heresies? Against alienation: paranoia. Against meaninglessness: conspiracy. It's all modernist mirrors: disinformation and counterintelligence. Beckett, Borges, and Nabokov; Conrad, Kafka, and *The Wasteland* . . . poor Fyodor: crime without punishment.

Oswald, of course, was the Underground Man. The deepest of covers is lunacy.

In Asia and the Middle East, in Latin America and in Dallas, *They* are writing our novel, our metafiction, and they are insane.

AIDS Is *Everywhere*

A SK GAYS, OF course, about AIDS coverage in the mainstream media, and they are outraged. Where are stories about the on-again-off-again federal funding of medical research depending on how scared the straights are *this* week? Or about an individual's right to privacy versus the profit motive of the insurance companies? Or about alternative medications, macrobiotic diets, bureaucratic hostility, exile in Mexico, the grotesque overpricing of AZT, and the ethics of placebo testing of people who've been sentenced to death? But nobody listens to victims; victims are prejudiced.

Instead, like Yang and Yin, or Punch and Judy, or Alphonse and Gaston, we get *Newsweek* and *Cosmopolitan*. *Cosmo* told us in January: "There is almost no danger of contracting AIDS through ordinary sexual intercourse." *Newsweek*, that bully pulpit for Masters and Johnson, begged to differ in a March 21 cover story: "AIDS is breaking out. The AIDS virus is now running rampant in the heterosexual community."

These are evil buffooneries, like the *People* cover story, also in March, on "AIDS and the Single Woman," with photos of twenty-one women, three black and one Hispanic, as if it didn't matter that female AIDS victims are 70 percent black and Hispanic. Perhaps *People* could do a similar job on Ethiopia, flying in a Concorde full of Parisian models to illustrate "Famine and Miss Goodbar."

But the media are how we think out loud about our plague years, and the cognitive dissonance is killing us. What *Cosmo* published was a sort of Pamper: protective packaging for the sore-at-heart who're straight, white, and middle class. "Penile penetration of a well-lubricated vagina" is still safe, so long as you stick to the missionary position, at least in places where *Cosmo*'s likely to be read. While heterosexuals in Africa *do* have an AIDS problem, *Cosmo* explains it's because "many men in Africa take their women in a brutal way. . . ."

This is anthropological and racist nonsense, but typical of a *Cosmo* Yuppie worldview, the view from the Cloud Club of the Chrysler Building or the Grill Room of the Four Seasons or the bold type in Liz Smith's gossip column, from which you can't see either Africa or America's own Third World, right here in the very city where Helen Gurley Brown discovered sex. If AIDS in California is 91 percent a gay disease, and in Texas 96 percent, in New York City it's the leading cause of death for women between the ages of eighteen and thirty-four. Twenty-six percent of them contracted the virus from infected men, not infected needles. The number of children with AIDS increased 50 percent in the past year. *Ninety* percent of these AIDS children are black or Latino. If *Cosmo* saw them, *Cosmo* would have to think about the ghetto.

After such fiddling, maybe Rome deserves to burn. And *Newsweek* will be there, pouring on oil. ("Not since Hitler's diaries . . ." said one incredulous staffer at the magazine.) According to Masters, Johnson, and Kolodny in *Newsweek*, 3 million Americans are AIDS-infected, which is double what we're told by the U.S. Centers for Disease Control; and 200,000 of these victims are non–drug-using heterosexuals, *seven times* the CDC estimate. AIDS is *everywhere*—in the bedroom, the brothel, the blood bank, not to mention French-kissing and maybe even dental floss.

The M&J survey sample of 800 drug-free heteros about which *Newsweek* huffed and puffed and blew its own horn was, of course, preposterous—a self-selected batch of volunteers, arbitrarily confined to four cities, with no follow-up interviews of HIV-positives, and no accounting for the tendency of people to lie about high-risk hanky-panky. Compared to the meticulous testing of millions of blood bank donors and military personnel, M&J might as well have spent a morning polling the first 800 names in the Gurley Brown Rolodex. All this was pointed out to devastating effect by Michael Fumento, an AIDS analyst for the feds, in the *New Republic* on April 4.

And what are we to make of a *Wall Street Journal* report that Masters and Johnson, before mongering these fears, had been refused the five-hundred-thousand dollars they asked for from the American Foundation for AIDS Research to develop an anti-AIDS spermicidal jelly? Such information has nowhere to go except into a deep depression. A reader of "Dear Abby" writes of an ad in the mail for "a disposable, specially treated paper towelette that will destroy the AIDS virus [on] public toilet seats, telephones, restaurant tables, silverware, and doorknobs." My own Board of Education passes out fifty thousand pairs of rubber gloves to protect teachers from their students. Local cops wore these gloves to break up a demonstration of gays at St. Patrick's Cathedral. (The gays hooted: "Your gloves don't match your boots!") *Newsweek* must have sold a lot of copies.

Maybe we'd prefer not hearing anything more at all about AIDS. Retina-eating cytomegalovirus and lung-choking Pneumocystis carinii and organ-rotting Kaposi's sarcoma: *yucky.* Hemophilia, anal abrasions, genital herpes, trichomoniasis, and nonoxynol-9: *gross.* Any causal relationship between poverty, prostitution, drugs, and disease ought not to be contemplated except by bleeding hearts whose secret mantra is the "s"-word: *socialism!* That we are as a nation ghettoized by race *and* sexual preference is an unacceptable injury to the self-esteem. (Isn't it against an amendment, or something?) No wonder we're hysterical, from denial or paranoia, depending on the magazine that's messing with our minds.

Unfortunately, what we think we know about AIDS will determine social policies that touch us everywhere we live—the government and public health; medicine and the Hippocratic oath; civil liberties and mandatory testing; immigration; the Church and gays, the bishops and condoms; network TV and commercials for contraceptives; how we collect blood, administer prisons, license marriages, apply for insurance, educate our children, and look into our mirror. Fear and loathing have already made a comeback in a country that was kinky to begin with about its private parts.

(Across the Atlantic, fear of AIDS, hatred of gays, and the usual Thatcherite contempt for civil liberties have metastasized into Clause 28 of the Local Government Bill, passed by both Houses of Parliament, forbidding the use of public funds in any way to "promote homosexuality." So much, then, for seeing a play like *Breaking the Code* in a state-subsidized theater, or borrowing a book by Jean Genet from the village library, or looking at David Hockney at the Tate.)

And what we think we know is determined entirely by *the* information environment, a killer buzz of the *Cosmos* and the *Newsweeks*. It's as if they're screaming at us from transistors in the cavities of our teeth, and they don't care if they're telling the truth or not. We haven't the tuners and amplifiers to steer through this static, no historical bifocals for a close reading of the facts, no previous experience nor any guru to help us feel our way. As perhaps never before, we are dependent on the conscience-less, retina-eating media for *all* the weather in our heads, while friends die. What this amounts to is a Kaposi's sarcoma of the epistemology: a shameful unknowingness, a crime.

On the Beat at *Ms.*

WHEN THE MINERAL Dukakis and the vegetable Bush are nominated in Atlanta and New Orleans, I won't be there. I haven't been to a political convention since Chicago, 1968, which spoiled me forever for jihads and the circus. After Wagner's *Ring*, who needs Gilbert and Sullivan? But there will be lots of other people looking on in 1988 who weren't invited twenty years ago, and that's terrific.

In Chicago in 1968 I was half of a two-person team from the *New Statesman*. My job was to report from the slaughterhouse floor. I'd sleep each night with the California delegation in the LaSalle Hotel. I'd wake each dawn to a phone call from a frantic editor who was positive—in London!—that Teddy Camelot was closing fast. I'd lurch each afternoon by chartered bus through barbed-wire checkpoints to a security frisk at the International Amphitheater, after which I'd find the press gallery already preempted by Mayor Daley's municipal goons. That was the Old Politics.

The New Politics was on the streets, where the *New Statesman* sent Nora Sayre. On the streets were 12,000 paranoid Chicago cops, 6,000 National Guardsmen, 1,000 agents of the FBI, and another 7,000 federal troops, including units of the 101st Airborne. Against such law and order agitated fewer than 4,000 dissidents, one in six an undercover Fed. Sayre and I would rendezvous to telex at the Hilton, with tear gas in our eyes. My convention was merely literary, as in Marat/Sade: The Persecution and Assassination of the Democratic Party as performed by the Inmates of the Asylum at Chicago. Sayre—down there in the middle of the magic and the blood, the cop paranoia, the Yippie freak-out, and the Castroite delusional systems of the New Left Pugachevs—got all the history.

Her report of it was brilliant. It was also (almost) singular. Except for Sayre, and Mary McGrory from the *Washington Star*, and Jill Krementz taking combat photographs, women didn't report Chicago. Without wanting to, I saw Norman Mailer for *Harper's*, Brock Brower for *Life*, Jean Genet and William Burroughs for *Esquire*, and Teddy White for God. The *New York Times* sent Harrison Salisbury, Tony Lukas, and Tom Wicker. The *Washington Post* sent Nick von Hoffman. Wilfrid Sheed, Garry Wills, and Terry Southern scribbled madly. Dan Rather and Mike Wallace were roughed up on the convention floor, and John Chancellor was arrested, and Walter Cronkite told the nation, "I want to pack my bags and get out of this city."

But it seems not to have occurred to a single important editor to solicit the opinion of a single female writer. The, ah, women's magazines ignored the show. *Ms.* didn't exist. Gloria Steinem was in Chicago, but working for McGovern. Betty Friedan was likewise there, but so was Ann Landers, neither on assignment. Elinor Langer was on the streets, but wouldn't write about it until 1973 in *Working Papers*. Who might have been asked?

Well, in 1968, Joan Didion had already written about the Black Panthers; Francine du Plessix Gray, about the Catholic Left; and Elizabeth Hardwick, about the march on Selma and the murder of Martin Luther King. Susan Sontag had already been to Vietnam, and so had Mary McCarthy. If McCarthy, why not Lillian Hellman? And if Hellman, why not Diana Trilling? Or Grace Paley, a veteran peace groupie? For some old-fashioned radical politics, Jessica Mitford would have been fun, with Ayn Rand for a reactionary rebuttal. M.F.K. Fisher was already an expert on Nixon's Whittier, and Pauline Kael had trafficked with Trotskyites in Berkeley, and Joyce Carol Oates was writing a novel about race riots in Detroit, and if any of this seems farfetched, ask yourself what Jean Genet was doing in Chicago?

It would have been easy, it didn't happen, but never again. The left in 1968, in spite of Kate Millett's *Sexual Politics*, was as male chauvinist as the rest of the nation. (See Stokely Carmichael's infamous *diktat*, "The only position for women in the Movement is prone.") But times changed with the Redstockings Manifesto and Marge Piercy's "The Grand Coolie Damn" in 1969, and Robin Morgan's "Goodbye to All That" in a feminized *Rat* in 1970, after which came *Ms.*

In Atlanta and New Orleans, you'll see Ellen Goodman for the *Boston Globe* and Molly Ivins for the *Dallas Times Herald*, as well as Sayre for *Grand*

Street and Jane O'Reilly for *Spy*. For the *New York Times* expect Felicity Barringer, Maureen Dowd, Julie Johnson, Judith Miller, Joyce Purnick, Robin Toner, and, of course, their national editor, Soma Golden. CBS is sending Betsy Aaron, Diane Sawyer, Susan Spencer, Lesley Stahl, and Kathleen Sullivan. For ABC, watch for Cokie Roberts; for CNN, Mary Alice Williams. . . . We ought, for once, to be pleased with ourselves.

Nan Robertson's *Getting Better*

J OHN CHEEVER SOBERED up in time to write one last short novel, *Oh What a Lovely Paradise It Seems*, in which the protagonist finds himself in a parish-house:

> . . . one of those places where the rummage sale would be held and the nativity play would be performed. He looked into the faces of forty men and women who were listening to a speaker at a podium. He was at once struck by his incompetence at judging the gathering. Not even in times of war, with which he was familiar, not even in the evacuation of burning cities had he seen so mixed a gathering. It was a group, he thought, in which there was nowhere the force of selection.

John Berryman didn't make it, killing himself before finishing *Recovery*, his novel of alcoholism. Saul Bellow remembers forcing a window at Berryman's house to find him facedown, rigid, diagonal on a double bed. "These efforts are wasted," said the poet; "We are unregenerate." But Bellow also remembers the poem "Surprise Me," in which the poet prayed for the "blessing gratuitous . . . on some ordinary day."

The blessing gratuitous on some ordinary day is what 2 million members of Alcoholics Anonymous seek in the parish-house or rectory, between rummage sales, in an underground network of church basements like the caves of the early Christians, in hospitals, union halls, bookshops, health clubs, high school cafeterias, the YMCA, the Friends Meeting House, a synagogue, the American Legion and the McGraw-Hill Building and the Port Authority. They've been selected by their disease. Their passion is sobriety. Two-thirds of them survive, and not by magic.

Nan Robertson, a veteran *New York Times* reporter, is herself a recovering alcoholic. She hit bottom after the death of a cherished husband. With AA's support she not only survived a nearly fatal attack of toxic shock syndrome, but wrote a magazine account of it that won her a Pulitzer Prize. She cheerfully admits she could not have done so alone. *Getting Better* is written, splendidly, in gratitude. Its lifesaving business is to celebrate and "demystify" her weave of steadfast friends.

Not a weird Druidic cult, nor penal colony, lynching bee, pop-psych seminar, convention of Jesus freaks, or fallout shelter for twitchy bums on their way to cirrhotic seizure, AA is everybody you've ever met, trying in small groups to help each other through the night. To qualify for membership, all you have to do is to want to stop drinking. In this amazing democracy, with more than its fair share of awful coffee and blue cigarette smoke, people tell stories. These many stories—of joblessness and paranoia, of smashed automobiles and nights in jail, of wife-beating and child abuse, of hallucinations and attempted suicide, of waste and pain and disconnection and the end of love—are really one: of the lost child in a black forest of bad chemicals.

AA began with an exchange of stories, in Akron, Ohio, in May 1935, between two drunks on whom the medical profession and the clergy had given up. Dr. Bob Smith, a local surgeon, and Bill Wilson, a visiting stock market "securities investigator," told each other the worst about themselves. Ever since, it's been an AA slogan that "you are only as sick as your secrets." AA slogans, like "One Day at a Time," "Keep It Simple, Stupid" and "It Works If You Work It," always strike the stranger as being, if not downright loony, at least a lot of baby talk. So, too, do the "12 Steps" seem to strangers as comically mystifying as "The Emerald Table" of the alchemist Hermes Trismegistus. We're too smart at first to grasp the practicality of the slogans, and to appreciate the terrifying simplicity of the Steps: be honest; change yourself; help others.) After these Founding Fathers were done with the First Meeting, they went into the world to talk to others like them, often dragging them out of hospital beds to do so.

Of the two, Bill W. is the more appealing, a Christmas tree of gaudy flaws. He'd go on sober to partake of spiritualism, niacin by megadose, Bishop Sheen, and LSD; to enjoy too much his crumbs at the tables of the Rockefellers; to drop names and, compulsively, to womanize. He was never sure himself whether his famous "conversion experience" was the sight of God in a blaze of "indescribably white light" or merely a "hot flash" of toxic psychosis. He lingered a decade too long as leader of an organization opposed on principle to any sort of hierarch, but when he died, in 1971, AA'd grown from two men in Akron to 475,000 men and women in eighty-nine countries.

The indefatigable Robertson, who seems to have gone to most of those countries for a meeting, serves notice in her full-bodied portrait of Bill W. that *Getting Better* intends to be useful rather than pious. She will entertain us with the history of the program, from its origins in William James's *The Varieties of Religious Experience* and the Protestant work ethic, to the publishing division by which it's become so self-sufficient it refuses outside donations and won't permit its own members to contribute more than five hundred dollars a year, to the fiftieth-anniversary festival in Montreal in the summer of 1985. She'll tell us as much as we need to know about alcoholism from Hammurabi and Chung K'iang—the first recorded "blackout" occurs in *The Bacchae* by Euripedes—to Dr. Benjamin Rush in 1784 and Betty Ford in 1978, with sidebars on toxicology, the "disease concept," genetic predisposition, cultural stress, and, of course, everything we've learned from our invasion of the privacy of identical twins. She's full of scary facts, encouraging figures, gallows humor, and hardy appetite. And there's an invaluable appendix of addresses and telephone numbers for the 72 million Americans—family and friends—whose hearts are broken by 18 million "problem" drinkers.

But AA—a citizenship seeking always to be innocent of politics—has had its problems, and we hear about them. How can you be all-inclusive and coherent at the same time? In the beginning, women weren't admitted. (They were too "nice" to be drunks, said Dr. Bob.) Nor were the young. (They hadn't "suffered enough," he said.) Addicts—of tranquilizers, speed, heroin, coke—weren't welcome, either. (And there is still some hostility, although many members came to understand in the inscrutable way members seem to, as if by body language and abrasion, that all chemical dependencies look alike in the dark.) From detox and rehab programs now paid for by health insurance, there are more bodies than there are basements. And the Children of Alcoholics movement, with its separate meetings and Speaking Bitterness, menaces the very civility of discourse that's one of AA's most astonishing achievements.

And then there's the God problem. Robertson devotes a chapter to it. Go to almost any AA meeting, and when they aren't talking about God, they're talking about "spirituality." A recovering alcoholic is supposed to turn over his or her life to a Higher Power. This Higher Power sounds suspiciously midwestern and Protestant. It needn't be. AA's a surprising success in Catholic Mexico and Brazil; and the Steps look a lot like what Maimonides and Rabbenau Yonah of Gerona had to say on repentance; and if you show up anyway, in rage and doubt, having derived your ethics from Tolstoy, Gandhi, and Einstein, and having found your awe in Bach and sunsets, nobody's going to quibble. AA, really, is sort of Buddhist, all about reciprocity; and also existential, except not chic. You are likely to have been alone for a long time, and the highest of powers is a community of those who went into that loneliness before you, and came back, and are mending.

Besides, if you're still uncomfortable, there are meetings for agnostics and atheists, as there are meetings for nonsmokers, and the deaf, and gays and lesbians, and meetings predominantly of doctors and lawyers, actors and writers, airline employees and prison personnel, clergy and merchant seamen—1,600 meetings of 650 groups every week in New York City alone. And you can always start a group of your own. All it takes, says Robertson, "is two drunks, a coffeepot, and some resentment."

What happens at a meeting? According to Robertson: love and service. Well, yes, but *how*? Somebody tells a story, maybe terrific, maybe not. Anybody else who wants to, shares. A hat's passed. There are bores and glory hounds, crybabies and monomaniacs, but there is also an etiquette, an unwritten encompassing, a respectful patience, a decorum hard to describe because it's in the very grain of the occasion, in the listening. You think about who are you, what you really mean, how you got here, like an athlete in training, and that you're probably not good enough to stay the course. The first weeks it feels like paying your taxes, an unpleasant duty done. Then, after a month or two, it feels like voting, something clean. Later on, or maybe all the time, it's a breathing space, a sanctuary, somewhere safe from ambush by the world you flunked, a parenthesis in which you are assisted at inventing a braver self by people variously sad and heroic who are sorry for your troubles, and forgiving, and available. Whether God shows up I wouldn't know, but somehow, in the collective wisdom, witness, and example of these friends of your affliction, there is Berryman's blessing gratuitous, a kind of grace. You are not quite so much a stranger to yourself, and so you go to bed, one midnight at a time, having chosen not to drink.

Salman Rushdie's *The Satanic Verses*

H EADLINES KEPT GETTING in the way. In Pakistan, reactionary nuts are using Salman Rushdie, and the dead bodies of some true believers, to destabilize Benazir Bhutto's government. In Iran, the Ayatollah Khomeini, with Rocks in his Dome, has put out a $5.2-million contract hit on the novelist. In South Africa, Saudi Arabia, and at Waldenbooks, *The Satanic Verses* is banned. For a couple of minutes, let's try to see the book through the bonfires of its burning.

As much as Islam, Salman Rushdie blasphemes Thatcherism. He's unkind, too, to V. S. Naipaul. "Pitting levity against gravity," altogether impious *The Satanic Verses* is one of those go-for-broke "metafictions," a grand narrative and Monty Python send-up of history, religion, and popular culture; Hindu cyclic and Muslim dualistic; postcolonial identity crisis and modernist pastiche; Bombay bombast and stiff-upper-liposuction; babu babytalk and ad agency neologism; cinema gossip, elephant masks, pop jingles, lousy puns, kinky sex, and schadenfreude; a sort of *Sammy and Rosie Get Laid* in Doris Lessing's *The Four-Gated City*—from which this slyboots Author-God tip-and-twinkletoes away, with a cannibal grin. "Who am I?" he asks us. "Let's put it this way: Who has the best tunes?"

The Satanic Verses lacks the ravening power, the great gulp, of *Midnight's Children* and *Shame*. It bites off the heads of its characters instead of digesting their essences. It's got too much on its troubled mind to make a symphonic noise out of so many discords. Of course, in its huge dishevelment, its *Leaves of Grass* lurchings and scourges, whistles and vapors, belly laughs and belly flops, it's infinitely more interesting than those hundreds of neat little novels we have to read between Rushdies.

What Modernism, the new alchemy, is all about is the inventing of a new self. But what if the machinery short-circuits? Is there a way out of these devolving cycles into lesser selves, meaner societies, deathward-spinning meta-systems? One suggestion, though I'm not sure how seriously Rushdie intends it, shows up in a book by Zeeny Vakil, Saladin Chamcha's Bombay art critic/girlfriend (the most interesting, least developed character in the novel): *The Only Good Indian* lambastes "the confining myth of authenticity, that folkloristic straitjacket which she sought to replace by an ethic of historically validated eclecticism, for was not the entire national culture based on the principle of borrowing whatever clothes seemed to fit, Aryan, Mughal, British, take-the-best-and-leave-the-rest?" It's Zeeny who tells Chamcha to get real: "We're right in front of you. You should try and make an adult acquaintance with this place, this time. Try and embrace this city, as it is, not some childhood memory that makes you both nostalgic and sick."

But this seems far too straightforward for a metafiction. I think Rushdie's also proposing something more botanical. When, in Gibreel Farishta's dream of Mecca and drowning, the Titlipur villagers leave their mothering banyan tree, they perish. Then there is, for Chamcha, "the tree of his own life," the walnut tree his father planted "with his own hands on the day of the coming of the son." Chamcha explains this tree to Zeeny: "Your birth-tree is a financial investment of a sort. When a child comes of age, the grown walnut is comparable to a matured insurance policy; it's a valuable tree, it can be sold, to pay for weddings, or a start in life. The adult chops down his childhood to help his grown-up self. The unsentimentality is appealing, don't you think?" As usual, Chamcha has missed the point. For his father, that tree was where his son's soul lived while the boy himself was far away, pursuing his unrequited love affair with England. Many pages later, Chamcha will watch a television program on gardening, and witness what's called a "chimeran graft," in which two trees—mulberry? laburnum? broom?—are bred into one:

> a chimera without roots, firmly planted in and growing vigorously out of a piece of English earth: a tree . . . capable of taking the metaphoric place of the one his father had chopped down in a distant garden in another, incompatible world. If such a tree were possible, then so was he; he, too, could cohere, send down roots, survive. Amid all the televisual images of

hybrid tragedies—the uselessness of mermen, the failures of plastic surgery, the Esperanto-like vacuity of much modern art, the Coca-Colonization of the planet—he was given this one gift.

For this, they want to kill him.

The Hit Men

I hope hundreds turned out yesterday at the PEN rally to support Salman Rushdie. We need something to wash the taste of gall and aspirin out of our mouths. It's been a disgraceful week. A maniac puts out a $5.2-million contract on one of the best writers in the English language, and how does the civilized West respond? France and Germany won't publish *The Satanic Verses*; Canada won't sell it; Waldenbooks and B. Dalton abandon ship and the First Amendment; and a brave new philistinism struts its stuff all over Mediapolis, USA, telling us that that Rushdie's unreadable anyway, besides being some sort of left-wing Indian troublemaker you never heard of till the Ayatollah gave him a bad review. And nobody seems in fact to have read *any* Rushdie—certainly not Cardinal O'Connor, nor Jimmy Breslin, nor Pat Buchanan.

In his first novel, *Midnight's Children*, Rushdie suggested that independence for the Indian subcontinent was ruined by the lunatic behavior of Muslims and Hindus. He also made fun of Indira Gandhi. And Indira Gandhi threatened to sue. His second novel, *Shame*, was a savage attack on the bloody coming to power in Pakistan of the Islamic fundamentalist Zia. Pakistan banned it. *The Satanic Verses* is likewise *contemporary*. Among other things, it's a Monty Python send-up of modern England, its money-grubbing and its racism. Maggie Thatcher's more of a target than Mohammed. And so is the Ayatollah Khomeini himself, in thin disguise. Just maybe, the blood-grudge of His Bearded Malevolence is personal. He'd surely have seen himself in Rushdie's portrait of the Imam. This Imam, in angry exile in the modern era in one of Europe's imperial cities, plots the overthrow of a Mideast state run by a Western-educated, secular-minded empress whom the Imam accuses of "sexual relations with lizards," and whom he confuses with the hated Mother-Goddess Al-Lat. He sounds like Tehran radio. Just listen to him: "History is the blood wine that must no longer be drunk. History, the intoxicant, the creation and possession of the Devil . . . the greatest of the lies—progress, science, rights—against which the Imam has set his face. History is a deviation from the Path, knowledge is a delusion, because the sum of knowledge was complete on the day Allah finished his revelation to Mahound." And: "Burn the books and trust the Book; shred the papers and hear the Word." And, after a revolution exactly like K.'s in Iran: "Now every clock in the capital city of Desh begins to chime, and goes on unceasingly, beyond twelve, beyond twenty-four, beyond one thousand and one, announcing the end of Time, the hour that is beyond measuring, the hour of the exile's return, of the victory of water over wine, of the commencement of the Untime of the Imam."

But all this has been ignored, like the fact that fundamentalist Pakistanis would be rioting to get rid of Benazir Bhutto, a Western-educated woman, whether or not Rushdie had ever written a word. And religious fanatics are killing one another's children in Belfast and Beirut without the excuse of a novel to hate.

You may recall that "assassin" derives from the Arabic *hashishi* ("hashish eaters"). The original assassins were an eleventh-century all-male Persian sect, fanning out from the Alamout mountain in northern Iran. They killed on command of Hassan Ibn Sabbah. What we've looked into for the past shameful week is an eleventh-century mind, an assassin's grin. We've averted our jumpy eyes, ducked our fuzzy heads, scuttled on all fours. Welcome to the Untime of the Imam.

On Thursday in England Roald Dahl, an author of wicked children's books, told TV cameras that Rushdie's novel should be pulped "to save lives"—as if the *novel* had killed anybody. On Friday, pulling *The Satanic Verses* from his shelves, B. Dalton CEO Leonard Riggio explained: "It is regrettable that a foreign government has been able to hold hostage our most sacred First Amendment"—as if Riggio weren't the hostage holder. (You'd think maybe the FBI might be interested in terrorist threats to bookstores and publishing houses, but not according to a Justice Department spokeswoman.) On Saturday in the *New York Post*, Pat Buchanan enjoyed himself at the expense of "the trendy leftist" Rushdie, suggested that he seek sanctuary among Nicaragua's Sandinistas to whom he's been so sympathetic, and allowed as how "the First Amendment has succeeded phony patriotism as the last refuge of the scoundrel"—as if that amendment, the glory of our republic, weren't precisely what protects the right of a Buchanan to his swamp fevers, the privilege of such pips to squeak.

And on Sunday in *Newsday*, Breslin, whom the vapors must have taken as they sometimes seize a Mailer, described Rushdie as "a horrid writer" whose "cheap apology" to Khomeini was "a wretched performance," a "groveling . . . perfectly consistent with Rushdie's dreadful sentence structure"—as if all the newspaper columnists in America could write for a thousand years, even unto the end of Untime, and ever produce a novel half as wonderful as *Midnight's Children*.

Monday we were told that Cardinal O'Connor would really rather we didn't buy the Rushdie book. We were also told that the cardinal himself won't read it. And where were the other world religious leaders? Not a single one seems to have spoken up on Rushdie's behalf. They may have deplored the Ayatollah's *fatwa*, but they spent more time sympathizing with the injured feelings of the Islamic multitude; and most thought the book should never have been published; and many in England agitated to expand the blasphemy laws. If the Vatican's performance was disgraceful, so was that of the Archbishop of Canterbury, the Chief Rabbi of the United Hebrew Congregations of the Commonwealth, the Cardinal of Paris, the Archbishop of Lyon, and Israel's chief Ashkenazi rabbi, Avraham Shapira. It's as if all of them overnight forgot about Erasmus and Spinoza, Jan Hus and Thomas More, Galileo and Martin Luther, not to mention Socrates and not even to think about Jesus Christ: free speech on the cross.

As Rushdie himself explains, right at the start of *Verses*, when Chamcha and Gibreel are blown out of the sky by terrorists: "Just two brown men, falling hard, nothing so new about that you may think; climbed too high, got above themselves. . . ."

Thomas Pynchon's *Vineland*

*V*INELAND—A MULTIMEDIA SEMI-THRILLER, a Star Wars for the counterculture—is easier to read than anything else by Pynchon except *The Crying of Lot 49*. Like *Crying*, it's a brief for the disinherited and dispossessed, the outlaws and outcasts of an underground America. Also like *Crying*, I suspect it's a breather between biggies. It doesn't feel like something obsessed about and fine-tuned for the seventeen years since *Gravity's Rainbow*. It feels unbuttoned, as if the Author-God had gone to a ball game. Another darker magisterial mystification is implied, maybe the rumored Mason-Dixon opus. This doesn't make *Vineland* a Sunday in the park with George, but at least it can be summarized without my sounding too much like an idiot.

1. Where is "Vineland"?

In the northern California redwoods, "a Harbor of Refuge" since the middle of the nineteenth century "to Vessels that may have suffered on their way North from the strong headwinds that prevail along this coast." It's also a republic of metaphors, a theme park of sixties obsessions— television, mysticism, revolution, rock 'n' roll, Vietnam, drugs, paranoia, and repression. And it refers as well to the Vinland of the old Norse sagas, what the Vikings called America. (I wasted time looking up the Vikings. How far did their dragon-ships get? Explain that Icelandic tower in Newport, Rhode Island, and those Minnesota runes. Was Quetzalcoatl actually a Viking? Is Pynchon singing some rock saga about another of his unmapped kingdoms, like Vheissu, the "dream of annihilation" at the heart of *V*?) Anyway, it's symbolic: a Third World.

II. What happens to whom, and when, in this "Vineland"?

In Orwellian 1984 midway through the Reagan gerontocracy, refugees from the sixties are having a hard time. Zoyd Wheeler, who used to deal dope and play piano in a rock band, is a "gypsy roofer" trying to take care of his teenaged daughter, Prairie. Prairie's in love with a heavy metal neofascist, and misses the mother she hasn't seen since babyhood. This mother, the almost mythical Frenesi, belonged in the sixties to a band of guerrilla moviemakers—the Death to the Pig Nihilist Film Kollective. But she was more or less abducted by the malign federal prosecutor Brock Vond and "turned" into an "independent contractor" for FBI sting operations. When Justice Department budget cuts "disappear" Frenesi from the government computer, Vond's frantic. Expecting her to show up in Vineland, he plots to frame Zoyd, kidnap Prairie, and scorch every pot plantation north of "San Narcisco." (Think of Panama.)

In other words, "the State law-enforcement apparatus . . . calling itself 'America'" declares total war on the leftover flower children. It's a made-for-TV rerun. Back in the sixties Vond's Feds destroyed a college-campus People's Republic of Rock 'n' Roll and trucked the student revolutionaries off to camps for a Political Re-Education Program (PREP). This is where Vond turned Frenesi. When Vond invades Vineland, Zoyd and Prairie are assisted in their resistance by the Woman Warrior DL Chastain; by the Japanese private eye Takeshi; by a DEA renegade and television addict Hector Zuniga; by the Sisterhood of Kunoichi Attentives, a convent of Ninjettes in the karmic adjustment racket; by Vato and Blood, who steal cars and traffic with ghosts; by punk rockers; Jesus bikers, Mafia hoods, and three generations of Left Coast Wobblies, including Frenesi's mother, Sasha, who may or may not be a member of the Party. . . .

III. Is any of this funny?

Of course it's funny. Not only does Pynchon know more than we do about almost everything—communications theory, stimulus-response psychology, rocket science, Catatonic Expressionism, entropy, gauchos and stamps—but what he doesn't know, he makes up. In *Vineland*, for instance, Ping-Ponging between the sixties and the eighties, he makes up TV movies: John Ritter in *The Bryant Gumbel Story*, Peewee Herman in *The Robert Musil Story*, and Woody Allen in *The Young Kissinger*. Not to mention a docudrama about the Boston Celtics, with Paul McCartney as Kevin McHale and Sean Penn as Larry Bird. And not even perhaps to think about *The Chipmunks Sing Marvin Hamlisch*.

There are, besides, the Bodhi Dharma Pizza Temple ("a classic example of the California pizza at its most misguided") and a controlled-environment mall called the Noir Center, with an upscale mineral-water boutique (Bubble Indemnity), a perfume-and-cosmetics shop (The Mall Tease Flacon), and a New York deli (The Lady 'n' the Lox).

Of all the funny names—Weed Atman, Ditzah and Zipi Pisk, Ortho Bob, Mirage—my favorite is Isaiah Two Four, Prairie's heavy metal squeeze named by his parents for the swords-into-ploughshares, spears-into-pruning-hooks passage from the Bible. No wonder Isaiah wants to start a chain of Violence Centers, each to include "automatic-weapon firing ranges, paramilitary fantasy adventures . . . and video game rooms for the kids." These centers would presumably compete with the "fantasy marathons" of the Kunoichi Sisterhood that feature "group rates on Kiddie Ninja weekends. . . ." I also laughed at a Sisterhood self-criticism session devoted to "scullery duty as a decoding of individual patterns of not-eating." And, of the many songs Pynchon's written for his various musicians, the funniest is "Just a Floozy with an U-U-zi."

IV. Can we count on the usual entropy, paranoia, and Manichaeanism?

Yes, as well as some terrific rhapsodies on water, cars, and parrots. And the paranoids are right. *They* (narcs, RICOs, Yuppies, television anchor-faces, earth-rapers, treekillers, random urine-sniffers, sexhating death-loving Wasteland thought police) are out to get *Us* (whomever: civil liberties, due process, readers of Pynchon and *The Nation*). *And* they use *Us* against *Us*. At PREP,

> Brock Vond's genius was to have seen in the activities of the sixties left not threats to order but unacknowledged desires for it. While the Tube was proclaiming youth revolution against parents of all kinds and most viewers were accepting this story, Brock saw the deep—if he'd allowed himself to feel it, the sometimes touching—need to stay children forever, safe inside some extended national Family. . . . They'd only been listening to the wrong music, breathing the wrong smoke, admiring the wrong personalities. They needed some reconditioning. . . . the long-haired bodies, men who had grown feminine, women who had become small children, flurries of long naked limbs, little girls naked under boyfriends' fringe jackets, eyes turned down, away, never meeting those of their questioners, boys with hair over their shoulders, hair that kept getting in their eyes . . . the sort of mild herd creatures who belonged, who'd feel, let's face it, much more comfortable, behind fences. Children longing for discipline.

Only this time *We* win. You have to understand entropy not just as the heat death of a culture, but also as *equilibrium*. As Pynchon clued us in his first famous short story with nods to Henry Adams, so he clues us here by quoting another American crazy, William James. According to *Varieties of Religious Experience*: "Secret retributions are always restoring the level, when disturbed, of the divine justice. It is impossible to tilt the beam. All the tyrants and proprietors and monopolists of the world in vain set their shoulders to heave the bar. Settles forevermore the ponderous equator to its line, and man and mote, and star and sun, must range to it, or be pulverized by the recoil."

For Pynchon, this is remarkably cheerful. But how are *We*, a bunch of dopers in the California redwoods, to prevail against the Geeks: Virgin versus Dynamo? See below.

V. Will we care any more about these characters than we did about, say, Benny Profane and Tyrone Slothrop?

Probably not, except for DL. Like a Buddhist or a Hume, Pynchon doesn't really believe in the "self." He's more interested in states of being and becoming. Zoyd attitudinizes, Frenesi's a computer dream of patterns. Takeshi's inscrutable. Hector's a clown, and Sasha's one of Tolstoy's supergoody clean old peasants; even Vond, "like any of the sleek raptors that decorate fascist architecture," adds up to little more than an upwardly mobile social-control freak with a flashy line of psychic yard goods. But as Vond talks to other men through the holes in women's bodies, so Pynchon talks to his readers through the holes in his cartoon zanies. What he wants to talk about is "official" reality (a media fabrication) versus "unofficial" alternatives (see below).

Frenesi is Pynchon's excuse to make fun of film. According to her "Kollective": "A camera is a gun. An image taken is a death performed. Images put together are the substructure of an afterlife and a Judgment. We will be the architects to a just Hell for the fascist pig. Death to everything that oinks!" Vond tells her, "Can't you see, the two separate worlds— one always includes a camera somewhere . . . the other always includes a gun, one is make-believe, one is real? What if this is some branch point in your life, where you'll have to choose between worlds?" To the People's Republic of Rock 'n' Roll the night of its destruction, Frenesi brought a gun *and* a camera, not to mention fast-film 7242 and a Norwood Binary light meter, for the helicopters and the troops in blackface and "the high-ticket production of their dreams." This is "Reality Time" versus "all that art-of-the-cinema handjob." She'll emerge from hiding and go to Vineland only because Hector promises to star her in *his* movie.

Hector is an excuse to talk about television. Although almost everything happens in *Vineland* in "sullen Tubeflicker," not always "Primetime";

and odd birds sit in palm fronds to sing back at the commercials; and Zoyd, dropping acid, hopes that Prairie will be there "to help him through those times when the Klingons are closing"; and Takeshi believes that television "mediates death"; and even Frenesi feels "that the rays coming out of the TV screen would act as a broom to sweep the room clear of all spirits"; and all over Vineland, rival cable TV riggers exchange gunfire, "eager to claim souls for their distant principals, fighting it out house by house"—only Hector is addicted, a Brady Buncher. When his wife kills their TV set with a frozen pot roast, Hector arrests her. He'll escape from a rehab for "Tuba-busers." Television is the white noise of the Garrison State, the elevator Muzak of Repression going down.

Zoyd is an excuse to talk about music, from rock ("romantic death fantasies . . . the terrible about-to-burst latency just ahead, the hard-on") to heavy metal ("nuke-happy cyberdeath," "Septic Tank and Fascist Toe-jam") to New Age ("audio treacle," "mindbarf"), even Bach ("the best tunes ever to come out of Europe"). And everybody's freaked by comput-ers. Prairie worries "how literal computers could be—even the spaces between characters mattered. She wondered if ghosts were only literal in the same way. Could a ghost think for herself or was she responsive totally to the needs of the still-living, needs like keystrokes entered into her world, lines of sorrow, loss, justice denied?" Frenesi, the absentee mother, is also metaphysical:

> it would all be done with keys on alphanumeric keyboards that stood for weightless, invisible chains of electronic presence or absence. . . . We are all digits in God's computer, she not so much thought as hummed to herself to a sort of standard gos-pel tune, and the only thing we're good for, to be dead or to be living, is the only thing He sees. What we cry, what we contend for, in our world of toil and blood, it all lies beneath the notice of the hacker we call God.

Whereas Sasha is Pynchon's excuse to talk about one of the alternatives to media reality—a lost history of radical politics in the American West, long before Pacifica or Savio or People's Park; the organizing of loggers and miners and canneries; the strikes against San Joaquin cotton, Ventura sugar beets, Venice lettuce; Tom Mooney, Culbert Olson, Hollywood craft unions, and fifties blacklists. This repressed progressive history and its media denial seem at first the subtext to *Vineland*. These people did more for the Revolution than sing about it, or dope themselves stupid. Nor did they surf.

But this is to reckon without the alternative (and competing) unofficial realities of the Indians and the dolphins and DL Chastain, the kick-ass Woman Warrior.

In every Pynchon novel, there is a woman we love—Rachel Owlglass in *V.* Oedipa Maas in *Crying*. Katje or Greta in *Gravity's Rainbow*—because in the satiric muddle she seems to point true north to a magnetic pole of decencies. DL is the one we care about here. Though trained in a variety of martial arts strategies, from the Vibrating Palm and the *Kasumi* Mist to "the Enraged Sparrow, the Hidden Foot, the Nosepicking of Death, and a truly unspeakable *Gojira no Chimopira*," and equally at home among the Kunoichi Sisters and the YakMaf, she is nevertheless Frenesi's loyal friend, *and* Prairie's resourceful protector, *and* Takeshi's eventual lover. Like her comrades on a rescue mission into "the Cold War dream" of PREP, we believe in DL's "proprietary whammies" the same way that "in those days it was possible to believe in acid or the imminence of revolution, or the disciplines, passive and active, of the East." She is also Pynchon's door to the Orient, into which, it seems to me, he disappears.

VI. Now I can sound like an idiot.

I haven't mentioned the Thanatoids, nor their Vineland suburb of Shade Creek. You reach Shade Creek by water and darkness, with the help of Vato and Blood, strippers of cars and souls. It's a ghost town, except the ghosts aren't dead yet. They are "an unseen insomniac population," refugees from history, residues of memory, the victims of "karmic imbalances—unanswered blows, unredeemed suffering, escapes by the guilty—anything that frustrated their daily expeditions on into the interior of Death, with Shade Creek as the psychic jumping-off town—behind it, unrolling, regions unmapped, dwelt in by these transient souls in constant turnover. . . ."

Thanatoids, instead of rock 'n' roll, sing songs like "Who's Sorry Now?" "I Got a Right to Sing the Blues," and "Don't Get Around Much Anymore." They watch television, although they learned long ago "to limit themselves, as they always did in other areas, only to emotions helpful in setting right whatever was keeping them from advancing further into the condition of death. Among these the most common by far was resentment, constrained as Thanatoids were by history and by rules of imbalance and restoration to feel little else beyond their needs for revenge."

Weed Atman, the Learylike mathematics professor who rose implausibly to guru of the People's Republic of Rock 'n' Roll before Frenesi betrayed him, is a Thanatoid. So are many Vietnam veterans, like Ortho Bob. Ortho Bob explains to Takeshi that "in traditional karmic adjustment . . . Death was the driving pulse—everything had moved as slowly as the cycles of birth and death, but this proved to be too slow for enough people to begin, eventually, to provide a market niche. There arose a system of deferment, of borrowing against karmic futures. Death, in Modern Karmic Adjustment, got removed from the process." Takeshi, like the Sisterhood of Kunoichi Attentives, sees the moneymaking possibilities of a "Karmology hustle." So, apparently, do Vato and Blood, Charons on the Shade Creek Styx. When Vond goes looking for Frenesi, he will meet Vato and Blood instead, while the leftover flower children are at a picnic with the leftover Wobblies and a Russian punk rocker who wandered into the redwoods. According to Takeshi, if none of the other stuff works, "we can always go for the reincarnation option." Takeshi's into *The Tibetan Book of the Dead*, with souls in transition, denying death, unable to distinguish between "the weirdness of life and the weirdness of death." So, of course, are Thanatoids. But . . .

In a way, everybody in *Vineland* is a Thanatoid, full of bad faith; guilty, resentful, and nostalgic; under ghostcover, in motion through varying thicknesses of memory and light toward a reckoning. Zoyd's sixties surfer band found "strange affinities" with the subculture of "beer riders of the valley": both rode a "technowave. . . . Surfers rode God's ocean, beer riders rode the momentum through the years of the auto industry's will." DL in her "Ninjamobile" has an LA freeway vision of screaming black motorcades, cruisers, huge double and triple trailer rigs,

> flirters, deserters, wimps and pimps, speeding like bullets, grinning like chimps, above the heads of the TV watchers, lovers under the overpasses, movies at malls letting out, bright gas-station oases in pure fluorescent spill, canopied beneath the palm trees, soon wrapped, down the corridors of the surface streets, in noctural smog, the adobe air, the smell of distant fireworks, the spilled, the broken world.

Frenesi dreams of a "Gentle Flood," of standing just above the surf,

> looking toward a horizon she couldn't see, as if into a wind that
> might really be her own passage, destination unknown, and
> heard a voice, singing across the Flood, this wonderful song . . .
> telling of the divers, who would come, not now but soon, and
> descend into the Flood and bring back up for us "whatever has
> been taken," the voice promised, "whatever has been lost". . .

But there were ghosts before the sixties—the Yurok Indians. Early
Russian and Spanish visitors to Vineland felt some "invisible barrier" the
Indians "might have known about but did not share—black tips of sea-
mounts emerging from gray sea fringed in brute-innocent white break-
ings, basalt cliffs like castle ruins, the massed and breathing redwoods,
alive forever . . . the call to attend to territories of the spirit." And there
were ghosts before there were Indians. Past the lights of Vineland, "the
river took back its oldest form, became what for the Yuroks it had always
been, a river of ghosts," with spirits called *woge*, "creatures who had been
living here when the first humans came," who went away, eastward over
the mountains, or "nestled altogether in giant redwood boats, singing
unison chants of dispossession and exile." Without warning, trails "would
begin to descend into the earth, toward Tsorrek, the worlds of the dead."
Ecofreaky Hippies tell Vato and Blood that

> this watershed was sacred and magical, and that the *woge* were
> really the porpoises, who had left their world to the humans,
> whose hands had the same five-finger bone structure as their
> flippers . . . and gone beneath the ocean, right off Patrick's
> Point in Humboldt, to wait and see how humans did with the
> world. And if we started fucking up too bad, . . . they would
> come back, teach us how to live the right way, save us. . . .

What's going on? If we put together Shade Creek, flood dreams, tech-
nowaves, porpoises, and *woge*, with Vheissu in *V,* and the Tristero underground in *Crying* (clairvoyants, paranoids, outcasts, and squatters swinging
in "a web of telephone wires, living in the very copper rigging and secular miracle of communication untroubled by the dumb voltages flickering
their miles") and the "Deathkingdoms" and "death-colonies" Blicero

apostrophizes in *Gravity's Rainbow* ("waste regions, Kalaharis, lakes so misty they could not see the other side," Original Sin, Modern Analysis), we end up with something that looks a lot like, if not a comic-book Bardo, then maybe that Buddhist "Global Novel" that Maxine Hong Kingston's been going on about recently in the pages of *Mother Jones* and on, gasp, The Tube. For that matter Zoyd, Prairie, Takeshi, DL, and the Wobblies look a lot like the 108 bandit-heroes of *Water Margin*, the Chinese Robin Hood Kingston has so much fun with in *Tripmaster Monkey*.

According to *The Tibetan Book of the Dead*, dying takes time. We experience the supreme void as pure light, and hope it takes us straightaway to Amitabha, which is for Buddhists what One Big Union was for Wobblies. If the pure light won't take us, we must wrestle with our past, our karma. Only after apparitions both beautiful and monstrous are done with our "conscious principle" will we be reborn—the "reincarnation option"—as something else, somewhere other, on the great wheel. Tom Pynchon calls this place, in the last word of *Vineland*, "home." Wouldn't it be pretty to think so?

Günter Grass: Bad Boys and Fairy Tales

THEY WENT AHEAD and did it anyway, the two Germanys—as if the Berlin Wall had been a chastity belt. They are in bed together again, a single two-backed beast, under the sign of the Deutschmark, in spite of Günter Grass, who told them not to. He has been telling them not to for thirty years. He agrees with the Frenchman who said he loved Germany so much, he was glad there were two of them. Which is why Grass has been called—to his face—"a traitor to the fatherland." He hates the very idea of a German fatherland. Look what the fatherland does when the lights are out all over Europe.

This is more than oedipal rage. These fugitive pieces dating back to 1961 all say the same thing. You may feel the war's over; let bygones be bygones, aren't some of our best friends Germans? But Grass began to write because of Auschwitz. Time passes, and Auschwitz hasn't gone away. Writing after Auschwitz, "against passing time," means using "damaged language in all the shades of gray": no more "black and white of ideology," "blues of introspection," "polished literary chamber music," "detergents of all-purpose poetry," but "shame on every page." Maybe another nation could have committed Auschwitz, but only one did. Unless we stuffed our ears with lottery tickets, we must have heard the screaming. "One of the preconditions for the terrible thing that happened was a strong, unified Germany. . . . We have every reason to fear ourselves as a unit." If to say this is to be a traitor to the fatherland, maybe even a "rootless cosmopolitan," well, tell it to the Scarecrow.

According to Grass, nationalism itself is a "bacillus." He'd rather see a confederation, "a linkage of provinces" sort of like Switzerland: "Germany in the singular is a calculation that will never balance; as a sum, it is a communicating plural." Such a plural could communicate in a mother tongue instead of a fatherland, as German-language writers—citizens of a state of mind—have communicated as far back as Grimmelshausen, who made fun of the Thirty Years' War, and as recently as Group 47.

In his fiction and nonfiction, he's often obsessed about Group 47, the German writers East and West who met sadly and briefly after the war. Some would try again, with beer and potato salad, between 1973 and 1977. They show up in *Headbirths* and he's even projected them backward, into the seventeenth century, in *The Meeting at Telgte*. At Telgte, we also met the first German novelist, Grimmelshausen, who gave Brecht the idea for Mother Courage and Grass the idea for a *Tin Drum*, a modern *Simplicissimus*. So has the notion of a commonwealth of writers, "a cultural nation" in the no-man's-land of Potsdamer Platz, been kicking about for years in his pages,

But oedipal rage there certainly is—in splendid excess. The Bad Boy of German Letters has been father-bashing, grandfather-bashing, and godfather-bashing since he left Danzig. At the gates of Buchenwald, listening to Bach, Nazis wept like wounded bulls. So much for the civilizing surplus value of High Culture. So much for Werther, Brahms, and *Buddenbrooks*, for geopolitical fairy tales and Black Forest *Unsterblichkeitsbedürfnis*. There's no forgiving the Mandarins, the ideologues, the lyric poets. He quotes in *Two States* from one of his *Dog Years* fairy tales. Nothing is pure: not snow, virgins, salt, nor Christ, nor Marx. If anything were pure, then the bones,

> white mounds that were recently heaped up, would grow immaculately without crows: pyramids of glory. But the crows, which are not pure, were creaking unoiled, even yesterday: nothing is pure, no circle, no bone. And piles of bones, heaped up for the sake of purity, will melt cook boil in order that soap, pure and cheap; but even soap cannot wash pure.

Against this shameful fatherland of the white mounds and the cheap soap, Günter Grass—pariah, traitor, Dennis the Menace—sticks out his Tin Drum. He will wash the taste of shame out of the mouth of the German language. This seems to me exemplary. We need more such brilliant Bad Boys, even if we lose a few great novels.

Grass grew up in a hurry: at fourteen, a Hitler Youth; at sixteen, a soldier in the Panzers; at seventeen, an American POW; at nineteen, an apprentice stonecutter, conscience stricken by "photographs showing piles of eyeglasses, shoes, bones"; at twenty-five, a poet and sculptor; at twenty-eight, off to Paris where—under the lash of Paul Celan—he wrote most of his amazing Danzig Trilogy.

If you know *The Tin Drum* (1959) just from Volker Schlöndorff's pious movie you'll have missed the gusto and maybe the point of this Danzig according to Breughel and Bosch, this rhapsodizing and guffaw, the punning and screaming. Nor am I about to belabor it here. But a brief visit in book two to the western front, where Oskar and Bebra look at the turtle-shaped pillbox Dora Seven, a compound of concrete and puppy-dog bones, gives you the flavor. A proud Corporal Lankes explains:

The centuries start coming and going, one after another like nothing at all. But the pillboxes stay put just like the Pyramids stayed put. And one fine day one of those archeologist fellows comes along. And he says to himself: what an artistic void between the First and the Seventh World Wars . . . Then he discovers Dora Five, Six, Seven; he sees my Structural Oblique Formations, and he says to himself, Say, take a look at that. Very, very interesting, magic, menacing, and yet shot through with spirituality. In these works a genius, perhaps the only genius of the twentieth century, has expressed himself clearly, resolutely, and for all time. I wonder, says our archeologist to himself, I wonder if it's got a name? A signature to tell us who the master was? Well, if you look closely, sir, and hold your head on a slant, you'll see, between those Oblique Formations. . . . All right, here's what it says. Herbert Lankes, anno nineteen hundred and forty-four. Title: BARBARIC, MYSTICAL, BORED.

And Bebra says, "You have given our century its name."

There's a disdain here for a lot of poetry, philosophy, psychology, and the nineteenth century's notorious Wagnerian bond with night and death. Oskar, a self-made dwarf whose voice shatters plate glass, isn't symbolic of Nazi culture; nor is he symbolic of what became of the Germans, poor puppy dogs, inside Hitler's thousand-year pillbox. Oskar instead symbolizes the German artist, who should have been the German conscience but who chose instead to stay three years old forever. Not by accident, as Oskar scrambles with his books up the railroad embankment to look at Dora Seven, does he admit to "losing a little Goethe" in the process. Goethe! *The Tin Drum* is the first of Grass's very Grimm fairy tales. As it ends, the Black Witch is gaining on the three-year-old times ten, in a loony bin: "Black words, black coat, black money."

Likewise I know what to make of Mahlke's grotesque Adam's apple in *Cat and Mouse* (1961). Mahlke's been asked to swallow too much, including the philosopher Fichte. He has swallowed so much, he needs an Iron Cross to cover it up. Nor, for all the time he spent in church and his fixating on the Black Madonna of Czestochowa, is Mahlke any sort of Christ figure, a Teutonic Billy Budd. As old and as useful to myth as a Son of God is the Scapegoat, someone who is blamed and punished and expelled from the social order. Scapegoats are usually Jewish.

After the Scapegoat in this fairy tale of history comes the Scarecrow. Amsel the half Jew constructs these scarerows in *Dog Years* (1963). They are mechanical marching men: the SA. Amsel will be betrayed by his "bloodbrother" Matern, "the bounceback man." Tulla, the satanic pubescent from *Cat and Mouse*, shows up again; and Dr. Brunies, the first in a long line of luckless Grass pedagogues; and many black German shepherds, leading to Hitler's favorite Prinz, and to the equally black Pluto, hiding underground after the war in Brauxel's mine, with an army of scarecrows, all of them waiting for emancipation and a reckoning.

Unfriendly references abound in *Dog Years* to Kant and Hegel, old Celtic Druids, Prussian oak-tree gods, "the goateed Husserl," and the Hoard of the Nibelungs. Besides, "Schopenhauer glowered between bookshelves." But listen to this:

> Has a thousand words for Being, for time, for essence, for world and ground, for the with and the now, for the Nothing, and for the scarecrow as existential frame. Accordingly: Scareness, being-scared, scare-structure, scare-vulnerable, scare-principle, scare-situation, unscared, final scare, scare-born time, scare-totality, foundation-scare, the law of scare. "For the essence of the scarecrow is the transcendental three-fold dispersal of scarecrow suchness in the world project. Projecting itself into the Nothing, the scarecrow *physis*, or burgeoning,

is at all times beyond the scarecrow such and the scarecrow at-hand. . . ." Transcendence drips from stockingcaps in the eighteenth stall. A hundred caustic-degraded philosophers are of one and the same opinion: "Scarecrow Being means: to be held-out-into Nothing."

And so the Danzig Trilogy ends with a wicked parody of . . . Martin Heidegger! Is this any way to talk to your Higher Culture? With a slingshot?

It's generally felt that Grass won't write another novel as completely satisfying as *The Tin Drum*. This is because, after the Trilogy, instead of staying put inside his characters, he was loose on the streets, agitating for social justice and Willy Brandt, animadverting Kiesingers and Globkes, off to Tel Aviv or Managua. John Updike tells us: "Those who urge upon American writers more social commitment and a more public role should ponder the cautionary case of Günter Grass. Here is a novelist who has gone so public he can't be bothered to write a novel; he just sends dispatches to his readers from the front lines of his engagement."

I'd be more comfortable agreeing for once with Updike if he hadn't missed the point of three of Grass's books. But yes, Grass has been on the barricades, and barricades get in the way of the lapidary. Personally, I'd blame movies almost as much as politics for the, ah, dishevelment of his subsequent fiction: the impatient cuts, irresolute fades, camera angles wider than subcontinents; a sacrifice of introspection.

But I also see a career in which novels and politics are twinned. He would democratize the language *and* the social order. He not only answers all the fire alarms in the culture, he often sounds them himself. And the vernacular in which he sounds them—vulgar, sarcastic, satiric, cajoling, blasphemous, absurd, iridescent; seaport street talk and Magic Realism on the Vistula—has about it the acid vehemence of another great German scourge. Think of him as Martin Luther with a sense of humor. Yes, of course, salvation for Grass is all works, and he'd probably rather sit down for beer and potato salad with Erasmus, but I can't help recalling the Ninety-five Theses nailed to the door of the Wittenberg church, the tract on Babylonian Captivity, and the famous farting contest between Luther and Lucifer. At least in part, the Reformation was all about metaphors.

And I do believe we're talking about a second Reformation in a West where every possible indulgence is for sale, plastic accepted.

In his own words, he is one of those writers who "bolt from their desks to busy themselves with the trivia of democracy. Which implies a readiness to compromise. Something we must get through our heads is this: A poem knows no compromise but men live by compromise. The individual who can stand up under this contradiction and act is a fool and will change the world." This almost mandates in his prose something messy, voracious, indulgent, hybrid, partisan, ad hoc, avuncular, treasonable and . . . well, heroic. How many Calvinos do we need, anyway? Or Robbe-Grillets and Tourniers? Enough, already, of this cult of the petty-bourgeois genius.

He wouldn't publish another novel for seven years. The political speeches were collected as *Speak Out!* (1968), and there's an important play to mention, *The Plebians Rehearse the Uprising* (1966), his account of the workers' insurrection in East Berlin, Leipzig, and Magdeburg. *Plebians* was disapproved of in the West because it hadn't followed our line of a popular revolt against Communism. It was despised in the East because it was anti-Stalinist, and asked the embarrassing question, Where was Brecht? Grass had to go all the way to India to see it performed again, twenty years later, in Bengali.

In *Local Anaesthetic* (1969), Eberhard Starusch, a fortysomething professor of "German and history," goes to a dentist. There's a TV set to distract the patients. On its screen, Starusch projects his life, his violent fantasies, and not a little German history and literature—Goethe again; Kleist and Buchner; "Hegel and Marxengels"; "the late Rilke—the early Schiller"; even Herbert Marcuse—between commercials. Sometimes, this private videotape is the only scheduled program. Sometimes the commercial products (deep freezers, hair rinse) represent abstract problems (memory, disguise). Sometimes the screen writhes in "live" coverage of antiwar demonstrators, including Starusch's brainy, disillusioned student, Scherbaum, who wants to burn his long-haired dachshund, in public, to protest against American napalm in Vietnam.

Surrogate fathers and prodigal sons: Starusch and Scherbaum educate each other into the basis for action and the requirements of decency. Being rational "doesn't prevent you from being stupid," but neither does being passionate and sincere. If, as we are led to believe, "humanity is terrorized by overproduction and forced consumption," the answer may not be the professor's "pedagogical prophylaxis" (because the modern eats history for breakfast), or the dentist's utopian/anesthetic "Sickcare" (because there will always be pain), but neither is the answer burning dachshunds, nor the mindless violence of the Maoist teenybopper Vero.

A passionate youth, a kindly elder, an accommodation. Imagine that, in the sixties. Not exactly, to pick at random, Irving Howe and the New Left; not even, to go all the way back to the fifties, Lionel Trilling and Allen Ginsberg. Pay attention in *Local Anaesthetic* to the counterpoint of quotations from Seneca and Nietzsche. Grass has his problems with Seneca, who was to blame, after all, for Nero. But he *hates* Nietzsche.

So much for Goethe, Heidegger, Nietzsche. Now for the Brothers Grimm. In *The Flounder* (1977), a swamp-monster history of nationalism, religion, nutrition, art, sex, and the author, Grass unbuttons himself, and it's quite a sight, like Rabelais and Levi-Strauss doing the dirty. His nine chapters are the months of pregnancy and the Ages of Man. They give birth, out of the sea and the amniotic soup, to the New Woman who may be almost as revolutionary as the potato.

Our flounder's borrowed from an old Grimm typically punitive and typically misogynistic folktale. He pops out of the Baltic, near (of course) Danzig, the first male chauvinist fish: immortal. In Grimm, the fisherman who caught this talking turbot was so impressed with its gift of speech he set it free. In gratitude, the fish promised to fulfill the fisherman's wishes. This good fortune was subverted by the greed of the fisherman's wife, Ilsebill, who asked for control of the moon and the sun.

According to Grass, the flounder, back in Neolithic times, hated matriarchy, and signed on as a kind of Kissinger to the fisherman, teaching him power politics, leaking the secrets of metallurgy and the Minoans, stirring up a stew of war and wanderlust—of restless Goths and final solutions. Like the fish, the fisherman is immortal, a masculine principle mindlessly replicating itself, and sexually allied down through the eons with successive Ilsebills: invariably cooks, invariably pregnant, invariably symbolic of the status of women from the Stone Age to 1970 in society, fantasy, and other metaphysisms. Thus a three-breasted Awa, who suckles man to happy stupor; Iron Age Wigga, who invents fish soup; Mestwina, reconciling paganism and Christianity; ascetic Dorothea, who bakes a Sacred Heart into High Gothic bread dough; Fat Gret, a goose-plucking nun, for whom "young sons of patrician families were an appetizer: tender asparagus tips"; Agnes the kindhearted, Amanda the potato-faced, Sophie the Virgin, Lena the Socialist, Billy the Lesbian, and Maria of the buttermilk.

We meet Opitz and Gryphius, the seventeenth-century poets who will reappear in *The Meeting at Telgte.* There are broad burlesques of the Teutonic epic: more godfather-bashing. And, before the talking turbot is tried by feminists for crimes against the distaff, there will be many odd recipes, including one for toads' eggs fried in the fat of stillborn baby boys. But we know now that what's really cooking is an entire culture, masculine and capitalist, ballsy and greedy. We eat our role models, those mushrooms, and that excrement. It makes a writer want to puke.

The Meeting at Telgte (1979), written as a seventieth birthday present for his old friend Hans Werner Richter, is more oedipal mayhem, anticipating much of what Grass says later on about mother tongues and fatherlands. In fact these poets never made it to Telgte in 1647 to talk about language and peace as the Thirty Years' War was winding down. Still, a novelist dreams: What if, like German writers in 1947, they'd met and drafted a statement? After all, poets alone "knew what deserved the name of German. With many 'ardent sighs and tears,' they had knitted the German language as the last bond; they were the other, the true Germany."

Meet Birken ("one wondered why so much beauty should have a need of theory"); Buchner ("so ponderously silent that his mute periods have been cited as figures of speech"); Gryphius ("thunder, even when he lacked lightning"); Rist ("Logau's wit was corrosive because it lacked wholesome humor . . . because it lacked wholesome humor it was no better than irony . . . because it was ironical it was not German . . . because it was not German, it was intrinsically 'un-German and anti-German'"). According to Grass, even the composer Schutz *could* have been there where he wouldn't have heard much music: "To set such a drama to music, one would have to unleash a war of flies." Eavesdropping—naturally—is Grimmelshausen. Grass identifies with Grimmelshausen as Mann identified with Goethe. This is because Grass and Grimmelshausen are both funny. (Goethe told us: "How dare a man have a sense of humor, when he considers his immense burden of responsibilities toward himself and others? However. I have no wish to pass censure on the humorists. After all, does one have to have a conscience? Who says so?")

Thirty years is a long war. These poets would actually *prolong* this war, in order to refine the German language and its "rhymed yearning for death." Instead of soup they "sank their teeth into phrases and sentences, easily satisfied word-ruminants, finding, if need be, satiety in self-quotation." Besides: "No one was willing to give up merely because reality had once again put in an objection and cast mud at art." Finally, of course: "This verdict of universal guilt amounted to a universal acquittal."

They perfect a petition, but as the inn burns down the petition burns up: "And so what would in any case not have been heard, remained unsaid." No great loss: less "soul-mush." But something in Grass is tickled by these poets' clubs: Fruit-bearers, Sweet-smellers and the German-minded, the Upright Cucumber Lodge, an Order of the Elbe Swans. Something in him looks among the beer kegs and milking stools and wanton wenches for a saving "thistle." Honor? Comrades?

Zeus had the first "headbirth," springing Athene. It's "a paradox that has impregnated male minds to this day." It's also a parable of art. Grass Zeusifies. His *Headbirths* (1980) is a lively mess, placenta and all. In no special order, though often in circles, *Headbirths* contemplates the 1980 elections in the German Federal Republic: a dead friend; movies, children; Asia, balls of thread; liver sausage; and a fictitious pair of civil servants, Harm and Dorte, who can't decide if they want a child and can't imagine what history will do to them and their Volkswagen.

Grass approves of children, having sired lots, but he isn't sure the world needs any more Germans, no matter how much authorities deplore a declining birth rate that makes necessary so many Turks to do the coolie work of the republic. After being a nuisance on the *Tin Drum* set, Grass went off with Schlöndorff to the Orient, thinking cinematic. Maybe they'd make a movie on overpopulation. Like nuclear reactors, overpopulation's bad for the ecology. Grass took these notes; we don't know what Schlöndorff did. The dead friend is Nicolas Born, from Group 47.

Meanwhile Zeus looks over his shoulder at critics who ask him to butt out of contemporary politics, as if this morning's news weren't a headbirth of history. At one point he makes himself ten years older than he really is in order to imagine the compromises writers of that age—Eich, Koeppeman, Kästner—must have made with Hitler. To the dead Born, he speaks out loud: "Now that you are dead I am aging more perceptibly. My courage, which was doing fine only yesterday, has furled several sails." (Don't believe him.) And: "I'm ashamed." (He's the only one.)

Mobius on a bender gets looped. In Shanghai, among eleven million bicycles, he wonders, What if the populations of China and the two Germanys were reversed? If there were only eighty million Chinese . . . and a *billion* Germans in "the alarming process of self-discovery"? But the Germans, unlike the Chinese, are dying out. Will they end up stuffed in their own museums? On your left, Hittites, Sumerians, Aztecs; to the right, Germans who were "not mere warlike barbarians concerned only with sordid gain, mere function without spirit," but victims of an industrial society that depended parasitically for its extravagant standard of living on a South (oil; Turks) which it exhausted. Ought those Germans to have *denied* themselves *anything*?

Grass imagines Harm and Dorte as teachers who met at a sixties rally against the war: liberal puppy love. Harm will quote Marx on the capitalist law of accumulation through redundancy, and deplore "the lack of long-range views." Dorte frisks among computer projections, and deplores "the lack of meaning in general." Both feel bad about their civil-servant privileges, and vote against Franz Josef Strauss. Since Grass needs them to go to overpopulated Asia to "tabulate and classify" the squalor, he will also invent a Sisyphus Travel Agency, to arrange "destitution as a course of study." Harm and Dorte will be booked into slums from Bangkok to Bombay.

Grass directs: "Long shot of the Indian subcontinent. She, cut off at the waist, covering half the Bay of Bengal, all Calcutta and Bangladesh, casually takes the pill: 'It's safe to say that birth control . . . has been a failure in India.'" It's also safe to say that Grass has more fun with his impossible screenplay than he does with Harm and Dorte, who will weary any reader. When Dorte, inside a Cave of Bats, undergoes a mystical conversion to the cult of the Mother Goddess and withholds her sexual favors from Harm till he agrees to procreate, even Grass is exasperated. With her ball of thread, can't she knit herself a child? Only a movie could make us care about these two. And movies, Grass suggests, are a substitute for the imagination. Take that, Schlöndorff.

But so, Grass implies, are card files and data sheets a substitute for the imagination. They furnish a "vacuum." And the worst possible substitute for the imagination is a politics-as-usual of neglect, a headbirth metastasized. Grass fumes: What nonsense to seek disarmament through rearmament, to combat an energy shortage by stepping up production, to breed reactors instead of Germans, to pile up pork and butter mountains in a world where fifteen million children starve to death each year. If he were in charge he would abolish compulsory education and "emancipate" all civil servants by firing them. To raise the birth rate he would cut off the electric current at night and reintroduce as bedware the traditional German nightcap, to save the heat that escapes through the holes in our heads. He would mandate a switch of political systems every ten years between Germanys East and West, giving the German Democratic Republic "an opportunity to relax under capitalism," while, under Communism, the FRG would drain off its cholesterol. More radically, he'd deal with property "as my spiritual property and that of others have been dealt with: 70 years after the author's (that's me) death, his (my) rights enter the public domain. I (as dictator) would extend this benefit by law to all earned or acquired possessions—house, factory, field—so that only the children and some of the grandchildren will be obliged to inherit it or hold it in usufruct. Ones born later will be exempt from this hereditary burden . . . they will be free to make a fresh start."

Ridiculous of course. Without surplus there can be no value. This is the sort of irresponsible antinovelistic "dispatch" digressiveness that so dismays an Updike he neglected to mention any of it in his review of *Headbirths*.

Finally, Grass would ordain a National Endowment, a Museum without Walls in the psychic space between the two Berlins, promoting the history and, much more important, the literature—the mother tongue—of all the Germanys. Writers, he says, are the best patriots; even a "wounded" language might somehow heal the body politic. "What's wrong with us is neither material nor social, but an emergency of the spirit." Dorte in her sarong confesses: "I'm afraid, Harm. Of us, of everything." Grimmelshausen would advise her: Read Holderlin. Or Trakl.

Having kissed off the Brothers Grimm in *The Flounder*, in *The Rat* (1987) Grass kisses off fairy tales period. No more ruined towers, magic mirrors, hungry ravens, dead trees, a comb, a belt, a cherry torte and those little bones left over after Adolf ate the sleeping princess. "All hope is gone," he says in one of the little poems that pepper the text, "for fairy tales / it shall be written here, / are dying with the forests." The forests are dying from industrial overdevelopment and acid rain. Without forests, of course, "children can no longer get lost."

In one of *Rat*'s subplots, fairy-tale characters seize power and demand a regreening of Middle Europe. They are exterminated. In another subplot, five feminists, on a barge in the Baltic, search for a vanished matriarchal city; they'll be vaporized. In a third subplot, Oskar the dwarf returns as a middle-aged producer of video cassettes on his way to Danzig-Gdańsk, where he will show films he has already made about the apocalyptic future; he, too, will be vaporized. In yet a fourth subplot, an artist who counterfeits Authentic Gothic for needy cathedrals is tried and convicted . . . of treason!

Where's the Social-Democratic novelist while all of this goes on? Either dreaming or marooned in a space capsule orbiting an Earth on which everything has been obliterated except rats, wood lice, a stinging bluebottle, and a flying snail. In either case, a scholarly She-Rat explains the future and disdains the past. We are also told of new punk religions, hybrid rat-men with blue eyes and blond hair, and the posthistorical significance of Solidarity, the then-outlawed Polish labor movement. (Who knew?) An alarmist Grass is having his black fun with movies as fairy tales, with literature as lies, with art and politics as forgeries, and with rats as symbolic of all the herrenvolk wants to get rid of, from scruples to children to, of course, the Jews. This is his own sort of poisoned apple: Wake up, before all of us turn into big, bad Germans!

Fed up with "frozen cheerfulness," "stylized warmth behind burglarproof glass," "Social Democratic neither/nor," not to mention people who obsess about the "half-life of their vegetables" and take courses in How to Cope with Grief, Grass sent himself for six months in 1987 to Calcutta, where he found more shame. In *Show Your Tongue* (1988), he measures everything, including himself, by Calcutta: "a city damned to offer lodgings to every human misery"; a city he loves, in spite of itself, for the Bengali lyrics, sitar melancholy, moonlit courtyards; a city that plummets "as if an Expressionist had invented this rush of streets for a woodcut of epileptic collapse. Only the sleepers remain real. "In a diary, in anguished little poems and violent smudgy drawings, he limns an "acrid smoke of open fires fed with cakes of dried cow dung"; vultures, crows and "child-bundles" living in a garbage dump: old women on funeral pyres at the crematorium, "sticking out from under the shrouds."

Even at the crematorium: "Only the rich can afford sufficient wood. The free-market economy, death as an overhead expense, like everything else." Temple-hopping with his sick wife; reading Lichtenburg, Schopenhauer, and Elias Canetti; among Bengali poets who can't understand a word of Tamil or Urdu, Grass is beside himself:

> If you lent (for a fee) one of these slum hovels, created from bare necessity, to the city of Frankfurt am Main and had it set down next to the Deutsche Bank highrise where the hewn granite sculpture by the artist Bill says yes, always yes to the towering bank, because as an endless loop it loves only itself, is incontrovertibly beautiful and immaculately endorses the circulation of money stamped valid for eternity—if, I say, you replaced that granite celebrating its flawless self, and set down instead one single slum hovel as authentic as want had made it right next to the glassy arrogance of the Deutsche Bank, beauty would at once be on the side of the hovel and truth, too, even the future. The mirrored art of all those palaces consecrated to money would fall to its knees, because the slum hovel belongs to tomorrow.

Who'll make the revolution that saves Calcutta? Not Marx, says Grass, nor Mao. He looks to Kali, goddess of destruction, "the terrible black mother" with ten arms and a sword, a spear, a shield, and a strangling noose, a necklace of skulls, and a girdle of severed hands. This is the Kali we see in the temples under layers of black enamel, palms red, eyes ringed, surrounded by women "equipped with Dracula teeth, holding child-sized men in their talons, biting off heads, hands, and cocks." In blood-drunk ecstasy, Kali cast down her consort, Siva, and danced on his stomach. And then, because she was ashamed of herself, she stuck out her tongue. So does Grass.

This is the good liberal, having met despair. V. S. Naipaul went to Calcutta once upon a time, and stayed a minute, holding his nose. Allen

Ginsberg went there, too, for a year, and became a nurse. Supposing a Norman Mailer went to Israel? Isn't this the sort of thing a serious writer ought to do—book himself into the nightmares of the century, the unconscious of history, after too many tours of the self? When Grass left town for Calcutta in August 1987, he was flying away

> from Germany and Germany, the way two deadly foes, armed to the teeth, grow ever more alike; from insights achieved from too close up; from my own perplexity, admitted only sotto voce, flying with me. And from the gobbledygook, the where-I'm-coming-froms, the balanced reporting, the current situations, the razor-elbowed games of self-realization. I am flying thousands of miles away from the superficial subtleties of former leftists now merely chic feuilletonists, and far, far away from myself as part or object of this public exposure.

And now look what they've done: Left and Right, do-si-do, buck and wing, danse macabre. He should be embarrassed. Instead he allows to be published these unrepentant fugitives—as if a lost cause mattered. As Martin Luther may or may not have told the Diet at Worms: "Here I stand. I can do no other." . . . *A rhymed yearning for death.*

Now that writers can talk, what shall they say to one another: Show me the way to the next BMW? We are advised by publicists for corporate capitalism that if the nonprofit police state is now bankrupt, so too, somehow, is social democracy. To be a good liberal, a practical radical, a ferocious democrat, a self-made orphan, a citizen without portfolio, and a prophet without honor; a Bad Boy and skeptic; a holy fool instead of a court jester; incapable of simplifying yourself in the gridwork of profit-taking and self-congratulation, ashamed of your very own white-male perks—well, it's very thick sausage. And certainly not advisable if you want a Nobel Prize.

In some ways it would be easier to write in opposition, from a prison or a psycho ward, in one of the Koreas or Latin Americas or the new black fascisms of emergent and depressing Africa—to have been, before everything changed utterly in 1989, a Konrad or Kundera or Sinyavsky. They'd forgive you then your urgency—review your courage instead of your cleverness. You'd not be asked for more than one masterwork. Fly the black flag, and everyone salutes. But in our postindustrialized, postmod-

ernized, post-semioticized, Post-Toastied fairy-tale West, a Grass is
needed more than ever, and more than masterworks. From men of color
in white societies, and from women everywhere, we expect dissent, abrasions of race and sex and class on a dominant culture, the music and sinew
of the Other. But how many white male writers of the first rank are Citizens before they are Author-Gods? How many put down the pen, pick up
a sword, cut through the fat, gather unto them the children and say:
There are wounds that will not heal?

Grass would hate this comparison, but look at France since the death
of Sartre. Primo Levi fell down a stairwell. Amoz Oz also comes to mind,
in *Slopes of Lebanon*: "What began with the biblical words 'Zion shall be
redeemed by law' has come to 'Nobody's better than we are, so they
should all shut up.'" Quoting Isaiah ("Your hands are covered with
blood") and Jeremiah ("For they had eyes but they did not see"), Oz
grins: "Veteran defeatists, both of them. Troublers of Israel. Self-hating
Jews."

Citizen Grass is stuck in both his Germanys, but he can look at him-
self. Now that the Wall isn't there, I see him jumping over it with Christa
Wolf to hold hands and to ban nuclear reactors. The talking turbot and
Cassandra. This picture makes me smile.

Peggy Noonan's
What I Saw at the Revolution

T HE FIRST THING to be said about Peggy Noonan, who rose from all-news CBS radio to the White House speechwriting staff in the first term of the Great Communicator and stuck around long enough to be lip-synched by two different presidents, is that she's a dandy maker of phrases, often sentences, sometimes whole paragraphs. Listen to her justify her job: "A great speech," she says, "from a leader to the people eases our isolation, breaks down the walls, includes people: It takes them inside a spinning thing and makes them part of the gravity." Listen to her describe the people who got in the way of her doing that job: "What I mean is," she says, "when men in politics are together, testosterone poisoning makes them insane." She can even be savage discussing hard-core conservatives on her ideological side: "Well," she says, "what you get is a bunch of creepy little men with creepy little beards who need something to seethe on (State Dept. cookie-pushers! George Bush! the Trilateral Commission!) some hate to live on. . . ."

The second thing to be said about Peggy Noonan is that for the purposes of this memoir, and her deliverance from ghosting into a more agreeable career, she's had to invent a literary persona, a sassy tone of voice, a cross circuit of Holden Caulfield and Fran Leibowitz, but right-wing smarty-pants, too, like *National Review* magazine, with some class animus for seasoning, a weakness for sarcasm, a bratty Irish appetite for grudge, and way too many exclamation marks. This persona works reasonably well, except it sometimes leaves her sounding dumber than she is, as if she had to apologize for her copy of Ezra Pound's *Cantos*, as if she really believed that all liberals are rich and guilty nitwits who went to

Harvard and Yale instead of Farleigh Dickinson, and all activists on behalf of the homeless are cruel manipulators of the insane, and only Republicans can talk to janitors, and Paul Johnson and Jean-Francois Revel are intellectual heavyweights, and George Gilder isn't an idiot when he babbles about "the humane nature of the free market." To have met Gorbachev and to tell us only that he looks like "a retired hockey goalie" is not just to miss the boat of history, but to jump off after it's under way, thumbing your nose as you drown. Take *that*, you Commie pinko.

The third thing to be said about Peggy Noonan is that, almost against her will, she does damage to the president she claims she loves. Reagan's White House is compared to "a beautiful clock that makes all the right sounds, but when you open it up, there is nothing inside." Of the president himself she says that his intellect was only "slightly superior to average"; that he didn't hear very much of what was said around him; and that the battle for his mind, and I quote again, "was like the trench warfare of World War I: Never have so many fought so hard for such barren terrain." Noonan quotes a friend of the president's: "Behind those warm eyes is a lack of curiosity that is, somehow, disorienting." And so is her memoir, however much fun, somehow disorienting. Her real gripe seems to be that they messed with her copy. That was John Reed's real gripe with the Russian Revolution, too. It always happens to flacks, after which they write for themselves or they die.

No Turning Back, Barbara Ferraro and Patricia Hussey, with Jane O'Reilly

NO TURNING BACK is a radical book in every respect. Barbara Ferraro and Patricia Hussey, who used to be nuns, strike at the roots of the Roman Catholic Church and its attitude toward women, its relationship to those secular societies of which it is a part, and its retreat from a commitment to the social gospel of peace and justice endorsed by the Second Vatican Council in 1965. Ferraro, the granddaughter of Italian immigrants, and Hussey, from an Irish American family, grew up in parochial schools; entered different convents of the Sisters of Notre Dame five years apart in the 1960s; took graduate degrees in social work, family therapy, and theology at Jesuit colleges; and served their religious order and their communities in factories, parish-houses, holding pens for runaway children, and shelters for the homeless. By thinking out loud, especially on the nature of their stewardship, they began to question a patriarchal Church hierarchy. By reading, especially books like *Bare Ruined Choirs* by Garry Wills and *The Feminization of American Culture* by Ann Douglas, they were politicized. By listening, especially to women who came to them for help, they were radicalized. These daughters of Pope John XXIII came to question the Vatican's refusal to ordain women as priests, its exploitation of nuns as a labor pool of poorly paid coolies, its condemnation of any form of contraception, and its bitter opposition to abortion for any reason whatever. In 1984 they signed a full-page pro-choice ad in the *New York Times*. By 1988 they were the only nuns to have signed that ad who hadn't recanted in the face of ugly pressure all the way from Rome. "We were the daughters of the Church," they explain, "and they were the fathers, and we were expected to be dutiful, as always." Ferraro and

Hussey continue, I quote: "Their surprise, and discomfort, and eventually their fury as we developed different ideas was as ferocious as any husband's was in the 1970s when he discovered that his wife was no longer interested in folding his socks." In order to serve their God, they had to leave the Sisterhood.

Ferraro and Hussey have told their story to the social critic Jane O'Reilly. O'Reilly, who wrote a wonderful account of her own Catholic girlhood and subsequent feminist discoveries, *The Girl I Left Behind*, so skillfully weaves the personal and the political that what we get is a unicorn tapestry. Here are convent days of passionate vows and mortification; consciousness-raising nights of High and Low Christology; the assembly line, the pregnant teenagers, the disturbed children; worker priests, liberation theology, and the Sanctuary movement; Boston and Charleston, Rome and Managua. But besides meeting these two remarkable women, through their eyes we are made to see a Church that refuses to *listen* to its congregation, to hear the witness of its own believers. The overwhelming majority of American Catholics are in favor of birth control; a solid majority disagrees with Rome on divorce and abortion; enrollment in Catholic schools and colleges steadily declines; there aren't enough priests to go around; and still, like Galileo all over again, the Church would punish its dissidents and those Sisters of Mercy out there in a burning world, bringing the Cross to the poor and the speechless, living the Gospel and the Sermon on the Mount, forming a circle to listen and to heed. How very sad.

Philip Roth's *Patrimony*

THREE YEARS AGO in *The Facts*, which he called "A Novelist's Auto-biography," Philip Roth let us know he wasn't really Zuckerman, or Tarnopol or Kepesh or Portnoy or any other character in any of his novels, no matter how closely those novels seemed to resemble his own life. What he had always done as a writer, he said, was to "set out spontaneously to improve on actuality in the interest of being more interesting." Thus, according to *Facts*, Philip was really a good boy, who wrote bad-boy books to keep his creative edge and save himself from being "desexualized." And there were passages in *Facts* where he made us believe him, especially when he wrote about his mother, into whose sleek black coat he'd wormed his way as a child, a "privileged pampered papoose . . . the unnameable animal-me bearing her dead father's name, the protoplasm-me, boy-baby, and body-burrower-in-training, joined by every nerve ending to her smile and her sealskin coat. . . . To be at all was to be her Philip." Of course, Roth almost spoiled it all by dragging in Zuckerman to criticize the manuscript of *Facts*, but I liked that mother.

She died in 1981. Philip's father, Herman, blind in one eye, deaf in one ear, started to die eight years later, of a tumor on the brain, and the good boy stopped writing novels, though he did take notes, to think about and care for him. *Patrimony* is his splendid account of that custodianship and its baffling emotions. Herman was difficult, but we don't choose our fathers. And unlike Zuckerman's father, he was fiercely proud of his novelist son. And the son discovers in this stubborn, brusque, and grudging old man surprising aspects of himself. There are several patrimonies— the old shaving mug handed down by generations of Jewish immigrants;

his incontinent father's own excrement, which Philip must clean up as once he was cleaned up after as a baby; an obsession with memory, with never forgetting *anything*; and equally important to a writer, a distinctive voice: "He taught me the vernacular," says Philip; "He *was* the vernacular, unpoetic and expressive and point-blank, with all the vernacular's glaring limitations and all its durable force." *Patrimony*, the book, sticks mostly to this vernacular. Neither ironic nor sentimental, it finds its effects in the perfect detail. Herman remembers relatives, neighbors, and bygone Jewish boxing champs. For him, says his son. "To be alive . . . is to be made of memory—to him if a man's not made of memory, he's made of nothing." They joke together about a survivor who has written "a pornographic bestseller about the Holocaust." There is a scene in which Philip sleeps with his father, as if a poultice to the wound. Zuckerman would have worried this bed with every imaginable ambiguity and embarrassment. The good son merely reports it. "He wasn't just any father," he says; "he was *the* father, with everything there is to hate in a father and everything there is to love." There's that word, so rare in Roth. He imagines his father's tumor, "the fingernail that had been aggrandizing the hollows of his skull for a decade, the material as obdurate and gristly as he was, that had cracked open the bone behind his nose and with a stubborn, unrelenting force just like his, had pushed tusklike through the cavities of his face." Love is just as hard, just as inexorable, like this book. His father dies, age eighty-six. Philip, at last, is all grown up.

Milan Kundera's *Immortality*

W E ARE AT the end of Europe, the end of history, the end of culture, and the end of this novel, in deck chairs at a health club with a swimming pool. We can look at ourselves in twenty-seven mirrors on three sides of the rooftop club, or we can look through the fourth wall at a panoramic view of Paris. Milan Kundera is talking to one of his characters in *Immortality*, the accused rapist and guerrilla tire-slasher Professor Avenarius. He seeks a metaphor. To Avenarius, he says, "You play with the world like a melancholy child who has no little brother." Avenarius smiles, very much like a melancholy child, and then remarks: "I don't have a little brother, but I have you."

And we have Kundera, a sixty-two-year-old melancholy child, a little brother of the bloody borders and the lost faith. He has written this novel in front of our eyes, out of chance encounters with enigmatic strangers, and radio news reports of anomalous events, and imaginary conversations among the lofty likes of Goethe and Hemingway, and snippets of books, and shards of memory. He has interpolated little essays—on journalism, sentimentality, coincidence, astrology, and the phases of the erotic moon— that turn out, of course, not to have been digressions at all. Everything fits inside with a satisfying snap, like the hasp on a jewel box or the folding of a fan. Left in the air, like smoke, are ghosts and grace notes.

I'm sure there's a musical analogue; there usually is in Kundera's fiction: Mozart's *Don Giovanni* or Beethoven's last quartet or any one of sixteen fugues by Bach. "Our lives are composed like music," Kundera told us in *The Unbearable Lightness of Being*, "and if we listen well, they will speak to us in the heightened language of secret motifs, which are really the accidents of our becoming, transformed into significance by a roused imagination."

Certainly, in *Immortality*, there's a lot of Mahler.

But along with linear time, Romantic poetry, modern art, the idea of progress, the ardor of revolution, and the consolations of nostalgia, he has also given up on music. "Music," we're told, "can be heard every time some statesman is murdered or war is declared, every time it's necessary to stuff people's heads with glory to make them die more willingly. Nations that tried to annihilate each other were filled with the identical fraternal emotion when they heard the thunder of Chopin's Funeral March or Beethoven's *Eroica*." Kundera himself explains that "music taught the European not only a richness of feeling but also the worship of his feelings and his feeling self. . . . Music: a pump for inflating the soul. Hypertrophic souls turned into huge balloons rise to the ceiling of the concert hall and jostle each other in unbelievable congestion."

Whether this constitutes a symbolic parricide—Kundera's father, mourned so lovingly in *The Book of Laughter and Forgetting*, was a musicologist—I can't say. But it leaves us lonelier in Paris than we were before we ever met Agnes (a computer expert and "the clear-minded observer of ambiguity") or her sister. Laura (an *haute couture* shopkeeper and "the addict of ambiguity") or Agnes's husband, Paul (a clever lawyer and "the simpleton of ambiguity").

Laura, because she thinks she loves Paul, plays Mahler on a white piano and collects money for African lepers in the Paris Metro system. Agnes, because she decides she doesn't love Paul anymore or not enough, leaves Paris for Switzerland, where her father and her money are both stashed. Paul, who's come to deplore Mahler as much as rock 'n' roll, and to despair of Western civilization, drinks too much. Professor Avenarius meets Laura in the Metro when she's humiliated by *clochards*, seems never to have heard of Agnes, and hires Paul to defend him against the charge of rape. (Though there's always a lot of rape in Kundera novels, this one didn't happen.)

I neglect Rubens, who renounced art in favor of erotomania, because he is one of Kundera's several wicked surprises. So I won't tell you about his affair with the Lute Player, also known as the Gothic Maiden, and their stroll among "the severed heads of the famous dead." Besides, you've met him before. Like Zemanek in *The Joke*, Jaromil in *Life Is Elsewhere*,

Klima in *The Farewell Party*, and Tomas in *The Unbearable Lightness of Being*, he's a compulsive womanizer. There are signs here that Kundera is at last as weary of Don Juan and his roundelay of one-night stands as he wearied earlier of Don Quixote. But there are signs here that Kundera has wearied of everything else, too, even laughter. "Humor," says Avenarius, "can only exist when people are still capable of recognizing some borders between the important and the unimportant."

These people are unhappy because God is dead, and neither sex nor politics will guarantee them a life ever after. They're short on meaning and being. In all of European culture there are only fifty or so geniuses (fifty-one, counting Kundera) who deserve remembering after they have gone. Laura, Agnes, Paul, Rubens, and Avenarius are not among these happy few. ("Class inequality is but an insigificant shortcoming compared to this insulting metaphysical inequality.") Kundera plays them on his fiddle. Or, to stick to his own quite wonderful conceit of the clock in Old Town Square in Prague, with the twelve apostles and the bell-ringing skeleton, he pops them in and out of his narrative like marionettes. In a world of "many people, few ideas," not even their unhappiness is original. They've borrowed it like their gestures, from Goethe, Beethoven, and Napoleon; from Tycho Brahe and Robert Musil; from Marx and Rimbaud. In one thirty-page section midway through *Immortality* Kundera mentions Lacan, Apollinaire, Rilke, Romain Rolland, Paul Eluard, Knut Hamsun, Cervantes, Shakespeare, and Dostoyevsky. In spite of all this culture, Europe got Auschwitz and the gulag. Somebody must be doing something wrong, so everybody's punished.

According to Paul, who is about to be fired from a radio station where he has a commentary program,

> High culture is nothing but a child of that European perversion called history, the obsession we have with going forward, with considering the sequence of generations as a relay race in which everyone surpasses his predecessor only to be surpassed by his successor. Without this relay race called history there would be no European art and what characterizes it: a longing for originality, a longing for change. Robespierre, Napoleon, Beethoven, Stalin, Picasso, they're all runners in the relay race, they all belong in the same stadium.

To which the man who will fire him replies:

> If high culture is coming to an end, it is also the end of you
> and your paradoxical ideas, because paradox as such belongs to
> high culture and not to childish prattle. You remind me of the
> young men who supported the Nazis or Communists not out
> of cowardice or out of opportunism but out of an excess of
> intelligence. For nothing requires a greater effort of thought
> than arguments to justify the rule of nonthought. I experi-
> enced it with my own eyes and ears after the war, when intel-
> lectuals and artists ran like a herd of cattle into the Communist
> Party, which soon proceeded to liquidate them systematically
> and with great pleasure. You are doing the same. You are the
> brilliant ally of your own gravediggers.

This, of course, is Kundera's right brain talking to his left. Indeed the
novelist, eavesdropping on this exchange as if he hadn't made the whole
thing up himself, is reminded of another of his characters in another of
his novels, Jaromil in *Life Is Elsewhere*. Like Paul (and Rimbaud), Jaromil
felt it necessary "to be absolutely modern." He, too, was "the ally of his
gravediggers." Kundera counts on us to remember on our own that
Jaromil—an amalgam of Rimbaud, Lermontov, and the Czech "proletarian" poet Jiri Wolker—was everything the novelist despises about Modernism: its confusion of Youth, Poetry, and Revolution; its muddling of
the vanguard and the avant-garde. Since Jaromil, in the storied Czech
tradition of the Bohemian Catholic governors in 1618 and of Masaryk in
1948, was defenestrated, I'm somewhat surprised Paul doesn't take a
header out the panoramic window of the Paris penthouse. But the surprise death in *Immortality* is reserved for someone else. Paul, instead,
declares it is time "at last to end the terror of the immortals. To overthrow
the arrogant power of the Ninth Symphonies and the *Fausts*!"

Clever yes? Yes. And so are Kundera's "existential mathematics," his
listing of the varieties of coincidence—mute, poetic, contrapuntal, story-
producing, and maybe even morbid—he has employed to keep us turning
his pages. Equally clever is Goethe's reminding Hemingway, in the middle
of a chat in the afterlife, that they are both "but the frivolous fantasy of a
novelist who lets us say things we would probably never say on our own."

The trouble with this cleverness is that it also reminds us we've been here before, with the send-up of Pavel Kohout in *The Joke*; with the send-up of Dostoyevsky and Gide in *Farewell Party*; with the send-up of Nietzsche, Tolstoy, and Sophocles in *Unbearable*; with the send-up of Milan himself as the misogynist Boccaccio in *Forgetting*. The essay in *Immortality* on Imagology (ad agencies, public opinion polls) is inferior to the essay in *Unbearable* on "Kitsch" ("kitsch excludes everything from its purview which is essentially unacceptable in human nature"; "a folding screen set up to curtain off death," to "deny shit"). Just as the meditation on *Grund* (a German word for reason in the sense of a cause, "a code determining the essence of our fate") is inferior to the meditations in *Forgetting* on *litost* (a Czech word meaning "upsurge of feeling") and in *Unbearable* on *soucit* (a Czech word meaning "human co-feeling").

It's not as though he hadn't already told us in *Laughable Loves* that sex is powerless against socialism; or in *Elsewhere* that poets will always sacrifice shopgirls for the good opinion of the Revolution; or in *Farewell* that "Western culture as it was conceived at the dawn of the modern age, based on the individual and his reason, on pluralism of thought, and on tolerance," has come to a violent end; or in *Forgetting* that cultural progress is no longer possible; or in *Unbearable* that *"Einmal ist keinmal"*: The horror of history signifies nothing.

We've even been with him into swimming pools before, maybe for lightness of being.

Nor, really, do we need Laura's skirt flying over her head in the Paris Metro, among rioting *clochards*, to remind us of the humiliation of other women in other Kundera novels: Helena and laxatives; sex-starved Alzhbeta and sleeping pills; pregnant Ruzena and the poison capsules; the spinster, in "Edward and God," on her knees, and Tereza, in shame, on the toilet. Avenarius may be innocent of rape, but Lucie in *The Joke* was a victim of its viciousness, and we were encouraged to believe that Sabina, with her bowler hat, dreamt about it, and we can be pretty sure that Kundera does. About all his eros there is a sado- and a masochistic edge: the whistle of the whip. Even mothers tend to be monsters. Jakub in *Farewell* pictures his own birth: "He imagined his tiny body sliding through a narrow, damp tunnel, his nose and mouth full of slime."

Even women with whom we are expected to identify, like Tamina in *Forgetting*, like Agnes in *Immortality*, belong to men in the molecules of their memory: Tamina to her dead husband, Agnes to her dead father—

although there's an indication here that Kundera may have briefly entertained another role for his women to play besides the pathetic, one that's not so metaphysically insulting. I'll make fun of that in a minute.

If there is much that's familiar in *Immortality* from the other novels, there is also a great absence. That absence, except for the clock in Old Town Square, is Czechoslovakia, particularly Prague, the capital of Kafka and forgetting. We're in Paris, to which Kundera fled in 1970, but we might as well be anywhere. Place is irrelevant to *Immortality*, a deracinated novel, a sacred monster-ego, one of those severed heads of the famous dead by which Rubens and his Gothic Maiden stroll. This head makes witty remarks ("Napoleon was a true Frenchman in that he was not satisfied with sending hundreds of thousands to their death, but wanted in addition to be admired by writers"), but it floats, on the water, in the air, trailing its nerve-strings like cut cables.

There's no hint here of the intersection of the personal and political that made *Forgetting* a masterwork: the magic circle of Young Communists, levitating angels in "a giant wreath," from which Kundera fell; the slit throats of six ostriches and six poets; the passage of the totalitarian state from a Bach fugue to a twelve-tone "single empire" to the abolition of notes and keys; the statues of Lenin growing "like weeds on the ruins, the melancholy flowers of forgetting." This same intersection was also the key to *Unbearable*. Not all the violence belonged to the Russians; there was a lot of it in Tomas before the tanks came to Prague in 1968.

(Oddly, it was this personal violence that was omitted from the overpraised movie version of the novel. Yes, Lena Olin, as Sabina, did for bowler hats what Pythagoras did for triangles and Melville did for whales: She gave them a whole new meaning. But the old meanings got lost. In the novel, the bowler is a sex-games prop, a memento of her father, "a sign of her originality," and something else. When Tomas and Sabina look at each other in the mirror, at first it's comic. But, suddenly, "the bowler hat no longer signified a joke; it signified violence, violence against Sabina, against her dignity as a woman. . . . The fact that Tomas stood beside her fully dressed meant that the essence of what they both saw was far from good clean fun . . . it was humiliation. But instead of spurning it, she proudly, provocatively played it for all it was worth, as if submitting of her own will to public rape." Likewise, the movie lets Tereza swim in one of Milan's pools with other naked women, but leaves out her dreams about it, in which "Tomas stood over them in a basket hanging from the pool's arched roof, shouting at them, making them sing and do kneebends. The moment one of them did a faulty kneebend, he would shoot her.")

Last summer in Prague, Czech writers complained to us that not only had Kundera deserted them, but he was so busy designing himself a Nobel Prize, he hadn't managed to say a word on the Velvet Revolution, when history resumed, not having come to the end he had predicted; and so did European culture, but strangely without him. I don't know when he finished *Immortality*—the copyright is 1990—and therefore can't tell you whether he chose deliberately to ignore this astonishing and essentially nonviolent sea change, or it arrived too late to be thought about this time around, or he no longer cares at all anymore. Besides, Czech writers gripe a lot.

But history doesn't end; it *can't*; it's internalized, in nations and cultures and families and lovers. There's no reason to believe that we don't evolve, for better or worse, in the history of our cultures like the species in its Darwinian messiness, as much a consequence of chance, contingency, compromise, and quirk, as of necessity or design; with some adaptations that are nifty, and some inefficient, and some full of surprising surplus value. Surely cultures are their own feedback loop, susceptible to Chaos and Catastrophe Theory, capable of rearranging themselves in a hot flash after an idea or a bomb, like Islam, the Mafia, or the party line. And surely individual citizens tend to recapitulate the culture, as ontogeny recapitulates phylogeny. Or fractals . . . but let's not get into fractals. A Khmer Rouge was implicit in the brutal kings and the tenth-century Cambodian command economy of slaves that created in the jungle a sandstone cosmology and a vision of thirty-two hells, those golden lions, golden Buddhas, dancing girls, corncob towers, and serpent cults, which is probably why Pol Pot let stand so undisturbed those temples and tombs, the bare ruined choirs of Angkor Wat. Maybe despair, like so much else, is cyclic, millennial.

I can be lofty, too. For that matter, it doesn't seem to me that kitsch is anything new. What else are folk songs and fairy tales, lullabies and festivals, the shinbones of saints for sale on the roads to the cathedrals, or the comfort stations of the miraculous, in the Middle Ages? Wasn't "imagology" invented by great religions? Didn't the media, by sympathetic magic, help make possible what happened, another *Eroica*, in Eastern Europe in 1989? And yet in his very own bare ruined choirs, Milan Kundera feels himself beached; and this vastation he patrols in a canary yellow Spenglerian doom buggy.

What we get in *Immortality*, instead of any Czechoslovakia, is a lot of Goethe. Why, you may wonder, so much Goethe? For two reasons. First, he was

> the great center . . . a firm center that holds both extremes in
> a remarkable balance that Europe will never know again. As a
> young man, Goethe studied alchemy, and later became one of
> the first modern scientists. Goethe was the greatest German of
> all, and at the same time an antipatriotic and a European.
> Goethe was a cosmopolitan, and yet throughout his life he
> hardly ever stirred out of his province, his little Weimar.
> Goethe was a man of nature, yet also a man of history. In love,
> he was a libertine as well as a romantic. And something else . . .
> Goethe knew how and with what materials his house had
> been constructed, he knew why his oil lamp gave off light, he
> knew the principle of the telescope with which he and Bettina
> looked at Jupiter. . . . The world of technical objects was open
> and intelligible to him.

Not since Mann has another writer wanted so much as Milan to reincarnate Weimar's wise guy, trashed by Modernism. (Never mind that Kundera belongs more to Vienna at the turn of the twentieth century than to Weimar on the straddle of the eighteenth/nineteenth: to Ludwig Wittgenstein and the Secessionists. His novels are peopled with Schieles and the wild-haired women of Klimt.)

The second reason for so much Goethe is that Kundera has borrowed, with credit, his brand-new role for women right out of Part II of *Faust*. According to Paul at the swimming pool on top of Paris, "Woman is the future of man." (Without knowing it, though Kundera does, Paul quotes Aragon.) Paul has been drinking and thinking about his daughter and his granddaughter:

> Either woman will become man's future or mankind will per-
> ish, because only woman is capable of nourishing within her
> an unsubstantiated hope and inviting us to a doubtful future,
> which we would have long ceased to believe in were it not for
> women. All my life I've been willing to follow their voice,
> even though that voice is mad, and whatever else I may be I

am not a madman. But nothing is more beautiful than when someone who isn't mad goes into the unknown, led by a mad voice . . . *Das Ewigweibliche zieht uns hinan!* The eternal feminine draws us on!

How seriously are we supposed to take this? Not very. Paul, after all, the "simpleton of ambiguity," is the one who says it. Kundera can't help adding that "Goethe's verse, like a proud white goose, flapped its wings beneath the vault of the swimming pool." I can no more imagine this novelist buying into the Eternal Feminine than I can see him abandoning the (dead) cultures of the great cities for some woodsy totem worship under the sign of Gaia, the Mother of Titans. And the last thing women need done to them, anyway, is another abstraction, another metaphor.

But where does that leave the severed head? Being melancholy, being brilliant, dreaming of gestures. As much as Thomas Mann at the end, he reminds me of Vladimir Nabokov—another exile, another Bolshie-basher, another father-phile, another disdainer of the determinisms of Marx and Freud, another sacred monster of immortal art, opposed to the very idea of a "future," inventor of Zemblas. Nabokov's magic kits were also full of masks and mirrors, artist-madmen and artist-criminals, insanity and suicide, strangled wives and slaughtered sons and debauched nymphets. But I am also reminded, more surprisingly, of Ingmar Bergman.

What tales Bergman tells on himself in his autobiography. He grew up on masks and ghosts and guilt and Strindberg. Death instead of a cuckoo popped out of the clock in the dining room. His first memory is of vomit. His prayers to get rid of pimples and stop his masturbating "stank of anguish, entreaty, trust, loathing, and despair." He hated a brother, tried to kill a sister, almost never sees his many children by his several wives. When he sleeps, he's afflicted by loathsome dreams: "murder, torture, suffocation, incest, destruction, insane anger." Insomnia is worse: "Flocks of black birds come and keep me company: anxiety, rage, shame, regret. . . ." Autoanalysis, Lear-like rage, a madness to see through prison walls to an absent God: The greatest movie director in the history of the world has found the only cure for his dread of the dark in "film as dream, film and music. . . . The mute or speaking shadows turn without evasion towards my most secret room. The smell of hot metal, the wavering picture, the rattle of the Maltese cross, the handle against my hand." All this compensatory genius, from a little boy afraid to die in the dark.

I think *Immortality* is Kundera's *The Seventh Seal*, a game against death. I think he'd feel bad anywhere, like Bergman. (I am also charmed by the title of Bergman's autobiography, *The Magic Lantern*, which was, of course, the name of the theater where Havel, and the rest of the Czechs who hadn't left Prague, sat down to revise their social contract, to write a civil society instead of a novel.) Kundera jumped ship before it suddenly set sail into new meanings and new beings. All his borders are scheduled to disappear next year. Somewhere Marx says that when the train of history turns a corner, all the thinkers fall off. This included Marx. And Kundera. And many other lonely severed heads.

Norman Mailer's *Harlot's Ghost*

I N 1976 IN *New York* magazine, Mailer sneezed black-magic metaphors all over Watergate and the CIA, Marilyn Monroe and Howard Hughes, Kafka and the Mormons. At once a shaman and an exorcist, he changed shapes and split the lips of his wound: "Is America governed by accident more than we are ready to suppose, or by design? And if by design, is the design secret?"

> Trying to understand whether our real history is public or secret, exposed or—at the highest level—underground, is equal to exploring the opposite theaters of our cynicism and our paranoia. . . . What a crazy country we inhabit. What a harlot. What a brute. She squashes sausage out of the minds of novelists on their hotfooted way to a real good plot.

Harlot's Ghost is the elephantiasis of that article: a lot of sausage, spicy and nourishing as far as it goes, but not going far enough. On the book's own calendar, it's still short twenty years. Mailer will try to talk his way around this gap. His editor, Jason Epstein, has already told the *New York Times* that *Harlot's Ghost* is a "test for reviewers—one that I fear will find many of them wanting." But this is preemptive condescension. After thirteen hundred pages of often brilliant tease—Popol Vuh and Victorian gothic, Vico and Nietzsche, Italian opera and Mahler symphony, Book of Kells and Book of the Dead—Mailer fails to deliver the ultimate intimacy. TO BE CONTINUED, he tells us, but we've waited almost as long for his CIA novel as we waited for his Egyptian novel and it's like waiting for Zapata or the Red Sox.

I was not in the CIA to become a bureaucrat but a hero.

—Harry Hubbard

Suppose Julien Sorel had joined the CIA instead of the Roman Catholic Church, or C. P. Snow had written *Strangers and Brothers* about modern-day Templar spooks instead of social-climbing slide rules. The "Company" may be America's Prep School and Episcopal Church, our Counterreformation and our Fourth Crusade, but it is also Norman Mailer's spirit world—his Scathach and Xibalda, his Jigoku and Jahannam, his karmavacara and his Universal Baseball Association.

Just kidding. Or am I? "Irrationality," Mailer says, "is the only great engine of history." So much for the class struggle. Skip the next several paragraphs if you hate a plot synopsis.

New England blueblood Herrick "Harry" Hubbard joins the CIA in 1955, fresh out of Yale and "as pretty as Montgomery Clift." He is joining his father "Cal" (a Robert Lowell reference I don't pretend to fathom) and his godfather "Harlot" (Hugh Tremont Montague, who brightened Harry's boyhood by teaching him to climb rocks). Harry is posted to Berlin at the time of the Tunnel, where he consorts with pistol-packing William King Harvey; to Montevideo, where he trafficks with the Arbenz-bashing E. Howard Hunt; to Miami, in time for the Bay of Pigs, the Cuban missile crisis, and Operation Mongoose, where he beds down with playgirl Modene Murphy (an avatar of Judith Campbell Exner), thus communing with Sam Giancana, Frank Sinatra, Jack Kennedy, Fidel Castro, Howard Hughes, and Marilyn Monroe. What happens to Harry after the assassination of JFK is not entirely clear because most of it's been omitted. *A thirteen-hundred-page novel about the CIA leaves out Vietnam, Watergate, Nicaragua, and Iranamok, not to mention running drugs, laundering money, and fingering Mandela.* This much, we are vouchsafed:

Between 1964 and 1984, Harry saves the life of Harlot's wife, Hadley Kittredge Gardiner Montague, who is not only "an absolute beauty," a Jackie Kennedy look-alike, but also a "genius" who develops her own anti-Freudian theory of personality while working of course for the CIA. After Harlot kills his son and cripples himself climbing more metaphorical rocks, Harry steals Kittredge for himself, while continuing to counterspy for Harlot. In 1984, Kittredge, in turn, is stolen by Dix Butler, an Agency "asset" and bisexual megabucks *übermensch*, and Harlot's body, with its face shot off, washes up from Chesapeake Bay. Did Harlot kill himself? Was he murdered? Or has he, in fact, defected to the KGB? Harry leaves Maine for Moscow, to find out. In Moscow, among these many mystifications, he is abandoned by his Creator. And that's all I'm going to tell you because from now on, instead of reviewing this novel, I intend to haunt it, like the pirate ghost Augustus Farr, like the CIA in America's kinky closet. (We are *spooked*!)

> *What, indeed, did Picasso teach us if not that every form offers up its own scream when it is torn?*
>
> —Norman Mailer

We learn about the trouble with Harry from two manuscripts—a shortie called "Omega," set in Orwell's 1984, and a gargantua called "Alpha," maybe the longest flashback in world literature, covering everything else up to 1964. These manuscripts correspond to the two halves of the human psyche as identified by Kittredge for the CIA. They also try out almost every narrative form known to the Mother Russian Novel: picaresque and epistolary; *Bildungsroman* and *roman à clef*; the historical, the gothic, the pornographic; the thriller and the western. There are also journal-jottings, cable traffic, interoffice memoranda, and transcripts of wiretaps.

For so many species of story, there are as many tics of prose; seizures and afflatus. When his battery's charged, Mailer windmills from one paragraph to the next—baroque, anal, Talmudic, olfactory, portentous, loopy, coy, Egyptian; down and dirty in the cancer, the aspirin or the plastic; shooting moons on sheer vapor; blitzed by paranoia and retreating for a screen pass, as if bitten in the pineal gland by a deranged Swinburne, with metaphors so meaning-moistened that they stick to our thumbs, with "intellections" (as he once put it) slapped on "like adhesive plasters." When he chooses to, he also speaks in tongues. Harlot sounds like Whittaker Chambers. Modene Murphy sounds like Lauren Bacall. Bill Harvey sounds like L. Ron Hubbard or Lyndon LaRouche. The guilt-ridden Uruguayan double agent Chevi Fuentes sounds like Frantz Fanon and Octavio Paz. Harry sounds like Rousseau's Emile when he isn't sounding like Wilhelm Reich, and Kittredge sounds like Flaubert's Salammbo when she isn't sounding like Hannah Arendt, and together they sound like Nichols and May. And everybody sounds like Mailer, as if picking up

quasar signals from Sirius the Dog Star through a plate in the head; as if
bodies, vegetables, and objects all had distinctive vibrations, special stinks
and personal divinities, angels in the meatloaf, demons in the Tupper-
ware. Even money comes "in all kinds of emotional flavors." Ghosts!
Pirates! Indians! Animism! Alchemy!

You either like this stuff or you don't, and I do.

Nor are the usual obsessions neglected, like boxing, bulls, and booze.
And Marilyn Monroe: Harry's father, Cal, has a theory that Hoffa bumped
her off, hoping to pin the rap on Bobby. And Hemingway: Cal says he
beat Papa at arm wrestling one dark and stormy Stork Club night. And
LSD: Kittredge seems to have invented it in a lab at Langley. And Martin
Buber: I'm convinced Mailer has rendered Harry, for all his Waspishness,
"one-eighth" Jewish just so Harlot can tell him to read *Tales of the Hasidim*.
And of course manhood: Like all Mailermen, who are happiest in motion,
in boats, and in beds, Harry finds that "happiness is experienced most
directly in the intervals between terror," which may be "our simple purpose on earth." If we "surmount that terror . . . we can, perhaps, share
some of God's fear."

This means a lot of rock climbing, some polo, and an invasion of Cuba.
Thinks Harry:

> So many of these soldiers had spent their lives getting ready for
> a great moment—it was as if one lived as a vestal virgin who
> would be allowed to copulate just once but in a high temple:
> The act had better be transcendent, or one had chosen the
> wrong life.

If this Prep School Ethos is hard on Kittredge, tough darts:

> I gave up the thought of explaining to her that the natural con-
> dition of men's lives was fear of tests, physical even more than
> mental tests. Highly developed skills of evasion went into keep-
> ing ourselves removed from the center of our cowardice. . . .
> So I could not help it—I admired men who were willing to live
> day by day with bare-wire fear even if it left them naked as
> drunks, incompetent wild men, accident-prone. I understood
> the choice.

It's even harder on Castro, but he's so Neolithic macho, he will surely understand:

> I would mourn Fidel if we succeeded, mourn him in just the way a hunter is saddened by the vanished immanence of the slain beast. Yes, one fired a bullet into beautiful animals in order to feel nearer to God: To the extent that we were criminal, we could approach the cosmos only by stealing a piece of the Creation.

You need no longer wonder: Why Are We in Vietnam? Or Iraq. Or Marilyn Monroe.

> *I could say, to stretch a point, that we were being schooled in minor arts of sorcery. Are not espionage and magic analagous?*
>
> —Harlot

If paranoia is our culture's weather, all that lightning, then Mailer, bless him, puts up a kite instead of an umbrella. But having grown up on him, we already know that we have enemies. It's harder to amaze us. It's a tough break for the old exorcist that Don DeLillo, Joan Didion, and Stan Lee in *Dunn's Conundrum* have already covered so much of his territory; that Robin Winks has already written his book about Yale and the CIA; that Tom Mangold has just published a biography of James Jesus Angleton; that Robert Gates twists in the Senate wind; that Pete Brewton's S&L stories, and the magnitiude of the BCCI scandal, are so much more fantastic to contemplate than the CIA conspiracy in *Harlot's Ghost* to finance itself by cashing in on insider tips on when the Federal Reserve Board is about to fiddle with the interest rates. What's *new*, Norman?

Well, he really likes these guys. And why not? If you can identify with Gary Gilmore, not to mention Menenhetet, how hard can it be to identify with Allen Dulles? Besides, the old Social Bandit has been soft on WASPs since the moonshot, when he mindmelded with the astronauts. And he's summered forever in New England with its sermons, charades, and whalingship watergames. Of course: Harry will lose his innocence and Harry *is* America—that's the point of these many pages—but what a boys' club it seems to him at the start, what a Skull and Bones, a *safe* house, a happy hunting ground of Hopelites, Berserkirs and Samurai, storm-cloud

Maruts and Taoist warrior-sages, Gilgamesh, Achilles, Arjuna, Crazy Horse—with secret books, sacred seals, and nifty computer graphics. It's Rosicrucian, Kabbalistic, Druidical! I mean, they have castles on the Rhône, châteaux in the Loire, temples in Kyoto. Why not great Baals with glowing redhot bellies and Tantric miniatures depicting Kundalini; Nuremberg Maidens with heartsful of nails; ramsing, the horn of Tugs, hanging from a banyan; the altar of sacrifice to Yaldaboath; menhirs, tesseracts, an orgone box, a Swedenborg deathmask, a black Celtic virgin (for Sergius O'Shaughnessy) and, in the reliquary, the foreskin of Hermes Trismegistus? (I'm sorry; it's catching.)

But what we get instead is Harlot. Harlot seems to be Mailer's version of James Jesus Angleton, the Fisher King of counterespionage. Like Angleton, he's suspicious of everybody else at Langley, and was taken in by Kim Philby, and doesn't really believe in the Sino-Soviet split. As Angleton was referred to variously at the Agency as Mother, Poet, Fisherman, and (aha!) Gray Ghost, so Montague is referred to not only as "Harlot" but also as "Trimsky" (for a Trotskylike salt-and-pepper mustache), and "Gobby" (for "God's old beast"). Instead of orchids, rocks.

Angleton shows up as a character in dozens of fictions, from Ludlum to Bellow. Even after he was forcibly retired in 1974, he was still obsessed that a Soviet "mole" had penetrated to the nation's very cerebellum. Everywhere he looked, he saw "doubles." If *he* could imagine it, *they* must be doing it. It's with Angleton that we associate the phrase "wilderness of mirrors." He had been, after all, a Futurist poet at Yale, and published a literary magazine, *Furioso*, full of difficult Modernists like Pound, whose enthusiasm for Mussolini was apparently contagious. T. S. Eliot was a buddy of young Angleton's; Thomas Mann came to lunch. No wonder that when he looked in the Labyrinth at Langley for the pattern in the magic carpet, all he saw were "doubles" and "moles," counterfeit identities, masks of the Other. Dostoyevsky, Conrad, Kafka, Nabokov, Wastelands: alienation of the self, by the self, against the self. And no wonder writers love him so much: What else is Modernism but Counterintelligence? Our paranoia is a *text*.

In *Libra*, DeLillo imagines an "occult" of intelligence agencies, a "theology of secrets," the latest in Gnostic heresies, gone to holy war against nihilism, terrorism, inauthenticity, and incoherence. Robin Winks tells us in *Cloak & Gown* that John Hollander, then on the Yale faculty, was so struck while reading Sir John Masterman's *The Double-Cross System* by the code names in the book (Mutt and Jeff, Brutus and Bronx, Zigzag and

Tricycle) that he sat down and wrote a book-length poem, *Reflections on Espionage*, "with spies standing for writers and thinkers, living a kind of hidden life in the actual world," with Pound and Auden and Lowell in code.

This is weird stuff, made to order for gonzo novelizing. But Mailer shies away from most of it, as he shies away from seeing Latin America or Europe as anything other than geographies of the Agency mind, pale-fire Zemblas. Yes, he has fun with the minor players. If Howard Hunt isn't quite as flamboyant here as his own alter egos in his own David St. John thrillers, Bill Harvey comes on like Henderson the Rain King. The old shaman has even more fun with code names: In Berlin: BOZO, GIBLETS, SWIVET, and CATHETER. In Montevideo: AV/OCADO, AV/ANTGARDE, AV/OIRDUPOIS, AV/EMARIA. And in Miami, to sort out the bedfellowship of Mafia and Camelot in Operation HEEDLESS, Jack Kennedy is code-named IOTA, Sam Giancana is RAPUNZEL, Murphy/Exner is BLUEBEARD, and Frank Sinatra is STONEHENGE. I love it.

But the old Druid hasn't given Harlot enough juice to be an Angleton, a paranoid synecdoche. Harlot's supposed to wow us, as he wows Harry, Dix, and Arnie Rosen in their early Agency days. But when he talks about a Third World still clinging "to pre-Christian realms—awe, paranoia, slavish obedience to the leader, divine punishment," or explains that the CIA buys up bankers, psychiatrists, narcs, trade unionists, hooligans, and journalists because "our duty is to become the mind of America," he seems to belong more to a Bill Buckley/Blackford Oakes penny dreadful than a John Le Carré requiem mass. Just once, brooding on relations between Dzerzhinsky, the godfather of the KGB, and the White Russian Yakovlev, does Harlot sound like an Angleton:

> When seduction is inspired . . . by the demands of power, each person will lie to the other. Sometimes, they lie to themselves. These lies often develop structures as aesthetically rich as the finest filigrees of truth. After a time, how could Yakovlev and Dzerzhinsky know when they were dealing with truth or a lie? The relationship had grown too deep. They had had to travel beyond their last clear principles. They could no longer know when they were true to themselves. The self, indeed, was in migration.

But that is the last we hear from Harlot on this subject for another eight hundred pages. And then there's what I take to be the crucial exchange between Harlot and Bill Harvey, although they are talking to Harry instead of each other, from opposite ends of the novel. First, we get Harlot:

> The aim is to develop teleological mind. Mind that dwells above the facts; mind that leads us to larger purposes. Harry, the world is going through exceptional convulsions. The twentieth century is fearfully apocalyptic. Historical constitutions that took centuries to develop are melting into lava. Those 1917 Bolsheviks were the first intimation. Then came the Nazis. God, they were a true exhalation from Hell. The top of the mountain blew off. Now the lava is starting to move. . . . Lava is entropy. It reduces all systems. Communism is the entropy of Christ, the degeneration of higher spiritual forms into lower ones. To oppose it, we must, therefore, create a fiction—that the Soviets are a mighty military machine who will overpower us unless we are more powerful. The truth is that they will overpower us if the passion to resist them is not regenerated, by will if necessary, every year, every minute.

Later, it's Harvey, larger-than-life like DeLillo's David Ferrie, a paranoid's paranoid:

> There is opposition to entropy. The universe may not necessarily wind down. There is something forming that I would call the new embodiment. Entropy and embodiment may be as related as antimatter and matter. . . . Yes, the forms deteriorate and they all run down to the sea, but other possibilities come together in their wake to seek embodiment. Blobs are always looking to articulate themselves into a higher form of blob. There is a tropism toward form, Hubbard. It counters decomposition.

What does this mean? Jason Epstein has found me wanting. On Mailer's last page, we are told that Harlot is *Harry's* embodiment, but otherwise this sounds remarkably like one of those rough beasts slouching out of a Yeats poem to be born-again, a mystagogic man-god. And Harry has gone to Moscow to sit at Dzerzhinsky's feet, and this embodiment of Harlot would seem to be whispering that God is the Ultimate Spy, that evolution is just a Cover Story, that the universe is basically Disinformation. Maybe, but the novel itself has no more got us to such a realization than it has bothered to flesh in the migration of Harry from the innocence of Lovett in *Barbary Shore* to the savage savvy of Rojack, that American Dreamer. And I can't help identifying with a character in DeLillo's *White Noise*, the ex-wife of the professor of Hitler Studies, whose job it is to review books *for* the CIA, "mainly long serious novels with coded structures."

> *Curiously, yet logically, there is one vice . . . that tempts both narcissist and psychopath. It is treachery.*
>
> —Kittredge

I like Modene more than Kittredge, who is Omega to Harry's Alpha. Besides being a tease, Kittredge is snotty. She hates Lenny Bruce, makes fun of A. J. Ayer, and condescends to Freud. Harry has his doubts about her, too, wondering if she began her affair with him "because she wanted to learn whether she could run an operation under [Harlot's] nose and get away with it."

This cross-referencing of sex and espionage is one of the novel's principal conceits. Harlot tells his boys: "Our studies move into penetralia. We search for the innermost sanctum, 'the shuddering penetralia of caves.'" The old Orgone Boxer is asking us to think of spies as voyeurs; of the double-backed beast as another double agent; of adultery as a sort of treason; of sex itself as quest and conspiracy, guerrilla warfare and the coup d'état. Our behavior in history has a lot to do with our behavior in bed. Politics is a sex crime. Imperialism is a gang bang.

Sex can also be divine: Coupling with Kittredge, Harry tells us, is a "sacrament," letting him "see God when the lightning flashed and we jolted our souls into one another." And sex, of course, is death: Harry smells "the whiff of murder beyond every embrace of love"; Sam and Modene even make it in a graveyard, on top of his dead wife's mausoleum.

It seems to me that the trouble with sex as the ground of being is that it puts too much of a burden on sex; we all still have to go to work in the morning, even spies. But I'm not ready yet to discuss Mailer and sex. That comes last. What *about* Alpha and Omega?

Well, according to Kittredge, they aren't metaphors. They are, in each of us, separate unconsciousnesses, with their own egos and superegos.

Alpha is our male component, "creature of the forward-swimming energies of sperm, ambitious, blind to all but its own purposes . . . more oriented toward enterprise, technology, grinding the corn, repairing the mill, building the bridges between money and power, *und so weiter.*" Whereas Omega, our female component, "originated in the ovum and so knows more about the mysteries—conception, birth, death, night, the moon, eternity, karma, ghosts, divinities, myths, magic, our primitive past, and so on."

In other words, double the trouble and goose the guilt, but also someone else to blame it on when things go wrong. What isn't right-brained/left-brained in this, or gussied-up Carl Jung, or old-fashioned schizophrenia, seems, as so often happens when the vapors take Mailer, to be a kind of Trojan zebra, foisting more of his Manichaean dualisms on the unwary reader—courage and fear, sex and death, Alpha and Omega, Simon and Garfunkel—the way Aristotle once foisted the unconscious dualisms of Greek grammar on an unsuspecting cosmos.

What the hey. If Yeats can believe in faeries, Pound in funny money, Doris Lessing in flying saucers, and Saul Bellow in Rudolf Steiner, the old Rosicrucian has a right to his Alphas and Omegas, however much they remind me of Randall Jarrell on W. H. Auden: "The theological ideas which Auden does not adopt but invents are all too often on the level of those brownpaper parcels brought secretly to the War Department in times of national emergency, which turn out to be full of plans to destroy enemy submarines by tracking them down with seals."

But Mailer as usual is out to get Freud. Freud, says the insufferable Kittredge, "really had no more philosophy than a Stoic. That's not enough. Stoics make good plumbers. The drains go bad and you've got to hold your nose and fix them. End of Freud's philosophy. If people and civilization don't fit—which we all know anyway—why, says Freud, make the best of a bad lot."

This is bumptious. It omits, among many other important matters, Freud's tragic pessimism. Okay, the guy was saying that civilization depends on a certain amount of repression of the instincts, and Mailer would like to think that he operates entirely on instinct, so he's bound to resent this bad news, as well as civilization, at least since the Enlightenment. (Mailer belongs, in fact, to Isaiah Berlin's team of anti-Enlightenment "swimmers against the current" like Vico and Hamann and Herder, like Moses Hess and Georges Sorel.) But you'd think that as much as he identified in

Ancient Evenings with Menenhetep on the Boat of Ra, he'd identify even more with a brave pariah who dropped by bathysphere *into himself* to see why people hurt the way they do; the dream-decoder; the first Deconstructionist. Isn't this Mailer's own detective method, a consulting of the suspect self, plowing through magnetic fields, lighting up the wounds of God?

Besides, Harry in *Harlot's Ghost* has to kill off two fathers.

I wish the old Kabbalist had spent less time thinking about Hemingway, and no time writing about Marilyn, and some years working through Freud, after which he could take on Marx, thus killing off, instead of kissing off, both *his* fathers. (Anyway, if Jean-Paul Sartre could churn out eight hundred pages on Freud when John Huston asked him for a screenplay, think what Mailer might have managed, especially with his old buddy Montgomery Clift as Sigmund.) Nor has he really ever answered the shrewd question put to him by an interviewer in *Pieces and Pontifications*: "Why can't the unconscious be as error prone as the conscious?"

Just because Kittredge had ghostsex with the pirate-shade of Augustus Farr, who "submitted me to horrors," doesn't mean Harry has to heed her every fatuity. He's better off listening to Chevi Fuentes. Among other good advices, Fuentes warns Harry against the labyrinth-maker Jorge Luis Borges: "Never read him. In five pages, in any of his five pages, he will summarize for you the meaninglessness of the next ten years of your life. Your life, particularly."

> Capitalism, says Fuentes, is essentially psychopathic. It lives for the moment. It can plan far ahead only at the expense of its own vitality, and all larger questions of morality are delegated to patriotism, religion, or psychoanalysis. "That is why I am a capitalist," he says. "Because I am a psychopath. Because I am greedy. Because I want instant consumer satisfaction. If I have spiritual problems, I either go to my priest and obtain absolution or I pay an analyst to convince me over the years that my greed is my identity and I have rejoined the human race. I may feel bad about my selfishness but I will get over it. Capitalism is a profound solution to the problem of how to maintain a developed society. It recognizes the will-to-power in all of us."

Chevi used to be a Communist back in Montevideo, before Harry "turned" him. By the time he tells Harry that he's a capitalist, in Miami, Chevi has also become a homosexual. Listen up:

> You will judge me adversely for being a homosexual, yet it is you who is more of one than any of us, although you will never admit it to yourself because you never practice! You are a homosexual the way Americans are barbarians although they do not practice barbarism openly. They keep their newspaper in front of the light. They go to church so as not to face death, and you work for your people so that you will not have to scrutinize yourself in the mirror.

Our Harry? What's going on? Sure, Kittredge is a drag. Still, isn't there Modene? But something, at the very least androgynous, seems to have happened to Mailer since he came back from Egypt. If you used to worry about his preoccupation with anal sex, as we all of course have worried about Updike's preoccupation with oral sex, you are entitled to worry even more.

In Berlin in 1956, after taking him to a seedy S and M bar where the house speciality is "the golden shower," Dix Butler, Agency *übermensch*, makes a pass at Harry. Harry declines this invitation, not because he isn't excited, but because he fears such an act would oblige him "to live forever on this side of sex." Dix goes both ways, we are told, because he was raped as a child by his brother. But later it's clear that Arnie Rosen, another of Harry's schoolmates in Langley's entering class of 1955, is also gay, and by choice, although forced in the fifties to be furtive.

This isn't to suggest that the CIA goes in for ritual pederasty—as seems to have been the case among Spartans, Celts, and the Sambia of New Guinea, if you believe Rick Fields in *The Code of the Warrior*—though it's not hard to imagine, at the Agency, as in prep school, a homoerotic bonding of the blue-eyed boys, reading their spagyrics and their necromantiums, pulling on their Tomar Towers and their Luxor Obelisks, speaking their Vattan cryptosystems. To join the eighteenth-century Bavarian Illuminati, you underwent a trial by a knife. Their candles were black, their hoods were white, and they bound up your testicles with a poppy-colored cordon: standard Skull and Bones hotstuff. However, I digress.

No. Mailer evokes the fugitive sensibility as yet another metaphor for the
secret life: undercover, as it were; the double or fictitious identity. But think
for a minute about Chevi. In being "turned," wasn't he raped, like Dix? And
hasn't he seen Harry in action on another front, too, smitten by the notorious prostitute Libertad, who turns out to be a hermaphrodite? And, suddenly, one begins to wonder what all these men, like STONEHENGE and
RAPUNZEL, are really up to. And I must explain the *Tequila Sunrise* Paradigm.

In the movie *Tequila Sunrise*, Mel Gibson and Kurt Russell are high-
school buddies who grew up on opposite sides of the law. They compete
for Michelle Pfeiffer. If not to them, what's clear to us is that Gibson and
Russell really want to go to bed with each other. Since they can't, they
go to bed with Pfeiffer. She's the go-between, the trampoline, a universal
joint, a portable gopher hole, a surrogate, and a Chinese finger puzzle.
Once you have seen it in the movie, you'll see it everywhere. In Pynchon's *Vineland*, for instance, it's obvious that Vond, the fascistic prosecutor, is murmuring to Zoyd, the rock piano player, through the holes in
poor Frenesi's body. The *Tequila Sunrise* Paradigm might even explain
serial killers like Bateman in *American Psycho*, unless you believe that
when Yuppie Bateman rapes the Aspen waitress with the can of hair spray,
nails Bethany's fingers to the hardwood floor, and sodomizes a severed
head, he is really criticizing Late Capitalism and the Fetishism of Commodities. (And I'm the king of Bavaria.)

Now take a look at the relationships in *Harlot's Ghost*, not just among
Harlot and Harry and Kittredge and Dix, or Dix and Harry and Chevi
and Modene, or Modene, Jack, Frank, and Marilyn, but, let's say, *historically*. Just suppose that Sam Giancana really wanted to go to bed with
Frank Sinatra, and Sinatra wanted to go to bed with Jack Kennedy, and
Kennedy wanted to go to bed with everybody, including that "beautiful
animal," Fidel Castro. And Marilyn and Modene (or Judith) were the
closest they could get, except, of course, for an invasion. There is no question, even in the pages of Arthur Schlesinger, Jr., that the Kennedy Boys
had a hard-on for Castro.

Talk about spooky. It shudders the penetralia of caves. Whatever else
he's done or failed to do in *Harlot's Ghost*, Mailer—our very own Knight-
Errant, Don Quixote, Tripmaster Monkey, Zapata, and Scaramouche—
has at last made the personal political. Which leads one to wonder
whether, all this time, he really wanted to play ball with Arthur Miller
and Joe DiMaggio.

Ed Sullivan Died for Our Sins

All fixed, fast-frozen relations, with their train of ancient and venerable prejudices and opinions, are swept away, all new-formed ones become antiquated before they can ossify. All that is solid melts into air, all that is holy is profaned. . . .

—Karl Marx

EACH WEEK SINCE October 1988, I've delivered myself of a five-minute "media criticism," a sort of sermonette, on *CBS Sunday Morning.* A dozen times in those eight years a stranger has stopped me on the street, at a movie, or waiting in line for a glimpse of Matisse to ask: "Do you write your own stuff?" To which I have learned to reply, passively-aggressively, "Well, they didn't hire me for my looks." But at least it's a human question. More often and more mystifying is the suspicious stare, the abrupt nod, the pointed finger, and the accusation: "I saw *you* on television." After which, *nothing.* Not "I liked what you said," or "You're full of crap," or "How much do they pay you?" Just "I . . . *saw you.*" And then the usual New York vanishing act, like Shane. This used to bother me a lot, as if the medium lacked substance, or I did, or the spectral street, maybe even Matisse. Lately, though, I've begun to wonder whether what such strangers really seek on the surprising street is assurance. The problem is epistemological. *They saw me on television. I am real. Television might also be.* After almost half a century of looking at the ghosts in our machines, we are agnostics about reality itself.

Never mind docudramas, re-creations, staged news, creative editing,

trick photography, computer enhancements, or commercials that sell us
cars by promising adventure and sell us beer by promising friendship. Our
dubiety about television probably started with the quiz show scandals in
1959. Oh how they wept, like *Little Mermaids*. That's one of the things I
remember most about television in the fifties. Nixon cried in his Checkers
speech. Jack Paar cried about his daughter. And Charles Van Doren cried
because he'd been caught. So did Dave Garroway cry on the *Today* show
because he was upset about Van Doren, the English instructor-son of a
famous poet-professor, who'd parlayed his *21* winnings into a job as a
"guest host" on Garroway's very own program. And because Dave was
upset, so was his chimp, J. Fred Muggs. Who says men don't have feelings? "A terrible thing to do to the American public," cried Dwight D.
Eisenhower on finding out that Van Doren, Patty Duke, Dr. Joyce Brothers, and even Major John Glenn, before he ascended into space and the
Senate, had all been fakes. This was some months before Ike lied to us
himself about those U-2 overflights. Nor had Ike been exactly above-
aboard about the CIA in Guatemala and Iran. But big government and
big business have always been more creative than big TV, e.g., Watergate,
Abscam, Chappaquiddick, Iranamok, BCCI, S&L, Whitewater, and the
Gulf of Tonkin. As Reagan apparatchik Elliott Abrams once told Congress: "I never said I had no idea about most of the things you said I said
I had no idea about."

Enough fifties nostalgia. As much as we may have loved Lucy, what
we did to our children was Howdy Doody and Captain Video. When
John Cameron Swayze died recently, we ought to have been reminded of
how bad TV news used to be back when his *Camel News Caravan* was
"hopscotching the world for headlines," before he went on to pitch Timex
("takes a licking and keeps on ticking"). Even the Golden Age of TV
drama was full of home-shopping Ibsens like Paddy Chayevsky and
greeting-card Kafkas like Rod Serling, of bargain-basement Italian neo-
realism and kitchen-sink Sigmund Freud, where everybody explained too
much in expository gusts, yet all were simultaneously inarticulate, as if a
want of eloquence were a proof of sincerity and an excess of sincerity
guaranteed nobility of sentiment, like a bunch of clean old Tolstoy peasants. And how clean were they, really? So clean, you never saw a black
face, not even on a railroad porter. So clean, that Chayevsky's own family
in *The Catered Affair* had to be Irish instead of Jewish, as the butcher in
Marty was somehow Italian. So clean that when Serling wanted to tell the

story of Emmett Till, a black Chicago teenager lynched for whistling at a Mississippi white woman, *U.S. Steel Hour* turned it into a pawnbroker's murder in a Thornton Wilder sort of *Our Town*. So clean, that the Mars candy-bar company would not allow a single reference on *Circus Boy* to competitive sweets like cookies or ice cream, and *The Alcoa Hour* was so solicitous of a good opinion about aluminum it wouldn't let Reginald Rose set a grim teleplay in a trailer park, and, most famously, the American Gas Company insisted on removing any mention of "gas chambers" from a Playhouse 90 production of *Judgment at Nuremberg*.

A better beginning for any discussion of American television's childhood and prolonged adolescence in the Age of Faith is the original Mr. Ed. They didn't hire him for his looks.

From 1948 to 1971, every Sunday night at eight o'clock, a man who couldn't sing, or dance, or spin a plate entertained fifty million Americans. Never before and never again in the history of the republic would so many gather so loyally, for so long, in the thrall of one man's taste. As if by magic, we were one big family. And what a lot of magic there was, as well as animals and acrobats, ventriloquists and marching bands, David Ben-Gurion, Brigitte Bardot, and the Singing Nun. All by himself on CBS, hand-picking every act, Ed Sullivan was a one-man cable television system with wrestling, BRAVO and comedy channels, Broadway, Hollywood and C-SPAN, sports and music video. We turned to him once a week in our living rooms for everything we now expect from an entire industry every minute of our semiconscious lives. Such was his Vulcan mind meld with his audience, one thinks of Chairman Mao.

Tiresome as the Boomers are, celebrating from their electronic nursery the nitwitticisms of *Leave It to Beaver*, *Gilligan's Island*, *The Brady Bunch*, *The Partridge Family*, and *Happy Days*, they have intuited a truth about television as a timeline in our secret lives. It's as if this reservoir of images, consumed since childhood, stored on memory tape, amounts to something like the "pottery clock" of the archeologists, like clam-bed fossils and dinosaur teeth, Irish peat bog and California bristlecones, rings of trees, layers of acid, caps of ice, and the residue of volcanic ash. We carbon-date ourselves. I was ten years old when I first saw Sullivan, in 1949, talking to Jackie Robinson on a tiny flickering screen in my uncle's Long Beach, California, rumpus room. I was twelve when I realized that he'd be around forever, or at least a lot longer than your average step-father. We were living then—after the rooms above a bowling alley in Washington, D.C., a ranch in New Mexico, a northern Wisconsin fishing lodge, and a southern California Cubist sort of pillbox through whose portholes blew breezes of orange rind, petroleum, and cow dung—in Queens, New York, behind a tavern, lullabied to sleep each night by Johnny Ray on a jukebox, singing "The Little White Cloud That Cried." On the portable Zenith my mother really couldn't afford, except that her latchkey children needed something warm to come home to after PS 69, there was Ed, chatting up Margot Fonteyn before she became a dame. As the following year he'd chat up Audrey Hepburn, before or after, I can't remember which, he laughed out loud when an Automat ate Jackie Glea-son. I was probably too busy to sit still for longer than *Crusader Rabbit*. I had my socialist newspaper, the *Daily Compass*, and my toy telescope to look at Sagittarius at night from the apartment house rooftop for signs of Velikovsky's multiple catastrophisms. At least a mock-heroic *Crusader Rabbit* made fun of the internal contradictions of the ruling class. Ed on the other hand . . . how could he have been back there in California and right here in Queens? And around, too, later on with Elvis in 1956, when I was flunking volleyball and puberty rites in high school? As, like the FBI, he'd find me wherever I went, in Cambridge, Berkeley, even Green-wich Village, chatting up Buddy Holly, Ernie Kovacs, Noël Coward, Stevie Wonder, Sonny and Cher, Cassius Clay, Eskimos, and Beatles. Ed was my first inkling that henceforth all of us everywhere would simulta-neously experience everything that is shameful or heroic about our coun-try on one big headset; as if, in a nomadic culture, the TV screen were the windshield of our mobile home, and all America a motor lodge.

There were only three channels to turn to at the start, duking it out for the most desirable hour of the television week. Ed's prime-time competition took the high road (*Philco Playhouse*, and Steve Allen) and the low (*Bowling Stars* and *The Tab Hunter Show*). Jimmy Durante, Perry Como, Eddie Cantor, Bob Hope, and Dean Martin and Jerry Lewis, *Sir Francis Drake*, *Bill Dana*, *Dragnet*, *National Velvet*, *Jamie McPheeters*, *Broad-side*, *Buckskin*, and *Wagon Train* came and went while Ed stayed put. James Garner in *Maverick* beat him two years running in the ratings, then col-lapsed from nervous exhaustion. Back in the days when corporations owned entertainers like trademarks or tropical fish—when Arthur God-frey belonged to Lipton Tea, Milton Berle to Texaco, Bob Hope to Pepsodent, Dinah Shore to Chevrolet, and Jack Benny to Jell-O; when Kraft, Lux, Revlon, G.E., Westinghouse, Magnavox, Budweiser, Armstrong Circle, and Johnson Wax all had *Theaters*; Bell Telephone, Twentieth-Century Fox, and U.S. Steel had *Hours*; Philco, Schlitz, and Prudential had *Playhouses*, Geritol an *Adventure Show Case*, DuPont its *Show of the Month*, Hallmark a *Hall of Fame*, Twin Toni a *Time*, Firestone a *Voice*, and Pabst Blue Ribbon *Bouts*—Colgate Palmolive spent $50 million on a *Comedy Hour* to knock Ed out of his Lincoln-Mercury. But he won his time period every week until Colgate bought a slice of him themselves.

Like Eddie Lopat, the crafty Yankees southpaw, Sullivan seemed to throw nothing but junk, and still they couldn't hit him. How did he do it, this spinning of the public like a plate?

They were making up TV as they went along, by accident and some sort of bat sonar, without focus groups, market surveys, "Q" ratings, or Betsy Frank at Saatchi & Saatchi. "A door closing, heard over the air," wrote E. B. White at television's dawn, "a face contorted seen in a panel of light, these will emerge as the real and true. And when we bang the door of our own cell or look into another's face, the impression will be of mere artifice."

Imagine at any moment in those prime-time years a six-room suite on the eleventh floor of Manhattan's Delmonico Hotel, where Ed and his wife, Sylvia, seem to have lived forever, with a Renoir landscape, a small Gauguin, autographed snaps of Cardinal Spellman and Ella Fitzgerald, and an original Disney cartoon in which Ed plays golf with Donald Duck. He gets up at 11:00 A.M.; breakfasts invariably on artificially sweetened pears, iced tea, and a room-service lamb chop; reads the papers and makes hundreds of telephone calls, dialing them himself. He puts on one of his Dunhill suits—numbered like his shirts and ties, so that he can tape a new introduction to an old rerun without looking as though he'd dropped in on his own program for a surprise visit from Kurdistan—and a pair of buckled loafers. (His favorite shoes were a gift from George Hamilton, whose feet he once admired.) He lunches invariably between 3:30 and 4 P.M. at Gino's on Lexington Avenue on roast chicken from which he detaches and pockets a drumstick, which he'll nibble later on. (From a childhood bout with scarlet fever and a high-school football injury, he developed permanent sinus trouble: America's tastemaker can't smell or savor his own food.) He hasn't a manager, an agent, a chauffeur for his limo, or even a limo. He likes to talk to cabbies about his show and to Lincoln-Mercury dealers. On his way to the studio, he will carry his own change of clothes on a wire hanger in a garment bag. After a movie screening or a Broadway play, he'll supper with Sylvia at the Colony, Le Pavillon, or La Grenouille. They order sweet wine, which Ed improves with hoarded packets of Sweet 'N Low. And then they are off to the Yonkers harness races and the frantic nightlife of the clubs.

We aren't talking about a Rupert Murdoch, a Michael Eisner, a Ted Turner, a Barry Diller, a John Malone, an Aaron Spelling, or any other morning star pedaling his epicyle in a Ptolemaic universe of hype according to which the very heavens buzz in eccentric orbits around the need of a vacuous public for gas. Ed is a regular guy. Except . . . he's made somehow of air.

Almost from their first date, a heavyweight prizefight, Ed and Sylvia were self-sufficient, a mollusk of a marriage. They never ate in. Nobody cooked. The only domestic help they needed was the hotel maid. Isn't this odd? Not just the single chop for breakfast, the drumstick in the Dunhill pocket, the Sweet 'N Low for wine, but this peculiar weightlessness, as if the Delmonico were an aquarium: artificial sweetening; artificial light. As in a Hollywood movie or TV action-adventure series or experimental novel, nobody had to wash a dish or make a bed. Till she was twelve their daughter, Betty, never ate with them; she ate at Child's with a paid companion. Days and nights always had this *floating* quality, like the dream life of athletes and gangsters, actors and comics, showgirls and sports, hustlers and swells; of songwriters, gag writers, and ragtime piano players; of men who gambled and women who smoked; guys and dolls. Ed and Sylvia were children of the roaring jazz-age twenties, that nervy postwar adrenaline-addicted Charleston state of mind confabulated in New York by admen, poets, and promoters, and then nationally syndicated by Broadway columnists like Damon Runyon, Walter Winchell, Louis Sobol, and Ed himself—men who had gone to newspapers instead of college.

Newspapers and Broadway: together as Ed came of age, they were inventing twentieth-century American popular culture. Whatever else might go on behind the shades of a Puritan-genteel New England, a Calvinist-Victorian Heartland, a Pentecostal small-town South, or the desert-western wastes—and probably a lot more *did* go on than anybody guessed, except the expatriate novelists—Broadway was the big time and the hot ticket, where they dreamed for us all those imperial city dreams of license, celebrity, and scandal; of crossing race, class and gender boundaries into the demimonde and the forbidden; a floating operetta; a rilly big shew.

Or so we were told by the columnists. Because the newspapers moved to Broadway, too, and magazines like *Vanity Fair, Smart Set,* and *The New Yorker*. Broadway was invented by *Variety,* the showbiz daily, and by Runyons and Winchells who covered the theater, nightclubs, and crime waves the way they covered sports. The columnists had all been sportswriters, anyway, before they went to Broadway; they reported the neon night as if it were one big game, in a permanent present tense, with its own peculiar slanguage of ballpark lingo, stage idiom, underworld argot, immigrant English, fanspeak, black-talk, promoter hype, and pastrami sandwich. That's about all they reported, too. They certainly didn't report the political corruption and the racism that have always been the big city's biggest stories, not even the real-estate swindles attending the construction of the IRT subway that brought those crowds to Times Square to begin with. What they wrote, in a Broadway Babel pastiche of "suckers," "bogus," "lowdown," "scoop," and "who sez?" were press releases for a saloon society of singers like Caruso, fighters like Dempsey, and mobsters like Lansky; a fictitious twenties where the long legs of the chorus girls went on forever and all the gangsters were as cute as Gatsby.

If not from novels like *The Big Money* and *Ragtime,* then surely from biographies like Neal Gabler's *Winchell: Gossip, Power, and the Culture of Celebrity* and Jimmy Breslin's *Damon Runyon,* or such dazzling social histories as Jackson Lears's *Fables of Abundance* (on advertising as the "folklore," "iconography," and "symbolic universe" of market exchange) and Ann Douglas's *Terrible Honesty: Mongrel Manhattan in the 1920s* (on the convergence of "formalism" and the hard sell, of "avant-garde innovation and media smarts" to create "an egalitarian popular and mass culture"), we ought by now to suspect that some of this was fantasy: the raffish flipside of Tin Pan Alley songs about Easter bonnets and grand old flags and of Hollywood films about home towns full of nuclear families. While the ad agencies that gave us Aunt Jemima for pancake mix and Rastus for Cream of Wheat may have been entirely WASP, the songs were composed and the movies produced mostly by the children of immigrants, who marketed these American myths as a form of wish-fulfillment—as if the melting pot were a centrifuge for spinning cotton candy, from which we'd all emerge uniformly pink and squeaky clean. Later, after a twist of the color-adjustment knob to achieve the perfect Aryan fleshtone, TV sitcoms would be pink fables, too. As much as the popular culture craves velocity and sensation, it's also a state of longing.

But everybody drank too much and wrote fiction or ad copy (what Jackson Lears, wittily, calls "Capitalist Realism"). In the era of photojournalism and jazz-age novels, Edward Steichen and J. P. Marquand worked for J. Walter Thompson, and F. Scott Fitzgerald for Bannion, Collier. Sherwood Anderson was a copywriter before *Winesburg*; Dorothy Parker wrote underwear ads for *Vogue*; Maxfield Parrish painted General Electric calendars and Jell-O ads; Joseph Cornell designed perfume double-spreads for *Harper's Bazaar* and *House & Garden*; Alexander Woollcott plugged Muriel cigars; Georgia O'Keeffe pushed Dole pineapples, and Rockwell Kent, Steinway pianos. (Dr. Seuss and Jim Henson also got their start in advertising. So did Philip Rahv, in southern California, before coming east to coedit the *Partisan Review*. Allen Ginsberg was in market research correlating supermarket sales of toiletries with the money spent on ads by his toothpaste and baby-powder clients when he wrote "Howl." For that matter, George Bernard Shaw, Arnold Bennett, and H. G. Wells all flacked for Harrod's department store, James Joyce sold ad space for a Dublin newspaper—"What is home without Plumtree's Potted Meat? Incomplete!" recalled Leopold Bloom in *Ulysses*—and Bertolt Brecht wrote radio jingles for a German car company.) Even reportage of the time verged on the fictitious. From Breslin, we learn that while Damon Runyon's father, in a wild American West, had reported the truth about that gloryhound, George Custer, his son *didn't* report it about such gloryhounds as Pershing in Mexico and Patton in Europe. Runyon's famous and shameless rules for the journalism of *his* time were: Never bite the hand that feeds you, and Go along to get along. Pistol-packing Winchell hardly stirred from his reserved table at the Stork Club, except to tool around town in a squad car listening to cop radio. Most of what he needed for the columns that let him bed down with showgirls and ruin the careers of homosexuals got leaked to him by eager publicists or confided to him by that matched pair of sinister buddies, J. Edgar Hoover and Lucky Luciano.

This was Ed's gaudy, buoyant world—of the first book clubs, record charts, opinion polls, IQ tests, and birth-control clinics; a *Wasteland* with jumping beans—from 1922 at the *New York Evening Mail* to 1947, when he was discovered as a *Daily News* columnist who happened to be emcee-ing the annual Harvest Moon Ball, while a fledging CBS just happened to be trying out its primitive cameras. Serendipity! Like showbiz, sports, or war, like organized labor, organized crime, and organized religion, tabloid journalism had been an agency of upward mobility. But TV would prove to be a trampoline . . . a flying carpet.

It's instructive if not surprising to note how many pioneers of early televi-sion, as of early radio, came directly out of advertising, just like the jazz-age novelists: "Pat" Weaver, father not only of Sigourney but of the *Today* and *Tonight* shows; Grant Tinker, who invented MTM; and the wonderful folks who gave us the quiz show scandals, after which the networks took the programming away from the ad agencies. William S. Paley bought CBS to begin with, in 1928, because radio advertising had doubled his cigar company sales. No other nation in the world had turned over its airwaves to advertisers, in a tidy-wrap package of mass production and mass persuasion. These men didn't know exactly what to do with their new toy except to make it spin and sizzle so that the public would sit still staring at it long enough to be stupefied into desiring all the goodies a feverish market might disgorge. Like Mickey Rooney and Judy Garland, like a Mad Avenue Crusader Rabbit, they wanted to put on a show in their garage. Ed already did so.

Except with critics and sponsors, *Toast of the Town* was a hit from its get-go on June 20, 1948. Nobody knew why, nor did they credit Ed. Emerson Radio hated him and CBS shopped the show, with or without the host, to anybody who'd take it. (When, after three months, Emerson bailed out and Lincoln-Mercury took over, Ed was so grateful to the Ford Motor Company that he would log more than a quarter million miles in the next five years as its "ambassador," landing on Boston Common in a chopper, floating down the Mississippi on a Royal Barge to the Memphis Cotton Festival. From Paris, he sent picture postcards to every Ford dealer in the nation.) But that first Sunday, from a firetrap studio on Broadway, was the prototype for the next 1,087—Dean Martin and Jerry Lewis, headliners; Rodgers and Hammerstein, volunteer guests; pianist Eugene List; balle-rina Kathryn Lee; singing fireman John Kokoman; boxing ref Ruby

Goldstein; Ray Bloch and six of June Taylor's neediest dancers, calling themselves Toastettes.

And like every other Sunday to come, Ed had decided how many minutes each of them got at the morning dress rehearsal, after which one audience was chased out of the studio, and another seated for the real thing. Over two decades much changed in the technical production of the hour—it was the first show with a permanent chorus line, the first to introduce celebrity guests from the audience, the first with overhead cams and rear-screen projection, the first to hit the road for remote telecasts, and the first to play with high-resolution cameras, a zoom lens, and videotape—but not the dreaded rehearsal, which was Ed's initial look at the lineup. As quick as his temper, so, too, was his judgment snappy. If a rehearsal audience didn't laugh, a wiseguy was gone, and the singer got an extra song. Add a mime; lose the hippo. Ed agreed with George Arliss: when crowds assemble together "their mass instinct is perilously close to intelligence." Public opinion, he said, "is the voice of God." What's amazing in retrospect is how seldom God, Ed, and the mass intelligence missed the Royal Barge to Memphis. If Nat "King" Cole and Dinah Shore got booted off the show because they wanted to plug their *new* songs instead of singing Ed's hit parade favorites, well Pearl Bailey rose from a sickbed fever of 103° to perform, and Alan King could be counted on to fill any other sudden holes. King was so reliable he didn't even have to rehearse, and refused to appear on any program with a rock group.

Nothing pleased his critics. Fred Allen: "Sullivan will be a success as long as other people have talent." Joe E. Lewis: "The only man who brightens up a room by leaving it." Jack Paar: "NBC has its peacock, and CBS has its cuckoo. . . . Who else can bring to a simple English sentence such suspense and mystery and drama?" Even Alan King: "Ed does nothing, but he does it better than anyone else on television." But when Fred Allen came back to shoot the wounded—"What does Sullivan do? He points at people. Rub meat on actors and dogs will do the same"—Ed was stung to reply, and did so tellingly: "Maybe Fred should rub some meat on a sponsor."

So he looked funny. Even his best friends called him Rock of Ages, the Great Stone Face, the Cardiff Giant, Easter Island, and Toast of the Tomb. He had been, in fact, a handsome man, before an auto accident in 1956 knocked out his teeth and staved in his ribs. In his early days he'd been often mistaken for Bogart. But after the crash there was always about him a shadowy wince, like Richard Nixon's, or Jack Nicholson's in the

Batman movie, playing the Joker *as* Nixon. An ulcer didn't help, despite which he drank and smoked. (Like his old enemy Runyon, he would die from cancer.) Nor did the belladonna he took in his dressing room help: While it expanded the duodenal canal, it also dilated the eyes. Later, hearing problems and arteriosclerosis accounted for some forgetfulness and those famous malapropisms.

Yet the public loved him, the stars showed up, and his critics couldn't really attribute the success of the show to his column. Maybe, in the first few years, Sullivan did bully guests into appearing, as Winchell and Louella Parsons and Elsa Maxwell had bullied them onto their radio programs with the promise (or threat) of syndicated clout. But it quickly became obvious that appearing on TV was more of a career-maker than getting mentioned in any newspaper column. This was good news for CBS, and bad news for print journalism.

And his success isn't so very complicated. He was the best producer of his era. Television is a producer's medium, as movies used to be a director's medium, before the bankers took over, which is why all the best writers for the medium, in order to have some control over their own material and some of the profit as well, turn into executive producers whose names alone are all we see frozen on the screen after each episode of a series program like the sign of Zorro: *Steven Bochco.* It is also why the writing so often declines in the second or third season of even the best series. The executive producer has gone off to dream up another pilot and to executive-produce another series. But all Ed cared about was Sunday night on CBS, forever, reinventing his show each new season for a tribe of ghostly millions. His other talent was the transparent kick he got out of it, as pleased to be exactly where he was as we'd have been. Like Upton Sinclair's Lanny Budd, Woody Allen's Zelig, or Tom Hanks's Gump, Ed made every crucial scene, and didn't put on airs about it. If he had to leave town, he brought back something he knew we'd like because *he* did: a bicycle, a puppet, a Blarney Stone. From France, Edith Piaf. From Scandinavia, Sonja Henie. From Mexico, Cantinflas. From Italy, Gina Lollobrigida. From the moon, astronauts.

There used to be more high culture on television because there was less television, and we would watch almost anything, and middlebrows like Ed felt they had some dues to pay. Besides, Ed's father had loved grand opera and what the twenties had been about was a cross-pollinating of high arts and low: T. S. Eliot and Groucho Marx: Freud and *Krazy Kat.* Maybe as a by-product of all those passionate nineteenth-century Italian tantrums, divas especially had the star quality prized by the celebrity culture Ed was helping to create, even if he had to wait a few years for a Maria Callas to glamorize opera the way Arnold Palmer had glamorized golf. Certainly Roberta Peters, "the little Cinderella from the Bronx," was a terrific front-page story after her walk-on triumph as Zerlina in *Don Giovanni.* As was Itzak Perlman, whom Ed discovered on the streets of Tel Aviv. And Van Cliburn, the surprise American winner of a Moscow piano-playing contest. And Rudolf Nureyev, just off the boat from the Evil Empire. Who will ever forget Jan Peerce, singing "Bluebird of Happiness"? Or Joan Sutherland, on stage with Tanya the Elephant?

Unless you spent the fifties watching *The Voice of Firestone* and the sixties watching *The Bell Telephone Hour,* you weren't hearing much serious music anywhere else on commercial television. Ed cut a deal for first refusal rights on anything imported by Sol Hurok. Nobody else on network TV was ever better for serious dance. On no other show save *Omnibus* could we count on seeing any at all, from Agnes DeMille to Maya Plisetskaya. The Joffrey and the New York City Ballet were around the corner; Jerome Robbins was always available; San Francisco, Denmark, London, Florence, Hungary, and Japan sent companies. The (overrated) Bolshoi was a smash hit. And when Ed went away, who'd step in to hold the middle of that brow? Except for an occasional White House gala, and Eugenia Zuckerman on *CBS Sunday Morning,* classical music has vanished from network television. Ballet only happens on BRAVO and PBS, though not ever during pledge week when they switch to folkies. Likewise opera, with the added insult of Peter Sellars tarting up Mozart. Symphony orchestras, like regional theaters, local dance troupes, and jazz quarters, have to be subsidized by the oil companies and the feds. Even our libraries are closed after dark. Somewhere along the line to junk bonds, leveraged buyouts, and hostile takeovers, middlebrows stopped trying harder and ad agencies decided that "elite" culture lacked a desirable demographic profile and America settled for, or maybe even turned into, a greedhead musical comedy.

Ed gave us Helen Hayes mourning her dead daughter, in a scene from *Victoria Regina.* And Joshua Logan confessing on stage, ad lib, to his own nervous breakdown. And Judith Anderson as the world's most difficult mother, *Medea*. And Oscar Hammerstein tinkling a plaintive rendition of "The Last Time I Saw Paris." And Richard Burton, when the Welsh vapors took him, declaiming Dylan Thomas. And Sophie Tucker, singing with the Ink Spots. Plus half the cast from *West Side Story* and the whole tribe of *Hair*. From the start, Ed and the legitimate theater he covered for his column were allies. As early as 1950, on back-to-back Sunday nights, he brought *Member of the Wedding* to television, black and white together, and a bit of the *Tobacco Road* revival. Selections followed from *Of Thee I Sing* and *Guys and Dolls*. By 1952, he was even saving shows like the musical comedy *Wish You Were Here* and the Pulitzer Prize–winning play *All the Way Home*. But if Ed was good for Broadway, Broadway was better for Ed; his ace in the hole competing with Colgate's *Comedy Hour* was all the talent down the block, young and able, tried and true, and almost always available for Sunday morning rehearsals of a little this and a little that from *Carousel*, *My Fair Lady*, or *Mame*. It was on Sullivan's show that most of the country first heard of Cornelia Otis Skinner; where Yul Brynner visiting from *The King and I* became a pop-culture icon; where, before their musicals were turned into movies, the American public outside New York first saw Ethel Merman, Carol Channing, and Gwen Verdon. After *Guys and Dolls*, as if at a benefit for one of the more popular diseases, all the best Broadway musicals showed up, from *Brigadoon* to *Pajama Game*, meaning that Gertrude Lawrence, Joel Grey, Elaine Stritch, Stanley Holloway, and Mary Martin also sang and danced in our living rooms. So what if we never saw Beckett or Pinter? Ed just wanted us to clap our hands if we believed in Tinker Bell.

Hollywood hated TV before TV moved there. It was Ed's genius to convince a studio tinpot like Goldwyn that TV was free publicity, that clips of forthcoming films would entice millions to neighborhood theaters, that actors on Ed's stage could promote their careers without dissipating their mystery. Beginning in 1951, long before the rich and famous had "lifestyles," there were "biographies" of them on Ed. When he decided as a ratings gimmick to devote whole programs to Bea Lillie, Cole Porter, Walt Disney, and Bert Lahr, he inadvertently invented the "spectacular," by which TV graduated from vaudeville, radio, and Broadway into a humming ether all its own. The result was a steady stream of Bogarts, Grables, Hepburns, and Pecks; a Liz Taylor and a John Wayne. Gloria Swanson appeared to tell an astonished nation that she did, too, believe in God.

Such intimacy! Such presumption! But celebrity is what a democratic society has instead of aristocrats. We may feel today that we're no longer safe anywhere from the stars and starlets so ubiquitous on *Good Morning America*, the *Today* show, Phil, Oprah, Joan, Geraldo, *Entertainment Tonight*, *Live at Five*, the late-night eye witless news and Letterman and Leno, who babble on forever about alcoholism, drug abuse, incest, and liposuction in the weeks before, during, and after their new film opens for the skeptical inspection of teenaged mutant ninja mall mice. But back then it *was* magic in our living rooms, as if the gods had come down from their pink clouds, the generals from their white pedestals, and the vamps from our fantasies, to schmooze, giggle, and weep. And this same star-making machinery turned "unstar" Ed into an aristocrat himself. You will have noticed that TV news personalities like Edward R. Murrow, Walter Cronkite, and David Brinkley, from a synopsizing of the quotidian on our small screen, get *heavier*, taking on the gravity of what they report. Their faces become front pages, etchings of all they have seen. History thickens them to a density that exerts a mighty pull on our frayed attention. Through their images we are accustomed to trafficking with the momentous.

So it was for Ed, too, case-hardened and at last secure in his celebrity, a glaze of so much pleasure rendered, so many heroes of the culture having been consorted with; an odd radiance of well-being; the kind of hum heard only in the higher spheres, as if he had levitated out of other people's talent into a gravity all his own. They sang hymns to him in *Bye Bye Birdie*, and almost made a movie of his life, and he did show up in the Hollywood version of *The Singing Nun*. Not bad for a boy from Port Chester. But there was a difference. Ed was not in his celebrityhood the least bit remote. He was one of us, not so special that we couldn't have been there, too, ourselves, singing along with Birgit Nilsson, hoofing with Gene Kelly, playing Jack Benny's straight man or a fourth McGuire Sister. That's why we forgave him when he found himself suspended in midair by the illusionist Richiardi, or landing on the deck of an aircraft carrier in a helicopter, or riding around in a chariot as if in ancient Rome, on the *Ben Hur* set. If it could happen to Ed, it could happen to anybody. That spinning plate was a flying saucer: I saw *you* on television.

A white man wrote "Bill Bailey, Won't You Please Come Home." As George Gershwin wrote "Swanee" and Al Jolson sang it. Irving Berlin, who was Jewish, wrote both "White Christmas" and "Easter Parade." As well as a New York neighborhood, Tin Pan Alley was a wiseguy state of mind. Whatever you wanted, they'd write it: sentimental ballads, comical immigrant medleys, Broadway show tunes, ragtime, even "coon songs." They also wrote the score for Ed's home movie of an innocent and consensual America. Creepy to remember, but no other singer appeared on his show as often as Connie Francis. Nor did we lack for Bing Crosby, Dinah Shore, Perry Como, Rosemary Clooney, Gordon MacRae, Patti Page, Wayne Newton, Vikki Carr, Liberace, and Tiny Tim. For the longest time, even black entertainers like Nat "King" Cole and Leslie Uggams sounded as pink and squeaky clean as Pat Boone. It wasn't exactly elevator music. Ethel Merman and Pearl Bailey could blast through the wax in our ears. What Ella Fitzgerald or Sarah Vaughan did to standards was what alchemists had tried and failed to do to base metals. When they weren't stopping the show, Lena Horne and Nina Simone knew how to slow it down and make it think. At least Broadway musical comedies came with dancers like Fred Astaire, Cyd Charisse, Bojangles, and Chita Rivera. Not to mention a peppering of Copa Girls, can can, and all those folk dancers who arrived, as if by cargohold and forklift, from Warsaw, Prague, and Oslo; Mexico, Portugal, and Ireland; Romania and Bali. But each appearance of a "mongrel" music, the distilled sound of an aggrieved subculture outside Ed's Dream Palace, had a fugitive quality, as if Dave Brubeck and Stan Kenton, Count Basie and Duke Ellington, Mahalia Jackson and Miriam Makeba, Johnny Cash and Odetta, were souvenirs, and Ravi Shankar a kind of curry. When Nashville and Motown learned at last how to plug their own songs on radio, they'd do terrible things to Tin Pan Alley. Rock, of course, would take elevator music down to hell, and Ed's show with it.

But without pop standards there would have been no show. They were more than the punctuation of the program; they were its sculptured space. Anything *might* happen, but someone *always* sang. And what got sung was the latest hit. Ed was *about* hits, and to make sure he had an uninterrupted flow of them, he had entered into a mutual assistance pact with Tin Pan Alley that amounted to a codependency. He needed the top ten. And, by appearing on his show, you *stayed* in the top ten, the way a book on the *New York Times* best-seller list will sell enough copies to remain there for months; it *must* be good. Besides, showing up twice a year on Ed guaranteed a singer year-round club dates, plus constant play on the radio and jukebox. This was less hanky-panky than a synergetic shakedown of mass-communications conglomerates. (If you *need* hanky-panky, look to CBS Records, with whom Ed had a cozy deal, which is why we heard so much *My Fair Lady* and so little Frank Sinatra, who belonged to Capitol.) As if to signify this codependence, Ed ordered fancy sets built for every singing act, and no set was ever used a second time. In other words, music video. But you had to go live and couldn't lip-synch. Because Mary Tyler Moore insisted on synching, she was banished from the show, a sort of premature Milli Vanilli.

Well then, rock. Ed passed on Elvis the first time around in 1955, at a loose-change price of five thousand dollars. In July 1956, however, a terrible thing happened to him on his way to the Trendex ratings. Elvis appeared on Steve Allen's brand-new Sunday show directly opposite Ed. The Monday news was Ed, 14.8; Elvis, 20.2. To reporters calling for his reaction Ed said, "I don't think Elvis Presley is fit for family viewing." But that afternoon he was on the phone to Tom Parker, striking a fifty-thousand-dollar deal for three spots. And, contrary to what you think you remember, when Elvis showed up for the first of these, in September, we saw all of him. Having been burned in effigy in St. Louis, hanged in effigy in Nashville, and banned, at least his lower body parts, in the state of Florida, the full-frontal Elvis didn't seem so awfully shocking. It was the second Elvis appearance that got shot from the waist up only, because producer Lewis had heard a rumor that a playful Elvis had taken to hanging a soda-pop bottle in the crotch of his trousers. Ed actually decided to like Elvis after a press conference in which a reporter asked if he were embarrassed when "silly little girls" kissed his white Cadillac. The King replied: "Well, ma'am, if it hadn't been for what you call those silly little girls I wouldn't have that white Cadillac." Like Trendex, this was something Ed could appreciate.

But did any of us appreciate what else was going on? With an Elvis, Ed not only opened the gates to the ravening chimeras and barbaric hordes of rock; he had also unlocked the doors to the attic, the bedroom, and basement of the Ike culture. After a long sedation, all that sexual energy seemed to explode. It may have been acceptable to cross-pollinate the races and classes in Times Square. It was something else again when long-haired, poor white Southern trash insinuated a rockabilly/hubcap-outlaw variant of R&B and "dirty dancing" into the ears, hearts, and glands of the Wonderbread children of a bored and horny suburban middle class. What Elvis meant, along with Kerouac, Ginsberg, and the motormouth Beats, was that the sixties were coming, an animal act that rattled everybody's cage and couldn't be contained on any consensus television program that doled out equal time to competing but acceptable subcultures in a median range of American taste. Some chairs were going to be broken, some categories, some heads, and some hearts.

By the time rock got to Sullivan, the world was changing and so was television, and not, so far as he could see, exactly for the better. He *loved* Motown, especially the Supremes, in whom he seems to have found a dreamy mix of gospel and Tin Pan Alley. Rock, he merely put up with, because Bob Precht insisted: Even the Dave Clark Five (fifteen appearances) was no threat to Pearl Bailey (twenty-three), Theresa Brewer (twenty-seven) or, impossibly, Roberta Peters (forty). As for the Beatles, they were cute kids, if only they'd left their deranged teenyboppers back in Liverpool. The story goes that late in 1963 Ed and Sylvia, wandering through Heathrow Airport, ran into forty thousand screaming nymphets. What was up? "Beatles," an airline employee said. Ed: "Well, can't you get some spray?" But as the *New York Times* once explained, "whatever Lolita wants, Sullivan gets." That Christmas he agreed with Brian Epstein on three shows at four thousand dollars each. The rest was more compelling as pop history than as network television. In oddly Edwardian suits, with freshly laundered moptops, on their very best behavior, the Beatles were looked at by 74 million Americans in a single squat. What frightened Ed were the shrieking groupies—including, in his own studio, the daughters of Leonard Bernstein and Jack Paar. After the Beatles, he refused to let anybody into the theater under age eighteen without a parent or a guardian. Which didn't keep fans of the Stones from pushing Mick Jagger through a plate glass window in 1967, or the Doors from misbehaving after they had promised not to. (Told they'd never appear again on the show, Jim Morrison said: "Hey, man, we just worked the Sullivan show. Once a philosopher, twice a pervert.") And the worst sign of an approaching apocalypse was when Herman's Hermits came to town. A high-school student hung around backstage with a borrowed press pass, and then left by the stage door, where he was mistaken for a Hermit. The mob tore at his clothes. Fighting free into street traffic, he was killed by a passing car. To have died for Herman's Hermits—What was wrong with these people?

What was wrong was that his audience, in the studio and at home, had gone to civil war. Parents and their children not only watched different TV programs on different sets in different rooms of a house divided, but these children seemed to live on different planets with alternative gravities, under bloody moons like Selma and Saigon. Pop music was no longer edifying, and not even harmless. For every Woodstock, there seemed, alas, an Altamont. Children of Ed Sullivan, flower-smoking media Apaches like Abbie Hoffman (a revolutionary Dennis the Menace who said that he'd prefer to overthrow the U.S. government by means of bubble gum, "but I'm beginning to have my doubts") and Jerry Rubin (the poisoned Twinkie who announced, "Sirhan Sirhan is a Yippie!") took over campuses and parks, the Stock Exchange, and evening news. No wonder Ed looked tired, even sullen, toward the end: Where was the coherence?

Elvis, the Beatles, and the Doors signified the confusion to come of politics and culture. The juvenile delinquents had their own tribal music, and it wasn't "Sentimental Journey." Rock was political—and hair, and sex; even whales. This confusion perceived itself to be in a profound opposition to a tone-deaf, anal-retentive, body-bag establishment. To a child of the sixties, Ed's last decade, *they* had the guns and *we* had the guitars. If the seventies belonged so depressingly to disco, just waiting for the eighties were metalheads and punks, shape changers and androgynous shamans who would scrawl graffiti and sometimes swastikas all over the walls of the malls. Rap and hip-hop would tell us things about the mythical America that Tin Pan Alley had done its best to cover up. By the end of the eighties, no less than Harvard University would publish a book on the Sex Pistols. We each listen now to our own musics, on wavelengths designer-coded for age, color, class, sex, and sneer, through Sony Walkman headsets, on skateboards, Rollerblades, and Harleys— when we aren't tuned in to hate radio. Do we miss Ed and his consensus? Sure we do, like Captain Kangaroo and Ferdinand the Bull and the Great Pumpkin and all the other imaginary friends of our vanished childhood.

Ed was a democrat and a *fan*. From Harlem, Port Chester, and Broadway; from the ballpark, the saloon, and the tabloid, all he cared about was talent, no matter what it looked like, where it came from, or how he pronounced it. Forget the feuds with Arthur Godfrey, Frank Sinatra, Jack

Paar, Steve Allen, even Walter Winchell. What we saw on his screen was an encompassing, the peculiar sanction of the democratic culture. By being better at what they did than everyone else who did it, however odd or exotic, anyone could *achieve* his show, but nobody inherited the *right*. Ed's emblematic role was to confirm, validate, and legitimize singularity, for so long as the culture knew what it wanted and valued, and as long as its taste was coherent.

During the Cold War, he was absolutely typical. When the blacklist hit the entertainment industry, he was as craven as the times and as his own network. (At CBS, the Ed Murrows were few and far between. They fired Joseph Papp as a stage manager because he refused to talk about his friends to a congressional committee.) Attacked in 1950 by Hearst columnist Cholly Knickerbocker for booking dancer Paul Draper and harmonica player Larry Adler, both of whom had been accused of unspecified "pro-Communist sympathies," Ed, through his sponsor's ad agency, apologized to the public: "You know how bitterly opposed I am to Communism, and all it stands for. . . . If anybody has taken offense, it is the last thing I wanted or anticipated, and I am sorry." Draper and Adler had to leave the country to find work. When conductor Arthur Leif refused to tell the House Committee on Un-American Activities whether he had ever been a member of the Party, Ed dismissed him from the orchestra pit right before a performance of, ironically, the Moiseyev Dance Troupe, fresh from Moscow. Again in 1961, folksinger Leon Bibb was dropped from the show when he wouldn't apologize for his political past to American Legion Post No. 60 in Huntington, New York. Bibb, too, had to leave the country. Sean O'Casey was dumped from a St. Patrick's Day tribute in 1960, for left-wing anticlericalism. Bob Dylan dumped himself, in 1963, when he wasn't permitted to sing "The Talking John Birch Society Blues." Throughout a disgraceful blacklist period, Ed submitted performers' names for vetting to the crackpot Theodore Kirkpatrick, editor of *Counterattack* and author of *Red Channels: The Report of Communist Influence in Radio and Television*, a report slandering half of the entertainment industry, from Leonard Bernstein and Aaron Copeland to John Garfield, Uta Hagen, Lena Horne, Burl Ives, Zero Mostel, Dorothy Parker, Howard K. Smith, and Orson Welles.

But then there was the other American obsession: race. At Harry Belafonte, Ed drew a line against the blacklist. From his earliest newspaper days Ed had been a brother. In his column he attacked New York University for agreeing to keep its one black basketball player on the bench in a game against the University of Georgia. When his friend Bojangles Robinson died, he paid anonymously for a funeral at the Abyssinian Baptist Church and organized a parade afterward to the Evergreens Cemetery in Brooklyn with an all-star cast of foot soldiers that included Berle, Merman, Durante, Danny Kaye, and W. C. Handy. When Walter Winchell savaged Josephine Baker, who had been refused service at his favorite Stork Club watering hole, Ed declared a war on the *Mirror* columnist that wouldn't end till a memorable night in 1952 at that same club, when Ed hustled Winchell into the men's room, pushed his head down a urinal, and flushed him—as if to signify and celebrate the triumph of TV over Hearst. And, obliging though he had always been to his sponsor, Ed was contemptuous of those Ford dealers in the South who objected to his hugging of Ella Fitzgerald on camera, his kissing of Diana Ross and Pearl Bailey. With Louis Armstrong, he'd go anywhere in the world: Guantanamo, Spoleto. From Duke Ellington to Ethel Waters there wasn't an important black artist who didn't appear on Ed's show, just like famous white folks.

But as television expanded—let a hundred channels bloom!—the culture fell apart. It was as if the magic once so concentrated in a handful of choices had managed somehow to dissipate itself, like an expanding universe after the Big Bang, into chaos, heat death, and fractals. By the end of the sixties there were twenty variety shows on TV, and that wasn't counting the bloody circus of Chicago 1968, the porn movies from Vietnam and *Götterdämmerung* in Watts. Instead of Irving Berlin, Joan Baez; instead of Broadway, Newark. *None of this was Ed's fault.* For more than two decades he had not only kept the faith but he had every week renewed it, telling us what was funny, who was important, and how we were supposed to feel about the world he monitored on our behalf. But that world had detonated, concussing even our own homes, where we went in separate furious sects to separate electric altars, alien dreamscapes, and bloody creepshows.

Where's the coherence, much less the consensus, when the people who watch *The X-Files* on Fox and the people who watch ice hockey on Sports Channel and the people who watch the *News Hour* on PBS don't even speak to the people who watch Guns N' Roses on MTV? Of the nation's 95.4 million TV households, 70 percent have more than one set and 11 percent have four or more. Who needs Ed when we can become famous for nothing more compelling than having already been on television?

How amazing that such a show ever existed at all: such innocent bonds, such agreeable community, so much Broadway, Tin Pan Alley, and Port Chester. Can you imagine a prime-time variety hour like Ed's trying to make the nation feel more like a family, seeking some gentle like-mindedness in, say, fin-de-siècle Vienna, the world capital of dessert and alienation? Freud! Herzl! Schnitzler! In our studio audience, take a bow: Ludwig Wittgenstein! Instead of June Taylor Dancers, Gustav Klimt's witchy women, combing their Secessionist nerve-strings, whipping us with their hair. After too many Strauss waltzes, twelve-tone music. After too much operetta, psychoanalysis. After an overmuch of puffy pastry, blood in the Sacher torte. History *mit Schlag*! Or, more daunting yet—a *Toast of the Town* for the Weimar Republic with Kurt Weill and Lotte Lenya singing Hindemith golden oldies, Thomas Mann in a bully pulpit, and Rosa Luxemburg battered to death with a revolver butt on her way to prison, dumped in a canal. Behold the poet-*dompteur*: Wearing his signature steel-rimmed spectacles and his cute little leather cap, direct from the Black Forest where he ate Rilke like a mushroom—Bertolt Brecht. Let's hear it for the Reichstag fire! Not to mention Adolf and his laughing gas.

Ed had Liza Minnelli on his show—he even had her mother!—and held out as Joel Grey for twenty-three years, but life stopped being a cabaret.

Sometimes late at night, in the rinse cycle of sitcom reruns, cross-torching evangelicals, holistic chiropodists, yak-show yogis, and gay-porn cable, surfing the infomercials with burning leaves in my food-hole, I think there must be millions like me out there, all of us remote as our controls, trying to bring back Ed, as if by switching channels fast enough in a pre-Oedipal blur, we hope to reenact some Neolithic origin myth and from the death of this primeval giant, our father and our Fisher King, water with blood a bountiful harvest and civility.

Dear Bill (on the Occasion of His Inauguration)

MOLLY IVINS TELLS me that you actually *listen*. So I'm suggesting some people who need to be heard. And I'm not going to bother you with my own interest group, the "delirious professions." I went down to Washington, D.C., for a meeting of the National Council on the Arts, shortly after your election, and they could hardly wait. No more rifling of filing cabinets and knocking over desks truffling for lesbians. A vigorous nation invests in the arts not because it's cost-efficient (a sort of seeding for a gross national product of mystery and magic), but because that's how we dream our Republic. These difficult people constitiute an antimarket. Their business, instead of selling short, is to surprise us. If we could imagine what they will do next, we wouldn't need them, and we do, not only for pleasure and beauty, or to bind up our psychic wounds, but to bear witness and discover scruple and imagine the Other—all those archeologies of the unspoken and enciphered. And they are also stormbirds, early-warning systems on the seismic fault lines of the Multiculture, before the cognitive dissonance and the underground tremors convulse us.

But artists are noisy. You'll hear them whether you want to or not. I'd like you to listen to the dispossessed. The world is full of them—Haitians, Palestinians, Muslims in Bosnia, Turks in reunited Germany, Daw Aung San Suu Kyi in obdurate Myanmar, old dry bones of high-school principals cannibalized by Red Guards in the Guangxi province of China, everybody on the Indian subcontinent, and, especially, Salman Rushdie, a Flying Dutchman astronaut of all our fevers—but we know you've got the Justice Department to fix up first off, and then health care, and after that (who knows?) maybe campaign financing so that the greedhead lobbyists won't disembowel every other program you propose. So I'll stick here to the domestic dispossessed, even though, now that you've finished *One Hundred Years of Solitude*, it's time to read *The Satanic Verses*.

I suppose I don't have to remind you to listen to the women, not with Hillary around. Nor to the children, not with Marian Wright Edelman standing right next to Hillary. But you ought to be listening to the inner cities, at which you blew smoke from your saxophone after the Day of the Locust in Los Angeles. And what you will hear from those inner cities is *not* a demand for enterprise zones. Enterprise zones! More tax breaks and zoning variances for a handful of fast-buck businessmen to build something ugly on cinder blocks, surround it with barbed wire, bring in a few managers from outside the neighborhood for the high-paying jobs, hire a couple of hundred locals at minimum wage (nonunion, of course; no health plan), and so compete, on a Third World level, with the sweatshops of Santo Domingo and Singapore.

The median household net worth for Anglos in Los Angeles in 1991 was $31,904; for non-Anglos, the median household net worth was $1,353. Imagine that. In the last decade, a million immigrants have crammed into older black Chicano slum housing, without the ghost of a social policy to accommodate them, with federal housing asssistance slashed 70 percent since 1981, *without a single new public housing unit since the 1950s*. In black Los Angeles, unemployment has risen by nearly 50 percent since the early 1970s, *in a city that spends* nothing *on social programs for the poor*.

Nobody at your economic summit on C-SPAN seemed to have read Michael Katz's *The Undeserving Poor*, and so nobody mentioned that only 0.8 percent of our gross national product is spent on welfare, mostly for Social Security. That, since 1972, Aid to Families with Dependent Children has *declined* 20 percent. That most poor people, 69 percent, are white, though almost half of all black children live in families with incomes below the poverty line. That, between 1970 and 1980, the birth rate of unmarried black women *dropped* 13 percent, while the birth rate of unmarried white women *increased* 27 percent.

Barbara Ehrenreich has pointed out that the number of rich white men who have never married is almost exactly the same as the number of poor black single mothers: "In the absence of all the old-fashioned ways of redistributing wealth—progressive taxation, job programs, adequate welfare, social services, and other pernicious manifestations of pre-Reaganite 'big government'—the rich will just have to marry the poor."

Listen to the homeless. They're invisible again, but you can hear them if you really want to: at least a million out there; as many as 3 million homeless off and on; as many as 7 million at "extreme risk." Although most are single men, many of them Vietnam vets, single women are increasing, and about a third of the homeless are families with children. This is the way we've dealt with the problem in New York City: Grand Central Station has reduced its public seating to six benches. The Port Authority Bus Terminal refuses entry to anybody, after 1:00 A.M., without a bus ticket. The transit cops have cracked down on anyone trying to beg, sleep, or sing in the subways. In the parks, we burn them alive.

If you can't bring yourself to listen to these dispossessed, then at least listen to Molly Ivins, who told me you're such a listener. In Molly's opinion "there's not a thing wrong with the ideals and mechanisms outlined and the liberties set forth in the Constitution of the United States. The only problem is the founders left a lot of people out of the Constitution. They left out poor people and black people and female people. It is possible to read the history of this country as one long struggle to extend the liberties established in our Constitution to everyone in America."

Include us; exalt us—your office an agency of levitation.

Meeting David Grossman

EARLY ON IN *The Book of Intimate Grammar*—before he has fallen in love with Yaeli in her black leotard, before he is betrayed by his best friend Gideon, before his father, with a hammer, attacks the face of modern art, before his country goes off to the Six-Day War—in a schoolroom in West Jerusalem during English class, young Aron Kleinfeld discovers "the present continuous": "I em go-eeng, I em sleep-eeng. You don't have that *eeng* tense in Hebrew."

> "I em jum-peeng. . . ." Jumping far, far out in space, halfway to infinity, and soon he was utterly absorbed and utterly alone; jum-peeng; it was like being in a glass bubble, and someone watching from the outside might think Aron ees only jum-peeng, but inside the bubble, there was so much happening, every second lasted an hour, and the secrets of time were revealed to him and the others who experienced time the way he did, under a magnifying glass.

The "present continuous" is Aron's stream of childhood consciousness. By a process he calls "Aroning," he will henceforth "dive in" as often as possible, to float, to swim, to drown in this "intimate grammar" of pumpkin seeds and elevator shoes and Mozart, where he's a magician like Houdini, a spy in Egyptian intelligence, or the first Israeli bullfighter; where every surface of the Holy City throbs with subcutaneous meanings, coded messages, invisible writing, Kabbalistic signs; where red shirts on a laundry line semaphore of friends in need, and scribbles on a sidewalk signal airplanes overhead; where food is a sacramental menu of values and emotions ("the sugars of friendship and the starches of perseverance and the carbohydrates of loyalty"); where time is so relative that minutes on a clock have not only different speeds, but animistic phases (between a slow horse and a vanishing atom, phases of fox, of mouse, mosquito, and germ); and where words, pronounced "with deep devotion," have lazy halos and can be plucked like strings:

> There is a little light in everything, even the steel wool of scrubbing panels has a mysterious spark, even the dark grapes have a dusky gleam, or a thick drop of blood on the tip of your finger . . . and certain words, if you know how to pronounce them in a special way, not from the outside but as though you were calling their names, right away they turn to you, they show you their pink penetralia, they purr to you and they're yours, they'll do anything you want; take "bell," for instance, he rolls it over his tongue as though tasting it for the first time ever, "bellll," or "honeysuckle," or "lion" or "legend" or "coal" or "melody" or "gleam" or "velvet," melting on his tongue, sloughing off their earthly disguises, till suddenly there is red heat, a cinder of memory spreading its glow as it slowly disappears into his mouth, for Lo, this hath touched thy lips, and thine iniquity is taken away, and thy sin is expiated.

Like David in *Call It Sleep*, Aron has visions. Like Alex in *Portnoy's Complaint*, he spends too much time in the bathroom. Like Oskar in *The Tin Drum*, he refuses to grow up. At first he can't; later he *won't*. (Such a shrimp, his Uncle Loniu worries at the bar mitzvah: "Is this why we came to Israel with the sun and the vitamins and the oranges?") But who needs it? Pimples on the face, hair in the armpit, cracking of the voice, pornographic playing cards, patriotic sloganeering, Picasso's *Guernica*? Better to go "Aroning." With his imaginary dog, his broken guitar, his "jinxed shoes," and the blood covenant he strikes with Gideon in the cave where they bury the basalt stone, he will revel "in the possibilities that glittered between the wires, flitting in and out, to and fro; and in the process something would melt, and unfold to him in all its glory, yes, oh, yes, that's what he wanted, free passage through the fortified wall."

You think immediately of Momik in *See Under: Love*. Aron is his secret brother. As Momik was a child of survivors in Tel Aviv in the 1950s, so is Aron a child of survivors in Jerusalem in the 1960s. As Momik, in order to assuage a Nazi Beast he believed to be waiting in his cellar to devour Jews, would sneak down at night to feed yogurt, cucumbers, and chicken drumsticks to hedgehogs, lizards, turtles, and a raven, so Aron, in the Kleinfeld bomb shelter, seeks to raise a vegetarian cat, no meat and no bones. Nor is this cat Aron's only experiment. He tinkers as well with his tear ducts and laugh glands. He collects and smokes the butts of cigarettes to cause and assess a sneeze. He steals a giant magnet from the science lab at school and sleeps with it under his pillow. He establishes, in the bush, his own hospital for wounded words.

But Momik grew up to be a writer, looking for Bruno Schulz. Whereas Aron, who might have been, if not Babel's Di Grasso, at least a Gimpel out of I. B. Singer, won't grow up at all. He is exactly the same height and weight, after his bar mitzvah, as he had been at age ten and a half. Once upon a time he had a knack, but "the wunderkind has lost his wunder." Pouring the kiddush wine on Friday nights, his hand trembles; the wine spills. He is afraid of the electric eye at the supermarket that opens the glass door. He is "misclassified with a hasty glance" by movie ushers, substitute teachers, the new nurse, little old ladies, and "the crow that raids the trash bins who isn't quite sure whether Aron has reached the age where they stop throwing stones." It's as if he had been pickled and jarred, as his mother, with the banana hairdo, pickles and jars everything in the vegetable kingdom: peppers, olives, sauerkraut, carrots. While his father, a paper-pushing clerk who used to work in a bakery, moons over the neurasthenic Miss Edna Bloom next door "shivering like a delicate salamander." And his grandmother, crazy Lilly, who used to dance in a Polish nightclub, whose high heels Aron hides in the cellar, wants to give him a fire engine for his bar mitzvah. And his older sister, overweight Yochi, deserts him for the army. And his best friend, the green-eyed, "pure and noble" Gideon, will no longer play their games. And the love of his young life, the exquisite Yaeli, in whose likeness he has fashioned a sweet challah, prefers the company of Gideon, with his geopolitical expansiveness and Boy Scout warrior strut. (Poor Tonio Kroger, alone with his difficult art!) There is a buzzing, a "chirring," in his ears:

> You don't stand a chance. . . . There's nothing in the world that isn't me. I'm the things of the world and the people who use them. I'm steel and rubber and wood and flesh. I'm cranks and

valves and gears and pistons. I'm the blade that cuts. I'm the
screws you have to remember which way to turn on the first try.
I'm the knots in your shoelaces and the cord for the blinds. . . . I
am the scourge of the broken plate and the light bulb exploding
in your hand and the glass that shatters when you clink l'chaim.

Well, puberty. God help us. And there are certainly enough of them to
go around, gods that is, in Jerusalem. And absolutes. And so many fortified
walls between Aron and free passage: the Bet ha-Kerem housing project,
the hospital where they send crazy Lilly, the school where time is relative,
the cave of the childhood covenant, the abandoned refrigerator in the junkyard. And if not God, then Freud: Enraged by his mother, Aron strikes at
her hands, which hold bottles full of milk. Massaged with too much enthusiasm by his sister Yochi, he is frantic, thrilled, almost abused. Grappling
with Gideon, he is so much the lover scorned he might have been reading
Leslie Fiedler. And when his father undertakes to knock down a wall in
Edna Bloom's apartment, with its rug-checkered floors, its ivory figurines,
its black leviathan of a piano, its volumes of Indian art, its reproductions of
Degas, van Gogh, Picasso, and Magritte, those snow-filled globes of swans,
clowns, dancers, and children trapped under glass—after first fiddling with
her fig tree (come *on*, Grossman!)—and ends by reducing the whole flat to
dust and rubble in an orgy of furious destruction, we have passed with Aron
through and beyond a Viennese underground of eros and thanatos into the
medieval realm of the *Sefiroth* and *Zohar*, of transcendental sexuality. No
wonder that Aron, walking, eating, sleeping, Aroning, dreams of a "misty
courier" crossing a white plain, a scaffolding of bones, a red-black sea of
clotting blood, and a fissured egg of yellow coral covered with a frosty film:
"Aron to Aron, where are you now, over . . ."

Not quite so suddenly, sex disgusts him, and food, too (custard, falafel,
and salami; Creambo and Yemenite *skhug*); the "code of mass" and "the
canon of the flesh." How would you feel if what you really wanted for
your bar mitzvah was a new Yamaha guitar, and what your father gave
you instead was "very special": the army shaving kit with the razor, the
foaming block, and the little tray he used during the Sinai campaign? To
accompany, perhaps, the key ring in the shape of a Mirage jet given out
in honor of Independence Day by the Delek gas company. Because war
fever is heating up all over Israel, except in Aron's head. Even words have
lost their savor: *longing, wandering, heron, diamond, autumn, lonely*—"all

culled from the Hit Parade on the radio, an excellent source of words; in the middle there was news, Nasser Kasser Basser Yasser, and later that afternoon he would be releasing 'lamb' and 'twilight' and 'midnight' and 'kiss me by the sea.'" Comes the dark, however, and no place for Aron in Nighttown in Jerusalem:

> Noisy shouts and patriotic songs blared over the loudspeakers, and the smell of burning in the air after the fireworks, how the night suddenly burst into color, with a pang of longing he thought of Yaeli, and people kept bumping into him, saying, Hey, kid, watch where you're going; he was out of step, out of sync, he always ruined everything, someone hit a sour note on the accordion: "Sing, oh water/Flow to the Negev." "Flow," that's nice, and there are public showers there but what about the flow of blood, and carefully he extricated the word "flow" from the general clamor, stripping it gently and whispering it backward thrice with great intensity; "Wolf wolf wolf," his mouth clamped shut so none of the outward pollution would infiltrate, the tumult and the smoke and the crowds, till the dusty, sweaty sheath of "flow" dropped away like a cast-off skin, with its shrill notes and dissonances and random undertones; he hid it inside him, in the intimate new center, quickly checking over the other words he had smuggled in over the past few days: "supple," "lonely," "gazelle," "profoundest secrets," "sacrifice," "tears," words that had welled out of an endless stream, and now "flow"; for seven days he would refrain from saying it aloud, till it was purified, till it was his, his alone.

But Aron hasn't seven days, not even Six. He must engineer his exodus, his shaman Houdini disappearing act and Great Escape, from a maze of meanings and a wheel of signs. He is acquiring too much density even as he cracks. With Roman coins and onion skins in his pockets, and nylon bags on his fingers, and magnets under his pillow, Aron—who wants only to tell stories, interpret dreams, fend off famines, lead children in song with his golden flute, and "trap the lustrous auras of this world in glassy marbles"; for whom language is contaminated and food constipating and flesh corrosive; who declines to grow up even as Israel in the Six-Day War is about to burst its borders, to break down Edna's walls; terrified of the

sexuality and aggression of adulthood, the lust for power and appetite for
territory of modern statecraft, the destructive dissonance of modern art,
the raging hormones of gluttonous history itself—Aron falls inward, on a
spiral track through voltages of feeling and magnetic fields of words,
down to an abandoned refrigerator in a West Jerusalem junkyard, to await
deliverance by magic, like an angel in a cyclotron.

So: Did Aron perish in that locked box in 1967, or somehow, with a broken guitar instead of a tin drum, prestidigitate himself?

This is the wrong question to ask David Grossman, on the outdoor
terrace of the King David Hotel on a summer Sunday afternoon of ice
cream and sparrows. He has dodged it too often in the three years since
The Book of Intimate Grammar was originally published in Israel, where
high-school students already read it before sitting down to final exams;
where A. B. Yehoshua teaches a seminar on Aron at his impasse. Grossman still thinks about Aron; he may not be done with him any more than
he is done with Momik. But Aron is an imaginary character. A residue,
a caution, and a confabulation, he belongs now to the readers of his grammar, who'll have to make up their own minds. Anyway, if Aron *weren't*
alive, his book could never have been written. And if he *has* survived, it
is at a price. To be normal, after having been Aron, is to be coarsened. To
fit in is to be diminished.

Besides, while Grossman was waiting for the poet and perfectionist Betsy
Rosenberg to finish her loving translation of *Intimate Grammar* into English,
he wrote and published two more books—*Sleeping on a Wire*, a series of
interviews with troubled Israeli Arab citizens, and *The Zig-Zag Boy*, a novella
for children on Israel's adult best-seller list. Red-haired, horn-rimmed, affa-
ble and evasive, he would have us believe that Aron's problems are existential, not political. I'm not buying it. I've been Aroning myself, in the *past*
continuous. Grossman was thirteen years old himself during the Six-Day
War, living like Aron in Bet ha-Kerem. "I was terrified," he says, "when
they told us on the radio, on the Hebrew-speaking station in Cairo, that they
would throw us into the sea. I was a child in Jerusalem. I didn't know how
to swim very well. I took it in a concrete way, this threat. I am sure that I'm
not going to live until the next Rosh Hashanah."

At age thirteen, he had already been a child actor on Israeli radio for
four years, after winning a Sholem Aleichem contest, standing on a spe-

cial "Grossman box" to reach the microphone and to speak in tongues. Following army service just in time for the Yom Kippur War, he returned to radio to become the anchor of a popular newsmagazine program, from which he was dismissed, to which he was restored, in a pattern of trouble-making that continues unto this summer Sunday. Imagine devoting your first novel to Israel's morally corrupting occupation of the West Bank. And daring in your second to write about the Holocaust when your parents weren't even survivors. Jewish Defense League hoodlets disrupted his American tour for *The Yellow Wind*. In the middle of the Gulf War, when the PLO made common cause with the Beast of Baghdad, as Scuds came down on Tel Aviv, still, on television, he insisted that peace was possible "only if we listen to the Palestinian suffering and misery. . . . We were shaped by the same wound for almost a century."

But Grossman today would really rather talk about his son, who'll be waiting for him after soccer. And the Slavic planes of my wife's face, from the Pale of Settlement. And the redheaded Syrian soldiers he met during the Lebanon mess, an odd camaraderie of carrottops.

It occurs to me that the last time I was in Israel, for the Jerusalem Book Fair in 1983, in the middle of that very same Lebanon mess, Grossman's novel *The Smile of the Lamb* hadn't yet been published, although it was about to be. Missing the story, as usual. Inquiring, instead, at the Sling-Shot Bar of this very same King David, where Edmund Wilson and Saul Bellow both got haircuts, where V. S. Naipaul had gloomed in the lobby, where Menachem Begin once planted a bomb, exactly how one went about meeting the famous mayor. Being told: Just stand still; he'll find you. And of course he did, minutes later, Teddy Kollek with a tree in one hand, a caduceus in the other, and a minivan outside to make sure we didn't miss an important goat. "Balzac would have taken to the mayor," wrote Bellow in 1976. "Kollek is to Jerusalem what old Goriot was to daughters, what Cousin Pons was to art objects." They've dis-elected Teddy now; installed in his stead a bloodthirsty clown, Ehud Olmert, who will defend against a visit by Arafat with a wall of West Bank settlers. I did see Citizen Kollek the other day at breakfast. And guess who walked right by his table without noticing? Alan Dershowitz himself, in town for a presidential forum on Israel-Diaspora relations, and probably billing O. J. Simpson.

My best moment in 1983 may have been seeing the Western Wall with Swifty Lazar at midnight. Or, barefoot at Haram esh-Sharif, my first two

mosques. Or Masada, like the Alamo. My worst moment . . . maybe not
at Fink's, a bar for journalists and Eurotrash, where I declined the offer of
a hitch by jeep to the Lebanon front. Maybe at the party in Amos Elon's
flat, full of Peace Now people, all of whom were bad-mouthing Jacobo
Timerman. You recall Timerman. For being the sort of Jewish troublemaker who published in his Buenos Aires newspaper the names of the
"disappeared," he was kidnapped by the sort of people who believe in a
Zionist plot to gobble up Patagonia; and spent the next thirty months
"talking to Susan," a machine that applies electrodes to one's genitals; and
was then sent off by bloody parcel post to Israel, where he wrote *Prisoner
Without a Name, Cell Without a Number*, in which he just happened to
mention the acquiescence in his abuse by Argentina's silent Jewish community. Well, this ingrate had chosen in 1983, in the pages of *The New
Yorker* and in a book called *The Longest War*, to criticize Israel's invasion
of Lebanon—for which, by Peace Now people in Amos Elon's flat, he was
now reviled. How *dare* he, having arrived so recently, having skipped not
only the Holocaust but 1948, 1956, 1967, 1973 . . . "I see," I said. "He was
tortured in the wrong language."

Jacobo Timerman went back to Argentina. "He should have stayed,"
says David Grossman, who hasn't even left Jerusalem, though A. B.
Yehoshua has gone to Haifa for quiet time and peace of mind, and Amos
Oz, after the reviews of *Fima*, is hiding out in the desert, and as we sit
with our fingers crossed—Peace Now!—I'm semi-ashamed of myself.
How is anyone here to know, and why should anybody care, that I was
once upon a time a dilettante (or delicatessen) Zionist, a secular-humanist
sabra-in-my-head, before Edward Said and Lebanon and the *intifada*?

Where have you gone, my blue-eyed goy? If you grew up lonely on
the beach in southern California in the 1950s, as alienated as an Aron from
the sports-car culture and the pompons, the drive-in church and the
grunion and surfer cults, you chose your emancipating fantasy from a rich
debris of driftwood: James Dean, Jackie Robinson, Robert E. Lee,
Mahatma Gandhi; bog-Irish semi-poet singing "Danny Boy"; Wobbly
with cowboy boots; Bolshevik, but like Trotsky, scribbling as the alpen-
stock came down; *Mr. Keen, Tracer of Lost Persons*. It is really no more
preposterous, after a boyhood reading of Arthur Koestler's *Arrow in the
Blue* and *Thieves in the Night*, George Eliot's *Daniel Deronda*, and Theodor
Herzl's *The Jewish State*, to have dreamt yourself a kibbutznik, some sort
of soldier-scholar, reading Marx and listening to Mozart after you've

milked the cows . . . before communal sex. Instead of sand dunes and swamps, orange trees and potash; the white donkey and the red heifer and socialism with a suntan. Adolescence is all injury anyway; wounded feelings; blank incomprehension. So you appropriate the sufferings of a people to whom crimes beyond imagining have already occurred, and lay claim simultaneously to the great realms of modern thought, to the tragic determinisms of Marx and Freud, Einstein's relativity, Kafka's paranoia. And then you do something about it. Europe didn't work out. Let's start over again, from scratch. It's as if you turned the pages of *Partisan Review* with a sword.

But *all* of this is Aroning: Megiddo and catacombs and citadels of David; the Jerusalem Star restaurant, full of Palestinian intellectuals, across the street from Ariel Sharon's house in the Arab quarter of the Old City; Masada, where the Zealots might have been better off hiking down the road to the Ein Gedi Spa for a mud pack, a sulfur rinse, and a Dead Sea float. It is possible on a single day to spend the afternoon at the Dome of the Rock, looking down; an evening hour at the Western Wall, looking up; to still have time for dinner in East Jerusalem and be back at the swimming pool at the King David before you hear a ram's horn. Two religions are on top of each other, a third next door, archeologists digging underneath, and what they've opened is a vein. Solomon built the First Temple, and Babylonians destroyed it. Herod built the Second; Romans did it dirt. The Wall is all that's left, propping up the plateau with the Mosque of Omar, built by Greek slaves. From the rock where the gold dome sits, the Prophet went to Heaven on a white horse. When the Crusaders came in the eleventh century, Muslims fled to the roof of the Dome, where they were slaughtered anyway. Inside the Dome, as if inside an ornate clock, under the golden mosaics and gaudy Ottoman tile work, there's something scary. Let your eyes go into an arcade, stare at a vine scroll. What it sees are the insignia of vanished empires, the breastplates, crows, and double-winged diadems of Byzantium and Sassanid. In stocking feet, you get the creeps. The Dome is a trophy case: Look what Daddy brought home from his Holy War. They have been throwing rocks at the prophets in this desert for three thousand years. Only the Uzis and napalm are modern. A secular-humanist Israeli literature may have come of conscience and of age—David Grossman's Aron is everybody's wunderkind—but the Age of these politics is Bronze.

Eduardo Galeano Walks Some Words

IN A LATIN America rampant with Magical Realists, Eduardo Galeano calls himself a Magical Marxist—"one half reason, one half passion, a third half mystery"—which may explain why, in *Walking Words*, after the affair of a white rose, a sprig of coriander, and a police truncheon, José is convicted of a "violation of the right of property (the father's over his daughter and the dead man's over his widow), disturbing the peace, and attempted priesticide." And why Calamity Jane leaves South Dakota for a Comayagua brothel where, with a magic lasso, she ropes her very own archangel. And why in Haiti anyone telling a story before dark is disgraced: "The mountain throws a stone at his head, his mother walks on all fours." And why a cowboy who turns himself into a jaguar finds it afterward impossible to "disenjag." If Jesus on His Second Coming is not a happy camper ("They want me to jump without an umbrella. . . . A pancake from God"), it's even worse for the bandit Fermino. While Fermino's soul goes straight to heaven,

> On earth his corpse was split in two. The body was thrown to the vultures and the head to the scientists. . . . Their analysis revealed a psychopathic personality evidenced by certain bulges in the skull characteristic of cold-blooded assassins from the mountains of obscure countries. [His] criminal destiny was also apparent from one ear that was nine millimeters shorter than the other, and from the pointed head and oversized jaws with large eyeteeth that continued chewing after he was dead.

Whimsy with a sting: This Magical Marxist began his vagabond life as a newspaperman, in Montevideo and again in Buenos Aires, always leaving town a step before a dictatorship got him. On that road, he became a historian. His *Memory of Fire* trilogy is famously anecdotal and juxtapositional, a rollercoaster and Ferris wheel. (Imagine an account of our century that leaps in a single bound from Superman to the Bay of Pigs, while keeping one eye on General Trujillo as he reviews the troops at West Point with an ivory fan, another eye on Carmen Miranda dancing for the king of Belgium with a banana, and a third on Pancho Villa reading the *Arabian Nights*.) Late in the 1980s, however, after completing *Century of the Wind*, Galeano turned to something different—still political, still literary, still anthropological, but a lot more personal.

In *The Book of Embraces* (1991), we heard about his thinning hair, his heart attack, and his wife, Helena, for whom at night "a line formed of dreams wishing to be dreamed, but it was not possible to dream them all." We got gossip about such buddies as Pablo Neruda, Julio Cortázar, and Gabriel García Márquez. And, as if Latin American boom-boom had for a night cohabited with Pascal and Lichtenberg, there were eavesdroppings, aphorisms, minitexts, and footnotes on friendship, courage, muscle, wind, theology, art, silence, a snowy beach in Catalonia, and the culture of terror. "There is a division of labor in the ranks of the powerful," Galeano explained; "The army, paramilitary organizations, and hired assassins concern themselves with social contradictions and the class struggle. Civilians are responsible for speeches." And: "In the final analysis, it doesn't bother anyone very much that politics be democratic so long as the economy is not." And: "We are all mortal, until the first kiss and the second glass of wine." He also collected graffiti. On a Bogotá wall: "Proletarians of all lands, unite!" (And, scrawled underneath in another hand: "FINAL NOTICE.") Or, in Montevideo: "Assist the police. Torture yourself."

Walking Words is an anthology of stories about "ghouls and fools," derived from the urban and rural folklore of the Americas, with "windows" between chapters for the stray paradox and sneaky afflatus, and woodcut illustrations, like sarcophagus rubbings, by the Brazilian *cordel* artist José Francisco Borges: a kind of commonplace book of mysterious transcendence. But it could also be thought of as a line of dreams wishing to be dreamed by Helena. Besides Jesus and Calamity Jane, shoemakers, coachmen, fishermen, wine sellers, coffee grinders, and socialist-realist poets dream about tango dancers, soccer stars, and Moon People; frogs with feathers and parrots "born from grief"; St. George on a Yamaha motorcycle, warlocks on seahorses with vests of burning fat, and a Virgin at sea so busy resuscitating the drowned that "she didn't have time for bad luck on dry land." Often these dreamers feel awful, as if "dirty water rains inside me." Or like a tabloid headline: "KILLED MOTHER WITHOUT GOOD CAUSE." A cure for the blues will not come cheap: "Candido charged for his miracles in advance. He was no cheap saint. 'What do they want?' he'd grumble. 'A favor from God for the price of a banana?'"

Yet always, somehow, there is levitation: "Memory eats the dead. The vulture, too. Just like memory, the vulture flies." Besides: "We come from an egg much smaller than the head of a pin, and we live on a rock that spins around a dwarf star into which it will someday crash. But we're made of light, as well as carbon and oxygen and shit and death and so much else." Finally, wonderfully: "The Church says: *The body is a sin.* Science says: *The body is a machine.* Advertising says: *The body is a business.* The body says: *I am a fiesta.*" It's oddly Rabelaisian, with a Kurtness of Vonnegut—as if magic tricks and peasant cunning were still capable of subverting the greedhead warlocks and the banal surfeit and oppressive patterning of the admass media/consumer grid. One dreams so, like Helena.

Amos Oz in the Desert

N OT SO LONG ago in London, Amos Oz told reporters that a recon-
ciliation between Jews and Palestinians had to be Chekhovian,
"with everybody a little disappointed," so that it wouldn't be Shakespear-
ean, "with bodies littering the stage." Would you believe, instead,
Megiddo? By bus bomb and assassination Ultras and Hamas got what they
wanted, which was Bibi and Likud, meaning more settlers on the West
Bank, more soldiers on the Golan Heights, and more archeologists and
tourists tapeworming into the traumatized bowels of Al-Aksa, while a
lizardly Arafat bans books by Edward Said, and a rubber-bullet Olmert
pretends to be the bandit prince Bar Kokhba, and the Pillsbury Doughboy
in his Oval Office feels their pain. An earlier Amos prophesied a fire upon
Judah, "and it shall devour the palaces of Jerusalem."

But Oz has been in the desert, hiding out from the reviews of *Fima*
(1993), reconstruing marriage, children, and silence. In the dusty Negev
new town Tel Kedar (pop. 9,000), an hour or so away from Beersheba and
the daily papers, he has dreamed his way into the heads and hearts of
Theo, a sixty-year-old semiretired civil engineer, and Noa, a forty-five-
year-old teacher of literature. Theo, a tidy, gloomy insomniac, is so patient
mixing a salad he might as well be painting it. Noa, a scatter of pages and
ideas, is in such a rush she often fails to finish sentences, so worn out she
falls into bed as if axed. Although they're not legally married, the relationship they've settled for is more intimate than most licensed monogamies—
an almost hydraulic exchange of skeptical caution and heedless zeal; part
pendulum and part crossruff. Although they are childless, Theo is as much
Noa's father as her lover, and Noa, picking up stray children on the rainy

highway, listening to Mahler's *Kindertotenlieder*, feeling guilty about her students, seems to mother half the Middle East. And although neither spends more than a minute thinking about, say, Arabs, Zionism, Judaism, or Jerusalem, their separate peace is about to tested.

One of Noa's dreamier students, the introverted Immanuel Orvieto, either falls or jumps to his death, perhaps because of drugs. When Immanuel's father, Avraham, either a military advisor or an arms dealer, arrives from Nigeria for the burial, he also proposes to bankroll, as a memorial, a clinic for adolescent drug users—if Noa, Immanuel's favorite teacher, agrees to do the scut work. Remorseful at having barely noticed Immanuel while he was alive, Noa flings herself into the project. With his connections, Theo could help. A long career of planning settlement areas, industrial zones, and leisure complexes has taught him how to deal with local and district councils, and from "the old days, when this country was nothing but sand dunes and fantasies," he even knows the mayor. But Theo, typically, is skeptical. He also knows Noa will resent his help. And so while the teacher plunges headlong into comical committee meetings, bureaucratic farce, archeological memory digs, and self-recrimination, the engineer makes salads, plays chess, listens to BBC news radio, and stares all night at the desert.

We shall presently try to imagine what he sees there, populating absences. But *Don't Call It Night* is a novel of domestic accommodation—almost a convalescence. From Tel Kedar, we can't see Hebron or Gaza, much less the Caracas where Theo and Noa met eight years ago. It's as if the fevers of eros and history had wasted them. In a town without a past, they are going through the motions. At least these motions—drinking iced tea or mulled wine, stopping at the Paris cinema or Entebbe bar, making rosebuds out of radishes—are reassuringly reciprocal. As they address us in alternating chapters (and Oz watches them watch each other), even the parentheses in their monologues are compensatory. Inside separate chambers, on either side of a hermetic seal, they mimic the same rotary wave. Theo longs for peace of mind. Noa lusts for significance. Eventually, he'll take a hand in her project. Predictably, she'll then develop doubts. (Why not an old people's home instead?) Finally, they discover their interdependence, which is also their consolation.

Meanwhile, we have met a town: Elijah, so-called because every five minutes in the post office queue he asks, "When's Elijah coming?" Blind

Lupo, who apologizes to his own dog for kicking it. Muki, a lecherous investment consultant with sky-blue shoes. Avram, a falafel seller with a brand-new *shawarma* machine. Chuma, the militant vegetarian with "a particular hatred of potato crisps, mustard, and stuffed intestines." Not to omit the newsagents, poets, bookbinders, garage mechanics, bank clerks, pharmacists, notaries, a Hungarian cantor, a Russian-emigré string quartet, the former weight-lifting champion of Lodz, and a piano tuner who's writing a book on *The Essence of Judaism*. As always in Oz, Israel teems with spinning types who kick against the cartoon bubbles limned around them. As always, there's a sort of moral blackmail to which the victims too eagerly submit. As always, there are missing mothers—Oz's own committed suicide when he was twelve—and thus a wounded emblematic child like Boaz in *Black Box*, with "the look of Jesus in a Scandinavian icon"; like Dimi in *Fima*, a "slightly cross-eyed albino child-philosopher"; like Immanuel in *Night*, seeming "to live inside a bubble of winter even in summer." And also as always there is his oddly *angry* lyricism. His physical world has an astonishing thickness of texture and scent. His feel for olives, lizards, candles, eucalyptus, marble, and moonlight is almost wanton. Yet this appreciation of surprise beauty is so masculine that it seems to resent its own esthetic shock, to want somehow to bite the face of grace.

> *It is both a garrison state and a cultivated society, both Spartan and Athenian. It tries to do everything, to understand everything, to make provision for everything. All resources, all faculties are strained. . . . These people are actively, individually involved in universal history. I don't see how they can bear it.*
>
> —Saul Bellow, *To Jerusalem and Back*

What's missing—one of those absences on purpose—is politics. Or what Oz prefers to call "ethics." *Black Box* (1989) was consumed by West Bank settlements and Orthodox theocracy. Gideon, "tasting *schadenfreude* like expensive whisky, in small sips," has even written a book, *The Desperate Violence: A Study in Comparative Fanaticism*. In his opinion, we annihilate ourselves and will soon wipe out the species "precisely because of our 'higher longings,' because of the theological disease. Because of the burning need to be 'saved.' Because of an obsession with redemption. What is the obsession with redemption? Only a mask for a complete absence of the basic talent for life." *Fima* couldn't go to the movies without seeing Palestinians on a private sonar screen: "We're the Cossacks now, and the Arabs are the victims of the pogroms, yes, every day, every hour." Fima, the poet who works in an abortion clinic, "the Eugene Onegin of Kiryat Yovel," who would give away the whole of South America's magical realism, "with all its fireworks and cotton candy," for a single page of Chekhov—this tortured Fima explains:

> We must not become like the drunken Ukrainian carter who beat his horse to death when the beast stopped pulling his cart. Are the Arabs in the Territories our workhorses? What did you imagine, that they would go on hewing our wood and drawing our water forever and ever, amen? . . . Every Zambia and Gambia is an independent state nowadays, so why should the Arabs in the Territories continue come Hell or high water quietly scrubbing our shit-houses, sweeping our streets, washing dishes in our restaurants, wiping arses in our geriatric wards, and then saying thank you? How would you feel if the meanest Ukrainian anti-Semite planned a future like that for the Jews?

And that's just the recent fiction. For Oz in nonfiction like *In the Land of Israel* (1983), nationalism is mankind's curse: "Shall we aspire to rebuild the kingdom of David and Solomon? Shall we construct a Marxist paradise here? A Western society, a social-democratic welfare state? Or shall we create a model of the petite bourgeoisie with a little *Yiddishkeit*?" He'd be happier in a world "composed of dozens of civilizations, each developing in accordance with its own internal rhythm, all cross-pollinating. . . ." Israel after the Six-Day War was "crude, smug, and arrogant, power drunk, bursting with messianic rhetoric, ethnocentric, 'redemptionist,' apocalyptic—quite simply, inhuman. And un-Jewish. The Arab human beings under our dominion might never have been." And then this remarkable apostrophe:

> I study the elusive cunning of the Biblical charm of this landscape: and isn't all of this charm Arab, through and through? The lodge and the cucumber garden, the watchman's hut and the cisterns, the shade of the fig tree and the pale silver of the

olive, the grape arbors and the flocks of sheep—these picturesque slopes that bewitched from afar the early Zionists like
Yehuda Halevi and Abraham Mapu; these primeval glades that
reduced the poet Bialik to tears and fired Tchernichowsky's
imagination; the hypnotic shepherds who, from the very
beginning of the return to Zion, captured the heart of Moshe
Smilansky, who even called himself Hawaja Musa; the tinkle
of the goats' bells which entwined, like magic webs, the hearts
of the early Zionist settlers, who came from Russia thirsty for
Arab garb and to speed on their horses toward this Arab Bib-
licality . . . the tales told around the campfires of the Palmach,
the enchanted groves of Amos Kenan and the longed-for cis-
terns of Naomi Shemer, yearning for the bare-faced stony
mountain, for merger into the bosom of these gentle, sleepy
scapes so very far removed from *shtetl* alleyways, so very far
from Yiddish and the ghetto, right into the heart of this Oriental rock-strewn tenderness.

He is if anything unhappier in the collected broadsides in *The Slopes of
Lebanon* (1987). The 1982 invasion of Lebanon—like "a timely investment
in the stock market," like *The Empire Strikes Back*—enraged him. Not a
pacifist, nor an admirer of the PLO, and equally disdainful of a secular
left that "offers peace to the Israeli public as one part of a package that
includes . . . the rights of nude sunbathers," he still favors a separate Palestinian state: "If only good and righteous people, with a 'clean record,'
deserved self-determination, we would have to suspend, starting at midnight tonight, the sovereignty of three-quarters of the nations of the
world." King Solomon, after all, gave away twenty cities to Hiram of
Tyre, yet Solomon was not struck down, nor condemned by the prophets.
Besides, "Hebron and Nablus will not be ours whether or not the prophets once walked there, whether or not the stones our ancestors liked to
throw at the prophets still lie scattered there." So what if Palestinians
deceive us? "It will always be easier . . . to break the backbone of a tiny
Palestinian state than to break the backbone of an eight-year-old Palestinian stone thrower."

At desperate issue on almost every page of *The Slopes of Lebanon* is
Israel's soul and the Zionist ideal of a just society: "What have we come
here to be?" If the logic of statecraft is that ends justify means, and the

rule of thumb is that "it all depends," then "What began with the biblical words 'Zion shall be redeemed by the law' has come to 'Nobody's better than we are, so they should all shut up.'" He quotes Isaiah ("Your hands are covered with blood") and Jeremiah ("For they had eyes but they did not see"). "Veteran defeatists, both of them," Oz says: "Troublers of Israel. Self-hating Jews."

I suggest that some of this is what a sleepless Theo sees, staring at the desert. Never mind that "on the other side there is a forbidden valley containing secret installations." He's turned his back on more than Tel Kedar. He was asked himself to help plan Tel Kedar, back in the late sixties. By the light of a pressure lamp at the foot of a cliff, he sketched "rough preliminary ideas for a master plan that was intended to get away from the usual Israeli approach and create a compact desert town, sheltering itself in its own shade, inspired by photographs of Saharan townships in North Africa." For which he was ridiculed by his boss: "Same old Theo, carried away by his fantasies, it's brilliant, it's original, creative, the trouble is, as usual you've left one factor out of account: when all's said and done, Israelis want to live in the Israeli style. Desert or no desert. Just you tell me, Theo, who do you imagine suddenly wants to be transported back to North Africa? The Poles? The Romanians? Or the Moroccans? The Moroccans least of all. And just remember this, chum: This isn't going to be an artist's colony."

Theo's days as a senior planner in the Development Agency were obviously numbered, in spite of the British police stations and radar installations he'd once upon a time blown up in the Zionist cause. This great-grandchild of a Ukrainian gravedigger, with a couple of Herod's master-builder genes, would leave Israel as "a special advisor of regional planning"—to "develop" Veracruz, Sonora, and Tabasco; to redo Nicaragua after an earthquake; to wonder about atrophy, torpor, barrenness, and exile in Peru: "When he came across cruelty, corruption, barbarity, or grinding poverty he passed no judgment . . . he had not come here to combat injustice but, as far as possible, to attain professional perfection and thereby perhaps, however minutely, to reduce disasters. Honor, the labyrinth, and death were ever-present here, and life itself sometimes flared up like a festive firework display or a salvo of shots in the air: ruthless, spicy, noisy, and cheap." But not for Theo until, in Venezuela, he met Noa—that Noa who comes home at night in one of two ways, either "setting up a row of electric lights in her path as though to illuminate the runway of her landing" or "as if she had flown into this room by mistake and now she's in such a panic she can't find the window. Which is open as it always has been."

And the Tel Kedar they made without Theo? It's hard to believe Elijah would come to such a place: Fifteen identical streets off Herzl Boulevard, with caged poinciana saplings wrapped in sackcloth against sandstorms; "a few eucalyptus trees and tamarisks, blighted by droughts and salty wind, hunched towards the east like fugitives turned to stone in midflight"; green streetlamps and matching municipal benches; a solar panel on every roof, "as if the town were trying to appease the sun's blaze in its own language"; balconies shut up with cement, plaster blasted desert-gray; a chic northwest residential district "with projections, surrounds and arches, rounded windows and even weathercocks on gables, sighing for forests and meadows"; a commercial southeast of corrugated-iron huts, cement-block sheds, workshops, and junkyards; a billiard parlor for lottery tickets; a library, where only Noa seems to go; and a monument in memory of the fallen, with a cypress at each corner of the concrete column on which metallic letters read, THE BEAUTY OF ISRAEL IS SLAIN UPON THE HIGH PLAC S: "The penultimate letter is missing."

No wonder Theo's eyes are on the desert. As development novels go, *Don't Call It Night* is up there with Norman Rush's *Mating*, and maybe Voltaire's *Candide*. And what Theo is probably looking for across the scrub and desolation, on slate slopes in the blue distance and dark scree, besides Arabs and meaning, is the Zionist dramaturge himself, a vanishing act like Shane.

I experienced strange sensations, I saw and heard my legend being born. The people are sentimental; the masses do not see clearly. A light fog is beginning to rise around me and it may perhaps become the cloud in which I shall walk.

—Theodor Herzl

Before there was a Herzl Boulevard in Tel Kedar or anywhere else in Israel, there had to have been the godfather of Zionism—Theodor, the crackerjack journalist, mediocre playwright, "inveterate" misogynist, and manic-depressive brought so vividly to life in Ernst Pawel's biography *The Labyrinth of Exile*. Worshipped by his mother, doted on by his father, innocent of Marx and Freud, "amazingly untouched by winds of change

that revolutionized philosophy, literature, and the state in his own generation," he loved Wagner, feared women, and foresaw the cattle cars and
death camps. We can't understand him, says Pawel, without also understanding Prague, where he was born into ambivalence, and Vienna, with
its "apocalyptic temper," and Paris, too, where as a reporter he discovered
anti-Semitism (the Dreyfus case) and anarchism ("the voluptuous pleasure
of a great idea, and of martyrdom"). Pawel rereads his lame utopian novel,
Altneuland; finds in his diaries those "idea splinters" that created the "vatic
visionary"; sorts out the original plan (a mass conversion to Christianity!)
from subsequent revisions proposing to settle the Diaspora anywhere from
Argentina to Uganda; follows the argonaut to Paris, London, Rome, St.
Petersburg, and Constantinople as he petitions popes, emperors, sultans,
czars, and Rothschilds; and sits in on the assemblies where the playwright
hit on an "alchemy of mass manipulation" that "successfully transmuted
fantasy into power." Worn out at age forty-four, Herzl essentially killed
himself for the cause. He was nonetheless, says Pawel, "the first Jewish
leader in modern times." And what's more: "Thus far, the only one.
Those who came after him were politicians. Still, Jewish politicians in a
country of their own."

From Michael Berkowitz's enriching exploration of the rhetoric and
imagery of *Zionist Culture and West European Jewry Before the First World
War*, we get a broader picture of what Herzl and his brilliant and difficult
fellow disputants wrought at Basel in spite of Martin Buber. Against all
odds and despite a language question (Yiddish versus Hebrew), a built-in
Talmudic hostility to pluralism, the deepest Pale of Settlement suspicions,
and competing claims from revolutionary socialism, they composed an
entire mythopoeic *Gesamtkunstwerk*. They composed this total theater out
of European nationalism and German drinking songs; out of the idea of
the Promised Land and a cult of male friendship in student dueling fra-
ternities; out of paintings of the Wailing Wall and photographs of Palestinian flora; from selling books, trees, menorahs, kiddush cups, spice
boxes, and Holy Arks—not to mention merchandising an iconography of
Herzl himself, whose manly visage showed up on postage stamps, candy
wrappers, canned milk, and packs of cigarettes. As if to schoolmarm this
new macho image of an "orientalized" warrior Jew, on horseback with a
rifle and Arab headdress, they brought back the matriarchs: Sarah, Rachel,
Rebecca, Leah. It was agitation and it was propaganda, but it was also as
thrilling as Impressionism. "First," said Herzl to Nahum Sokolow, "there

has to be a home and peace for the Jews, then let them choose the culture they want. They will, of course, bring along with them many cultures, like bees who suck honey from different flowers and bring it all with them to one beehive; precisely this mixture will be far more interesting than one monotonous culture."

Just how interesting not even a playwright could have imagined, especially a playwright who somehow managed to forget there were Arabs already residing in this dreamscape, for whom Rachel's Tomb and David's Tower were as meaningless as Herder's moonshine on folksy essence or a postcard from Vienna with the angel Zion wearing a Star of David as her halo, pointing from a shtetl in Eastern Europe to a harvest in sanctified Palestine. Even so, before peace and before home, the Zionists did create a culture with heroes, songs, symbols, and a flag with blue stripes borrowed boldly from the *talit*. Berkowitz is flabbergasted: "A strange nationalism of the twentieth century—in the face of more aggressive and exclusive ideologies—which proclaims that the community producing the finest books, the most sublime poetry, a comprehensive research university, and an advanced agricultural-experiment station would 'win' a country."

Oz recalls what it felt like in his childhood: summer evenings and neighborhood scholars in his parents' garden; Revisionists from Odessa, socialist Zionists from Bobruisk, scholars of mysticism and of deserts, interpreters of Maimonides, Hegel, Nietzsche, Marx, Lassalle, and Jabotinsky; "atheists, vegetarians, and other assorted world reformers, each with his own personal plan for the salvation of the People and the Reform of Humanity in one fell swoop. Everyone knew exactly what had to be done—and at once. . . . When the Hebrew State was born it must be such-and-such, and if not, there would be no point to it." But: "All this is finished here."

Some of this fizz just didn't travel, as those of us who grew up pretending to be Jewish cowboys slaughtering Arab Nazis have reason to know from a visit to Ben Yehuda's pedestrian mall in Jerusalem after our rented car has been stoned on the Sabbath. Cypress and honeysuckle, vineyards and olive groves, vipers and goats, chalk and salt—"Not 'the land of the hart,'" Oz has pleaded, "and not 'the divine city reunited,' as the clichés would have it, but simply the State of Israel. Not the 'Maccabeans reborn' that Herzl talked of, but a warm-hearted, hot-tempered Mediterranean people that is gradually learning, through great suffering and in a tumult of sound and fury, to find release both from the bloodcurdling nightmares of the past and from delusions of grandeur, both ancient and modern."

So many wars, and before and after each, the scavenging of the bonepickers.

> *This generation has created a new religion, the religion of history, a belief in the history of its people as a religious faith. . . . It would not be an exaggeration to say that they fought with verses from the Bible. Through archaeology these people discover their "religious" values; in archaeology they find their religion, they learn that their forefathers were in this country 3,000 years ago. This is a value. By this they fought and by this they live.*
>
> —Yigael Yadin

This is what those Temple Mount tunnels are all about, besides a provocation and a real-estate expulsion scam. From Neil Asher Silberman's *A Prophet from Amongst You: The Life of Yigael Yadin*, we gather that for most of this century archeology in Israel has been a Zionist dig, an identity-politics daydream of a glorious antiquity segregated into ethnic cultures with unchanging racial characteristics. Think of the Dead Sea Scrolls as a ticket of admission and a warrant. Not for nothing did Yadin's father spend his student days at the University of Berlin. Translating "The War of the Sons of Light Against the Sons of Darkness," he might as well have been reading a right-wing newspaper. And his soldier son improved on him; a veteran of so many battles, including Irgun versus Palmach, a Lawrence of anti-Arabia, he must have imagined himself a Bronze Age warlord, especially at Hazor, in whose rubble he deciphered a rousting of inconvenient Canaanites. Yadin loved it; what afflatus: to stand at Megiddo, where Solomon built a temple on the ruins of Tuthmose III. To burrow into the caves of Nahal Hever and find a basket of skulls left over from the bandit prince himself, Bar Kokhba. To glory in Masada—never again. From fallen columns, charred beams, headless statues, smashed pottery, shattered frescoes, ceramic fragments, bronze coins, goatskin bags, incense shovels, Roman tunics, and some Aramaic scribbled on papyrus, to intuit Eretz Israel—the Covenant as Deed in Perpetuity, handed down by archers, cavalry, charioteers, catapult stones, and a battering ram. Never mind dissenting archeologists like Yohanan Aharoni, who counter-imagined a "gradual migration" of the Israelites into Canaan and a "social process" of assimilation instead of a turf war of gloryhounds with shofars for shillelaghs. Joshua was Yadin's kind of guy, a Little Big Horn in reverse.

Amazing that the ultra-Orthodox, for whom Mahmoud from East Jerusalem collects garbage and fixes sewers, should so much hate the bonepickers—"Death to the Hitlerite archeologists!"—who shovel the same sand-dune fantasies. On the other hand, Oz has also talked to the settlers, who sound like a column by A. M. Rosenthal:

> As soon as we finish this phase, the violence phase, step right up, it'll be your turn to play your role. You can make us a civilization with humanistic values here. Do the brotherhood-in-man bit—Light unto the Nations—whatever you want—the morality of the Prophets. . . . Be my guest. That's the way it is, old buddy: first Joshua and Jephthah the Gileadite break ground, wipe out the memory of Amalek, and then maybe afterward it's time for the Prophet Isaiah and the wolf and the lamb and the leopard and the kid and that whole terrific zoo. But only provided that, even at the end of days, we'll be the wolf and all the gentiles around here will be the lamb. Just to be on the safe side.

Is it any wonder that Theo can't sleep? That he needs Noa, who insists on knowing, "And where are we meant to be shining, and by whom is our shining required?" So what if their love isn't epic theater or grand opera or a Song of Solomon? That the best they can hope for is more modest than messianic—an autumn sonata, some rock-strewn tenderness, and maybe "the basic talent for life"? *What have we come here to be?* Oz himself wants to be Chekhov. He can't be, of course. He is magnanimous enough, but not exactly gentle. Still, trying to be Chekhov in a century written by Dostoyevsky is a kind of heroism. *L'chayim!*

Family Values, Like the House
of Atreus

Or the brothers Karamazov.

You will remember the scandalous goings-on of the best known family in the glory that was Greece, adultery being the least of it for Agamemnon and Clytemnestra, Aegisthus and Cassandra, Orestes and Elektra. Incest, infanticide, patricide, matricide, cannibalism, and other gaudy dysfunctions were almost all that Aeschylus ever wrote about, as if to hype his ratings. Nor do the soaps have anything on Sophocles. I mean, Oedipus murdered his father and married his mother, after which he was visually challenged. These are behaviors as lurid as Caligula's, who tried to marry his sister. Or Claudius, who, when it didn't work out with Messalina, had her tried for treason. Or Nero, who wasted his mom. Byzantine family life specialized in stranglings of heirs apparent in their bubbly baths, as well as many lopped-off hands. The best of their emperors, Justinian, married Theodora, the daughter of a bear keeper and a circus acrobat, who, before she showed up in Ravenna mosaics, is said by Procopius in his *Secret History* to have indulged in "bestial practices [and] unnatural traffic of the body," afterward complaining that Nature had short-changed her with only three apertures for intercourse. (Moreover, as if for pay cable: "Often in the theatre, in full view of all the people, she would spread herself out, and lie on her back on the ground. And certain slaves, whose special task it was, would sprinkle grains of barley over her private parts; and geese trained for the purpose would pick them off one by one with their beaks. . . . ") Richard III! Borgias! Romanovs! Medea and Catherine the Great were both Mommie Dearests. St. Augustine deserted a wife and two mistresses. Rousseau dropped off each of his five children by Thérèse at a foundling hospital. To get on with physics when times were tough, Einstein abandoned his baby daughter and never gave her another thought unless we count the theory of relativity as a sublimation. What Susano-o did in the cave of his Japanese Sun-Goddess sister Amaterasu was not only unspeakable but also bad for matriarchy. The Bible is a how-to manual on abusive sex and crazy violence in a sun-stunned, goat-munched desert.

Or the Mafia. There was an episode of *The Rockford Files* on NBC in 1977 called "Requiem for a Funny Box." Like many *Rockford*s, it involved the Mob. It took James Garner most of the hour to figure out that the Mob had been responsible for the murder of a comedian because the comedian had been conducting a homosexual affair with the son of a Mob boss. Confronted by his outraged capo father, the son with chilling dignity explained that he had felt this way about men since age seventeen and had even tried to talk about it to a father who refused to listen. This son also pointed out that, considering the deplorable nature of the family business, putting on high moral airs about *anything* was a bit thick. So the father ordered the son shot, too.

As old as any family value is the family curse. Most of our violence, like most of our sex, is domestic. But we *think* about both more than we *do* either, which is why we've got novelists, playwrights, poets, movies, and television. Naturally, gathered around the burning storyteller log in our home-entertainment centers, there is a part of us—kind, dutiful, thrifty, hygienic, repressed—that we'd like to see affirmed. But there is another part that is trapped, sad, and furious. This part seems to enjoy seeing all the bad stuff acted out by somebody else in public, as if the bloody fate of kings and queens were a caution; and the bad luck and hurtful sex of the undeserving rich, unfairly talented, and callously handsome were a comfort; and the punishment of the boring and the blameless by random evil and dreadful chance were somehow emancipating, an opportunity to start over after decks are cleared and worlds collapse—*as if we were fans of excessive behavior.* Who knows which kind of television is better for the domestic tranquility? Or what it means that TV itself, that sleek console full of contorted faces, is the most domestic of our distractions? Perhaps how families present themselves *to* the box is as important to think about as how those families are presented *on* the box. We are since the fifties more *fluid* in our homes, floating in and out of rooms like ghosts, according to the rhythms of spectacle on demand; more *episodic*

and *discontinuous*, like impatient vagabonds, choosing to tune in to fictitious lives and counterfeit experiences on the shape-shifting menu at the
electric Automat; *deritualized*, as if no longer grounded in our kitchens,
dining rooms, front porch, backyard, or stoop, as casual about eating as
we are about relationships, zapping emotions in a microwave for a quick
thaw or a loud pop; *vertiginous*, from a lightness of being.

Though situation comedies are now and always have been mostly about
families, they didn't start out as socializing agencies. That was what parents were for, and schools, churches, synagogues, armies, therapists, and
jail. From our bygone radio days through the first two decades of network
television, the best we could hope for from a sitcom, chugging along like
a choo-choo on its laugh track, was a certain rueful wisdom. As in the
slightest of John Cheever's short stories, perfectly nice people, who played
golf and raised flowers and never forgot to stock seed in their bird-feeding
stations, might cry "at the death of a cat, a broken shoelace, a wild pitch,"
but real pain and genuine suffering were "a principality, lying somewhere
beyond the legitimate borders of western Europe." Of course, in almost
every Cheever story, something happens to darken the screen. Men
drown and fall off mountains. Fifteen-year-old boys commit suicide. A
wife shoots her husband as he is about to hurdle the living room couch.
Someone is arrested for confusing a young woman with a Lucky Strike
cigarette. Someone else is devoured by his own dogs. A killer sings commercial jingles. Innocents incinerate when a can of charcoal igniter
explodes at a barbecue party. In the swimming pool: an undertow. In the
liquor closet: skeletons. In the tossed green salad: lighter fluid instead of
vinegar. In the snow: wolves.

   But not on TV. Sitcoms hardly daring to do more than suggest coping
mechanisms for such routine domestic crises as incompetence and mis-
chief were not about to explore the mysteries of intimacy, much less
promote a secret social agenda in favor of working women, class war, teen
sex, racial justice, secular humanism, gay rights, and spotted owls. We
aren't talking about art *or* politics. Can you really imagine gag writers in
New York or Hollywood trying to come up with two jokes a minute,
forty-four jokes for every half-hour sitcom, with time out for commercial
breaks, while simultaneously sneaking in subversive snippets from
Adorno or Wilhelm Reich? Then, as now, gag writers were trying to sell

a fail-safe concept to network programmers, who were selling audiences in the tens of millions to ad agency account executives, who were selling floor wax and reek to a benumbed republic and themselves to greedy clients. Then as now these gag writers read the same magazines and newspapers, saw the same movies, listened to the same music and skimmed the same reviews of the same best-selling books as everyone else. They also stole from each other. Yes, *if* a concept survived pilot-testing, *and* the public liked the actors, *and* the series lasted a couple of seasons, *and* the nation in its living room was ready to tolerate a NutraSweet version of the ideological fevers that already raged on the streets outside, then and only then, and even then only maybe, would the private pain, politics, and passion of the writer surface in a pointed wisecrack, a problematic new character, or a surprising ambiguity. And always *after* the culture already knew that it had major trouble on the event horizon, after the zeitgeist had already sneezed that sneeze.

For instance, the sixties: In a decade of civil-rights turmoil, the *only* lead character on a network sitcom who happened to be black was a high-school teacher on *Room 222*. In a decade of rioting on city streets, we sat down to watch *The Beverly Hillbillies*, *Green Acres*, and *Petticoat Junction*. In a decade of consciousness-raising and militant feminism, the small screen seethed with dreamy genies, kitchen witches, magical nannies, and flying nuns. In a decade of youthful opposition to war in Vietnam we got Gilligan, Dobie, Beaver, Dennis the Menace, *Hogan's Heroes*, Batman and Martians, *My Mother the Car*, and a spy who talked to his shoe. When, in the sixties, the angry and the disaffected petitioned the media for redress of grievance, we heard about it not on sitcoms but on the evening news with those images of water cannons and police dogs, or on *The Smothers Brothers Comedy Hour*, from Pat Paulsen and Pete Seeger, before they were canceled in favor of *Hee Haw*. Only after the election of Richard Nixon did sitcoms take a turn toward the subversive, as only after the abdication of Ronald Reagan would westerns make a comeback. Does this mean that television is a *counter*-culture?

But I can shuffle these concepts like a pack of cards and deal out almost any hand I want to. I can toss the cards in the air and assign arbitrary meaning to a random scatter. Why did black Americans disappear from sitcom television in the sixties? (After *Amos 'n' Andy* and *Beulah* in the fifties, it was perhaps a mercy.) Why did urban working-class Americans likewise vanish, after *The Life of Riley* (aircraft factory), unless we count

The Honeymooners (buses, sewers), till *Alice* (diner), *All in the Family* (tool and die), *Laverne & Shirley* (brewery) and *Taxi* (garage) in the seventies, after which of course *Roseanne* (plastics)? (We know they're working class because they go *bowling*.) Why are so many sitcoms set in TV newsrooms or on talk shows or at radio stations or in ad agencies, even once at a talent agent's, and why have so many of the male leads been newspaper columnists, usually covering sports? (Write what you know, like Herman Melville and Jackie Collins.) Once sitcoms moved out of the kitchen and into the living room, how come we always saw the same couch, directly facing the camera, as if the characters were laughing at us instead of the TV set *they* never seemed to look at, while *we* did little else? (Think of the screen as a looking-glass, with Alice on one side and Narcissus on the other, both thinking about Heidegger: in one sense obviously "being-there" [*Dasein*] but in another sense, just as obviously, "not-at-home" [*Unheimlichkeit, Nicht-zuhause-sein.*]) What was it about the eighties that caused so many dreadful sitcoms to succeed, while the best of them (*Frank's Place*) failed, and the hour-long dramatic series went into one of its cyclic tailspins? (I would blame it on King Babar and Queen Celeste in the White House and Ollie North in Neverland. What was Iran-Contra but a high-concept Tom Clancy–S. J. Perelman sitcom?)

Late in the seventies, a New York know-it-all with a flashy line in psychic yard goods, for whom TV criticism was merely a part-time indulgence, a kind of avuncular moonlighting between serious books on loftier subjects, I flew coach to California to present a paper at a conference on "Television and Human Sexuality" (Was it good for you? More taste! Less filling!) sponsored by a foundation that felt there was room for improvement. A car awaited me at LAX. This is because it's necessary in California to drive for two hours whether you want breakfast or transcendence. In my case, it was two hours north to Ojai, where golf links lay like a rug in a lap of little hills and swimming pools shivered like sheets of undulant tin. We slept at night in bungalows carved out of pastel chalk and candle wax, and rose at dawn to put on leopard-spotted Bermuda shorts and troop to tape-recorded T-group sessions. Among psychologists, sociologists, network veeps, and by-the-numbers tele-playwrights, I was the only media smarty-pants. In Wilfrid Sheed's savvy novel about a critic, *Max Jamison*, we were told:

He was in love with the way his mind worked, and he was sick of the way his mind worked. The first thing that struck you about it . . . was the blinding clarity, like a Spanish town at high noon. No shade anywhere. Yet not altogether lacking in subtlety. Very nice filigree work in the church. This was the mind they were asking him to blow.

You've heard such riffs. I was clever at the expense of those nuclear-family sitcoms of the fifties wherein it was permissible to cry but never to divorce and certainly not to die, not on *I Love Lucy, The Life of Riley, Mama, The Goldbergs, The Aldrich Family, Father Knows Best, The Trouble with Father, The Adventures of Ozzie and Harriet, December Bride, I Married Joan, My Little Margie, Blondie, Leave It to Beaver,* and *Make Room for Daddy.* Several exceptions proved semicontagious. In *Mr. Peepers* and *Our Miss Brooks,* Wally Cox and Eve Arden found families in the schools where they taught. And in *You'll Never Get Rich,* Phil Silvers, as Sergeant Bilko, found one in an army platoon. The idea that you could enlist or be drafted into a family led in the sixties to sitcom families on ships at sea (*McHale's Navy, Mister Roberts*), in marine barracks (*Gomer Pyle*), in prison camps (*Hogan's Heroes*), cavalry forts (*F Troop*), high schools (*Room 222*), a convent (*The Flying Nun*), and a spy agency (*Get Smart*). The nuclear family nevertheless kept on trucking in the sixties, from *Dick Van Dyke* to *Peyton Place,* missing the occasional parent (*Doris Day, Julia, The Courtship of Eddie's Father,* and *The Partridge Family*), adding the occasional animal (*Mister Ed, Gentle Ben, Flipper,* and *The Monkees*) and the occasional monster (*The Munsters, The Addams Family*). But nobody on the small screen smoked pot, dropped acid, seized a college building, burned down a ghetto, or fragged a Bilko in 'Nam.

As Wally and Phil were exceptions in the fifties, *That Girl* was the exception of the sixties, with Marlo Thomas as a wage-earning alternative to Donna Reed, Ann Sothern, and *Gidget. That Girl* made it possible in the seventies for a mysteriously single Mary Tyler Moore to have a career and even sex; for Diana Rigg, briefly, to be divorced; and for Bea Arthur's Maude to have the first and the last abortion on a prime-time series till *Picket Fences* in 1994. (Even so, marriage and childbirth still goosed ratings. As it had been for a raucous Lucy and a bewitched Samantha, delivering babies in the fifties and the sixties, so it was for Rhoda's wedding in 1974, and so it would be for Murphy Brown's baby Avery in

1992.) Mary, Valerie Harper, Linda Lavin, Cloris Leachman, Karen Valentine, Sandy Duncan, Loni Anderson, Penny Marshall, and Cindy Williams found surrogate families in the seventies on radio and at TV stations, in dress shops, ad agencies, law firms, acting studios, beer halls, and consumer groups, as did Hal Linden at a police station, Gabe Kaplan at a high school, Dick Van Dyke on a soap, Bob Newhart in group therapy, and Alan Alda in Korea. Not that the family burden didn't remain primarily nuclear: *All in the Family, Good Times, Happy Days, Benson, The Jeffersons,* and *Mork & Mindy.* Briefly, even Don Rickles came home from *his* ad agency to a wife and child who pretended to want him. But there were at least more working women, more black faces, and some fallout. As *Maude* faced up to abortion, and *M*A*S*H* to war, and *Good Times* to heroin, *All in the Family* sought to "cauterize" bigotry with taboo-busting incantations of "spic," "coon," "dago," "hebe," and "fairy."

So, I said, television is catching up with America. And because everybody in Ojai is afraid of our keynote speaker, Germaine Greer, all we have talked about, so far, is what this means for women. And certainly—if we duck our heads in order not to see the network movies whose only premise is a female menaced, in a lonely bedroom late at night in an empty suburban house, in a stalled car on the deserted road in a surprise monsoon, in a telephone booth on a mean city street in a problematic neighborhood, in a high-rise elevator or, especially, the underground parking garage—the women we see on TV more closely resemble the women we meet in the world than they used to: Instead of Harriet Nelson, Jane Wyatt, Barbara Billingsley, Betty Furness, Grandma Moses, the Miltown tranquilizer, or a White Tornado, they remind us of Annie Oakley, Amelia Earhart, Margaret Sanger, and Eleanor Roosevelt. Next year in Burbank: Antigone.

But what about men? Why is it on sitcom television, between, say, Robert Young and *The Waltons,* that the American father is so generally a mishap, such a Dagwood Bumstead antihero sandwich? From Desi Arnaz in *I Love Lucy,* Stu Erwin in *The Trouble with Father,* Ozzie Nelson in *The Adventures of Ozzie and Harriet,* William Bendix in *The Life of Riley,* Charles Farrell in *My Little Margie,* and Danny Thomas in *Make Room for Daddy,* to Carroll O'Connor in *All in the Family,* Tom Bosley in *Happy Days,* John Amos in *Good Times,* Sherman Hemsley in *The Jeffersons,* and Redd Foxx in *Sanford and Son,* the Sitcom Dad can't lace up the shoe on the foot in his mouth without falling off his rocker, into contumely.

According to the theater, we are James Tyrone in *Long Day's Journey Into Night* and Willy Loman in *Death of a Salesman*. According to the movies, we have devolved from Gregory Peck in *To Kill a Mockingbird* to Charles Bronson in *Death Wish*. According to the men among our novelists, well, from Melville and Twain and Henry James to Malamud, Mailer, and Vonnegut, they've been either silent or evasive. Faulkner violently engaged the generations, but his children were flowering curses, clocks wired to bombs. Fitzgerald and Hemingway were bright little boys to the bitter end, waving wooden swords. (Who knew from *Gatsby* or *Tender Is the Night* that Scott was writing such splendid letters to his daughter? Only after Papa ate a gun would he worry, in a posthumous novel, about what fathers do to sons.) In Updike, a child is for feeling guilty about after a father commits adultery. Bellow's no help. Both Eliot Nailles, in Cheever's *Bullet Park*, and Robert Slocum, in Joseph Heller's *Something Happened*, commute to dispiriting jobs in New York from homes in exurban Connecticut to which they've removed their families to spare them the frightful city. Slocum's boy stops talking to him: "He used to have dreams, he said, in which the door to our room was closed and he could not get in to see us. Now I have dreams that the door to his room is closed, and I can't get in to see him." Tony Nailles goes to bed and won't get up: "I just feel terribly sad." Neither father can protect either son—from what, exactly? From Dad, perhaps: so fearful of failure that he secretes it. Failure is his homespun art.

Anyway, the next morning at Ojai, we were asked in our T-group by the "facilitator" with the kindly voice and the gentle beard to close our eyes and talk about our sex lives. What? Yes. Well: very nice filigree work in the church. After which, three of the very best writers in the sitcom business, James L. Brooks, Allan Burns, and Ed Weinberger, fresh from *The Mary Tyler Moore Show*, *Maude*, *Lou Grant*, and *Taxi*, on their way to *The Cosby Show*, *Alf*, *The Simpsons*, and *The Critic*, ganged up on an NBC vice-president for broadcast standards (a censor). Brooks had heard that any script submitted to NBC touching in any way on the subject of homosexuality was sent by the net for vetting to *a gay dentist in New Jersey*. Could that possibly be true? *Not* true, the veep replied: In New Jersey, he may once upon a time have been a dentist, but he was now a *psychotherapist*. We stared for a while at the clouds in our coffee. Then Weinberger waggled a hand. "You mean," he said, "you mean . . . there really *is* a Tooth Fairy?"

The point here is not to stamp one's foot at a wisecrack that may be offensive to gays, or to dentists, or to New Jersey. When push comes to shove, at Stonewall or on Rodeo Drive, Brooks, Burns, and Weinberger are likely more liberal than the rest of us NIMBYs and certainly more fun to talk to, even in a T-group, than most of the people you meet at a New York literary cocktail party, obsessing about real estate. The point is, this is what sitcom writers do. They turn everything, even censorship, into wisecracks. It should not surprise us that Diane English and Jerry Seinfeld turned O.J.'s white Ford Bronco into a sight gag in the fall of 1994. Can you imagine what the gang at Sid Caesar's *Your Show of Shows*—Carl Reiner, Mel Brooks, Neil Simon, Larry Gelbart, Woody Allen—would have done to O.J.? To Michael Jackson? To a John Wayne Bobbitt? Or, for that matter, to Woody, Mia, and Soon-yi? *That's what they get those big bucks for and why Chekhov doesn't.* From *Cheers* did you really expect the loneliness of the long-distance runner or a goalie's anxiety at the penalty kick? From *Home Improvement*, a class-action suit against the Ford Motor Company for exploding Pinto gas tanks? The surprise ought not to be that nothing under our sun is safe from the trivializing one-liner. The surprise is that, every once in a sitcom while, there is actually something new under that sun, like Hawkeye's nervous breakdown in an episode of *M*A*S*H*; or Judd Hirsch on *Taxi* falling in love with the radio voice of an obese dispatcher and learning just how thin our culture is, how starved for sympathy; or Jane Curtin's discovering late in *Kate & Allie*'s run what it felt like to be homeless; or Tim Reid on *Frank's Place* taking the paper bag test to see if his skin color was light enough for membership in the New Orleans men's club; or Dixie Carter on *Designing Women* opening her mouth to deliver an impassioned aria on Anita Hill and Clarence Thomas; or Roseanne opening *her* mouth to kiss Mariel Hemingway.

A decade passed before I dared again to leave the house for another conference, this time at Brown University in Providence on "The Changing American Family." There's no reason why I couldn't have repeated the same growl about dumb dads—Know-It-Alls are invited to summit meetings in order to repeat themselves and secure a niche; it's like performance art—updated, maybe, with a new emphasis on "the single father epidemic." While single fathers have always been around on network television, more often widowed than divorced, from *My Little Margie, The*

Rifleman, and *Brave Eagle* in the fifties; to *My Three Sons, Bonanza,* and *The Andy Griffith Show* in the sixties; to *Nanny and the Professor, The Courtship of Eddie's Father, Sanford and Son,* and *Hello Larry* in the seventies, they had seemed in the eighties to undergo a fruit-fly proliferation—*Benson, Coach, Empty Nest, Silver Spoons, You Again, Rags to Riches, Dads, My Two Dads, Paradise, Free Spirit, Raising Miranda, I Married Dora,* and *First Impressions.* (The odd trend would spill over into the nineties with *Blossom, City, Uncle Buck, American Dreamer, Sunday Dinner, It Had to Be You, Second Half, Me and the Boys, Daddy's Girls,* and *The Critic*). What could this possibly mean? Although divorce was catching up to death as an excuse for single fatherhood, and many of these dads at least had rudimentary nurturing skills, the facts were out of whack. According to the U.S. Census Bureau, 25 percent of all children in the Real America lived with single parents in 1989. But in this same Real America *89 percent* of all those single parents were *women.* Moreover, 57 percent of the children who lived with single parents were black and 32 percent Hispanic. Whereas, in TV America, more than 90 percent of all the Little People with just a single Big One in the backyard bomb shelter seemed to be yogurt-colored.

It would also have been necessary to face up to the two most important television fathers of the eighties, neither bearing much resemblance to reality for the rest of us. One, of course, was Bill Cosby. Cosby had originally proposed a blue-collar sitcom. ABC turned him down. He then upwardly mobilized the concept to white-collar professional, starring himself as Dr. Heathcliff Huxtable, an obstetrician practicing out of his Brooklyn Heights brownstone; Phylicia Rashad as Clair, his lawyer wife who left that home to toil nobly every day for Legal Aid; and five children for whom a wise, if sarcastic, dad would always be there, whether they wanted him or not. ABC turned *that* down, too. NBC was shrewder.

The other important father of the eighties was Edward Woodward as Robert McCall, in *The Equalizer:* a retired intelligence agent who set up shop, in a Manhattan apartment to die for, as a last-resort detective, bodyguard, and avenging angel, doing good as a way of doing penance for his nasty past in Latin America, Southeast Asia, and the Middle East. While McCall's relations with his own son, Scott, were strained, it was amazing how often the children of strangers in trouble happened on his classified newspaper ad and left desperate messages on his answering machine. To which messages he invariably responded. This was post-Freudian and deeply satisfying: the mythic father all children wish for and none of us has ever had, *or ever will have*, who promises to protect us from the Dark Side—exactly like Ronald Reagan.

But not many of us work at home in such agreeable neighborhoods as Brooklyn Heights with friends like Stevie Wonder, B. B. King, and the Count Basie Band to drop in. Even fewer of us are guilt-stricken intelligence operatives, any more than we are a Captain Ahab or the Lone Ranger, which is why we watch television instead of leading insurrections. We don't even work for ad agencies. We are, like an Al Bundy and a Homer Simpson, less thrilling. Not old enough yet for a reptilian retirement in Florida, we seem never to have been as young as the demographically desirable NYPNS (Neat Young People in Neat Situations), DINKS (Double Income, No Kids), or what the mystery novelist David Handler calls YUSHIES (Young Urban Shitheads). Did I really have to think about Yup instead of fatherhood? Of course I did. As a professional critic, it was my zeitgeist duty to think about *whatever* the crybaby boomers were thinking about, which was always their conflicted, Y-person selves. As a guy said to a gal in the TV movie *Bare Essentials*: "The only food-gathering you've ever done is at a salad bar."

For instance: *thirtysomething*. Sensitive Jewish Michael and supermom Hope and bearded Elliot and blonde Nancy and red-haired Melissa and long-haired Gary and careerist Ellyn felt bad every Tuesday night from 1987 to 1991 about children, adultery, Thanksgiving, computers, and the sixties. Growing up hurts so much you want to suck your big toe. They rode their anxieties, like Melissa's Exercycle. Or wore them, like Hope's Princeton T-shirt. They played parent the way they played mud volleyball or laser tag. For all the smart talk, their frontal lobes seemed full of video rentals instead of books or politics; medium tepid instead of *Big Chill*. They were as lukewarm and secondhand in their erotic fantasies as in their attitudinizing, as if they'd bought the whole Xerox package of other people's prefab experiences already market-tested by Michael and Elliot at, of course, their ad agency. There was no true north in them, nor any bravery.

Who needed this in my living room? I could leave the house, and go to the corner, and find an overmuch of such people in my own yupscale neighborhood: sun dried as if in extra-virgin olive oil, crouched to consume their minimalist bistro meals of cilantro leaves, medallions of goat cheese, and half a scallop on a bed of money; gaudy balloons of avarice and ego tethered by their red suspenders to all that's trendiest, waiting with twenty-four-carat coke spoons for Tom Wolfe or Dave Letterman. By day this block belonged to barbers, dry cleaners, shoemakers, and locksmiths. But at night, in the sports bars, pubs, and ethnic restaurants, the Y-people bloomed like henbane or belladonna and you heard their wounded wail: "Gimme, gimme." For their many sins, they had been punished on a Black Monday with the stock market crash of October 1987. But they'd forgiven themselves and promptly risen, almost the very next night, with an hour of prime-time television of their very own, like a platinum American Express card.

Why was *thirtysomething* such a popular success and *The Days and Nights of Molly Dodd* a network flop, shuffled off to cult status on Lifetime cable? Wasn't Blair Brown a boomer, too, eating Chinese, teaching piano, listening to rockabilly in a West Side apartment building where the elevator never quite properly stopped to meet the floor, as Molly never quite met life at the proper angle? But Molly was a poet, divorced from a jazz musician. And worked in a bookshop, where D. H. Lawrence was actually spoken. And then at a publishing house, where she wasn't on the best-seller fast track. And dated, instead of an account executive or a pork-belly future, a black cop, whose name was Nathaniel Hawthorne. And was lusted after by her own psychiatrist, who happened also to be female. And went out after work to night school and museums instead of sports bars. A brave and baffled Molly made her own experiences. You'd never catch *her* in silk jacquards, tapered Lord & Taylor tunics, tobacco-suede Euforia boots, and Lady Datejust Oyster Perpetuals, eating steamed skate and pumpkin seeds on Columbus Avenue, smelling like the guts of a sperm whale. And yet the television culture disdained her almost as much as it had disdained Geena Davis and Alfre Woodard as storefront lawyers in *Sara*, or the Linda Kelsey who had quit the rat race to teach preschoolers in *Day by Day*.

However, by the time I got to Providence I was a humbler and chastened Know-Only-Some-of-It. In Kyoto, in front of Takanobu's *Portrait of Taira no Shigemori*, a Japanese scholar told André Malraux that "You want to be *in* the painting, whereas we want to be outside it. European painting has always wanted to catch the butterflies, eat the flowers, and sleep with the dancers." As if television were my European painting, I had spent a good portion of the eighties alone in my house, wanting to catch, eat, and dance with those butterflies, flowers, and dancers. I was hitting bottom, and then in the beginning stages of a recovery from alcoholism.

Never mind the horror stories about hospitals and estrangement. You have already seen their equivalent, if not in your own lives, then certainly in the TV movies: a wife hiding out in a West Side loft, with her spices and her afghan; the children in exile in Madison, Prague, and Taipei; the X-rays, EKGs, and CAT scans; the old people who seemed, in their tatty bathrobes, to be practicing a martial art on the lawn each morning and the young people of the adolescent wing who roamed in packs at night in their fluted Ionian deathgowns; the withdrawal dreams of basilisks, scorpions, and ravens' heads; of peacock tails and Pontic rhubarb. In Saul Bellow's *More Die of Heartbreak* one character asks another: "Uncle, how do you picture death—what's your worst-case scenario for death?" Uncle replies: "Well, from the very beginning there have been pictures—inside and outside. And for me the worst that can happen is that those pictures will stop."

When I came back from the hospital to an empty house, television no longer seemed an upstart medium, amusing in its presumption, about which to sermonize and smarty-pant. There were, to be sure, the video cassettes that arrived now by messenger and express mail, the same size and as self-important as the books I spent the other half of my professional life reviewing. I no longer had to leave the house and visit the networks and wait around in darkened anterooms for a member of the appropriate craft union to replace a cartridge and punch up a preview tape. I had only to consult the clock of my convenience, settle my fragile self in front of the VCR, and, like a car alarm, anticipate being burgled. But tape was not enough, nor was there enough tape, to fill all the holes in my apprehension. I needed TV in a different way. And it was like looking through the window of a washing machine during a spin-dry cycle, at tumbles of bras and socks, at twisted arms and severed heads. I was, suddenly, watching TV as a civilian. I fell into it, as if to water bed. After a decade of passing out and coming to, I couldn't sleep at all. Like some Aztec Mother Serpent, my metabolism was shucking skins. There are only so many books and tapes a pair of eyes can read or watch, so many words a pair of hands can process, so many walks a pair of feet can plod, around the block or to a meeting. At those amazing meetings, in an underground network of church basements, over the cardboard cups of lousy coffee in a blue smog of cigarette smoke, we told each other stories to get us through the night. These many stories were really merely one, about a lost child in a black forest of bad chemicals.

None of this was television's fault. But enough of it showed up on television to suggest to a disordered mind, if not coincidence or causality, at least an eerie series of correspondences, a hanging-together of related metaphors as the metaphors had bunched up in, say, Nahuatl poetry, or Roman and Gothic worldviews, among Mings and Renaissance Florentines. So I watched *Hill Street Blues* not only because it was the best TV series of the eighties and not even because Daniel J. Travanti as Frank Furillo and Joe Spano as Henry Goldblume had assumed the Alan Alda Hawkeye role model of the New Man Who Has Non-Predatory Feelings, but because Furillo was a recovering alcoholic, and when Kiel Martin's LaRue finally got himself to an AA meeting, there was Frank already in The Rooms. I watched *Cagney & Lacey*, not only because such a partnership of class-conscious fast-talking street-smart feminists was so singular as to have become Gloria Steinem's favorite show, nor because anyone could have guessed that Sharon Gless and Tyne Daly in New York would make Thelma and Louise imaginable in Hollywood, but because Chris Cagney so obviously had a drinking problem, and when she finally got around to doing something about it after her father's death, the series dogged her every step of the difficult way, all twelve of them. Toward the end of the decade, while I liked everything else about *Murphy Brown*, its breezy nonchalance on the matter of Murphy's drinking ticked me off, as if alcoholism were another of her quirks or cranks. In the pilot, Murphy was just back from Betty Ford. Thereafter at Phil's she drank designer water. One New Year's Eve, subtracting scotch, she was minus a sense of humor. Otherwise the flagrant behaviors of her drinking days were recalled by her officemates as comic romps. So much for recovery. It's as easy as having a baby, if you forget about both for weeks at a time. And having a baby, of course, was another half-baked, unbright idea that occurred to *Murphy*'s writers and shouldn't have, not for fear of ruffling Dan Quayle's indignant feathers but because even the sleepiest of us knows a real-world Murphy would have aborted. Compare such glibness to the gallows-humor sitcom fashioned for the nineties by John Larroquette—*Under the Volcano* with *Barney Miller*'s laugh track—from his own experience of bottoms and recovery, which partook of memory, process, and duration.

On the other trembling hand it was hard for me to watch either *Cheers* or *St. Elsewhere*. I needed never again to be in bars or hospitals: those dreamlike Easter Islands, with their long-eared priest-kings, their birdman cults, their ancestor worship, their megalithic petroglyphs, those great stone faces under black-rock top hats on Cubist penguins with their goofy, abstract, Bob Hope look. For the only time in my life, I sounded even to myself like Goethe: "How dare a man have a sense of humor when he considers his immense burden of responsibilities toward himself and others? I have no wish to pass censure on the humorists. After all, does one have to have a conscience? Who says so?" But whatever a Jackie Gleason drank on stage in the fifties and a Dean Martin in the sixties and seventies, it wasn't funny, as Sid Caesar, Carol Burnett, Dick Van Dyke, Susan Saint James, and Don Johnson had strobelit reason to know.

Obviously, this is no way to review television. You have to watch *St. Elsewhere* so that you will be prepared when some of the same writers come up with *Homicide: Life on the Streets*, as you have to watch *A Year in the Life* to understand where *Northern Exposure* and *I'll Fly Away* came from. But it is also an important way that civilians *do* watch television, as if by periscope under the heavy water of our own vagrant needs and monomaniacal compulsions, down where we are bottom-feeding like octopods on the fluffy bacteria and tube worms of everything we feel bad about, all those thermal vents in a problematic self. While I was reading and reviewing Gabriel García Márquez, Salman Rushdie, Toni Morrison, Milan Kundera, Nadine Gordimer, Don DeLillo, Günter Grass, Christa Wolf, Kobo Abe, and Cynthia Ozick, I was afraid of *Cheers*. What if I were coming home from teaching English as a second language in an overcrowded public school, or an assembly-line factory job, or milking cows and greasing tractors? What if after a hostile takeover, leveraged buyout, or obsolesence, I hadn't a job at all? Or grew up uncertain of my sexual identity? Or was running out my string in a geriatric gulag where, like a rhododendron, I was misted twice a day? Or were poor, black, gay, Inuit, Rosicrucian, or a mixed grill of the above? What then would I require of television? How would it, all unwitting, muddle with *that* mind?

Years ago, when my daughter was five, together we watched *The Littlest Angel*, a Christmas special about a shepherd boy who dies, goes to heaven, returns briefly to earth to collect his box of favorite things, and then gives that box to God (E. G. Marshall) as a birthday gift for the Christ child. While I remember objecting to the idea of all that polishing and vacuuming in heaven (the Protestant ethic of drudgery even unto afterlife), *The Littlest Angel* seemed otherwise harmless. Not so to my daughter. First, when the shepherd boy looked around at the other angelic gifts, he was so ashamed of his, he tried to hide it. God, of course, noticed. "God is sneaky," my daughter said. "He can see around corners. He'd *never* lose at hide-and-seek." Next, after the program, she burst into tears and couldn't sleep. It took me an hour to find out what upset her so. She had noticed that when the little boy returns to retrieve his box of favorite things, his parents can't see or hear him. That must be what death is.

We hadn't watched the same program. I couldn't protect her from *The Littlest Angel*; no one protected me from *The Yearling*. Childhood isn't *Sesame Street*, nor adulthood sitcoms. Suppose Amy hadn't eventually graduated from *The Brady Bunch*, *The Partridge Family*, and the afternoon soaps she taped all through college, to trade in her prurient preoccupation with Jim Morrison of the Doors for an equally obsessive crush on Martin Luther and become a doctoral candidate in Reformation history? Suppose, instead, she had turned into a professor of American Studies at Hampshire College, like Susan J. Douglas. Douglas published in 1994 a remarkable meditation on growing up female with the mass media, *Where the Girls Are*, in which she watched the same TV programs, went to the same films, read the same magazines, and listened to the same music as every other alert munchkin. Through her eyes, what sort of television culture do we see? She had to wait a long time, from Molly Goldberg and Alice Kramden, for a Joyce Davenport. Why did Stephanie Zimbalist need a "Remington Steele" in the first place? What is a young girl being told by *Queen for a Day*, *The Newlywed Game*, June Cleaver, Elly May Clampett, and Lily Munster? By Connie Stevens as Cricket in *Hawaiian Eye* and Diane McBain as Daphne in *Surfside Six*? By *Police Woman* and *Wonder Woman* and *Bionic Woman*? There's nothing *abstract* about Douglas's gratitude to NBC News for Liz Trotta, Norma Quarles, and Aline Saarinen, nor her celebration of *Kate & Allie*, *Cagney & Lacey*, *China Beach*, and *Designing Women*. While I saw *The Equalizer* as a Superdad, Douglas resented him as a collector of wounded women. While I was admiring a bionic Lindsay Wagner for her lioness graces, the violin string of restless intelligence that refined the shadows and planes of her good-bones face, Douglas deplored the dumbing-down of "liberation" into narcissism: Buns of Steel! On the other hand, while I disdained *Charlie's Angels* as a harem fantasy (except for Kate Jackson, the Thinking Angel with a whiskey rasp of a voice, the Lauren Bacall–Blythe Danner erotic croak), Douglas identified with a trio of adventurous and resourceful young women who saved themselves and each other while occasionally cross-dressing.

Periscopes! Like God and television, we see around corners. In the popular culture, we all play hide-and-go-seek. We find our models in the oddest places: a glint here, a shadow there, a scruple, a qualm, some style and attitude. Douglas reminds us that pop culture is more than TV. She found an abundance of possible selves in music: in the Shirelles and Cyndi Lauper; in Joan Baez, Diana Ross, and Janis Joplin; in Aretha Franklin, Bette Midler, and Madonna. But also at the movies with Joan Crawford and the Hepburns (Kate in *Pat and Mike*, Audrey as Holly Golightly); in books by Pearl Buck, Simone de Beauvoir, Betty Friedan, and Susan Brownmiller; in sports, with Billie Jean King, and in politics with Shirley Chisholm. And so was the enemy everywhere. To save her own sanity, Douglas had to swim out from under magazines like *Cosmo*, *Seventeen*, *Glamour*, and *Redbook*; from Revlon and Victoria's Secret; from *Mary Poppins*, James Bond, and biker movies; from Norman Mailer, Hugh Hefner, liposuction, and Ultra Slim-Fast.

To which we might add a *Whole Earth Catalog* of other shadows on our blameless childhoods. As much as the fifties were *I Love Lucy*, Howdy Doody, and Davy Crockett's coonskin cap, or Dick Nixon and Charles Van Doren in prime-time tears, they were also Korea and *Peanuts*, Marilyn Monroe and Rosa Parks, Joe Stalin and atom-bomb air-raid drills, Joe McCarthy and polio, hula hoops and Grace Kelly, Levittown and Ralph Ellison, Edsels *and* Sputniks, Castros and Barbies. (From M. G. Lord's 1994 "unauthorized biography" of that doll, *Forever Barbie*, we would learn that Mattel Corporation practically invented the advertising of children's toys on television in 1955, committing most of its entire net worth of five hundred thousand dollars to commercials for a jack-in-a-box, a Burp Gun, and a Uke-A-Doodle on *The Mickey Mouse Club*, paving the way for Mortal Kombat.) Instead of Barbie, I had a Lone Ranger atomic bomb ring with a color snapshot of the mushroom cloud, available in the late forties from General Mills for a couple of Kix cereal box tops. I also loved those horror comics that so alarmed congressional committees and psychiatrists like Dr. Frederic Wertham in the early fifties, as if they'd never heard of Grimm's fairy tales. Nowadays, we only pay attention to cartoons if they show up on TV, like *The Simpsons* on Fox or *Beavis and Butt-head* on MTV. We haven't noticed, at the candy store or the head shop, Swamp Things, Freak Brothers, the Flaming Carrot, Reid Fleming (World's Toughest Milkman), Elektrassassin (Cold War Beast), Dr. Manhattan (the Princeton physicist who fusions himself into a human hydrogen bomb) or *Love and Rockets* (lesbians who wear combat boots and speak barrio Spanish). Plus any number of musclebound acid-heads into the superheroics for the money, the sex, the violence, the publicity, and the chance to dress up in their underwear.

For that matter, as much as the sixties may have been about Dylan and Joplin and Vietnam, they were also about *Blow Up*, Kurt Vonnegut, and Twiggy. As the seventies were about disco and the eighties about AIDS. Think of jet planes and birth control pills, of drive-ins and drive-bys, of transistors and malls. As Billy Joel once explained: "We Didn't Start the Fire."

This much can still be said for our troubled culture: the sexual abuse of children not only turns the stomach and breaks the heart; it wounds the soul as well. It can't be figured according to any ordinary moral arithmetic. The violation of a child also violates our fundamental notions of ourselves as guardians, what we owe to the innocent and defenseless, how we feel about family and authority, who we want and need to be. Faced with such violation, our helplessness is both a personal nightmare and a subversion of the social fabric. We want to avert our eyes. No wonder Dostoyevsky's *The Possessed* was published for decades without Stavrogin's confession.

Something About Amelia started it on television, in 1984, with Glenn Close as the incredulous mother, Roxanne Zal as the abused daughter, and Ted Danson, already two years into *Cheers*, as the father who promised never, ever, to do it again. But between *Something About Amelia* and the close of the 1980s an odd thing happened. In spite of facts we knew perfectly well—acts of domestic violence occur every fifteen seconds; 4 percent of American families are abusive to children; almost 3 million cases of suspected child abuse were reported in 1992; more than a third of American girls are sexually molested, *usually by men they trust*—the focus on television somehow shifted from family to strangers. And so did the blame except insofar as parents were at fault for entrusting their children to these strangers. Especially culpable were moms who insisted on punching a clock or playing tennis when they should have been home with their angelfood cupcakes—unless of course they were *welfare* mothers, who didn't *deserve* children. (Although we can't ever *prove* anything about pop culture and the zeitgeist, we can at least point to a *correspondence* between this new network emphasis and the great porn scare, the Christian fundamentalist backlash, homophobia, "victimology," and a Reagan-Bush antifeminist agenda.) *Amelia*'s own Ted Danson was part of the shift, when he coproduced a 1986 TV version of Jonathan Kellerman's novel *When the Bough Breaks*, starring himself as the child psychologist who tracked down and smashed a ring of well-heeled, politically connected pedophiles. Suddenly, as in *I Know My First Name Is Steven*, kidnapping made a comeback. Or, in *Judgment* (1990), the Roman Catholic Church was accused in court of covering up for a Louisiana priest who'd seduced altar boys ("We're going to sue God!" exulted Jack Warden), as the mother church and Canadian provincial government itself would go on trial in *The Boys of St. Vincent* miniseries (1994). Worst of all in these paranoia sweepstakes, in both *Do You Know the Muffin Man?* (1989) and *Unspeakable Acts* (1990), preschool day-care centers were nests of pedophilic vipers. Behind Tiny Tot's locked doors at afternoon naptime . . .

But the revised emphasis elsewhere was on the barbarians who cruised outside the gates. *I Know My First Name Is Steven*, the 1989 NBC miniseries, was a very Grimm fairy tale at the end of which everybody was eaten up by guilt instead of wolves. (What are fairy tales, anyway, if not coded fables of child abuse?) In real life, a dreamy and troubled seven-year-old Steven Stayner was kidnapped in 1972, on his way home from school in Merced, California. In real life, in motels and shacks all over northern California, he was sexually abused. In real life, he escaped *seven years later* and only when his captor stole another little boy. And in real life, he couldn't go home again. He wasn't the same boy, his family wasn't the same family, and the very idea of "home" had been violated. TV told this savage story without a fabric softener. As Steven's father, John Ashton was all but destroyed by bewilderment. As Steven's mother, Cindy Pickett found you can't love somebody back to health. As Parnell, the horn-rimmed, chain-smoking kidnapper, Arliss Howard was a soft-spoken monster with delusions of divine afflatus. As teenaged Steven, Corin Nemec came back to Merced a self-blaming wild boy. By devoting as much time to what happened after his homecoming as to the abduction, *I Know My First Name Is Steven* did the uncompromising work of art. It was as if Spielberg's *Empire of the Sun* had gone on to tell us the future of the blank-eyed boy who survived the war. Steven's kidnapping seems to have corrupted everybody. They didn't know how to feel about what they would rather not imagine. It's not just that the Brothers Grimm taught us to fear Black Forests, nor that we have always been fascinated by tales of wild boys raised by wolves, as we've been fascinated since the start of our country by the captivity narratives of children stolen by Indians and of slaves in the Middle Passage; and, since late in the nineteenth century, by Freud's seduction theory; and, since the middle of the twentieth, by death-camp horrors. Family itself is a kind of ecology, an interdependence of organisms in an environment. No matter how arbitrary that environment is, the organism adjusts or dies. *People*, unfortunately, can adjust to almost anything, and yet hate our own adaptations. Like Steven, we may not forgive ourselves. It's one thing to tell our children not to talk to strangers. It's another if the *child* is a stranger, to us and to himself.

Even scarier, because more artful, was *The Boys of St. Vincent*. Just minutes into the first hour of a nightmare miniseries about an orphanage in Newfoundland in the 1970s, the janitor tells the superintendent: "There are things in life that are broken and can't be fixed." Halfway through, what's broken beyond fixing has come to include the little boys abused by the All Saints Brothers *and* the very idea of accountability. The police suppress a report of their investigation. The Church and the Ministry of Justice conspire at a cover-up. Brother Lavin, who insisted that his "special boy" call him "Mother," is permited to leave both the Church and Newfoundland for Montreal where he will father children of his own. When I first saw *The Boys of St. Vincent*, at a screening of Banff Television Festival prize-winners, most Canadians hadn't. Its broadcast up north had been delayed until the conclusion of the trial in the case that inspired director John N. Smith, who cowrote the script with producer Sam Grana and poet Des Welsh. More than a legal nicety, this delay seemed a scruple. So powerful was the film, trapped in dream-speed, drugged with menace, painterly yet visceral, you wanted to lay about you with an ax. So mesmerizing was Henry Czerny as Lavin, handsome, even dashing, princely but satanic, that you saw him in your cutthroat mirror like an evil eye. So corrupt were the agencies charged with protecting these abandoned boys, for whom there was neither appeal nor meaning, that you felt orphaned yourself: bereft. Part I was medieval: Never mind the telephone or the swimming pool where a ten-year-old discovered what being Brother Lavin's special boy really meant. At St. Vincent's, 1975 could be 1275, all passion and agony in a gothic vault of skeletal shafts, stained glass, and morbid candles; gargoyles and Gregorian chants. With a crucifix slung in the belt like a cudgel, in cassocks like black sails, the brothers patrolled corridors and tucked-in barracks beds as if they were cowboy Templars. Obedience had nothing whatever to do with God; power was sickly erotic; the only gravity was despair. Part II jumped to 1990: We met the damaged boys grown up around their wounds, and their corruptors at bay in the headlines. The modern imagination tried to come to grips with age-old evil in the distinctively modern manner, with a courtroom trial, a royal commission, a psychiatrist, and a call-in radio talk show. But the mind fell down like a torn black kite. So much for *Boys Town*.

No such art, but similar fears, applied to *Do You Know the Muffin Man?* and *Unspeakable Acts*. Until *Muffin Man*, we had not seen on television so many children so vilely used, so numb and inward, so trapped in shame, so disbelieved by so many adults, so tormented by their peers, so ridiculed on cross-examination by a hateful defense attorney. Nor had we experienced to such an excruciating degree the corresponding powerlessness of parents unequipped to make "the bad thing" all right, cancel it out, even to exact revenge. At a *preschool*, of all places . . . the hooded figures, burning candles, and pornographic Polaroids. About the "satanic" component of *Muffin Man*—the magic names (Virgo, Isis) and murdered rabbits, the bloody altars and black-mass pentagrams—I expressed some reservations in a magazine article in October 1989. But this was the lazy agnosticism of the armchair critic. You make reservations, but never actually go anywhere. Besides, had not *Muffin Man* been "inspired" by a "true" story? Hadn't we already read in the papers about similar cases of "ritual abuse" in Los Angeles, El Paso, and the Bronx?

Three months after the murdered bunny rabbits in *Muffin Man* on CBS came a dead chicken in *Unspeakable Acts* on ABC. As chickens go, this dead one was a red herring, introduced early in a TV movie "based on" accusations of child abuse at a day-care center in Dade County, Florida, and then dropped before the trial, as if a Chicken Little in Burbank were having second thoughts. I certainly was. We were asked to believe the children, which ought to have been easy. After all, they accused Gregory Sierra, who had brought with him to the TV movie all those bad vibes from his many lowlife roles on *Miami Vice*. But looking at the therapists who coached the children in their testimony, the screen got smaller. It was impossible not to suspect the therapists themselves of something ulterior: Brad Davis, with his self-righteous little blond ponytail, and Jill Clayburgh, on some sort of Simone Weil starvation diet, seemed almost to slither, in thrall to an extraterrestrial music. Their eyes glistened, as if from esoteric rite. They were . . . creepy.

We've come to an interesting intersection of television and other

American cultures. The Movie of the Week (MOW) had not, of course, invented alcoholism, cancer, wife-beating, child abuse, madness, murder, or rape. On the other hand, although we lack the helpful statistics, it's hard not to imagine that a steady diet of such movies encouraged more Americans to report intimate crimes; leave abusive homes; go into therapy and twelve-step programs; petition courts, legislatures, and the media for redress of grievance; feel anxious and speak bitterness and sue. Because MOWs as a genre tend to emphasize the vulnerability of women and children, they also doubtless contributed by feedback loop to what critics came to characterize as a "victim psychology" and "political correctness." (Amazing really that sensitivity to other people's pain should somehow turn into a whole new rhetoric of ridicule, as if empathy and old-fashioned "knee-jerk liberalism" were any threat to the paychecks, perks, and power games of a muscular patriarchy; as if feeling bad on behalf of the aggrieved were simultaneously lily-livered and totalitarian. Or even worse: un-hip; less than way-cool.) But in the related hysterias about incest and satanic ritual abuse, television was far behind the cultural curve, so late it was out of any loop.

We first heard about ritual child abuse in February 1984, when news-papers, radio, and TV excitedly reported accusations that for two decades teachers at the McMartin Preschool in Manhattan Beach had tortured and raped small children and killed their bunny rabbits. (Bunnies were to ritual abuse scenarios of the 1980s what black helicopters would become for right-wing militia fantasies in the 1990s.) That spring, in Jordan, Minnesota, there were twenty-four arrests for membership in a kiddie-porn sex ring said to murder babies, drink their blood, and toss their corpses into a river. In April, a janitor and three teachers at Chicago's Rogers Park Day Care Center were accused of boiling and eating babies. In May, in Reno, a Montessori day school was shut down on account of satanic rites and a "naked movie star game." In Memphis in June, a teacher's aide and a Baptist minister at the Georgian Hills Early Childhood Center were brought up on charges of sexual assault and animal sacrifice. All that sum-mer, from Malden, Massachusetts, to Sacramento, California, from West Point to Miami, hysteria spread. According to *Satan's Silence*, an angry account of "the Making of a Modern American Witch-Hunt" by Debbie Nathan and Michael Snedeker (1995), accusations of ritual abuse triggered criminal cases in more than a hundred communities between 1983 and 1987. On the one hand, forks, spoons, screwdrivers, Lego blocks, monster masks, mind-altering drugs, feces-eating, and urine-drinking; on the other, battered-child syndrome, rape-trauma syndrome, child-sexual-abuse-accommodation syndrome, and post-traumatic stress disorder. Janet Reno prosecuted the Country Walk case in Dade County, Florida. When Kelly Michaels's conviction was overturned in 1995, the aspiring actress and part-time worker at the Wee Care Day Nursery in Maplewood, New Jersey, had already served seven years in prison, with another forty to go, for atrocities that supposedly ranged from licking peanut butter off children's genitals to playing piano in the nude. As for the case that started it all, after seven years in court and $15 million in expenses, nobody associated with the McMartin Preschool was ever convicted on a single count of anything—not of sodomy, rape, group sex, satanism, or even excessive fondling; not of "Goatman," the Alligator Game, the ritual murder of a horse with a baseball bat or the cutting off of the floppy ears of bunny rabbits and making munchkins drink their blood, much less membership in what the media had called "a nationwide conspiracy of pedophiles in day-care centers."

The counterattack actually began on television. In 1990, in the churchgoing community of Edenton, North Carolina (population five thousand), seven defendants at the Little Rascals day-care center were charged on 429 separate counts of abusing children with knives, forks, scissors, needles, and hammers. Public-TV producer Ofra Bikel went to Edenton and talked, on camera, to almost everybody—accused, accusers, relatives, neighbors, lawyers, therapists, even many of the children named in the indictments—and the result was a 1991 *Frontline* documentary, "Innocence Lost," that won not only an Emmy and the Columbia University–Alfred I. duPont Silver Baton but also scared the hell out of those of us who had been predisposed throughout the eighties to believe whatever children said or whatever their therapists had coached them to say. After a mixed bag of guilty verdicts in 1993, Bikel returned to Edenton for another batch of interviews and to *Frontline* with a four-hour reconstruction, overview, and cry of rage. After the first program, it's amazing anyone in North Carolina would talk to her again, but most just couldn't help themselves, including a judge with hindsight doubts and five troubled members of the jury that sent Bob Kelly, the co-owner of Little Rascals, to prison for twelve consecutive life sentences.

Because of Ofra Bikel, We the Jury know more than the actual jury did about Edenton as a frazzled community, about social-service agencies with their own agendas, about cops wanting to close an ugly case, about psychiatrists with ego investments, about similar cases falling apart in other states, and even about jury irregularities in Edenton itself. To our watching, we bring some history and respond (again, not ignobly) with a visceral rush. We start taking everything personally. For instance, I didn't much care for the shifty-eyed Kelly. His wife, Betsy, seemed nicer, although she grew old before our eyes. And Betsy's passionate younger sister, Nancy, was immensely appealing. Whereas Bob's principal accuser, Jane Mabry, was somehow operatic and ulterior. And many of the parents who turned against the Kellys, including Bob's lawyer once he was told that his own child might have been a victim, were clearly hysterical. (Well, wouldn't you be, if you thought for a minute . . . ?) After which electronic personalizing, we all turn into advocates: No way, looking at such Little Rascals caretakers as Robin Bynum and Dawn Wilson, could we believe either capable of such devil-worship horrors. Hadn't they been offered a plea bargain, even *after* the verdict on Bob Kelly? Knowing she was innocent, Wilson rejected such a bargain, and was sentenced to the max. How come? Jurors told Bikel they hadn't trusted what little there was of medical evidence. (Of physical evidence, there was none.) Nor did they credit certain details of the children's testimony. (Like Bob shooting babies.) But they took into their deliberations the lurid reports of the therapists, and these had apparently been decisive. Bloodlust, besides, has its own momentum, and so does bad faith. (If Bob was guilty, didn't Dawn have to be?) And now everybody felt bad.

No one felt worse than Bikel, who refused to let go of her subject. Two years later in April 1995, she returned to *Frontline* with four more hours on "Divided Memories." She interviewed dozens of adult "victims" who, after years of "repressing" memories of childhood sexual trauma, "recovered" these memories in therapy. She interviewed members of the families of these "victims." She quizzed the therapists themselves, careful to sort out differences between hypnosis and "reparenting," between "reparenting" and "age regression." She talked to psychologists who blame Freud for having abandoned his seduction theory and to lawyers who are suing everybody, including, to their indignant surprise, the therapists themselves. It turns out that some of these patients "recovered" memories of ritual abuse in *previous lives*. It also turns out that, if any of these therapists had the slightest doubt whatsoever about the nightmare tales to which they had given such color and shape, they didn't think factual accuracy really mattered. What the patient felt was all that counted. "Confabulation," defined by the dictionary in its strictly psychiatric sense as "replacement of a gap in memory by a falsification that the subject accepts as correct," seems to be contagious—as it had been among teen-aged girls in Salem, Massachusetts, in 1692, and was again among goat-faced Bolsheviks at Stalin's show trials in the 1930s.

There hadn't been a more depressing program on television since Edward R. Murrow's *Harvest of Shame*. Until, that is, May 1995, the very next month, when HBO aired its McMartin docudrama, *Indictment*. Enter Oliver Stone, executive producer. And Abby and Myra Mann, who wrote an angry script in the best tradition of TV agitprop. And Mick Jackson, directing in the slam-bang take-no-prisoners style of Stone himself. And James Woods as Danny Davis, a lowlife lawyer more accustomed to defending "drug dealers and other scumbags," who would seem to have ennobled himself by representing three generations of McMartins. And Mercedes Ruehl, as the prosecutor who would do anything to advance the political ambitions of her DA boss. Not to mention a strong support-ing cast that included Lolita Davidovich as a therapist who coached the children at their confabulations; Chelsea Field as a member of Ruehl's team who began to have doubts; Sada Thompson as the grandmother Virginia McMartin; Shirley Knight as her daughter Peggy; and Henry Thomas as her grandson Ray, who forgot sometimes to put on his under-wear and was caught with a skin-mag centerfold.

Well, they *looked* guilty: "Perfect typecasting," said a prosecutor; "they could be Buchenwald guards." So what if their accuser was a hysterical alcoholic who may have been covering up for her own abusive husband? So what if the prosecutors neglected to screen the unlicensed therapist's videotaped interviews with the kids? So what if that therapist misrepre-sented the contents of those interviews besides sleeping with a tabloid-TV reporter and feeding him pillow-talk scoops? And so what if sad-sack Ray spent five years in jail before getting bail? "A client's a client," explained Woods in his *Salvador/True Believer* raw-meat mode, before he saw beyond the lizard eye of law as usual to the light of a just cause like a moral corona. No medical evidence of any variety of abuse at the McMartin Preschool was ever produced in court, not a single porn Polaroid, not a single sight-ing of an underground satanic cavern, nor the least residue of hot wax and singed fur. And who was to blame for these witch hunts? According to *Indictment*: parents, cops, prosecutors, therapists, and the vampire media.

To which list, according to Frederick Crews in two long articles in the *New York Review of Books* in 1994, we must add Sigmund Freud. An emeritus professor of English at the University of California, Berkeley, Crews had been hounding in hot pursuit after Freud for years, to punish him for the many sins of a subdivision of literary criticism bent out of shape by psychoanalytic concepts. To be sure, Crews was equally disdainful of Marxist, feminist, structuralist, and postmodern literary criticism— those kaleidoscopic lenses through which the trendier academics are accustomed to peering at every artifact of the culture in order to find it guilty of something. But the "recovered memory" controversy was a chance to up the animus ante. Feminists had an investment in the incidence of incest. Fundamentalist Christians had an investment in the existence of satanic ritual. And therapists had an investment in vulgarized Viennese voodoo. In this conspiracy of true believers, the victims weren't texts; the victims were families and careers and human rights and common sense—all because of "recovered memory" techniques based on a theory of repression for which, like psychoanalysis as a whole, there was no empirical evidence and, thus, no scientific validation.

We would seem to have strayed from two-dimensional television into a swamp. Well, you can't watch television, raise children, think about Freud, and fend off Frederick Crews, all at the same time, without starting to suspect that the culture's constituents connect, collide, and ramify in messy ways, and that interrelatedness may be the normal respiration of intelligence. In May 1996 the *New York Times Magazine* devoted an entire issue to swatches of wounding memoirs by writers like Susan Cheever, Mary Gordon, Mary Karr, Chang-rae Lee, Leonard Michaels, Joyce Carol Oates, Luc Sante, and Art Spiegelman. The editor of this special issue, James Atlas, seemed mildly susprised to find so much emphasis on dysfunction, alcoholism, incest, and mental illness. He seemed also to blame the contemporary novel, for no longer "delivering the news." He simply hadn't been watching much television. He might also have been reading the wrong novels.

When Crews at last published his essays in a book, *The Memory Wars*, in the fall of 1995, I put on another of my hats, as coeditor of the literary pages of *The Nation*, and shipped it out for review, along with *Satan's Silence*, to an anthropologist at the University of Washington. What we got back from Marilyn Ivy and published that December still strikes me as the sanest take on the topic so far. After synopsizing both books, Ivy used them as booster rockets. So psychoanalysis isn't scientific? Well, we have known for years "about the tension in Freud between his interpretive modalities and his scientism. . . ." Nevertheless:

> Crews' Popperian valorization of science makes him uncomfortable indeed with ambiguity, not to mention undecidability. He can only imagine two alternatives: that there is real sexual abuse, or that psychotherapists plant false memories of abuse in children's (or "recovering" adults') minds. Having foresworn the murky depths of interpretation in favor of the transparent verifiability of science, he has no way to think about phenomena that don't readily resolve themselves into the stable objects of real science but that remain unstable para-objects: memory, sexuality, desire, and terror. It's true that we wouldn't have recovered memory therapy as it is today if Freud hadn't theorized repression. . . . [But] we also wouldn't have had a body of thought, with its still discomfiting assertions of child sexuality and the reality of fantasy, that directly disputes the primitive premises on which that therapy is based.

As Nathan and Snedeker suggest in *Satan's Silence*, what is also going on is "the systematic, class-based scapegoating of people who represent the intersection of the public sphere with the (ideally) privatized, sacrosanct sphere of the family: caretakers in day-care centers. In a nation in which an increasing number of women work, with the ongoing fragmentation of the nuclear family . . . the obsession with the sexual abuse of children in public places reflects widespread moral panic about the breakdown of gendered and generational boundaries." Ivy continues:

> What is clear from the record is that such moral panic could not have occurred without the intense investment in the pristine innocence of the "child" in late twentieth-century America. Recovered memories or no, the insistence on a wholly pure, sexually innocent child—and the terror that the potential defilement of that purity provokes—remains at the very heart of the ritual abuse panic (as well as the adult recovered

memory movement). What makes this insistence even more revealing is that it occurs under the immense sexualization of children within consumer capitalism: There is no more charged figure for the seductive and the seducible than the child. The effect of mass media and consumption on children's sexuality seems rarely remarked in the analysis of abuse cases, and not surprisingly. For to think about the child as a sexual object in capitalism is already to have violated the pristine space that the child must occupy to guarantee the crumbling social order. . . .

Freud, of course, taught us that children are sexual beings. And memories are narrative reconstructions, artful mixtures of event and fantasy. Put into language, they can be deceptive. But equally deceiving are the "rococo paranoia" and "socio-sexual fantasies" of parents, child support services personnel, therapists, law-enforcement officials, district attorneys, and doctors, who so easily imagine midnight masses, devil masks, and rape orgies:

> And along with those fantasies, an even stranger and stronger one: that of the untouched child, pristine and unaffected by the capitalized sexuality all around her. It is Nathan and Snedeker's book that powerfully unmasks this world of specifically American phantasms, in which the terrors of day-care abuse appear as fabulous, perverse displacements of the systematic— satanic?—societal abuse and neglect of millions of real kids.

In March 1996, unattended by any sort of fanfare, in an otherwise routine MOW on ABC called *Forgotten Sins*, network television came full circle after only six years. John Shea, who had starred as a tough cop convinced his son had been molested at a preschool in the 1989 TV movie that started the whole prime-time craze for ritual abuse, *Do You Know the Muffin Man?*, also starred in *Forgotten Sins*, once again as a cop, who this time out was somehow persuaded that he himself had abused his own daughters, and so had half of his buddies on the force, all of them belonging to a satanic cult into goats and swords, dolls and pitchforks, Viking helmets and sacrificial infanticide. Shea was encouraged in this delusion, unto prison, by religious nuts, crazed prosecutors, bullying therapists, and, of course, the vampire media. But "sociologist" William Devane had bearded doubts. Bess Armstrong, playing Shea's wife, only pretended to go along with the witch hunt so she could keep custody of her little boy. *You* wouldn't have believed one of these accusers, Lisa Dean Ryan, if she told you she'd gone to the bathroom. And while the ABC movie had nothing to say about a psychology that insists on the sexual innocence of children, an economy that sexualizes them, our need for Satan now that Stalin's gone, the perverse displacement of our fear of our own families onto surrogates like day care, or Little Red Riding Hood and the seduction theory, *Forgotten Sins* at least felt bad in all the right places.

Masks, mirrors, psychoanalysis, family values, consumer capitalism, the succubus media, and spectator sports . . . all show up on television because *everything* shows up on television because television can't help itself. In both directions, sending or receiving, it's always on: "The cat eats the bird; Picasso eats the cat; painting eats Picasso." Before the lost child on American television, there was the lost child in American culture, from the captivity narratives of New England Puritans kidnapped by Indians to Huck Finn, Little Orphan Annie, and Holden Caulfield. ("Though I have done other things through the years," we are told by the surprise parent in Anne Beattie's *Picturing Will*, "I still think of myself as the person who knelt so many times to tie your shoelaces. Who needed to see them double-knotted and to know that you were safe, again, from tripping. I could have identified your feet, and still could, I see them so clearly, in a lineup of a hundred children.") Before Freud, there was Kaspar Hauser, the Wolf Boy of Aveyron, and the punitive Brothers Grimm, (In *Absence*, Peter Handke remembers "how in childhood we had often hidden from others because we wanted them to look for us." Kafka's first novel, lost to us, alas, was called *The Child and the City*.) And previous to these Black Forests there was Goethe's Gretchen, who drowned her newborn before killing herself, not to mention the slaughter of the innocents and the sacrifice of Isaac in the Bible, or the ritual infanticide of the mother cults of the ancient Middle East, or a classical literature full of dreadful fantasies of mothers losing or killing their children and of maidens dragged by their fathers to sacrificial altars, dying of despair at abandonment, stoned because they were raped; of Niobes, Medeas, Iphigenias, Ariadnes, and Didos. Don't let's get started on Claude Lévi-Strauss and his embroidery of the Amazonian Tucuna myth about the baby-snatching frog and the honey-gathering cycle. TV, like fairy tales and structuralism, is how we dream out loud about ourselves. Sitting down to watch, we are also projecting. In *Possessing the Secret of Joy*, her scary novel about female genital mutilation in Africa, Alice Walker took as her epigraph what she described as a "bumper sticker": *When the ax came into the forest, the trees said the handle is one of us.*

When Studs Listens, Everyone Else Talks

Studs Terkel was eighty years old Monday night. So what Studs did was publish another book. *Race: How Blacks and Whites Think and Feel About the American Obsession.* And what some of the rest of us did was go to a party for him, which he wasn't permitted to tape-record. He had to sit there, being admired, which is one of the few things he isn't good at. If you stay put, you might miss the action. While we were admiring Studs, for instance, they abolished democracy in Peru.

About the party, I won't tell you everybody there, they already know who they are. Many of them have been fighting losing causes since the Spanish Civil War. But mention must be made of two celebrants I've never seen before in almost a quarter-century of New York literary cocktail parties. One was Pete Seeger, in the kitchen, without his guitar. The other was Kenneth Clark, who started testifying to the pathologies of American apartheid as far back as 1952, in Clarendon, South Carolina, when the NAACP began its legal suit to desegregate our public schools.

(Time flies away. Back in 1953, it was Ike, not Ronald Reagan, who had this to say about the American South to his new chief justice, Earl Warren: "These aren't bad people. All they're concerned about is to see that their sweet little girls are not required to sit in school alongside some big overgrown Negroes.")

Clark, who must have had another party to go to, wore black tie. Seeger, of course, did not. Studs was his usual vision of red checkerboard. The rest of us lacked such dash.

Imagine Studs in action on the Chicago streets, on foot because he can't drive, in a raincoat and battered hat, with a hearing aid and a tape recorder, bluffing his way into the Ida B. Wells housing project on the black South Side, sitting down in somebody's kitchen, talking about race.

America's premier oral historian is also one of the last of the integrationists—a throwback to Martin Luther King; and before Dr. King, to the left wing of the CIO; and before that, to Jewish socialism and the French Revolution. He's kept the faith by continuing to test it. He will talk to anybody, and he listens twice, first right there in the kitchen, and then again when he edits the tapes for his books, where intelligence is made somehow musical, where conversations become cantatas. I'm tempted then to call him an oratorio historian. This is what Walt Whitman must have meant when he said he heard America singing.

Not all the songs in *Race* are cheerful. Everybody, white, black, brown, and yellow, seems to agree that relations between the races are worse than they've ever been, worse than they were in the sixties riots. Most blame the go-go greedhead Reagan years and the drug epidemic. Farrakhan gets mentioned more often than I'd have thought imaginable or desirable. As if in counterpoint to Farrakhan, there's also a lot of country blues singer Big Bill Broonzy.

But nobody Studs talks to has given up. (Certainly not Emmett Till's mother, Mamie Mobley, who became a teacher after her son was murdered.) They have all got jobs to find, and children to raise, and neighborhoods to save, and a nation to recover from its waste of scruple, its conscience gone up in smoke like Puff the Magic Dragon.

Where does he find these people? Mostly, but not always, in Chicago. Some, but not most, he's talked to before. Male or female, without exception, it's their *working* lives that give them their perspective. They are paramedics, firefighters, and flight attendants; carpenters and computer software salesmen; steelworkers, musicians, hairdressers, medical students, hospital aides, and chauffeurs; union reps, evangelists, black separatists, and Ku Klux Klanners; ex-Communists, ex-priests, retired domestics, and many, many teachers, most of them despairing.

Each new Terkel book I make a big deal about this amazing democracy of occupations. Why? Because the brain, too, is a muscle and it's nice—it's more than nice, it's thrilling—to see it exercised by people who have never shown up on *Face the Nation* or Ted Koppel, where all we hear from are the male and pale with their credentialed technoblab of "underclass" and "trickle-down": the mellowspeak salesmen in their Beltway blisterpacks, pushing a capital gains tax cut as the pep pill/miracle cure for moral fatigue, social paralysis, and economic catastrophe.

Disappointed, hesitant, or driven as they may be, there's no doubt at all that America would be a better place if *everybody* listened to these working people, not just radical-humanist Studs Terkel, that passionate old man with the brave songs and the magic hearing aid.

Amazing Grace

THIS WAS AWHILE ago, on Second Avenue across the street from the Israeli Consulate, right next door to National Public Radio. From the window of a bus, I saw they were demonstrating—something about the *intifada*. So I got out and walked around and met the New Jewish Agenda and there, of course, was Grace Paley. I wanted to tell her to go home and write another story. I would agitate in her stead. For decades, no matter where, every time I went to a demonstration, she was already there. I also knew that when I didn't show up, she'd be there, anyway. Why not a bargain? Couldn't she call when she felt a demonstration coming on? I'd go for her. She'd stay home and invent another report for her friends and her children on "the condition of our lifelong attachments." I had nothing better to do with myself than a Grace Paley short story.

"Then, as often happens in stories, it was several years later." And here we are, in this lovely building that's not the least bit like the old Greenwich Village Women's House of Detention where, after sitting down to impede some military parade, she spent six days reading William Carlos Williams, after which she wrote that if there must be prisons, "they ought to be in the neighborhood, near a subway—not way out in distant suburbs, where families have to take cars, buses, ferries, trains, and the population that considers itself innocent forgets, denies, chooses to never know that there is a whole huge country of the bad and the unlucky and the self-hurters, a country with a population greater than that of many nations in our world."

I regret my presumption. And I'm glad I kept my mouth shut. Yeats said famously: "The intellect of man is forced to choose / Perfection of the

life or of the work." He wasn't happy about it, adding: "That old perplexity an empty purse / Or the day's vanity, the night's remorse." But it was
a male chauvinist piggy thing to say. The Grace Paley who wrote the
stories that I started reading in Berkeley, California, in 1960, on the rec-
ommendation of Tillie Olsen one afternoon at Pacifica Radio just after
Tillie asked us: "Oh why do I have to feel it happens to me, too? Why is
it like this? And why do I have to care?"—the Paley already telling us that
she had looked "into the square bright window of daylight to ask myself
the sapping question: What is man that woman lies down to adore him?"—
this is the same Grace Paley who grew up Russian-socialist-Jewish-
American in the East Bronx, wearing the blue shirt and red kerchief of a
Falcon. Who fought before she became a pacifist in gang wars between
the Third and Fourth Internationals. Who staged agitprop plays like
Eviction! Who was suspended from junior high school, at age twelve, for
signing the Oxford Pledge against war. Who would organize abortion
speakouts and missile site sit-ins and protest marches on Shoreham and
Seabrook. Who would face down signs that said: NUKE THE BITCHES TILL
THEY GLOW. THEN SHOOT THEM IN THE DARK. Who'd go to Russia, and to
Hanoi, and to Nicaragua, and even the Pentagon, "a kind of medium-level
worker in one tendency in the nonviolent direct-action left wing of the
antiwar movement," before ending up at town meetings in Vermont.
Who's probably devoted more time to Peace Centers, Cooper Union
lectures, Clamshell Alliances, War Resisters Leagues, and Madre than she
has to a literature that seeks to oppose people made of blood and bone to
connections made of oil and gold. Who tells her students to read Emma
Goldman, Prince Kropotkin, and Malcolm X and the rest of us to read
Christa Wolf and Isaac Babel. Who has explained not only that a tank
uses up a gallon of gas every seventeen miles, but also that "If you're a
feminist it means that you've noticed that male ownership of the direction
of female lives has been the order of the day for a few thousand years, and
it isn't natural."

Meanwhile of course there were men and children: "I own two small
boys whose dependence on me takes up my lumpen time and my bourgeois feelings." But if "the world cannot be changed by talking to one
child at a time, it may at least be known." And equally, of course, the
politics and the literature and the life converge. It's a patchwork quilt of
witness and example; of radiance and scruple; of astonishing art made out
of the sibilant clues of the whispering world in the room next door; of a

wild humor, a Magical Socialism and a Groucho Marxism, that subverts our weary ways of seeing: "Alongside him on one of those walks was seen a skinny crosstown lady, known to many people over by Tompkins Square—wears a giant Ukrainian cross in and out of the tub, to keep from going down the drain, I guess." Or: "Hindsight, usually looked down upon, is probably as valuable as foresight, since it does include a few facts." Besides: "It's very important to emphasize what is good or beautiful so as not to have a gloomy face when you meet some youngster who has just begun to guess." If she began by telling us what women really thought and felt, by rescuing the history of all our mothers for all our daughters, she ends with Mozart and horizons. Faith Darwin indeed, coming down from the trees. Or flying off, like a Stephanie Dedalus. "First they make something," explains one of her stories, "then they murder it. Then they write a book about how interesting it is." Not Grace Paley. She embarrassed me into being a better person than I'd have settled for. She has enjoined all of us, her wayward children: "Let us go forth with fear and courage and rage to save the world."

Morrison's Paradise Lost

S O ABUNDANT, EVEN prodigal, is Toni Morrison's first new novel since her Nobel Prize, so symphonic, light-struck, and sheer, as if each page had been rubbed transparent, and so much the splendid sister of *Beloved*—she's even gone back to Brazil, not this time to see the three-spoke slave collar and the iron mouth-bit, but to check out *candomblé*—that I realize I've been holding my breath since December 1993. After such levitation, weren't all of us in for a fall? Who knew she'd use the Prize as a kite instead of a wheelbarrow?

And I realize I've been holding my breath even on those occasions— under a tent at Caramoor, once in a cathedral—to which I've been invited as a designated partisan, after which I'm guaranteed a standing ovation because, of course, I'm followed by the laureate, who reads from her novel in progress, which begins: "They shoot the white girl first." All week long in Stockholm, after the embassy lunch and the postage stamp with her face on it, before the concert and the banquet, between madrigals and snowflakes and candle flames and the joyride in the Volvo limo behind a police escort to the great halls and the grand ballrooms and the singing waiters and the reindeer steak, I had thought of Pecola, pregnant with her father's baby, believing that if only she had blue eyes she'd be loved as much as Bojangles had loved Shirley Temple. And of Sula, who when she loved a man rubbed the black off his bones down to gold leaf, then scraped away the gold to discover alabaster, then tapped with a hammer at the alabaster till it cracked like ice, and what you felt was fertile loam. Of Milkman in *Song of Solomon*, who went south from Detroit to a ruined plantation and a cave of the dead, who learned from blue silk wings, red velvet rose petals, a children's riddle song, and a bag of human bones not only his own true name but also how to fly all the way back to Africa. Of the horseback ghosts of the blind slaves in *Tar Baby*, where Caliban got another chance against Prospero. Of Sethe in *Beloved* like a black Medea with a handsaw and Denver who swallowed her sister's blood and Beloved swimming up from blue water to eat all the sugar in the world: *Beloved*, that ghost story, mother epic, folk fable, fairy tale, and incantation of lost children, men like centaurs, lunatic history, and babies offered up like hummingbirds to shameful gods. Where had it been hiding, this book we always needed? Who now can picture our literature in its absence, between Whitman and Twain, the Other in Faulkner and Flannery O'Connor? Before *Beloved*, our canon was wounded, incomplete. Until *Beloved*, our imagination of America had a heart-sized hole in it big enough to die from, as if we'd never seen black boys "hanging from the most beautiful sycamore trees in the world." And finally *Jazz*: as if Sidney Bechet had met the Archduke Trio or Ellington gone Baroque; a novel that wrote itself by talking to us, a story that confided: "I love the way you hold me, how close you let me be to you. I like your fingers on and on, lifting, turning. I have watched your face for a long time now, and missed your eyes when you went away from me. . . . Look, look. Look where your hands are. Now."

After her dispossessions and her hauntings, her butter cakes and baby ghosts, her blade of blackbirds and her graveyard loves, Not Doctor Street and No Mercy Hospital and all those maple-syrup men "with the long-distance eyes": *Just look where she was now.* We stood at our banquet tables in Stockholm's City Hall, in white tie and ball gowns and trepidation. A trumpet fanfare sounded. Above us, past a gilded balustrade, the processional began. The winner of the prize came down the marble steps at last, on the arm of the king of Sweden. Never mind that I am pale and I am male. She'd taught me to imagine the lost history of her people, to read the signs of love and work and nightmare passage and redemptive music, to hear the deepest chords of exile. I was proud to be a citizen of whatever country Toni Morrison came from. And that night she gave lessons to the noble rot of Europe on what majesty really looks like.

All of this—up in the air, dancing on the vaulted ceiling.

"They shoot the white girl first." In her lecture to the Swedish Academy, she had spoken against the punishing speech of the organs of obedience, used to "sanction ignorance and preserve privilege"; against the "obscuring" and "oppressive" language of state, the "calcified language of the academy," the "faux-language of the mindless media," the "policing languages" of "racist mastery," and the "seductive, mutant language designed to throttle women, to pack their throats like paté-producing geese with their own unsayable, transgressive words." Rather than these obscenities, she proposed a tongue that "arcs toward the place where meaning may lie." Word-work is sublime, she said, "because it is generative; it makes the meaning that secures our difference, our human difference." Death may be the meaning of life, but language is its measure. Language alone "protects us from the scariness of things with no names. Language alone is meditation." Meditating, she had found brave words like "poise," "light," "wisdom," "deference," "generosity," "felicity," and "trust."

To these, we must now add "solace." Like Schopenhauer and the sorrow songs, *Paradise* seeks consolation. Part history and part Dreamtime, part opera and part Matisse, it would be surpassing and transcendent if only for the notion of a "Disallowing." But its rainbow parabola also includes Reconstruction and the Trail of Tears, Vietnam and civil rights, patriarchy and ancestor worship, abduction and sanctuary, migration and abandonment, sex and ghosts. Considering degrees of blackness, reversals of color-blind perspectives, and above all longings for home, it will raise a ruckus and rewrite God.

> *Bodacious black Eves unredeemed by Mary, they are like panicked does leaping toward a sun that has finished burning off the mist and now pours its holy oil over the hides of game.*
> *God at their side, the men take aim. For Ruby.*
>
> —Paradise

In a house shaped like a cartridge, in a state shaped like a gun, the fathers and sons of the nearby all-black town of Ruby shoot down running women as if they were deer. *They shoot the white girl first.* Not the least of many mysteries in *Paradise* is how hard it is to figure out which of the five women attacked by a fearful lynching party in a former convent in a godforsaken Oklahoma in the 1970s is, in fact, white. Slyly, Morrison is reminding us that skin color, about which we tend to get hysterical, is only a single datum, and maybe not the decisive one, in a universe of information. We do know the lynchers are "blue-black people," called "8-rock" after coal at the deepest level of the mines. To understand how it happened—this act of violence at the heart of every Morrison novel, the wound that will not heal—we must first learn the stories of the convent and the town, then the dreams of the players, and finally the template's design. We are vouchsafed all three simultaneously, in flashes of lyric lightning; in "the cold serenity of God's wrath"; and in raptures, seizures, or eruptions of volcanic consciousness ("You thought we were hot lava and when they broke us down into sand, you ran").

The "big stone house in the middle of nowhere" began as an embezzler's mansion, with lurid appointments of nude Venus statuary, nipple-tipped doorknobs, and vagina-shaped alabaster ashtrays. After this Gatsby's imprisonment, it was taken over by nuns and turned into Christ the King School for Native Girls, most of whom would run away from the God who despised them. But these nuns brought with them their own luridities, including an etching of St. Catherine of Siena on her knees offering up a plate of breasts. And when the last nun died—leaving behind only Consolata, the child they'd stolen decades ago from Rio's slums—the convent became, without even thinking about it, a sanctuary for young women orphaned or broken on history's wheel, a safe house for the throwaway, castaway female children of the sixties and seventies, on the road and looking to hide from angry fathers, abusive husbands, dead babies, boyfriends in Attica, rapists, Vietnam, Watergate, black water, and little boys on protest marches "spitting blood into their hands so as not to ruin their shoes."

Something will happen in 1976 to this haphazard ad hoc community of "women who chose their own company," these wild-thing Sulas—to Consolata in the cellar with her wine bottle and her bat vision; to Seneca in the bathtub, the "queen of scars," making thin red slits in her skin with a safety pin; to Mavis, who hears her asphyxiated twins laughing in the dark; to Gigi/Grace, who seeks buried treasure; and to Pallas/Divine, who could be carrying a lamb, a baby, or a jaguar. They are suddenly full of "loud dreaming." They chalk their bodies on the basement floor. They shave their heads and dance like holy women in the hot rain: *If you have a place that you should be in, and somebody who loves you waiting there, then go. If not stay here and follow me. Someone could want to meet you.*

And the nearby town: ah, Ruby. Although Morrison doesn't say so, the ancients believed that rubies were an antidote to poison, warded off plague, banished grief, and diverted the mind from evil thoughts. A "perfect ruby" was the Philosopher's Stone of the alchemists. We may also remember Dorothy's slippers in the movie of *The Wizard of Oz*. Ruby,

Oklahoma, is likewise a refuge as well as a fortress, a Beulah, Erewhon, or New Shangri-la, not to mention the promised land of Canaan, and the last stop of a long line that began with the passage from Africa, that included landfall, slavery, and civil war, Emancipation and Reconstruction—a proud community of freedmen, of gunsmiths, seamstresses, lacemakers, cobblers, ironmongers, and masons:

> They are extraordinary. They had served, picked, plowed, and traded in Louisiana since 1755, when it included Mississippi; and when it was divided into states they had helped govern both from 1868 to 1875, after which they had been reduced to field labor. They had kept the issue of their loins fruitful for more than two hundred years. They had denied each other nothing, bowed to no one, knelt only to their Maker.

In 1890, armed with advertisements of cheap land for homesteading—at the expense, of course, of the Choctaw, Creek, and Arapaho who happened to live there—they "took that history, those years, each other, and their uncorruptible worthiness" and walked to Oklahoma, fifteen families looking for a place to build their communal kitchen, to inscribe on this brick altar of an Oven a ferocious prophecy ("Beware the Furrow of His Brow"), to seed their fields and their women and make a home they called Haven—one of many all-black towns in the territory of the time, like Taft, Nicodemus, Langston City, and Mound Bayou. Following a specter into the wilderness, they'd endured black-skinned bandits, "time-sharing shoes," rejection by poor whites and rich Choctaw, yard-dog attacks, and the jeers of prostitutes. What they hadn't prepared for—a humiliation that more than rankled, that "threatened to crack their bones"—was the "contemptuous dismissal" they received from Negro towns already built. This was the infamous "disallowing." And the reason for it is the secret of Ruby, which is where nine of the families went next, in 1949, after the men came home from war to Haven, to find America unchanged: "Out There where your children were sport, your women quarry, and where your very person could be annulled." Disallowed like the ex-slaves before them, the ex-soldiers dismantled their Oven and pulled up their stakes and struck out again. For Ruby.

Prosperous Ruby: wide streets, pastel houses, enormous lawns, many churches (if only one bank), and flower gardens "snowed with butterflies"; household appliances that "pumped, hummed, sucked, purred, whispered, and flowed"; Kelvinators and John Deere, Philco and Body by Fisher. No diner, no gas station, no movie house or public telephone, no hospital or police, no criminals and no jail, no "slack or sloven women," nor, of course, any whites. "Here freedom was a test administered by the natural world that a man had to take for himself every day. And if he passed enough tests long enough, he was king." It was as if Booker T. Washington had gone to bourgeois heaven without having to die first dirt-poor. Because nobody ever dies in Ruby, either. That's the deal they made with God, the guy with the Furrowed Brow. It's payback for the Disallowing.

I'll explain the Disallowing in a minute. But you should know that something is also happening in Ruby in the seventies. A new reverend, a veteran of the civil rights movement, messes with the minds of the children. (He actually thinks that "a community with no politics is doomed to pop like Georgia fatwood.") Somebody paints, on their sacred Oven, a jet-black fist with red fingernails. Not only do daughters refuse to get out of bed and brides disappear on their honeymoons, but the women of Ruby begin to question the Fathers, who get angrier and noisier:

> They dug the clay—not you. They carried the hod—not you. They mixed the mortar—not one of you. They made good strong brick for that oven when their own shelter was sticks and sod. You understand what I'm telling you? . . . Act short with me all you want, you in long trouble if you think you can disrespect a row you never hoed.

Naturally, the convent women are blamed. Hadn't they shown up at a wedding reception to which they should never have been invited in the first place, "looking like go-go girls: pink shorts, see-through skirts; painted eyes, no lipstick; obviously no underwear; no stockings"? Haven't our own women, who can't drive cars, been seen on foot on the road going to or coming from secret visits there—for vegetables, for pies, and maybe even for abortions? "The stallions were fighting about who controlled the mares and their foals," thinks Billie Delia, who as a child rode bare-bottomed on a horse until they reviled her for it. Graven idols, black arts, narcotic herbs, lesbian sex!

Besides—"out here under skies so star-packed it was disgraceful; out here where the wind handled you like a man"—the women of the convent are not 8-rock.

> For ten generations they had believed the division they fought to close was free against slave, rich against poor. Usually, but not always, white against black. Now they saw a new separation: light-skinned against black. . . . The sign of racial purity they had taken for granted had become a stain. The scattering that alarmed Zechariah because he believed it would deplete them was now an even more dangerous level of evil, for if they broke apart and were disvalued by the impure, then, certain as death, those ten generations would disturb their children's peace throughout eternity.

The fifteen families on their way to the promised land were Disallowed by "fair-skinned colored men," "shooed away" by "blue-eyed, gray-eyed yellowmen in good suits," *because they were too black*: so black they must be trashy. And so they became "a tight band of wayfarers bound by the enormity of what happened to them. Their horror of whites was convulsive but abstract. They saved the clarity of their hatred for the men who had insulted them in ways too confounding for language." What this meant for Haven and for Ruby was that anyone marrying outside the coal-black 8-rock bloodlines, "tampering" with the gene pool, was an outcast, no longer welcome in a community "as tight as wax," no longer even represented in a Christmas schoolroom reenactment of the Nativity that hybridized the birth of Christ with the trek story and the creation myth of the 8-rock forefathers. So what if all those generations kept going "just to end up narrow as bale wire"? In Ruby, nobody dies.

Until they do. And even then, at least in *Paradise*, they don't. Because the midwife Lone is there to teach Consolata how to raise the dead. And Soane's boys who died in Vietnam are as likely to show up leaning on her Kelvinator as Mavis's twins, who died in the mint-green Cadillac, will be heard laughing in the convent dark. And Dovey has a "Friend," who may be the apparition that led the fifteen families to their Haven, who visits her in the garden on his way to someplace else. And the fire-ruined house in the wilderness where Deacon meets his secret love is full of ash people, fishermen, nether shapes, and a girl with butterfly wings three feet long.

And in the meadow where the convent women run from the guns of Ruby, there is a door. And on the other side of the door is solace and Piedade, who'll bathe them in emerald water and bring shepherds with colored birds on their shoulders "down from the mountains to remember their lives in her songs."

Something astonishing happens here. While, as usual, Morrison is complicating our understanding of black communities, with their very own scapegoats and pariahs as well as their raven-wing circles of sorrow, she also prestidigitates another kind of Reconstruction. Having reminded us in her Harvard lectures, *Playing in the Dark*, of the invisibility of black Americans in our classic literature—and yet their gravity and torque, and yet their ghostly resonance—she not only rewrites that literature (Hawthorne and Melville) but our history as well (from the Middle Passage of a *Mayflower* to colonial New England's City on the Hill to the destiny-manifesting westward Voortrek), and even our sacred texts (the Declaration of Independence, Lincoln's Second Inaugural). And in this rewriting, with its Xenophon and Moses and Balboa, odysseys and iliads, expulsions and displacements, lost tribes and diasporas, she dreams a second Republic "of longing, of terror, of perplexity, of shame, of magnanimity," in which white people are entirely spectral, a cloud on the water, a shadow mind.

Piedade; Pietà. Consolata; consolation. Hunted; haunted. Convent, covenant, coven. Morrison names: Seneca, Divine, Elder, Drum, Juvenal, Easter, Royal, Pious, Rector, Little Mirth, Flood, Fairy, Praise, Pryor, Apollo, Faustine, Chaste, Hope, and Lovely. She evokes: late melon and roast lamb, wild poppies and river vine, burnt lavender and broken babies, cherubim and body bags. And she redeems: There is a ghost for every family secret and every horror in history, and the language to forgive them. If we knew how she did it, we'd have literary theory instead of world radiance. I was holding my breath, and she took it away.

Ralph Ellison, Sort Of
(Plus Hemingway and Salinger)

U PON HIS DEATH in 1994, Ralph Ellison left behind some two thousand pages of a never-finished second novel—more than forty years of fine-tuning what his literary executor, John F. Callahan, calls a "mythic saga of race and identity, language and kinship in the American experience" and what the despairing rest of us, waiting for Ralph like Lefty or Godot, came to think of as The Invisible Book. Two decades of stingy excerpts, from 1959 through 1977, were followed by two more of enigmatic silence. Of course, in 1967, between teases, a book-length manuscript of "revisions" perished famously in the flames that consumed his Berkshires summer house. In the history of our literature, this misfortune has assumed the symbolic heft of a Reichstag fire, and maybe even the burning of the Library at Alexandria. Was it also Ellison's alibi for failing to follow up on himself? Only Albert Murray knows for sure.

While sitting on this second novel, he was otherwise not too arduously engaged in writing about Duke Ellington, Mahalia Jackson, Jimmy Rushing, Charlie Parker and the blues; lecturing on democracy, morality, and the novel; reviewing Mark Twain, Stephen Crane, Erskine Caldwell, and Gunnar Myrdal; rethinking the psychic kinks in his relationship with William Faulkner and Richard Wright; insisting, over and over again, that T. S. Eliot and André Malraux had influenced his sense of vocation more decisively; showing up at L.B.J.'s White House during the Vietnam War, speaking at a West Point commencement, getting himself interviewed. Almost everyone wanted, if not more *Invisibility*, then some other piece of him, some pound of black spokesperson. In the early sixties, there'd been an exchange of vituperations with Irving Howe, who thought he ought to be angrier. From the late sixties Willie Morris remembers, in *New York Days*, Ellison's being called an Uncle Tom at Grinnell College, in blood-thirsty Iowa. In the early seventies, I was an appalled witness at a literary cocktail party when Alfred Kazin told him he should spend less time at the Century Club and more at the typewriter, followed by a scuffle on the wet street, from which an equally appalled cabbie roared away without a fare, like the locomotive of history. And just last month, at a City University conference, a Rutgers professor who may have seen too many episodes of *The X-Files* actually suggested that Ellison, in his only novel, had said such terrible things about the "Brotherhood" of the Communist Party just to curry favor with a freaked public during the McCarthy shamefulness.

On the other hand, I also recall teaching *The Invisible Man* in paperback in the midsixties to a roomful of teenage girls in a belfry of an Epis-copal church in Roxbury, Massachusetts. These quick-witted, slow-burning, high-flying Afro-Caribbean birds of paradise had been discarded by the rac-ist Boston School Committee: bagged, tagged, and trashed. Yet they showed up two nights a week, a chapter at a time, to engage the selves they discov-ered in his pages, read aloud from their journals, write their own stories, and fall headlong into passionate disputation about metaphor and identity, poli-tics and work, even incest—and tell me things I didn't want to know about their streets. Much later I'd receive invitations to several graduations from colleges like Spelman and Shaw. But this was long after yogurt-faced liberals like me had been told to get out of Roxbury—in the spring of 1967, pursuant to the secret resolutions of the Newark Black Power Conference, which resolutions had been written by precisely those militants who would call Ralph Ellison an Uncle Tom even as he was saving the lives of their sisters.

"Writers don't give prescriptions," said the poet Ikem in Chinua Achebe's *Anthills of the Savannah*. "They give headaches."

Anyway, here at last is a respectable chunk of what he withheld to the grave. Personally, I wish Random House had published all two thousand pages, if not on a CD-ROM, then loose in a box for each reader to assemble on our own, according to our solitary need, like a customized mantra. Structure, about which he had been so finicky, be damned. Yes, from Ellison's notes and drafts Callahan has fashioned a shapely synecdo-che that coheres—a duet between "Daddy" Hickman, the black Southern preacher who's come to Washington in 1955 to warn a man he raised as a boy of impending violence, and Sunraider, the white New England senator who was brought up black but turned savagely on the color of this kindness; a Lincoln-haunted and Oedipus-inflected dialogue of down-home homilies, grandiose dreams, and primal crime; a dialectic of masked pasts and screened memories; a call-and-response antiphony of flimflam riffs; a matched fall of twinned tricksters into shared mystery, lost history, and filmed illusions. As in Faulkner, the past keeps happening. But gripped at the throat, *Juneteenth* also seems to long for choral movement and symphonic orchestration; breathing space and digressive license; clarification, specificity, amplitude.

Nevertheless, there's still a lot of wow.

> Once there was a series consisting of a man and a boy and a boar hog, a cat and a big hairy spider—all shot in flight as they sought to escape, to run away from some unseen pursuer. And as I sat in the darkened hotel room watching the rushes, the day's takes, on a portable screen, the man seemed to change into the boy and the boy, changing his form as he ran, becoming swiftly boar and cat and tarantula, moving ever desperately away, until at the end he seemed, this boar-boy-spider-cat, to change into an old man riding serenely on a white mule as he puffed on a corncob pipe. I watched it several times and each time I broke into a sweat, shaking as with a fever. Why these images and what was their power?

Imagine Bliss—a little white boy under a circus tent in a pine grove at a revival meeting of black Baptists, "a miniature man of God" inside a narrow box breathing through a tube. He is called Bliss "because they say that is what ignorance is." He is dressed to kill because he is presumed dead. The box he's in, with angels blowing long-belled trumpets and carved clouds floating in an egg-shaped space, is a coffin. When the singing stops, Bliss, his Bible, and his teddy bear will pop out "like God's own toast, to ask the Lord how come He has forsaken him":

> Hurry! They're moving slow, like an old boat drifting down the big river in the night and me inside looking up into the black sky, no moon nor stars and all the folks gone far beyond the levees. And I could feel the shivering creep up my legs now and squeezed Teddy's paw to force it down. Then the rising rhythm of the clapping hands was coming to me like storming waves heard from a distance; like waves that struck the boat and

flew off into the black sky like silver sparks from the shaking of the shimmering tambourines, showering at the zenith like the tails of skyrockets. If only I could open my eyes. It hangs heavy-heavy over my lids. Please hurry! Restore my sight. The night is black and I am far . . . far . . . I thought of Easter Bunny, he came from the dark inside of a red-and-white striped egg.

Like rabbits popping out of a magic top hat, Bliss come back from the dead is a regularly scheduled trick in Daddy Hickman's circuit show. Never mind how this little white boy ended up with the black evangelicals, on the nomadic road during the Great Depression from Oklahoma to Alabama to Georgia, among so many surrogate parents who raised him to talk and to walk as if he were Yoruban. (A captivity narrative!) Never mind how Hickman got himself transformed from a juke-joint jazz man into Bliss's designated father and "God's own trombone," blowing his horn in the devil's outback. ("No mercy in my heart. . . . Only the choking strangulation of some cord of kinship stronger and deeper than blood, hate, or heartbreak.") Never even mind the mock Resurrection. Christ already rose for these Baptists. What they really seek is a Second Coming of Father Abraham— the emancipating Lincoln who, in freeing the slaves, freed himself, and so truly became "one of us." According to Hickman, "We just couldn't get around the hard fact that for a hope or an idea to become real it has to be embodied in a man, and men change and have wills and wear masks." And so: "We made a plan, or at least we dreamed a dream and worked for it but the world was simply too big for us and the dream got out of hand."

But look at it from Bliss's point of view, a "chicken in a casket." Being dead is hard work for which he wants to be paid, if not in sex, about which he's begun to wonder, then at least some ice cream. And what does he get instead? On Juneteenth—the anniversary of the summer's day in 1865 when Union troops landed in Galveston, Texas, and their commanding officer told the slaves only two and a half years late that they were free, for which 5,000 colored folks have gathered in an Alabama swamp to eat 500 pounds of catfish and snapper, 900 pounds of ribs, 85 hams, a cabbage patch of coleslaw, and who knows how many frying chickens and butter beans, while listening as seven different preachers "shift to a higher gear," beyond the singing and the shouting into a territory of "pure unblemished Word," the "Word that was both song and scream and whisper," beyond sense "but leaping like a tree of flittering

birds with its *own* dictionary of light and meaning"—Bliss gets a white
woman, a complete stranger, who says that she's his *mother*, who claims:
"He's mine, MINE! . . . You gypsy niggers stole him, my baby."

So she isn't his mother. White people lie a lot. His *real* mother, as a
matter of fact, caused the death and mutilation of Hickman's brother, after
which baby Bliss was handed over as a sort of hostage to the jazz man,
who accepted him "as I'd already accepted the blues, the clap, the loss of
love, the fate of man." Why not? "Here was a chance to prove that there
was something in this world stronger than all their ignorant superstition
about blood and ghosts." Still, even to imagine such a mother, to conceive
of an ice-creamy white birthright, will lead Bliss to run away from Daddy
Hickman; to deny and rage; to hide in "surprise, speed, and camouflage";
to cut the string, scud high places, bruise himself and snag at times on
treetops but keep on sailing into shadows—first to make movies and illusions, then to make a vengeful son, and finally, as Sunraider, to make
hateful politics. Ellison asks us to remember Greek legend, folk literature,
and the entire Amerindian structuralist mythology of the stolen child.

But the swamp scene alone is enough to remind us of his remarkable
powers of sorcery. Though never a stranger to interior monologue, lyrical
afflatus, or angry agitprop, Ellison may be the greatest of jazz sermonizers
and homiletic blues guitarists ever to write fiction. He probably picked up
tips on how to do it from Melville in *Moby-Dick* and Joyce in *Portrait of the
Artist*, and passed them on for Toni Morrison to improve on when *Beloved*'s
Baby Suggs took to her sacred grove. As in the swamp, where on "this day
of deliverance" they look at "the figures writ on our bodies and on the
living tablet of our heart," so, too, at the Lincoln Memorial, with "the
great image slumped in the huge stone chair" and then again on the floor
of Congress when Sunraider in mid-demagoggle is attacked by the Great
Seal of the United States—by E PLURIBUS UNUM itself, with the olive
branch, the sheaf of arrows, the sphinxlike eyes, a taloned clutch, and a
curved beak like a scimitar—he dazzles us into a surreal sentience.

For Ellison, that Great Seal is a hybrid, a mongrel, an alloy, a scramble
of stew meats and a weave of sinews, cultures, language, genius, and love.
This is the bass line. Admixed America is a Tintoretto:

> You can cut that cord and zoom off like a balloon and rise
> high—I mean that cord woven of love, of touching, minister-

ing love, that's tied to a baby with its first swaddling clothes—but the cord don't shrivel and die like a navel cord beneath the first party dress or the first long suit of clothes. Oh, no, it parts with a cry like a rabbit torn by a hawk in the winter snows and it numbs quick and glazes like the eyes of a sledge-hammered ox and the blood don't show, it's like a wound that's cauterized. It snaps with the heart's denial back into the skull like a worm chased by a razor-beaked bird, and once inside it snarls, Bliss; it snarls up the mind. It won't die and there's no sun inside to set so it can stop its snakish wiggling. It bores reckless excursions between the brain and the heart and kills and kills again unkillable continuity. Bliss, when Eve deviled and Adam spawned we were all in the dark, and that's a fact.

The trouble with *Juneteenth* is that it's almost all sermons and jazzy dreaming. How did Bliss ever get into politics—in New England!—and become Sunraider? Surely there are pages, chapters, a whole other novel to explain his assassin, missing like the mothers. From *Invisible Man*, we knew what Tuskegee was like, Harlem, a paint factory, a cell meeting, and the sidewalk where Tod Clifton bled to death. *Juneteenth* asks us to intuit, from two men talking to each other and to ghosts, from nightmare passages and beseeching light, four hundred years of complicitous history that keeps Daddy Hickman from getting to the nation's capital in time to stop a fatal bullet. Charged by language alone to imagine the holy dove and winged bull, the Lion, the Lamb, and the Rock, what we see instead is "the devastation of the green wood! Ha! And in the blackened streets the entrails of men, women, and baby grand pianos, their songs sunk to an empty twang struck by the aimless whirling of violent winds. Behold! the charred foundations of the House of God."

Maybe he couldn't finish because America, lacking in comfort and radiance, fresh out of Lincolns, wouldn't let him. We amounted to less than he needed and believed. Or maybe, more dreadfully, baby Bliss is Jesus after all. And Sunraider is the Christianity he grew up to be.

Nothing ever stops; it divides and multiplies, and I guess sometimes it gets ground down to superfine, but it doesn't just blow away.

Still, let's be grateful for what we have, and consider how much worse it could have been. It could have been, for dire instance, something like the posthumous Hemingway of *True at First Light*.

Between the Pulitzer Prize in 1953, for *The Old Man and the Sea*, and the Nobel Prize in 1954, which he didn't bother to collect in person, Ernest Hemingway left Cuba for Africa with his fourth wife, Mary, to shoot something for *Look* magazine—a leopard, a lion, or a gazelle; maybe even himself, at least symbolically. We know now from his biographers that the British colonial rulers of Kenya made him an honorary game warden, and set him up in a privately stocked safari camp, to attract tourists who had been scared away by the Mau Mau. That, overweight and manic-depressive, with bad eyes, bad knees, and a distended liver, he was so drunk most of the time that he couldn't shoot straight. That he would crack up two airplanes, rupturing a kidney, dislocating a shoulder, crushing several vertebrae, and collapsing an intestine. Nevertheless, in the bush, Papa shaved his head, dyed his shirts a tribal pink and orange, and carried a spear to go courting a local Wakamba girl, the "lovely and impudent" Debba. And never stopped writing for his life.

True at First Light is his "fictionalized memoir" of that African sojourn, published thirty-eight years after his suicide—a sad book and a bloated one, even though it was more than twice as long before his son Patrick shrunk it to this size. The Papa we meet in its pages is a Great White Hunter, a tribal chief, and a wiseguy medicine man. He drinks beer for breakfast; swigs gin from a Spanish double cartridge pouch after gunning down baboons; eats breaded cutlets of lion tenderloin; makes nasty remarks about John O'Hara, vegetarians, homosexual playwrights, and sherry-sodden and "syphilitic" Masai; satirizes religion by making up one of his own; masters the secret Kamba handgrip; reads Simenon in French; remembers Paris and the Rockies, Orwell and D. H. Lawrence, Scott Fitzgerald and his old horse Kite; speaks babytalk to Mary and the natives, all of whom are infantilized, and bluster and blarney to his boozy white hunting buddies. He will get his leopard for *Look* magazine, as Mary will get her black-maned lion and marijuana tree for Christmas. But he will not, alas, because of local custom and propriety, ever get to sleep with Debba, his last chance for true "happiness."

No wonder he left this book in a drawer. I'm not saying that *True at First Light* is without grace notes. Although almost everybody talks as if translated from the Portuguese for a Dalton Trumbo screenplay about Spartacus or Geronimo, Hemingway did know how to *listen* to leopards and rhinos and the little boy he'd left behind. For instance:

> There are always mystical countries that are a part of one's childhood. Those we remember and visit sometimes when we are asleep and dreaming. They are as lovely at night as they were when we were children. If you ever go back to see them they are not there. But they are as fine in the night as they ever were if you have the luck to dream of them.

Still, the prose of stories like "A Clean, Well-Lighted Place" and "Hills Like White Elephants" compares with the prose of *True at First Light* as early photos of a vital Hemingway compare with snapshots of late Papa, trapped in the blubber of his celebrityhood.

So he couldn't escape his own cultivated image. No more vanishing acts from a marriage or an impasse: to Wyoming; to Spain; to the bush; to the sea; to bag another beastliness or kill the big fish. No more blaming his mother. No more bull. Only the black bottle and electroshock at the Mayo Clinic, after which he bagged himself. Like his own father, Papa ate a gun.

Hanging out at the Century Club begins to seem a whole lot healthier, and *Juneteenth* a lot less shameless. Maybe we're better off not knowing what's in the drawers of writers who blinked off into radio silence. Maybe, for another instance, J. D. Salinger has the right idea.

Salinger, who is fifty years older than his third wife, may still be writing in a magic tower full of peppermints and pipe smoke somewhere in rustic New Hampshire with the curtains closed against the mountain view. But he hasn't published a story since 1966. According to his daughter Peggy, this is because he can't stand criticism. Among the many other things her father can't stand are country clubs, Ivy Leaguers, holidays, charity, white bread, soft butter, "primitive" art, "coarse" Negroes, "trashy" poets like Langston Hughes, "ignorant" languages like Spanish, as well as anything that's "second-rate," that isn't beautiful or perfect (including all marriage and most women), anyone who interrupts his work (including his wives and children), and all the "parasites" who sponge off him (*especially* his wives and children).

His daughter Peggy—Margaret A. Salinger—has written a memoir, *Dream Catcher*, that would break the heart even if her father weren't the reclusive author of *The Catcher in the Rye*. Perhaps there is a gene for splendid prose. She is a mother herself, an Episcopal chaplain, a graduate of Brandeis, Oxford, and Harvard Divinity School, a former garage mechanic and union organizer, a worker in a home for abused and abandoned children, and an occasional singer at Tanglewood in the Boston Symphony chorus. But, starting with childhood, she has also survived everything from bulimia to chronic fatigue syndrome, from hallucinations to dehydrations, from a scary abortion to postpartum panic attacks, from alcohol abuse to attempted suicide. Since that childhood, she has slept with one eye open, seeing UFOs and fairies. Now, she watches her own son, hoping like the Native American dream catcher hanging over his bed "to filter out the nightmares in its web and let the good dreams drip down the feather on his sleeping forehead."

But Peggy's father *is* the author of *Franny and Zooey*. And Peggy's mother *did* set fire to the house, cooking the gerbils. And the real-child Peggy could never be as perfect as the fictional Glass bananafish. So we read *Dream Catcher* as we read the Ian Hamilton biography and the Joyce Maynard memoir, obsessively seeking clues to the writer who came back strange from World War II, having married and divorced a *Nazi*. Who insisted that one young woman after another abandon her family, her friends, and her possessions for him as if he were a cult. Who only sleeps in beds pointed true north, and has been a serial True Believer in Zen, Vedanta, L. Ron Hubbard's Dianetics, Wilhelm Reich's orgone box, Edgar Cayce, macrobiotics, and drinking urine.

"What are you doing," his daughter wonders, "that is so much more important than taking care of your kids and family?" The happiest she ever saw him was playing ringtoss with a dolphin. The only time he ever cried was when John Kennedy was shot. When she needed money for medical bills, he sent her a book by Mary Baker Eddy, a subscription to a Christian Science magazine about miracle healing, and a note saying she'd only get well when she stopped believing in the "illusion" of her sickness. Instead, she stopped believing in the illusion of her father.

Well, fathers—

It used to bother me that Ellison, in *Shadow and Act* and *Going to the Territory*, so seldom reviewed and never encouraged any of the other black

American writers of his time, which was a long one. Ambivalence about Wright, who gave him his start, was one thing. Silence on the rest, so many of whom grew up nourished by his breakthrough novel, seemed downright hostile. And this is not to get into what isn't any of my business—the continuing argument about the responsibility of black artists to themselves versus their obligation to an aggrieved community; about primitivism, stereotypes, street cred, protest novels, the black aesthetic, and art for art's sake. I see no reason why Zora Neale Hurston, W.E.B. Du Bois, Richard Wright, Ralph Ellison, James Baldwin, Lorraine Hansberry, August Wilson, George C. Wolfe, Alvin Ailey, Bill T. Jones, Gwendolyn Brooks, Amiri Baraka, Alice Walker, Spike Lee, and Julie Dash shouldn't disagree as much about fundamentals as any other miscellaneous bunch of extravagant talents, any other pantheon. Baldwin, speaking to white America, was certainly right when he said, "If I am not who you say I am, then you are not who you think you are." And so was Toni Morrison, speaking to everybody: "The best art is unquestionably political and irrevocably beautiful at the same time." And maybe, anyway, the best model for any modern literature is the letter of transit, the message in a bottle from exile, displacement, and dispossession. Aren't all of us, even Ellison, homesick?

I'm talking less cosmically, about teachers, mentors, friends. He seems almost to have felt that encouraging the children who cherished his example, and struggled with his shadow, would cost him some body heat. So he hibernated for the long winter, and sucked like Ahab on the paws of his gloom.

But *Juneteenth*, so unlike and yet in surreal keeping with so much that's happened in the last half century of African American writing, suggests those children got what they needed anyway. That Toni Morrison got sermons, jazz, the Civil War, the Reconstruction, magnanimity, and diaspora. That John Edgar Wideman got kinship, ancestry, basketball, deracination, Homewood, epiphany, Africa, and Caliban. That if Ellison neglected Martin Luther King, Jr., Charles Johnson would have to dream about him. And that a phantasmal version of Ellison himself shows up on the last page of Wesley Brown's wonderful *Darktown Strutters*, in the person of the nineteenth-century minstrel Jim Crow, slyly ruining a photograph they're trying to take at P. T. Barnum's Southland theme park—a museum of the American distemper that includes a NIGRA WENCH, a

HEATHEN CHINEE, a DUMB SWEDE, a DRUNKEN MICK, a SHYLOCKING JEW, a MURDEROUS PAISAN, and a DEAD INDIAN. Jim Crow is supposed to be THE CONNIVING UNCLE TOM. But just as the powder goes flashpoof, Jim executes a brand-new fancy step: not there; long gone; you might even say invisible, but dancing somewhere on a coffin.

Why Socialism Never Happened Here

A T A FREE concert in Battery Park in New York City in the first
spring of the twenty-first century, the British folksinger Billy Bragg
observed between Woody Guthrie riffs that the only signs of socialism he
had seen anywhere in these United States were the public library and the
car-pool lane.

If I were socialism, I'd have skipped this country entirely. Imagine an
eye in the sky—a phoenix, a dove, a stormy petrel, or a Sputnik—on a
scouting mission from the failed revolutions of 1848, or maybe the Paris
Commune. Looking down, canting counterclockwise on its powerful left
wing, what would it see? From sea to shining sea: long-distance loneliness . . . Deerslayers, cow punchers, whaling captains, and raft river
rats . . . Greedheads, gun nuts, and religious crazies . . . Carpetbaggers,
claims-jumpers, con men, dead redskins, despised coolies, fugitive slaves,
and No Irish Need Apply . . . Land grabs, lynching bees, and Love
Canals . . . Lone Rangers, private eyes, serial killers, and cyberpunks . . .
Silicon Valley and the Big Casino . . . IPOs and Regis.

Not exactly the ideal social space for a radical Johnny Appleseed to
plant his dream beans. Early on in *It Didn't Happen Here: Why Socialism
Failed in the United States*, Seymour Martin Lipset and Gary Marks quote
the historian Richard Hofstadter: "It has been our fate as a nation not to
have ideologies but to be one." And late in the game the authors speak for
themselves: "A culture can be conceived as a series of loaded dice," in
which "past throws" constrain the present. By then they have
comparison-shopped on the Labor-Left all over the world, consulted
everybody from Trotsky and Gramsci to Irving Howe and Ira Katznelson,

and outlined, rehearsed, staged, critiqued, summarized, reiterated, rewound, rerun, and Mobius-looped every conceivable scenario. The odds, they conclude, were so steeply stacked against socialism in America that its defeat was "overdetermined."

Lipset professes public policy at George Mason University and is a fellow at the Hoover Institution. Marks professes political science at the University of North Carolina and directs its Center for European Studies. They are fair-minded, open-handed, flat-footed, and lily-livered (that is, value-neutral). They aren't saying that socialism *deserved* to flunk our litmus test because there's something *wrong* with it. Nor are they saying there's anything *right* about it, either, unless its washout would help explain why we happen to be the only Western democracy without a comprehensive health-care system, the only one that doesn't provide child support to all of its families, and the worst offender on economic inequality—with a greater gap between rich and poor than any other industrialized nation, double the differential of the next worst down the list; the richest nation in the world, where, nevertheless, one child out of every five is born beneath the subsistence line. What they *do* say is that almost everything exceptional and distinctive about America made socialism a harder sell here than it was in, for instance, Australia. And that the pigheaded behavior of American Socialists only compounded the problem.

Be warned that Lipset and Marks say these things over and over again, after which they repeat them, in the approved reverse-gear style of academic monographs whose feet, like those of the legendary Mikea Pygmies of Madagascar, point backward to confuse their enemy trackers. And yet I can't think of any crime scene Lipset and Marks haven't dusted, nor any suspect they haven't cuffed.

The big picture is that, from the get-go, our "core values" glowed in the dark like Three Mile Island: an ethos of individualism, a weltanschauung of antistatism, and a blank check from God. We sprang full-blown from John Locke's higher brow, a natural-born hegemony of bourgeois money-grubbers—unscathed by medieval feudalism (with its fixed classes of aristocracy and forelock-tugging peasants); exempt from nineteenth-century Europe's ideological power-grabbing fratricides (by virtue of early white male suffrage, lots of land, waves of immigrants to assume the lousiest jobs while the native-born upwardly mobilized themselves, and a ragtag diversity that undermined nascent class consciousness while permitting the merchant princelings to play workers of different racial and ethnic backgrounds against each other in a status scramble); and insulated from revolting developments—insurgencies, mutinies, Jacqueries, even mugwumps and goo-goos—by a political system so partial to the status quo that it's almost arteriosclerotic (a winner-take-all presidency, a fragmenting federalism, a bought judiciary, and a two-party Incumbent Protection Society).

So everybody is measured by his or her ability to produce wealth, those who die with the most toys win, anyone who fails to prosper is morally condemned, and a vote for Ralph Nader, Ross Perot, John Anderson, George Wallace, Henry Wallace, or Robert La Follette—not even to mention Norman Thomas and Eugene V. Debs—is considered to be a waste of franchise.

To be sure, we have had more than our fair share of labor violence. Otherwise, we would never have needed Pinkertons. One recalls, at random, the Haymarket riot, the Homestead strike, and the Ludlow massacre; Harlan County and Coeur d'Alene; steelworkers in Chicago and Detroit, textile workers in Lawrence and Paterson, dockworkers in San Francisco, rubber workers in Akron, and gravediggers in New Jersey: Joe Hill, Big Bill Haywood, Tom Mooney, Mother Jones, Molly Maguires, and Wobblies. But the most depressing chapters in *It Didn't Happen Here* are devoted to a labor movement that had already internalized the all-American ethos of antistatist individualism before the first left-wing agitator explicated the first contradiction—a working class needing to lose a lot more than its chains. "I'm all right, Jack" and "Less Filling! Tastes Great!" don't add up to "From each according to his abilities, to each according to his needs."

Thus the whole idea of a labor party here, anything like those that developed in European nations or Canada and Australia, seems chimerical when we read how such radicals as the Knights of Labor and the Industrial Workers of the World—more anarcho-syndicalist than socialist or Marxist—disdained reform politics every bit as much as conservative craft unionists in the American Federation of Labor. The AFL, in its turn, worked just as hard to protect the skilled jobs of its white native-born membership from a lumpenproletariat of African Americans and immigrants as it did to wring concessions from rapacious employers. (The AFL, until the Great Depression, actually opposed minimum-wage legislation, state provision of old-age pensions, compulsory health insurance, and limitations on the manly work week. Nor should we ever forget a 1902 pamphlet that Samuel Gompers wrote himself: "Meat vs. Rice: American Manhood vs. Asiatic Coolieism: Which Shall Survive?")

Or when we read how the Socialist Party, as fetishistic about doctrine as any Protestant sect, refused to join in coalitions with allies like the North Dakota Non-Partisan League, the Minnesota Farmer-Labor Party, the Commonwealth Federations of Washington and Oregon, the Working Class Union in Oklahoma, or Upton Sinclair's Campaign to End Poverty in California—and in many localities went so far as to expel, for "opportunism," members who joined a union or, even worse, ran for office on a coalition ticket and *won* a municipal election. (Inconstant Debs, a five-time candidate for president on the Socialist line, was quoted famously: "There was a time in my life, before I became a Socialist, when I permitted myself to be elected to a state legislature, and I have been trying to live it down ever since. I am as much ashamed of that as I am of having gone to jail.")

Or when we read how the Depression-born alternative to the AFL, the more inclusive Congress of Industrial Organizations, alert to the possibilities of pro-labor legislation, nevertheless rushed into the co-opting embrace of F.D.R. so quickly and uncritically as to compromise its subsequent leverage on the Democratic Party, even after it was obedient enough to purge its own left wing in the late 1940s. (How prescient the old Socialist Norman Thomas seems now, having warned back then that the New Deal was "an elaborate scheme for stabilizing capitalism through associations of industries that could regulate production in order to maintain profits.")

So much for solidarity. In fact, only once in this century did organized labor desert the Democratic Party, after its nomination of the antilabor John W. Davis in 1924. Which was also the only national election year when the Socialists made common cause with another party, the Progressives. And so La Follette got 16.6 percent of the vote. And so the Democrats, learning their lesson, made sure to nominate a prolabor Al Smith the next time around. And yet how soon the left forgot about the practical payoffs that can sometimes accrue from rejecting the "lesser evil" thesis. And so now organized labor and disorganized labor, too, are both on the wrong side of the candy-store window, looking in from the Dumpster as megamerging downsizers, flyboy bond traders, and multinational vulture capitalists eat the truffles and sodomize the sales clerks. The typical chief

executive of a big company earns 170 times as much as the typical workers. One-third of the labor force earns less than fifteen thousand dollars a
year. The average hourly wage adjusted for inflation is lower today than
it was in 1973. The very definition of inflation has been helpfully
"adjusted" to exclude food and energy. And politicians of both bought
parties are in thrall to a Clairvoyant Master of the Temple of Karnak, a
High Priest of the Hermetic Secrets of the Sacred Science of the Pharaohs,
the Gnome of Fed: Alan (Chuckles) Greenspan.

But socialism had other difficulties. For one, while we tend to think
of immigration as a tide that brought us the socialist Germans of Milwau-
kee, the socialist Finns of Minneapolis, and the socialist Jews of New
York, never mind the socialist Dutch of Reading, Pennsylvania—and
how one cheers their radical initiatives of rural cooperatives and credit
banks; of state-owned terminal elevators, flour mills, packinghouses, and
cold-storage plants; of city-owned coal yards, ice plants, stone quarries,
and electric utilities; of cooperative housing, hot-lunch programs in the
elementary schools, and direct election of school board members; of civil
service standards for the police and fire departments, public works for the
unemployed, and free medical care—that same tide brought in the far
more numerous potato-famine Irish and southern Italians, most of them
Roman Catholics inclined to obey the priests of a Church whose anath-
ematizing of godless socialism had been codified in two different papal
encyclicals. And the Militia of Christ had more money to spend than was
ever discovered in a Wobbly strike fund.

For another, while Lipset and Marks call our electoral system a wash,
neither inhibiting nor encouraging socialism or any other third-party
alternative, they arrive at this judgment by apples-and-oranges analogy.
The logic of a primary-and-party-convention process, they inform us, "is
fundamentally similar to the two-ballot system" in many European countries: "Party factions, which in a two-ballot system would be separate
parties, can contest primaries and then coalesce with other factions in the
general election, or run independently as third candidates."

This is so much static, obscuring the fact that what our primaries do
is aggrandize the two-party system at the expense of outgunned, out-
manned, out-soft-monied Greens, Trots, Flat Earthers, and Right-to-
Lifers. To vote at all in a primary I must be registered in one or another
party, and choose only among its competing candidates. Whereas in
France, for example, any registered voter can vote for any party in the first

round. All those parties receiving one-eighth of the vote advance to the second round, with time off between to form coalitions with like-minded partners. Even the smallest of parties has a chance to advance during both rounds. In France besides, on a local level, half of all elected officials must now be women. More wondrous still, the passionate particularities of a party vote for the European Parliament will be reflected in their exact proportion to the total count, whether that proportion constitutes a majority, a plurality, a handful, or merely a single deputy. It's a mosaic instead of a duochrome; the grand theory accommodates and approximates its noisy fractals.

For a third, the American Socialist Party opposed the First World War. Many socialists, after all, had voted for Woodrow Wilson when he promised to keep us out of it. But he lied. And while socialists all over Europe rallied to the slaughter under their respective flags, the American party stuck to its principles, for which it was repressed—and not only by the usual firings of teachers, shutting down of newspapers, breaking up of meetings, and arrestings on suspicion, but by the infamous Palmer Raids, the refusal to seat duly elected representatives in Congress and state legislatures, and the jailing of Eugene Debs. Never mind that the American party was right (a point that seems not to have occurred to Lipset and Marks). So severely were they punished for opposing a criminally stupid bloodbath that the party never recovered. The authors insist that only the native-born white component of the movement suffered unto extinction, mostly out West; that the big-city ethnic enclaves hunkered down and kept on trucking. But American socialism lost its shock troops, its assembly-line and Deep South labor organizers, its youth brigades, and whatever élan it might have mustered for the the long struggle against not only metastasizing capitalism, but also serial-killing Stalinism.

Because of course it was the Stalinists who took over left-wing organizing in the Popular Front period, even as they lied about their ultimate loyalties. And when they, too, succumbed to Cold War paranoia and McCarthyite repression, there was nobody left to pick up the sticks and do any stitching. "We were, most of us, fleeing the reality that man is alone upon this earth," wrote Murray Kempton in his elegy for thirties radicalism. "We ran from a fact of solitude to a myth of community. That myth failed us because the moments of test come most often when we are alone and far from home and even the illusion of community is not there to sustain us."

I would like to feel the way Nadine Gordimer felt when Susan Sontag asked her, on public television in the late eighties, whether she didn't agree that the old categories of left and right had become outmoded. Gordimer smiled sweetly: "Well, Susan, I still believe with Jean-Paul Sartre—that socialism is the horizon of the world." But I am reluctantly persuaded otherwise. Obviously, the utopianism I concocted for myself in high school in the fifties—equal parts of John Dos Passos, the One Big Rock Candy Union in the fitful memory of an old Wobbly I met on the Pike in Long Beach, California, and the bad dreams of the United Auto Workers area rep who let me follow him around to local union halls while he popped Antabuse to keep from drinking himself to death because he felt guilty for surviving the CIO's left-wing purge—was all a bagpipe dream. How lonely the literature seems where I've made my makeshift home.

How full of hopelessness are Melville in *Benito Sereno*, Twain in *Pudd'nhead Wilson*, and Richard Wright in *Native Son*. How problematic our romance with money in the gangster novels of Saul Bellow, E. L. Doctorow, and William Kennedy. How improbably often the characters in our canonical fiction are on the run, like Ahab and Huck, or Neal Cassady and Rabbit Angstrom. How deeply weird and perverse is our fascination with the iconology of the filthy rich: the famous Steichen portrait of J. P. Morgan with a paring knife and an endangered apple; the Spruce Goose of Howard Hughes; the Rosebud sled of Citizen Kane; the death-in-the-saddle of Nelson A. (for Attica) Rockefeller; the severed ear of the kidnapped Getty; John Jacob Astor, who slaughtered all the otters in Hawaii before building us a library; Daniel Guggenheim, who cut a silver deal with Porfirio Díaz in Mexico and helped out King Leopold II of Belgium with his Congo before endowing us a museum; Andrew Carnegie, who before he gave us a music hall, also gave us the Homestead strike. . . .

We have seen the future and it's selfish. Lottery! Globocop! It seems to me that Lipset and Marks should be a lot sadder than they sound—but then they, too, are all right, Jack.

Maureen Howard's *Big as Life*

I N T H E L A S T panel of Maureen Howard's splendid new triptych of novellas—after the love affair between a professor and a foundation executive; after a Sligo mermaid flees a Wall Street stockbroker's gothic playpen to become a nurse; after church hats, folktales, property rights, banking secrets, and an altar of dandelions and wild garlic—*Big as Life* dreams itself into the nineteenth-century head of John James Audubon, the birdman who killed for his art. To which, as is her recent habit, Howard adds some memoir, recalling a sixteen-year-old Maureen who first looked at *Birds of America* in the Bridgeport Public Library in 1946, discovering there "an ardor brought to information of feathers, claws, beaks, flight, color, to song and violence, which was my natural world, too, though I hadn't known it."

Her winged world: from Bridgeport, Connecticut, "a vaudeville joke," and Irish America, a lacework bog, to delirious New York with its Potemkin bohemias. From sex and money as family secrets, to marriage and children as botched experiments, to art and history as magnetic compass points, to writing and teaching as the calisthenics of moral intelligence. "We may be creatures of our time and place," she has said, "but we make choices, not always for the best, when we love and work."

Love and work, songs and violence, class, politics, literature, and womanhood—on these grids, she plots us. At least since *Natural History* (1992), her brilliant project has been to superimpose one grid on another on a third, fourth, and fifth, for depth perception and spectrum analysis. "Exhaustive events," Artie wrote Louise in *A Lover's Almanac* (1998), "cover all possibilities. So that's where we must be . . . on the island of overlap in the beauty of intersection." *Almanac* was the first book in a projected quartet on a calendar grid—the seasons in symbolic rotation. Thus, after an *Almanac* winter of discontent and expiations, these three tales for spring, these complicated Easter bunnies of renewal and redemption.

Why Howard isn't cherished more is mystifying. It's as if, while nobody watched, Mary McCarthy had grown up to be Nadine Gordimer, getting smarter, going deeper, and writing better than ever before, and she was already special to begin with. Maybe it's bad timing—the feminist novel, *Bridgeport Bus*, a couple of years too early; the radical-sixties novel, *Before My Time*, coming to us after Watergate; the New York intellectuals novel, *Expensive Habits*, a sort of Ancient Mariner nobody wanted to listen to after all that selling out; the great postmodern pastiche, *Natural History*, obliged to compete near the end of the century with morose minimalisms and sullen memoirs. Or maybe it's her unpredictability and impatience—you just can't keep on leaving home, or minting earrings out of the exhausted vein of silver plate in the Irish American foothills, or rehearsing the same old road show of wayward girls, harmful husbands, angry academics, impudent strangers, suspicion of money, quarrels with the past, ambition, and corruption. Half card sharp, half Gypsy, she always finds another game.

And maybe it's her refusal to compromise. She hasn't learned, after all, "not to want the things I cannot have." To each new haunted house, she brings not only her outcast eye but also her child's hunger for grand passions, homely objects, happy endings, and big ideas; for contour, sinew, and resonance. Like Mary Agnes Keely in *Bridgeport Bus*, at her mother's deathbed, "I must contain it all—all—coolly in my mind while the artifice burns in my heart." She is almost too much for us. Like the Emerson she plundered for an epigraph to *Expensive Habits*, she dreams a dream of Eden's apple and of Newton's, too—"that I floated at will in the great ether and I saw the world floating also not far off, but diminished to the size of an apple. Then an angel took it in his hand and brought it to me and said, 'This must thou eat,' and I ate the world." But she is also Ben Franklin, the slyboots so crucial to *A Lover's Almanac*, the inventor of bifocals and lightning rods, rocking chairs and water wings. Rocking chairs and water wings!

Howard's chain-smoking, pill-popping, channel-switching father—with his seminary schoolboy smattering of rhetoric and apologetics and his adhesive grudge against a society that treated the Irish "like guttersnipes and cartoon drunks"—was "a terrible man," perverse and crude, who "never got out of his chair to get himself so much as a glass of water all his life." Or so his daughter told us in *Facts of Life* (1978). But he was also a detective, with a badge, a gun, and a railroad pass.

Her mother—fey, fragmented, "somewhat wistful" and "too fine for the working-class neighborhood that surrounded us"—graduated from Smith, quoted Schiller, and married down, for passionate love, at age thirty-three, after which she carried herself "like a grieving queen." But she was also artsy, with a "near perfect eye" for lotus pods and asparagus ferns. And when she wasn't washing twenty-dollar bills in dish detergent and drying them on a towel rack (because "money is so dirty"), she dragged her children to concerts by the Budapest String Quartet, rather than the circus.

One grandfather made a pile in the contractor business, married a department store clerk crazy about opera and horses, and conveyed his patriarchal self about town in a luxury Locomobile. The other, having failed to organize workers at Singer Sewing Machine, settled for a political patronage job and walked each day to the county jail.

So Maureen, playing Puck and Portia and reading Eugene O'Neill, knowing that she was "a sinner from the start, never one of the good girls the nuns fussed over," grew up a plump and pigtailed hostage to piano lessons and modern dance, in a household where mom carved Mary, Joseph, camels, and lambs out of bars of Ivory soap while dad sang "Danny Boy" with tears in his eyes and rooted for Joe McCarthy. She only went to work in the public library in the first place because she thought her parents needed the money—and then all of a sudden saw those Audubon prints, as Big As Life, and decided to fly away.

For a writer "at the beginning of my long caeer as an escape artist," this is a pretty good tool kit. "I am not the lady I was meant to be," she didn't have to tell us.

Her first novel, *Not a Word About Nightingales* (1960), was a Randall Jarrell campus production she would rather we ignored, like a first marriage, simply practice. But her second, *Bridgeport Bus* (1965), was a *Fear of Flying* before the feminist resurgence, as if Bridget Jones's diary had been written by Rebecca West, Maud Gonne, and Hildegard of Bingen, and very funny, like early Waugh. No American heroine has ever been more wayward, nor more pregnant, than Mary Agnes Keely, a white whale, a "Molly Mick." And in her pilgrim's progress from Bridgeport to Greenwich Village, from a job in a zipper factory to a job at Wunda-Clutch the miracle grip, from virginity to martyrdom and from reading to writing, Mary Agnes is more than a match for Studs Dedalus.

Maggie Flood in *Expensive Habits* (1986) is equally Irish (née Lynch), also a writer (including screenplays), has likewise not succeeded in telling the whole story, and may be dying at age forty-five. Before her heart is bypassed, she has amends to make: Her first husband didn't deserve her unkind first novel; her only son is owed "some uncorrupted text." But also scores to settle—with the editor who "took me to be raw material like sugar cane and refined me into a small bowl of salable white crystals to draw the ants." And the Hollywood director who turned her into a pretentious movie. And the left-wing New York intellectuals who patronized her. You may notice in these pages hanks of Lillian Hellman's hair, rags and bones of Philip Rahv and Hannah Arendt, and the passing resemblance of poor Pinky, the father of Maggie's child, to Robert Lowell and Dwight Macdonald. But *Expensive Habits* is best described as a self-punishing American version of Gordimer's *Burger's Daughter*.

Yet all her heroines are self-punishing, harder on themselves than we are. This is why they're so refreshing in the modern period of crybabies sanctioned by designer therapists. Even as they peel off the Irish, they accuse themselves of envy and class animus. They have no sooner buried their tin-pot fathers and cannibal mothers than they dig them up again to keen—the same sad song on the same damned harp; burning themselves instead of peat. Or, swimming up through fathoms of money to butter knives, serving plates, golf trophies, maybe a clavichord, probably Princeton, certainly a horse, they get the bends, as if they didn't deserve these goodies, as if anybody does. Don't look back on the potato famine or you'll turn into a bottle of Guinness.

And I should say "we" instead of "they."

So they try to read their way out of the discrepancies—Mary Agnes with the French poets; Laura Quinn with Frost, Freud, and Joyce; Maggie Flood with Plato, Tolstoy, Jane Austen, and *Anne of Green Gables*. And to politick: civil rights, Vietnam, Bed-Stuy, Woodstock, Pentagon. And to mediate: Mary Agnes writes parables and playlets, as well as ad copy, before her short stories, while all around her in a lofty Village, poets pose and artists arty. Laura's books include a novel, and she also tape-records a lot. Maggie goes from fiction to screenplays, before confessing all like Augustine, while Pinky in a basement full of alcoholic fumes compiles his secret archive: "family tales," "scraps of romance," "naive realism," "correspondences."

Which blasts the heath for *Natural History,* a multimedia novel asking why, in 1945 wartime Bridgeport, a socialite vamp with a Southern accent got away with murder. Because *Natural History* is an Oedipal mystery, keep your eye on the county detective. But spectacle and illusion are the bigger villains. Bridgeport, home of P. T. Barnum, Walt "Pogo" Kelly, Remington rifles, and Sikorsky aircraft, may have declined from an Arsenal of Democracy into needle-park housing projects and jai alai frontons. But not as seen through the self-deceiving eyes of the Irish Catholic Bray family, who imagine the city and themselves in children's stories, fairy tales, stage plays, film scripts, lives of the saints, and a double entry that mimicks the *Arcades Project* of Walter Benjamin, with narrative to the right while on the left we shop in a typographic mall of time-coded mugshots, history lessons, odd stats, snide asides, quotes, and jokes.

In this dreamscape of stage and screen, circus and rodeo, museums, marching bands, and even operatic stagings by the Catholic Church of our "primary narrative myth," nobody notices the real-life disappearance of Peaches, who turns coat hangers into wire effigies of men who abuse her mother. And when a name and an identity are both erased from a computer file, we sense that Maureen Howard is about to go digital, virtual, and World Wide Webby. And so she does.

A Lover's Almanac is the story of two pairs of lovers coiled in a double helix. Artie, a young mathematician, and Louise, a young artist, love each other, but are both so callow they let talk-show issues get in the way. Besides, neither is sure of being the real thing: the first-rate mind, the genuine original. Cyril O'Connor, Artie's grandfather, and Sylvie Neisswonger, an Austrian refugee, loved each other fifty years ago. But Cyril married Mae, the good Catholic daughter of his Wall Street boss, to escape his boggy origins (cop father drinks, mother is abused), while Sylvie went home to the nice man with the okay stepchildren. It is, however, a new millennium. Sylvie is alone in Connecticut. So is widowed Cyril in a leather chair in his Fifth Avenue apartment, reading the books he gave up for money. And so, briefly, they will put their stories together while Artie and Louise dream up ways to tear theirs apart. "It seems," says Louise, "you must reinvent yourself to meet love's impossible demands." Well, yes.

But *A Lover's Almanac* is also a captivity narrative, where everyone is kidnapped, if not by Indians, then maybe Freud, or Marx, or bad luck, or probability theory. To all her other intersecting grids, Howard has added mathematics and music, astrology and Egyptology, medical science, a Mayan calendar, and what she calls "The Endless Page." Scroll down, she tells us. And we do, learning a lot about dairy farms, number theory, conceptual art, Ben Franklin, Thomas Jefferson, Emily Dickinson, Thomas Edison, Darwin, Newton, and St. Paul. But we don't find out what happened to Sissy, orphan of the savage streets. Nor who Artie's real father was, back in the radically permissive sixties. So many data and coordinates, such a density of language, and I haven't even mentioned the machine-gun italics when the author wants to confide in us herself—and still we never know enough to be positive about anything.

Which is the point of this amazing novel. Knowing as much as may be humanly possible, and yet not enough to be absolutely sure, guarantees choice—free will's wiggle room.

I can't be sure (of course!), but I think we meet Sissy again in *Big as Life*, before she had to hit the streets and sleep at night in empty day-care centers. We certainly meet Mae Boyle, before she married Cyril O'Connor, the only creature in her father's house who isn't dipped in bronze, a prim tormented child who worships the Virgin at her own wild altar of buttons, garlic, and pigeon feathers. And Artie and Louise put in an extended reappearance, not yet married but the parents of a child, on a Long Island sabbatical from the delirious city. Artie plays games at a seminar with Fermat's Last Theorem, Euclid's Fifth, Riemann's Hypothesis, and the Parallel Postulate. Louise, in a garage, consulting her Audubon, dreams of Peaceable Kingdoms and does kinky things to an owl. Maureen looks on, eagle-eyed. While she clearly cares about them, she's itchy to have her own say.

After speaking in tongues of endings that are almost happy, in fables intended to remind us of Perrault and La Fontaine, Howard seizes her own stage. She will stick pins in Audubon, with his gun, violin, and dancing slippers. "I hardly call it a day," said the American Woodsman, the son of a slave trader, "if I have not shot a hundred birds." And in his journal: "Cuckoos, killed 5. Painted Buntings, killed 20." This is another, darker parable, and she is made to wonder: Killing for art, for science, for greed, for the blood-drunk lazy crazy hell of it? It is also the self-consciousness of a great artist in her own forest—more love, violence, work, and songs.

Bill Ayers's *Fugitive Days*

Every good hunter is uneasy in the depths of his conscience when faced with the death he is about to inflict on the enchanted animal. He does not have the final and firm conviction that his conduct is correct. But neither, it should be understood, is he certain of the opposite.

—José Ortega y Gasset, *Meditations on Hunting*

MY BLOODTHIRSTY STAGE, the warrior phase of a developing manhood, lasted from age six until age twelve. At six, I was the first little boy on my block, in Washington, D.C., to have a Lone Ranger atomic bomb ring. You peeked in at a color photograph of the mushroom cloud. In fact, owing to a mixup of breakfast cereal box tops in Battle Creek, Michigan, I had four Lone Ranger atomic bomb rings, one for every other finger on both hands. I only wish I could have quoted Sanskrit.

At age twelve, in 1952, I found myself wearing a WIN WITH KEFAUVER T-shirt in Joe McCarthy territory, at a hunting and fishing lodge in northern Wisconsin, when one of the black Labrador retrievers came back with a nose full of porcupine quills. Grim men in checkerboard motley took up arms in the forest primeval. I found the fierce porcupine, hiding up a tree. I shot it twice with a .22 rifle. It fell at my feet, not exactly a sweet kill. I can't remember if we ate it. But no bird sang, and neither did a Hemingway.

Robin Williams has since explained: "Kill a small animal, drink a lite beer." My son, who was born so fortuitously in 1962, describes himself today as the first Berkeley antiwar protest, or a draft dodge. I tell you this so that you will know just who's thinking out loud about Weatherman and the Days of Rage and the Greenwich Village townhouse explosion. In my opinion, they were all a bunch of Lone Ranger atomic bomb rings.

Bill Ayers takes a different view. He was himself a street-fighting Weatherperson, a rock-and-roll Tupamaro, a social bandit out of Hobsbawm, like Rob Roy, Pancho Villa, Jesse James, and the Opportune Rain Sung Chiang. He was in love with another Weatherperson, Diana Oughton, a former Peace Corps Quaker who died making bombs on West Eleventh Street. He then married a third Weatherperson, Bernardine Dohrn, a University of Chicago law-school graduate feared by J. Edgar Hoover ("the most dangerous woman in America") and American Rhapsodized by Joe Eszterhas ("our real babe in bandoliers"). And he's foster father to the child of a fourth, Kathy Boudin, who remains in prison for the 1981 stickup of a Brinks truck that killed four people. How he got to American Berserk, carrying a poem by Ho Chi Minh in his pocket, tattooed on his neck with the rainbow-and-lightning logo, and playing with the sticks of dynamite they nicknamed "pickles," is the subject of this unrepentant retrospection.

Up to a point, *Fugitive Days* is the frazzled story of almost any white middle-class sixties activist in the civil-rights and antiwar movements, written with a speed-freak rush between sometimes embarrassing apostrophes to Mnemosyne—memory "is a delicate dance of desire and faith, a shadow of a shadow, an echo of a sigh," when it isn't "a twig cut from a tree and tossed like a toy from crest to trough" on a murky "wine-dark, opaque, unfathomable" sea, or the "ghosts and fears that haunt us, floating desires and falsifying dreams more powerful and more compelling than hard reality will ever be," or "a mortuary," a "mystification," and maybe even "a motherfucker"—but true to the kids we were. At exactly that OK Corral point, however, when a movement devolved into a vanguard, when participatory democracy turned into a tantrum of the Leninist cadres, when Isaac Babel's Red Cavalry started looking like Don DeLillo's alphabet killer cult, Bill Ayers blinks.

Such swaddled beginnings: The middle child of well-heeled midwesterners—his "rising executive" father became CEO of Commonwealth Edison of Chicago—young Bill grew up in comfortably suburban Glen Ellyn, Illinois, playing football almost as soon as he could walk, catching crayfish and sticking frogs in the Du Page River, summering at YMCA camp or on Cape Cod, reading books like *The Runaway Bunny* and *Catcher in the Rye*, going to movies like *The Flying Leathernecks*, prepping at Lake Forest Academy, and, upon discovering in Ann Arbor that he was too small to cut the mustard on Michigan's Big Ten football team, dropping out to play instead for social justice.

Well, not immediately. He auditioned in Detroit for the Reverend Gabriel Star, who sent him to New Orleans, where Father Peter Paul Streeter couldn't figure out what to do with him, so he signed up as a merchant seaman on a freighter to Piraeus full of "Food for Peace." Rome was where he first read about Vietnam, in the *International Herald Tribune*. Back then to Ann Arbor and Students for a Democratic Society, being radicalized by his first bonfire, teach-in, sit-in, and jail time: "anarchists and street people, radicals and rockers." Not to mention Diggers, Wobblies, dope, hair, and his first tattoo, the red star on the left shoulder. Like Bob Moses and Martin Luther King, Jr., he would be "a nonviolent direct action warrior, in the spirit of the civil rights struggle. I was about to personally disrupt this war, and I tingled all over."

What this meant, at age twenty in 1965, was teaching young children in a freedom school and learning from a local leader of Women's Strike for Peace "the fine points of female orgasm." By age twenty-one, he was director of the Ann Arbor school and setting up a similar one in Cleveland—food and lodging paid for by church groups and labor unions, two dollars a week spending money and an expanding agenda that included a rent strike committee and a health-care project—when he experienced his first urban riot: "The strange thing was to live in an atmosphere simultaneously terrifying and deeply energizing." Alas, when Stokely Carmichael and Black Power came along, "I had to get out of the way"—which meant leaving both Cleveland and Jackie, the young black woman with whom he was sleeping. But he had seen enough:

> Night after night, day after day, each majestic scene I witnessed was so terrible and unexpected that no city would ever again stand innocently fixed in my mind. Big buildings and wide streets, cement and steel were no longer permanent. They, too, were fragile and destructible. A torch, a bomb, a strong enough wind, and they, too, would come undone or get knocked down.

So it was back to Ann Arbor, where he met Diana, just back herself from Guatemala. Not only could she worm dogs, can fruit, and drive a motorcycle, but she was as blond as Bill. About Bill, Diana wrote to her sister: "I'm afraid he's going to be a boy forever—he's got a Peter Pan complex, and no Wendy Girl in sight." Together, they "wanted to teach the children, feed the hungry, shelter the homeless, fight the power, and end the war." And yet, as the war worsened, so did their behavior. If Diana began to identify with Simone Weil, longing to parachute behind enemy lines, even cutting her long hair, Bill seemed to channel the "By Any Means Necessary" Malcolm X poster on the wall above their bed. In Washington for the 1967 demonstration, he told TV reporter Peter Jennings, who had paid for the steak he ate: "I'm not so much against the war as I am for a Vietnamese victory. I'm not so much for peace as for a U.S. defeat." Even before the assassinations of Dr. King and Bobby Kennedy, the Mexico City Olympics or the Chicago Democratic Convention, "everything seemed urgent now, everything was accelerating. . . . It fell to us—and we were just kids—to save the world."

You already know more than you want to about Chicago 1968. But Ayers makes clear the determination of the student radicals, wearing red headbands, carrying backpacks with Vaseline and goggles to protect them against tear gas, hammers to smash windows, slingshots, blackjacks, cherry bombs, and marbles (to scatter any cavalry charge), to bring down capitalism, racism, and imperialism by kicking butt. After which "smoke and rage," there was "fear, then naked panic," and, finally, "sheer joy and wild relief to be there cherishing every lovely blow." For those in need of an epiphany:

> The serpent of rage was loosed in the wide world, and it sank its passionate fangs deep into our inflamed hearts, power and corruption lying in the tall grass side by side along the pathway of wrath.
>
> Uncontrollable rage—fierce frenzy of fire and lava, blowing off the mountaintop, coursing headlong, in an onslaught of unstoppable chaos—choking rivers, overwhelming the living things in its disastrous path, consuming to exhaustion.
>
> Purifying fury, white-hot and cutting laserlike through illusion, burning a fine, straight tunnel to the very soul of things, illuminating anger, passionate and perceptive, eliminating all distraction and doubt, our burning shining pinpoint of lucid, absolute certainty at last.

This doesn't sound to me much like Bob Moses, Grace Paley, Allen Ginsberg, or Joan Baez. It sounds more like Big Ten football.

> *The sky was blue and the whips were black.*
> —Isaac Babel

Nor, trust me, do you really want to hear about the takeover of SDS by its Maoist faction, Progressive Labor, which scowled upon the "revisionism" of the North Vietnamese. It wasn't necessary to be a member of any wing of the Revolutionary Youth Movement, all of them waving their Little Red Books, to want to secede in 1969 from a lunatic state of mind. But Ayers and his buddies took up citizenship in a system almost equally delusional—with its rhetoric of "wargasms" and "an American Red Army," its ideology of pothead group sex and rubbishy machismo, and its dorky four-fingered fork salute. They brought the war home by invading high schools, trashing supermarkets, going to kung fu movies, hassling autoworkers on a beach, passing out leaflets at a Hells' Angels rally, burning an effigy of Henry Ford III at a Davis Cup tennis match, springing Timothy Leary from prison, accusing each other of reading poems or eating ice cream, blowing up police statues and themselves.

Diana had to be identified from the print on a severed fingertip.

Ayers might have told us why, looking back, he now thinks so many smart kids shape-shifted their shamanic selves from Dr. King to Dr. Strangelove, or Baader-Meinhofs and the Red Brigades. There is even reason to suspect that he knows things about himself he'd prefer to blame on Harry Truman and Hiroshima than to analyze out loud. For instance, even before he read Dickens, Twain and Hemingway, Ellison and Kerouac, Rousseau, Thoreau and Marx, even before his favorite films turned out to be *Bonnie and Clyde* and *The Battle of Algiers*, he seems to have had a crush on boom-boom. The Fourth of July was his favorite holiday because of cherry bombs—"and the rocket's red glare." At age fourteen, hanging with the neighborhood pool sharks and bumper tags, he proved himself an honorary "Italian" by keeping silent after he was accidentally set on fire by an exploding zip gun/pipe bomb, whose ingenious construction from match heads, firecracker fuses, threaded bolts, cotton wadding, and ball bearings he lovingly describes. To pass the time at

Lake Forest Academy, overprivileged preppies "trapped small animals in the woods and blew them up with candle bombs late at night." As early as p.21 of *Fugitive Days*, young Bill has already asked a poignant question:

> Could there ever be a really good bomb? It could not be built to hurt or kill. Maybe it could extract minerals from the ground. Maybe it could knock over an abandoned building, or maybe the Pentagon after everyone goes home. Simple earth-works, performance art, everyone standing back. Bombs away.

But Looking for Mr. Goodbomb will not entirely explain his memoir's prurient interest in pressure-trigger, alarm clock, magnifying glass, and nipple time bombs, in Bangalore torpedoes and homemade grenades, in nitroglycerin, ammonium nitrate, mercury fulminate, chloride of azode, and dynamite, not to mention hat pins, brass knuckles, garrotes, and saps, or, even after the death of Diana, the training in the desert with high-powered rifles and nine-millimeter pistols. The once-upon-a-time "nonviolent direct action warrior" has become his very own free-fire zone:

> This bizarre and violent time, this ritual of combat, this surreal setting combined with ferocious demons vomited into the dark-eyed night, pursuing me now with anonymous, deadly hatred. I was sure of only one thing: whatever happened next, I was choosing with eyes wide open, and while I might be wrong or foolish, limited and inadequate, mine would not be the suffering of the hapless victim. I might be crushed, but I would never complain and I would never bring suit. Life's tough, and I knew what was up. Get a helmet.

This is the cuckoo sprung from the clock of a Sumer warrior-king, a Butch Cassidy and the Sundance Kid psychology of masculine triumphalism. So it's no surprise, just lousy timing, that on the very morning of the terror bombings of the World Trade Center and the Pentagon, Bill Ayers should be quoted, in a smirking interview in the *New York Times*, as saying of his Weather days: "I don't regret setting bombs. I feel we didn't do enough." Maybe he's joshing again, as he assures the *Times* he must have been if he actually said in 1970, "Kill all the rich people. Break up their cars and apartments. Bring the revolution home, kill your parents, that's where it's really at." (Intended, he now says, as "a joke about the distribution of wealth.") His wife, Bernardine Dohrn, must likewise have been joking when she said in 1969, after the Manson gang murders: "Dig it! First they killed those pigs, then they ate dinner in the same room with them, then they even shoved a fork into a victim's stomach. Wild!" (Dohrn hastens to tell the *Times* that "we were mocking violence in America. Even in my most inflamed moment I never supported a racist mass murderer.") And Jerry Rubin told me in 1977 that he had only been joking in 1968, after Robert Kennedy's assassination, when he declared: "Sirhan Sirhan is a Yippie!"

After the Village townhouse explosion, when all the Weather balloons went underground, they resolved to be more careful: "No one at that safe house in those white hot days wanted to surrender, and no one argued for surfacing or disbanding. No one even thought that we should turn away from violence on principle. There was, however, a consensus growing that our actions would be strongest as symbols, a kind of overheated story-telling." So, while the last half of *Fugitive Days* is devoted mostly to the tradecraft of hiding from the FBI, mention is also made in passing of bombings of ROTC buildings, Selective Service offices, and the "corporate giants most clearly identified with U.S. aggression and expansion" like Standard Oil, United Fruit, Chase Manhattan, and IBM.

Each, says Ayers, was "hugely magnified because of the symbolic nature of the target, the deliberate and judicious nature of the blow, and the synchronized public announcements suggesting the dreadful or exhilarating news that a homegrown guerrilla movement was afoot in America." He insists that "I thought about the justification for each action. . . . [We] did our best to take care, to do no harm to persons and no more damage than we'd planned." I'm sure that all the other kamikazes of Kingdom Come say pretty much the same thing before they bomb another abortion clinic. Later, speaking of the Pentagon, Ayers tells us: "Because nothing justified their actions in our calculus, nothing could contradict the merit of ours." We've heard this before, too, from everybody in Belfast, Sarajevo, and Beirut who has ever killed a child because his Higher Power told him to.

Let's leave it simple. Let's valorize, instead of Weatherman, those who strung along with Gandhi on his Salt March to decolonize the Indian mind in 1930. And the Dutch doctors who refused, during the Nazi occupation, to screen for genetic "defects." And the Danes who declined to build German ships, feed the German army, or honor the Nazi racial laws, while whisking away their Jewish fellow citizens to Sweden. And the Fisk students who desegregated Nashville's downtown lunch counters in 1960 and thereby launched a second American revolution. And the Polish workers in Solidarity who occupied a shipyard in 1980, and, by insisting on their right to strike, began, without firing a single shot, the dismantling of the nonprofit police states of Eastern Europe. And those disenfranchised citizens of martial-law South Africa whose economic boycott spread from black townships to the conscience-stricken West, paralyzed the apartheid state, and led eventually to free elections. And those Chileans who ended Pinochet's dictatorship with street festivals, protest songs, union activity, vigils by the mothers of the disappeared, and a surprise plebiscite. Not to forget the women of Manila who shamed the tanks of Marcos with a fusillade of yellow flowers, and the Chinese students in Tiananmen Square, or what Aung San Suu Kyi is apparently accomplishing under Rangoon house arrest.

Everywhere it is written—in bullet holes and amputations, in shell shock and mushroom clouds, in brainwash and shrink-wrap—that political science is a clenched fist, that power flows from the mouths of guns, that bloodlust and servitude are coded in our genome, and that obedience or death is the inevitable trajectory of narrative. But there is another way to read this atrocious past century: the view from Gandhi's spinning wheel, in which, against tyranny and exploitation, occupation and oppression, popular movements of tens of thousands withhold their consent. They refuse, secede, mobilize, challenge, humiliate, disrupt, and disobey. And their principled civil disobedience—tactical, strategic, improvisatory, sometimes even whimsical—creates the very wherewithal of a civil society. When Václav Havel and his friends wrote a new social contract in 1989 in the Magic Lantern Theater in Prague, on a stage set for Dürrenmatt's *Minotaurus*, they weren't reading *Prairie Fire*. Nor were the students from Charles University, dressed comically as Young Pioneers in red kerchiefs, white blouses, and pigtails, calling themselves the Committee for a More Joyful Present, who joined these jailbird intellectuals when they were depressed and weary: "We have come," the students said, "to cheer you up—and make sure you don't turn into another politboro." And so the students gave to all the members of Havel's plenum little circular mirrors to examine themselves as they wrote the future of the Czech Republic to the music of the Beatles—in order to be on the lookout for you know whom.

Blowing His Nose in the Wind

I

Bob Dylan wrote "A Hard Rain's a-Gonna Fall" in the summer of 1962, in a matter of minutes, on Wavy Gravy's typewriter, after reading William Blake. "That song kind of roared right out of the typewriter," Wavy Gravy remembers. "It roared through him the way paint roared through van Gogh."

Wavy Gravy, in case you are wondering how to become a Ben & Jerry's ice-cream flavor, was the Merry Prankster who introduced young Dylan to everybody hip in Greenwich Village in the early sixties, from Allen Ginsberg to Lenny Bruce to Thelonius Monk. He was also heard to whisper, during Martin Luther King's "I Have a Dream" speech on the steps of the Lincoln Memorial in 1963, "I hope he's over quick, Mahalia Jackson's on next." And he later served as master of ceremonies at the 1969 Woodstock music festival. Bob Dylan actually happened to be living in Woodstock at the time of this pep rally, but chose to perform instead on the Isle of Wight, off the south coast of England, for fifty thousand dollars plus expenses—although he would manage to make it to Woodstock the Sequel, in 1994, for six hundred thousand dollars.

Anyway, Wavy Gravy's 1962 intuition of afflatus accords with Dylan's own. "The songs are there," the boy genius told *Sing Out!* "They exist all by themselves just waiting for someone to write them down." If "Hard Rain" painted itself, "Like a Rolling Stone" would come to him in 1965 like "a long piece of vomit." To Robert Shelton he explained in 1966 that "anytime I'm singing about people and if the songs are dreamed, it's like my voice is coming out of their dream." Much, much later, after being baptized in the Pacific Ocean, a born-again Bob would credit God. And then vandals stole the handle.

Given that I'm about to contribute to the literature of hyperventilation on the overwrought occasion of Dylan's sixtieth birthday, you ought to know where I stand. Because Joan Baez loved him a lot, I have to assume that he is not as much of a creep as he so often seems. But I'm entitled to doubts about anybody whose favorite Beatle was George. And don't tell me it's all about the music. The whole Dylan package has been marketed as attitude; wrapped in masks. Music is about music. Biographies are about behavior. Caring about the music is what makes our interest in the behavior more than merely prurient. If you'd really rather not have known that Pythagoras hated beans, Spinoza loved rainbows, and Ingmar Bergman was a lousy father, you're a better person than I am, although we both have a long way to go before we're as good as Joan Baez.

2

I wish that for just one time
you could stand inside my shoes
You'd know what a drag it is
to see you

Think of David Hajdu's *Positively 4th Street: The Lives and Times of Joan Baez, Bob Dylan, Mimi Baez Fariña, and Richard Fariña* as *A Little Night Music* scored for dulcimer and motorcycle. Or a pas de quatre, with wind chimes, love beads, and a guest-appearance entrechat by Thomas Pynchon. As Hajdu, whose biography of Billy Strayhorn, *Lush Life*, is an ornament of jazz lit, rotates among his principals until at last they settle down to play house in Carmel and Woodstock, he is such an ironist among blue notes, so knowledgeable about their performing selves on stage, in bed, and in our mezzotinted memories, that he seems almost to be whistling scherzos. So we follow Bobby Zimmerman, aka Shabtai Zisel ben Avraham, a Russian-Jewish college dropout who left Minnesota to look for Woody Guthrie, and Richard Fariña, an Irish-Cuban altar boy from Flushing, Queens, who majored in literary ambition at Nabokov's Cornell, as they advance their careers by sleeping with Joan Baez and her sister Mimi, the singing daughters of a Mexican-American physics professor who trained Cold War military engineers. And Hajdu also knows precisely where to stop the music, just this side of lapidary, in 1966, when a matched pair of motorcycle accidents—a zygotic twinship—killed off Fariña two days after the publication of his only novel, *Been Down So Long It Looks Like Up to Me*, and sent the substance-abusing Dylan into the first of his many gnomic seclusions.

This countercultural *Les Liaisons Dangereuses* began on a Greenwich Village street corner in 1961, when an unknown Fariña said to a little-known Dylan, "Man, what you need to do, man, is hook up with Joan Baez. She is so square, she isn't in this century. She needs you to bring her into the twentieth century, and you need somebody like her to do your songs. She's your ticket, man. All you need to do, man, is start screwing Joan Baez." To which an insouciant Dylan replied: "That's a good idea—I think I'll do that. But I don't want her singing none of my songs." It would end twenty-five years later—after Richard had dumped his first wife, Carolyn Hester, to get as close as he could to Joan by courting and marrying her teenaged sister Mimi; after Bob used Joan to get famous and then did everything he could think of to ridicule and degrade her, to which she responded with a love song, "Diamonds and Rust," that would have shamed any other cad this side of Dr. Kissinger's princely narcissism; after Vietnam, Watergate, and Ronald Reagan—when Brother Bob saw the Widow Mimi for the first time since Richard's death, and sought to comfort her with these apples: "Hey, that was a drag about Dick. It happened right around my thing, you know. Made me think."

And love is just a four-letter word.

Postdocs in Dylanology will most appreciate Hajdu's revisionist account of Newport in 1965. He blames the boos on a lousy sound system in worse weather. How could anyone have been surprised at Dylan's plugging himself in, when his new album, *Bringing It All Back Home*, with its hit single, "Subterranean Homesick Blues," had been on the charts for four months, and you couldn't turn on the radio without hearing "Like a Rolling Stone"? Assistant professors of *Gravity's Rainbow* will be delighted to hear from Tom Pynchon, who was a buddy of Richard's at Cornell, and best man at his wedding to Mimi in Carmel, to which he hitchhiked from Mexico because he didn't have a driver's license, and agreed to be interviewed for Hajdu's book by fax, and is quoted not only in a blurb for

Been Down So Long ("This book comes on like the Hallelujah Chorus done by two hundred kazoo players with perfect pitch"), but also in a personal note to the needy author:

> But to you, wild colonial maniac, about all I can say is holy shit. . . . This thing man picked me up, sucked me in, cycled, spun and centrifuged my ass to where it was a major effort of will to go get up and take a leak even, and by the time it was over with I know where I had been.
>
> If you want comparisons, which you don't, I think most of Rilke.

For those of us who are amateurs—that is, those of us who still enjoy the great songs but are inclined to believe that there are whole decades of Dylan more interesting to read about in Greil Marcus ("What is this shit?") than to listen to on our speaker systems—*Postively 4th Street* is a cohort story. I like cohort stories: about Partisan Reviewers, Abstract Expressionists, or the Beats; the New York Brat Pack and the Chinese Misties. I think it's terrific that young singers and songwriters, like young writers and artists, fester together in seedy nests or move in herds like thick-skinned ungulates across the inky savannahs of the culture, dodging potshots from the great white hunters at Establishment media. So what if they hurt one another while the rest of us are waiting to see which one turns into a unicorn? My favorite *Positively* scene is when Bob, Joan, Richard, and Mimi visit Henry Miller, the Tropic of Cancer himself rusticating in Pacific Palisades, whom only Richard has read. Henry, of course, wants either Baez (or both), but has to settle for playing Ping-Pong with Mr. Tambourine Man.

I also love their cover stories: Dylan, who grew up in Hibbing, Minnesota, with fine china, crystal glass, sterling silver cutlery, a spinet piano, and a chandelier, whose father bought him a pink Ford convertible and a Harley, whose only real job ever in the real world was as a busboy one summer at the Red Apple Café in Fargo, North Dakota, told everybody in Manhattan that he had been raised in foster homes, had Sioux Indian blood, sang for his supper in carnivals from age fourteen, played piano on early Elvis records, picked up guitar licks from a New Mexico blues musician named Wigglefoot, wrote songs for Carl Perkins in Nashville, and earned walking-around money as a Times Square hustler. Fariña, whose father was a toolmaker and whose first job out of college was at the J. Walter Thompson advertising agency, working on the Shell Oil account, advised the credulous that his father was a Cuban inventor and his mother an Irish mystic, that he had been born at sea, and had run guns for Castro, and had sunk a British sub for the IRA, and had been expelled from Cornell for leading a riot, and slept with a loaded .45 under his pillow in case of assassins.

Haven't we all fudged our résumés? But who knew that organized folksinging, like organized labor, organized religion, and organized crime, could be a medium of upward mobility?

3

They'll stone you when you're riding in your car
They'll stone you when you're playing your guitar
But I would not feel so all alone
Everybody must get stoned

Think of Howard Sounes's *Down the Highway*, on the other hand, as a surveillance tape. Or maybe a transcript of the black-box audio recovered from the crash site of the never-ending tour bus. Either lumbering way, it wants to be exhaustive, like a commission report or a Dreiser. (*An American Tragedy* comes to mind.) British journalist Sounes, who has also written a biography of Charles Bukowski, tracks Dylan from the four-year-old who used to entertain his family with a rousing rendition of "Accentuate the Positive" to the sixty-year-old who has authorized himself to sing "Forever Young" in a television commercial for iMac Apple computers. And besides mentioning every book, record, gesture, arrangement, or idea that Dylan ever stole in his lordly passage from Hard Rain to Sweet Jesus, Sounes will also name the names of every girlfriend, fraternity brother, business associate, disordered groupie, and discarded mentor or buddy; every musician at every gig or recording session; and every influence from Buddy Holly, Hank Williams, Little Richard, Muddy Waters, and Jimmy Reed, to James Dean and Marlon Brando, to Woody Guthrie, Pete Seeger and Odetta, to *Gunsmoke*'s Matt Dillon and Graceland's Elvis and the Beatles and St. Augustine.

Most of this you probably already knew from previous biographies by

Anthony Scaduto, Robert Shelton, Bob Spitz, and Clinton Heylin, whose ferociously opinionated *Bob Dylan: Behind the Shades* has just been "revisited" and updated for the birthday party and is lots more fun than Sounes. But some of it you didn't—such as his second marriage to one of his African American backup singers, Carolyn Dennis, to legitimize his sixth child, Desiree Gabrielle Dennis-Dylan. Moreover, after interviewing everybody in the vicinity at the time, Sounes suggests that Dylan's famous 1966 motorcycle accident might not have been as medically serious as previously supposed, but more of an excuse to drop out, sober up, and recharge, after *Highway 61*, *Blonde on Blonde*, and all that hash and all those amphetamines in Australia.

In fact, while heavy drinking seems to have been Dylan's biggest problem most of his career—he finally quit in the midnineties—1966 is associated in both books with everything from pot to speed to LSD and maybe even heroin, leaving Dylan "skeletal and green." (There is even a theory that "I Want You" in *Blonde on Blonde* was "about heroin" rather than a woman.) While we burned Dylan for fuel, he seems to have been running on fumes. The 1975 Rolling Thunder Revue, to which Baez, Allen Ginsberg, Sam Shepard, Joni Mitchell, and Stevie Wonder signed on, though they can't be blamed for *Renaldo and Clara*, sounds in Sounes like a coke bust waiting to happen to a tabloid. And by Thanksgiving 1976, when the Band let Martin Scorsese film *The Last Waltz*, they even had a backstage snorting room, painted white and decorated by noses cut out of Groucho Marx masks, with a tape of sniffing noises. Hajdu tells us that in 1964 and 1965, while Dylan was typing those "prose poems" that eventually added up to *Tarantula*, he got by on black coffee and red wine. But to compose what Baez thought of as his increasingly nihilistic songs, he chain-smoked marijuana. It's an odd division of labor enticements—sort of like Jean-Paul Sartre's staying sober to write his novels and *Les Mots*, whereas, for philosophy, he was usually doped up on a compound of aspirin and amphetamines called corydrane, stoning himself to kill God.

So now ask yourself if Dylan's notorious indifference to the niceties of cutting a record, to the relative merits of a multitude of sessions musicians, to the desires and opinions of his fans and audience, to whether he had any business on a stage, taking their money, when he was wired out of his skull, or in a recording studio, martyrizing thugs like Joey Gallo; combined with his disdain for former colleagues, ex-friends, and previous incarnations, contempt for other artists like Harry Belafonte and Theodore Bikel who cared about causes he could no longer use, like civil rights, and surliness unto Road Rage; even his unintelligible weirdness on such public occasions as his accepting the Tom Paine award from the Emergency Civil Liberties Union in November 1963 with a monologue that empathized with Lee Harvey Oswald—"But I got to stand up and say I saw things that he felt in me," which must be what inspired Jerry Rubin, five years later, to proclaim that "Sirhan Sirhan is a Yippie!"— well, ask yourself if some of this might have owed as much to chemicals as it did to authenticity. Elvis envy! Don't think twice.

Still, for those of us who aren't Dylanologists, there is much in *Down the Highway* that is wonderfully surprising. Did you know that Dylan's first song was about Brigitte Bardot? That his favorite film is *Shoot the Piano Player*, with Charles Aznavour? That his favorite artist is Marc Chagall? That his first wife had been a Playboy bunny? That Sid Vicious of the Sex Pistols seems not to have liked him? That Tiny Tim was a member of his Woodstock entourage? That after Jesus he took up sailing and boxing? That, with Bob's help and some high-grade pot, Paul McCartney not only discovered the meaning of life but also wrote it down? "There are seven levels."

It takes a lot to laugh; it takes a train to cry.

4

The geometry of innocence flesh on the bone
Causes Galileo's math book to get thrown
At Delilah . . .

Joan Baez, or so Hajdu quotes her mother, "always thought she was ugly." Even on Mt. Auburn Street in Cambridge in 1958, in her own mind "I was still the girl the kids used to taunt and call a dirty Mexican," so "pathologically insecure about her appearance" that she mugged at cameras in self-defense, and so self-conscious about what she imagined to be the small size of her breasts that she always wore a light floral jumper over her bikini. Joan Baez? I saw her with my own eyes in Cambridge in 1958, after I'd heard her with my own ears one warm spring night when "All My Trials" came through the window into the basement of the college newspaper on Plympton Street. It was the purest voice I'd ever heard,

like listening to the wild blue yonder. And when I rushed out to see what
such a voice looked like, she was, of course, beautiful beyond the speed
of light. And still is, like her fellow pacifist Aung San Suu Kyi.

This is the woman that Dylan and his coke-addled cohort chose to
humiliate on camera in D. A. Pennebaker's documentary *Dont Look Back*,
on their 1965 concert tour of England. She is also made to symbolize, in
both these books, a phony folkie subculture which Dylan, of course,
would rile and rock and raunch and roll. "The virgin enchantress," Hajdu
calls her, as well as "Glinda, the Good Witch of the North." How precious her flock, those middle-class flower children of a Harvard-educated
twelve-string banjo like Pete Seeger. What poseurs, like a bunch of Bam-
bis at some hootenanny salt lick, or a seminar on creative nonviolence at
a Quaker meeting of vegetarian carpenters. Over such a quilting bee, the
hermit-monk Dylan would ride roughshod, not sidesaddle, on his Golden
Calf—the Biggest of Boppers.

According to Hajdu the Newport Folk Festival in 1959 was "a popular
summer attraction for the suburban leisure class of the postwar boom
economy." And "the nascent discontent on college campuses" in 1962 was
"a mobilization in the name of political and moral principle that was also
a fashion trend and a business opportunity." And, by 1965 at Newport, if
Baez and Dylan weren't around, "no one poolside seemed to know which
way to point his lounge chair." Actually, I remember sleeping on the
beach because we couldn't afford a motel.

Sounes, who is English and may not know any better, arches his eye-
brow at 1963 Newport because the setting itself "underscored the gulf
between the proletarian roots of the music and the privileged lives of most
of the performers and the majority of the audience." I guess he missed
Dylan, later on, at Royal Albert Hall in London. And it's this same summer he's talking about when he speaks of "antiwar sentiments then in
vogue." Would that they had been in vogue, months before the assassination of John Kennedy, when the only Americans yet in Vietnam were still
called "advisors."

But more schematic than the books have been the reviews of them,
everywhere from the *Washington Post* to the online magazine Salon.com,
buying into an antithesis between folkies and rockers and plunking down
in belligerent favor of the snarl and the stomp, as if we couldn't listen to
both; as if in fact we hadn't been listening, not only to Seeger and Odetta
and Baez, but also to Motown and James Brown and the Drifters, even

before Bob Dylan, while nursing his hurt feelings that Carl Sandburg had never heard of him, was so stunned to pick up the Beatles on his car radio singing "I Want to Hold Your Hand" that he was moved to the Bob equivalent of a Gettysburg Address: "Fuck! Man, that was fuckin' great! Oh, man—fuck!"

Never mind the failure of anybody to take Joan Baez's Quaker pacifism seriously, from Joan Didion in 1966 to Jonathan Yardley in 2001. Never mind whose career looks more honorable and who's really posturing at the end of an awful century—those acoustic guitar players who went south for civil rights and tried to stop troop trains with their middle-class bodies, or the Macho Rubbish Rehab Ramblers with their amplified electric chairs and enough *attitude* to trash a hotel room and gang-bang a groupie. Never even mind that a whole lot of things are also always going on besides popular music; that there is news, too, on the wounded radio.

> *Mama's in the fact'ry*
> *She ain't got no shoes*
> *Daddy's in the alley*
> *He's lookin' for the fuse*

Besides telling us that "folk music is a bunch of fat people," these are the thoughts of Citizen Bob after the Kennedy assassination:

> All I can say is politics is not my thing at all. I can't see myself on a platform talking about how to help people. Because I would get myself killed if I really tried to help anybody. I mean, if somebody really had something to say to help anybody out, just bluntly say the truth, well obviously they're gonna be done away with. They're gonna be killed.

To which he added:

> You can't go around criticizing something you're not part of and hope to make it better. It ain't gonna work. I'm just not gonna be a part of it. I'm not gonna make a dent or anything, so why be a part of it by even trying to criticize it? That's a waste of time. The kids know that. The kids today, by the time

they're twenty-one, they realize it's all bullshit. I know it's all bullshit.

I'm not surprised he found God in 1979. It was a very seventies thing to do, like Rolfing, Arica, acupuncture, and biofeedback. Like tantric yoga and the hot tubs of Esalen. Or Jonestown and est. Like pet rocks, WIN buttons, smiley faces, and swine-flu vaccine booster shots. It led directly to power ballads and Ronald Reagan and the Last Tango on Mr. Sammler's Planet. Meanwhile, some of the rest of us were required to think about the women's movement, and read Toni Morrison, and poke at the meaning of a James Baldwin sentence: "If I am not who you say I am, then you are not who you think you are."

Baez has recorded this exchange with Dylan, in March 1965: "I asked him what made us different, and he said it was simple, that I thought I could change things, and he knew that no one could." It was a puerile thing to say, a species of adolescent fatalism, a waste of our precious time. No wonder he's back on the bus. If we really have to choose between, on the one hand, sex, drugs, rock 'n' roll, and the world exactly as it is and ever shall be, or, on the other hand, such sixties folkie fantasies as fishes and loaves, community and solidarity, peaceable kingdoms and rainbow coalitions, sanctuary, and, of course, Joan Baez—well, where do I sign?

Just like a woman.

Networks of Terror

A FTER A COUPLE of days of doing what they do best, which is grief therapy, the television networks and cable channels reverted to what they do worst, which is to represent the normal respiration of democratic intelligence.

Never mind the apocalyptic branding every producer of continuing coverage felt he had to inflict over, under, and around the multiple reruns, the endless nightmare feedback loop of jumbo jet, firebomb, and towers falling down. Soon enough, "America Under Dastardly Attack" would be succeeded by "The Empire Strikes Back." Nothing less can be expected of a commercial culture with a logo, a patent, a copyright, or a trademark on everything from pro athletes and childhood fairy tales to the human genome. What does surprise is that nobody thought of "Infinite Justice." What a brainstorm.

Still, television was our surrogate: a stunned witness, a black box, and also a storybook we needed. This is what it looked like, the Big Pixel, and the mangled steel and broken stone; the brilliant blue, unbearable sorrow, heroes in uniform, stalwart mayor—and an unmooring and a creepiness, as if a CAT scan had suddenly disclosed anomalies as unreadable as Rorschachs. So not even a girdle of oceans was enough to preserve our innocence. Nor could we flee in our pump-up running shoes. And what good were laser-beam defense shields against the guided missiles of our own passenger planes?

We gathered as we usually do in a parenthetical frame of mind, somewhere between the trauma and the stress syndrome. We have been there when we were merely curious: an Oscar or a Super Bowl. And when we have felt compelled: the Watergate hearings or the Berlin Wall. On exalted moments, like a moonshot. On dreadful occasions, like an assassination. It's a fix, and I'm not here to pick and choose among the performance arts of a Rather and a Brokaw and a Jennings. Bad news grays their skin beneath the powder, glooms their eyes staring at the Prompter, slows and thickens their aspect whether they're wearing a jacket or not— although it often seems that we also see through them, to the pentimento of every other terrible thing that ever happened while they had to sit there like an Easter Island emperor penguin.

I will say that Aaron Brown on CNN was the man I wanted standing on my roof, from whom I'd even buy insurance, while Bill O'Reilly factoring on Fox was a guy I wouldn't let in to check the Con Ed meter. But then CNN also still has foreign bureaus in those inconvenient places where the strangest people behave as though they have a purchase on history, too—like Kabul, from which only Nic Robertson was seen to be reporting, as only Peter Arnett had reported from Baghdad during the Gulf War.

But we needed the rapture of the feed. We needed the shadow on the scan.

And then the reversion. Before you could say Holy War, the screen filled with the usual pols, and their hierophants and sycophants. Bad enough that we had to listen on every channel to the same spin doctors explaining the same behaviors of a Flying Dutchman president. But we also had to listen to the pols we had booted out of office in previous elections: one last photo op for James Baker, Madeleine Albright, Richard Holbrooke, and Dr. Kissinger himself. What we didn't see—or at least I didn't, and I have more eyes than most flies—was any meaningful dissent from the tom-toms. End of dialogue.

We are apparently supposed to shut up and eat our spinach. Asking questions, proposing alternatives, making distinctions, arguing analogies, remembering history, or criticizing our stand-tall president is, for the moment, unpatriotic and maybe even unmanly. Wave that flag, stuff that qualm. The *Wall Street Journal* reported on September 19 that even such "peacenik" leftovers from the Vietnam era as Lee Weiner, one of the Chicago Seven, and Stew Albert, an original Yippie, were all of a sudden in favor of retaliatory violence and "surgical" military strikes. Grace Paley, on the other wonderful hand, suggests in the same article that we bomb Afghanistan with three tons of wheat, rye, and rice, since they are starving: "If we do it with a vicious attitude, maybe that will be enough for some people."

There can be no grievance that excuses the killing of innocents, either by terrorism or state violence, its Siamese twin. Any cause that does so is corrupt. The murder of children in Belfast, Sarajevo, Rwanda, Beirut, or anywhere else is beyond extenuation. Some of the West's best writers, from Dostoyevsky and Conrad and Malraux to Mary McCarthy, Heinrich Böll, Doris Lessing, Alberto Moravia, Nadine Gordimer, and Gabriel García Márquez, have tried to read the minds of what Don DeLillo in *Mao II* called "men in small rooms." All they've done is make those minds seem almost as interesting as their own, which of course they aren't. The kamikazes of Kingdom Come—the skyjackers, land miners, thumbscrewers, militiamen, death squads, and ethnic cleansers; the bombers of department stores, greengrocers, and abortion clinics; the Pol Pots, Shining Paths, and Talibans—have stupefied themselves. To imagine otherwise is to be as ethically idiotic as Karlheinz Stockhausen, the composer who told reporters in Hamburg on September 16 that the destruction of the World Trade Center was "the greatest work of art ever."

That said, our intellectual responsibility is to read our own minds. We are, we are told, at war. In wartime in America, civil liberties go out the window. Abe Lincoln suspended habeas corpus during the Civil War. During World War I, Woodrow Wilson's attorney general pushed an Espionage Act through Congress that kicked socialists out of state legislatures and sent Eugene V. Debs to prison. During World War II, Franklin D. Roosevelt wasn't at all troubled by the internment of thousands of Americans guilty of nothing else but Japanese descent. Even the Cold War was hard on radical schoolteachers and those government workers who could be blackmailed because they were homosexuals. And the War on Drugs has long since undermined constitutional protections against searches and seizures and a dozen other niceties of due process.

Let's hope a war on Osama bin Laden and his cancer cells is more successful than the war on coke and smack, although the difficulties seem at least as onerous and the prosecution likely to last even longer. But already 115 individuals are being held by federal authorities under the notoriously permissive gunslinger bylaws of the Immigration and Naturalization Service, without charges, bail, or even lawyers. (When in recent history have we seen so few lawyers, fetishizing an antiquated Bill of Rights?) Already Congress is falling all over itself to give attorney general John Ashcroft most of what he wants in roving wiretap legislation, e-mail, and other Internet peeping rights, detention and deportation of aliens based on secret evidence, and a gutting of statutes of limitation, not to mention the unleashing of the CIA to hire its own gang of thugs and to resume assassinating foreign leaders we don't like. And already the cry goes up for a technological deliverance from our grief and insecurity by the "biometrics" of fingerprinting, voice recognition, retinal scans, and racial profiling, not only at airports, but at train stations, sports stadiums, parks, schools, and reservoirs. Plus of course a national electronic ID "smart" card, capable of tracking our criminal history, our bodily motions, our financial transactions, and our driving speed. Previous "wartime" abridgements of freedom have been temporary, but will Infinite Justice mean Permanent Surveillance?

Somebody besides Congresswoman Barbara Lee must ask these questions. And why haven't I seen her on network or cable television?

About Afghanistan: On September 14, Tamim Ansary, an Afghani writer of delightful children's books who happens to live in Berkeley, posted a cri de coeur that has since been forwarded on tens of thousands of e-mail sites. He hates bin Laden and the Taliban equally. But he argues that a bombing attack will only kill women and children, including five hundred thousand orphans from all the previous wars. How then to snuff the mastermind? Ground troops, obviously. But these would have to advance from Pakistan, where bin Laden's sort of fundamentalists are perhaps stronger than the government. Which in turn could mean a fight to the death between Islam and the West, exactly what bin Laden lusts for.

Imagine Tamim Ansary talking to Larry King.

There are indications that Colin Powell may share these apprehensions, but even as I type, two dozen heavy bombers are circling what we think of as the crime scene and the aircraft carrier *Theodore Roosevelt*, with seventy attack planes, has left Virginia for an undisclosed location. And I wish each pilot could read not only Ansary's anguished essay but also a September 15th Internet communiqué from RAWA, the Revolutionary Association of the Women of Afghanistan, the underground feminist organization that has braved the wrath of the Taliban by teaching its own children and by smuggling out videotapes of executions to Western news outlets. RAWA asks us, please, to differentiate between the people of Afghanistan (70 percent women and children) and "a handful of fundamentalist terrorists."

But that's impossible, from an aircraft carrier or a bomber or the little blue fox full of Bill O'Reilly. It's especially impossible if nobody talks straight to us in the mainstream media. It's almost as though we don't need any legislation to curtail our dangerous civil liberties. Stunned by grief, we've shut ourselves up. If the ultimate contemptuous purpose of terrorism is to dominate and humiliate—to turn citizens into lab rats and cities into mazes—then bin Laden may have already won this round, because we seem to have acquiesced into playing his favorite game: bloodbath.

Richard Powers's *The Time of Our Singing*

ABOUT RACE IN America, about music in history, about atom bombs and "phantom mechanics"—curved space, loopy time, pure chance jump and flow—*The Time of Our Singing* is an astonishment but not a surprise. Richard Powers has been astounding us almost every other year since 1985, turning intellectual activity into imaginative literature in novels that ask homesick rangers and resident aliens to cope with everything from game theory, molecular biology, and artificial intelligence to such terrorisms as hostage taking and the behavior of "limited liability" corporations. We can no longer be surprised at whatever he dares to think in ink about.

Powers has been warming up for this novel in particular. *Prisoner's Dilemma* (1988) ended with a son looking for his sick father, who had run away into the atomic desert of Los Alamos. *The Gold Bug Variations* (1991) needed Johann Sebastian Bach's polyphony to crack the genetic code. And *Operation Wandering Soul* (1993) brought the nonwhite Third World home, to a pediatrics ward in a public hospital in Watts, Los Angeles. As if these sight lines were to triangulate on the American unmentionable—mixed race: "There isn't a horse alive that's purebred"—we now have the Stroms.

David Strom is a German Jew who has escaped the Nazi net to profess physics at Columbia University in New York, where his ability "to imagine what goes on inside the smallest matter's core," to hear the "harmonies in time" of forces and fields that curve and flow, will be useful during the war to atomic scientists like Rabi, Bethe, Pauli, Von Neumann, Szilard, Teller, and Fermi—"all of them boys, caught up in pure performance. The permanent urge to find and release." On Easter Sunday 1939, at the Lincoln Memorial in Washington, D.C., David Strom meets Delia Daley.

Delia is the brilliant daughter of a black Philadelphia doctor; she is also a daytime hospital nurse, a nighttime music student, and a part-time singer in church choirs, with a sound "that could fix the broken world." She should have had a concert career except that she arrived at the conservatory for her audition wearing the wrong skin. And she's come to the nation's capital for the same reason as David and 75,000 other people—to hear Marian Anderson sing in spite of the Daughters of the American Revolution. Against all odds, David and Delia decide to start their own revolution: "Maybe they could make an America more American than the one the country has for centuries lied to itself about being."

At least they make three more Americans: Jonah, "a year older, a shade lighter," than his brother, Joey, followed by their darker little sister, Ruth. And so long as all five are gathered around a piano in their derelict house in the northwest borderlands of Manhattan, playing "Crazed Quotations"—a musical game born of David and Delia's shared belief that "any two melodies could fit together, given the right twists of tempo and turns of key" and that, as Delia imagines it, "in the only world worth reaching, everyone owns all song"—they seem safe enough. But outside, "ever downward, from crazed to numb," race trumps love "as surely as it colonized the loving mind." These "halfbreed" children must sing not only for their supper but also for their mother, burned alive in an explosion before she has finished making her music.

"Honey-wheat" Jonah, sent away to music school in Boston at the insistence of Albert Einstein himself, is best at performing "whiteness," at singing Stockhausen and Schubert and even Palestrina, regressing in harmonic history throughout the novel, all the way back to Gregorian chant, as if his very own backyard hadn't grown a wonderful bastard music of spirit hollers, cabin songs, field calls, gutbucket, rag, blues, jazz, and scat. "Muddy milk" Joey, his sometime accompanist, has a harder time hiding out in concert halls from an America at race war. On one occasion, he finds himself playing show tunes in an Atlantic City dive. On another, more usefully, in a freedom school in Oakland, California, he teaches old stuff to street kids weaned on rap, for the first time doing work "that wouldn't have been done if I wasn't doing it."

Ruth? She has always lived in the burning world, the real history that torched her mother. While Jonah ("Orpheus in reverse") sings his way to the monastery, Ruth's history agonizes onward, from Marian Anderson to the Million Man March, with full stops at Emmett Till, "Bull" Connor, Medgar Evers, Birmingham, Newark, and Watts. Watts is where Jonah finally reads the score. So much for the Cloisters and unicorns. But Ruth is a Black Panther. It's her freedom school where Joey ends up teaching, and it's her son, of all the black children lost in space-time, who will be found in the wavelengths of color and pitch in the "somewhen" of his Jewish grandfather.

This is a Richard Powers novel, after all, and as such it must bend our minds as gravity bends time. Einstein on general relativity intersects with Leibniz on music. If, as David Strom dies hoping, most galaxies would rather rotate counterclockwise, then traveling back in folded time is possible, but only if we've already been whenever. If time is always now, so is music, "an exercise in occult mathematics by a soul that doesn't even know it's counting." And shame, too—shame is the very air we breathe, the normal respiration of our fearful tribal lungs.

Jacobo Timerman, Renaissance
Troublemaker

If you add up all the victims and victimizers, they form such a small per-
centage of the world population. What are the others engaged in? We
victims and victimizers, we're part of the same humanity, colleagues in the
same endeavor to prove the existence of ideologies, feelings, heroic deeds,
religions, obsessions. And the rest of humanity, the great majority, what
are they engaged in?

—Jacobo Timerman

E D ASNER WANTED to play Jacobo Timerman in a film version of *Pris-*
oner Without a Name, Cell Without a Number. I don't know why he
didn't, but he certainly would have been better than Roy Scheider in the
misbegotten 1983 TV movie that wasted the talents of Liv Ullmann, about
whom more in a minute, and Budd Schulberg, who insisted his name be
deleted from the credits after they butchered his script. Not only does
Asner *look* more like the Argentine editor, but he has generally behaved
more like him, too, making trouble and waves.

Timerman, who died last week at age seventy-six, was a Renaissance
troublemaker—something he carried with him in his Jewish-diaspora
DNA from the Netherlands, from which his family fled in the sixteenth
century to escape the Spanish Inquisition, to the Ukraine, from which
they fled in 1928 to escape the pogroms. Growing up in Buenos Aires, he
became a socialist and a Zionist in a country that was pro-Hitler in World
War II. As editor of *La Opinion* from 1971 through the 1976 military coup
until his kidnapping in April 1977, he was equally opposed to state

violence and sectarian terrorism, and insisted on publishing the names of the "disappeared" every day on his front page. And so he was seized, for thirty months, by neo-Nazi hoodlets who actually seemed to believe in a Zionist plot to gobble up Patagonia—chained to a concrete bed; beaten while blindfolded ("boarded up"); smashed against the wall by cops linked in single file pretending to be a locomotive ("the choo-choo shock"); chanted at ("Jew . . . Clipped prick . . . Jew . . . Clipped prick"); and obliged at regular intervals to "chat with Susan" (a machine that applied electrodes to his genitals). International pressure by everyone from Amnesty and Solzhenitsyn to Kissinger and the pope finally secured his release, after which he was stripped of his newspaper and his citizenship and shipped off by bloody parcel post to Israel.

Where he wrote *Prisoner . . .* (1981). Had it been only a witness to torture and deranged anti-Semitism, it would still have been a noble document on humanism at the end of its tether and the pornographic intimacy of violence, where "memory is the chief enemy of the solitary tortured man," "hope is synonymous with anxiety and anguish," and "goodness is madness": "Do I not, I ask myself, wind up being suspect in my own eyes for having undertaken that impossible choice, that permanent vigil of my own despair, experiencing a kind of omnipotence in being the victim? The Victim. Didn't that hatred of all those who'd caused me to surrender the best of myself, my courage and sacrifice, didn't that hatred wind up asserting itself within my fear, leading me at times to believe that perhaps there was indeed some underlying motive, something that had escaped me—some vague guilt hidden behind my principles . . .?" But troublemaking Timerman was just as hard on his fellow Jews, three hundred thousand of them in Argentina, whose silence he saw as an acquiescence in his torture. They were, he suggested, as fearful, obedient, and tongue-tied as the Judenrat during the Holocaust. Well: Hannah Arendt all over again.

To compound his offenses, from Tel Aviv he had a clear view of the 1982 Israeli invasion of Lebanon, in which his son, Daniel, was a soldier. Timerman expressed his sorrow and anger at Israel's "messianic concept of geopolitics," first in a dispatch to *The New Yorker* and then in *The Longest War*: "Now history is Palestinian," he wrote after the massacres at Sabra and Shatila, this man whose first Hebrew teacher in Buenos Aires had been murdered in the Negev by a Palestinian terrorist. Those of us who happened to be in Israel in the spring of 1983 can testify that, for his black ingratitude and moral presumption, Timerman was as much reviled as Arafat, even at Peace Now cocktail parties during Jerusalem's Book Fair. How dare he bad-mouth the country that gave him sanctuary? After all, he hadn't lived through the Holocaust, or 1948, or 1967. ("But does the key to it all lie in the scale?" he asked in *Prisoner*.) Obviously, he had been tortured in the wrong language.

Upon the restoration of democracy in Argentina in 1983, Timerman returned and went to court to accuse his tormentors. But he wasn't done stepping on toes and minefields. In 1987, he visited Chile for the first time since the assassination of his friend Allende. In *Chile: Death in the South*, he told us the usual horror stories of Pinochet's dictatorship—brutalization; rape as an instrument of state policy; murder as a *norm*—but also spoke of the numbed psychology of the afflicted, of the powerfully destructive grip of nostalgia on the imagination of the liberal parties, and of the impotent romanticism of the exiles who'd gone helplessly home again. Besides saying outrageous things about writers as various as Neruda, García Márquez, and Mario Vargas Llosa, he declared (correctly, it turned out) that Pinochet would not be dislodged by "phantom armies" of the left, "pseudo-guerrillas" who had persuaded themselves they could overwhelm the military when all their violence did was "grease the wheels of the killing machine." Left extremists trying to make themselves appear more dangerous than they were had managed to motivate the armed forces in Chile, Uruguay, and Argentina "to genocide."

This was news, from a man of the left: You can't hate torture while at the same time rooting for, or excusing, terrorism. It is news that seems not yet to have reached Colombia.

Worse was to come, in 1989, from *Cuba*. He'd known Fidel since 1959. A reacquaintance after thirty years appalled him—brainwashing, alienation, and hypocrisy; megalomania at the highest levels and informers on every city block; "re-education camps" for homosexuals and the suicide of old revolutionary comrades like Haydee Santamaria and Osvaldo Dorticos. In the arts community, toadyism; among journalists, self-censorship and despair. In Havana in 1989, you couldn't even buy a *Soviet* magazine that might be full of news of glasnost and perestroika.

Language consumed this bad-news bear, because the corruptions of language and the corruptions of power were joined like monstrous Siamese twins. Why were so many Cuban writers in prison or exile: Carlos Franqui, Herberto Padilla, Cabrera Infante? He was especially hard on

García Márquez, "one of the greatest writers of our time," who *had* helped Padilla get out of the country alive, but who was otherwise complicit in his buddy Fidel's dictatorship, even disgusting in "his public eulogies with their byzantine hyberbole." Personally, Timerman identified with an ex-journalist who prefered to work as a fumigator instead of a reporter: "He'd rather poison garden insects than Cuban minds."

The death of his wife and the bottom of a bottle slowed him down in his last decade and now we will probably never get those memoirs. Never mind the offense he gave to the caudillos, to the left-romantics, to Sharon and Likud, to some of my favorite writers, even to me. (I only met him once, at lunch in 1981 with the publisher of the *New York Times*, where he was as full of impatience and reproach for me, at my having insufficiently emphasized in my review of *Prisoner* the silence of the Jews, as he was for Hilton Kramer, who suspected him of being somehow soft on Tupemaros. In 1983, in Tel Aviv, he didn't answer the phone.) But what about Liv Ullmann?

He met her in New York only a month after his release, in the backseat of a big black car on a rainy night after a lecture by Elie Wiesel. And he explained to her that she, of all people, had done him the most harm while he was in prison. Her autobiography had arrived behind their bars—on the outside enhanced by a photograph of her gentle face, in that ungentle place; on the inside so full of tenderness toward her daughter, when he couldn't see his sons. Even its title, *Changing*, had been offensive to him, because he couldn't. The very "tenderness" of which Ullmann seemed so proud in her book was the "enemy" of a victim of torture. In the "biology" of his survival, "the intoxication of tenderness is tantamount to death, madness, suicide."

Timerman didn't tell Liv Ullmann that he had hated her, but he wanted to. This seems to me so radical an opposition to our habit of ingratiating ourselves to anyone, our licking of the boots of war criminals and egomaniacs and psychopaths, as to amount to a new religion with its own liturgy: *Always the truth.* After "a chat with Susan," we speak a different anguish.

Jonathan Lethem's *Men and Cartoons,*
The Disappointment Artist, and
The Fortress of Solitude

I

In *The Fortress of Solitude*, his great white whale of a novel, Jonathan Lethem chased after childhood, neighborhood, and the American leviathan of race relations. In *Men and Cartoons*, a grab bag of his stories, he paddles a kayak downstream over waters not exactly rapid. Old friends from elementary school reappear in order to deplore the compromises and corruptions of their former classmates. Bygone parents are revealed to have been capable of secret, sexual exultations. Young lovers in a burgled house go to bed with the ghosts of past relationships made visible by magic spray. Artists, agents, editors, opticians, and a talking sheep named Sylvia Plath negotiate dystopias of gridlock—a character in "Access Fantasy" lives in his car in a citywide traffic jam on the wrong side of a One-Way Permeable Barrier—and topographies of dork and cool.

But the joke's on Hemingway. According to Lethem, men without women employ comic books to compensate. When his characters aren't listening to Frank Zappa and Talking Heads, or dreaming up scenarios for interactive video games, or hiring out as "advertising robots" at the local Undermall, or destroying the world with air bags made out of cabbages, they are thinking about Stan Lee and R. Crumb, Spider-Man and the Fantastic Four, Daredevil, Dr. Doom, and Captain America. If Norman Mailer, Thomas Pynchon, Walt Whitman, and Carl Jung show up in "Super Goat Man," the most ambitious of these stories, they are really only red herrings or highbrow beards in an epic tale of an Electric Comics cartoon crusader from the 1970s who is reduced in the nineties to teaching a college seminar on "Dissidence and Desire: Marginal Heroics in American Life, 1955–1975."

Mostly, though, the comics mentioned in *Men and Cartoons* aren't published by Electric. Or DC, Raw, or Fantagraphic. They are Marvel-branded, "which anyone who read them understood weren't comic at all but deadly, breathtakingly serious. Marvel constructed worlds of splendid complexity, full of chilling, ancient villains and tormented heroes, in richly unfinished story lines." Lethem's nerds entered into those complex worlds back in grammar school and junior high, between the ritual humiliations of pubescence. In years to come of pink slips, eviction notices, and deleted icons, of fax machines and vibrators, these Marvel worlds are the vistas in their mediated heads. They see in panels, talk in balloons, and feel in lurid colors. But how can a Columbia professor who plays party games (in "The Vision"), a museum director for acquisitions of drawings and prints (in "Vivian Relf"), or a cartoonist for a free music magazine published by a record-store chain (in "Planet Big Zero") ever be expected to compete with the likes of Vision, the android in the *Avengers* series who could vary the density of his body from bullet-stopping diamond-hard to blue-smoke phantom fuzzy? Or Black Bolt, the noblest member of a band of outcast mutants known as the *Inhumans*, whose superpower was speech itself:

> The sound of his voice was cataclysmic, an unusable weapon, like an atomic bomb. If Black Bolt ever uttered a syllable the world would crack in two.

In other words: once there were giants, with magical powers, secret identities, Technicolored underwear, and swishy capes. Male adulthood proved to be much less fun than the masked dreams of pop culture had led little boys to believe. Growing up stunted us. The primary emotions and psychic wounds of the Marvel superhero are as drums and trumpets to the disappointed marimba tinkle and sneezy regrets of the fortysomething salaryman. Perhaps, says Lethem, "superheroism was a sort of toxin, like a steroid, one with a punitive cost to the body"—but we can't help feeling that we traded in living large (James Dean, Godzilla) for the poignant (a wild pitch, a broken shoelace) and the ignoble (cowardice, envy: "Bite my crank, Super Goat Man!"—as two sozzled frat boys taunt the aging comic book hero, on a clock tower, waving a giant phallic paper clip).

Sad-making. Pop nostalgia clings like kudzu to everyone who ever grew up feeling alien-freaky . . . all of us who somehow knew we were born to die uncool. Having posted my sugar-bomb box top to Battle Creek, Michigan, in 1947, I was the first little boy on my block to own a Lone Ranger atomic bomb ring. I examined the color photo of a mushroom cloud while listening, on the radio, to "Mr. Keen, Tracer of Lost Persons." Such a perfect dorky pathos . . . and this was long before marijuana made everything seem more interesting than it really is.

Even so, from a young writer as clever as they come and as crafty as they get, who skinwalked and shape-changed from Kurt Vonnegut into Saul Bellow before our starry eyes, whose Huckleberry Brooklyn novel brought municipal fiction back from the dead, the whimsies in *Men and Cartoons* look like arrested development. And *The Disappointment Artist*, a collection of Lethem's journalism and reminiscence, seems at first to be more of the same. Whole chapters are devoted to John Ford's westerns, Philip K. Dick's science fiction, *Star Wars*, John Cassavetes and Stanley Kubrick. Page after page celebrates such recording artists as Chuck Berry, David Bowie, the Beatles, Elvis Costello, Brian Eno, Pink Floyd, and Cheap Trick, and such science-fiction writers as Frank Herbert and Jules Verne. And when the loftier likes of Kafka, Borges, and Lem, or Faulkner, Beckett, and Joyce, or Cynthia Ozick, Grace Paley, and William Gass are mentioned at all, they will be fingered in brusque passing as "professional Bartlebys." It's not as if he's never met them; they show up in his novels, wearing turtlenecks and trench coats; they hang in his closet. Yet not one is worthy here even of a paragraph.

Do we care that Lethem saw John Ford's *The Searchers* twelve times and *Star Wars* twenty-one, or that his "fever for authenticity" led him to Anthony Newley, or that he still believes the Fantastic Four superheroes were the Rubber Soul and the White Album of comics? (Do you care how many times I have seen *The Umbrellas of Cherbourg,* or what's going on in my head while I watch Sara Evans sing "Suds in the Bucket" on the country music cable channel?) Is it so unreasonable to want to know more of what he thinks about Julio Cortázar and less of how he feels about Obi-Wan Kenobi? To wish for a few words explaining why he stopped reading Don DeLillo, rather than thousands more on Red Sonja, Howard the Duck, and Marvel's "existential loners"? And then this, as if Jean Genet instead of Jonathan Lethem were Marveling in the seventies:

I'm breaking down here. The royal *we* and the presumptive *you* aren't going to cut it. This is a closed circuit, me and the comics which I read and which read me, and the reading of which by one another, me and the comics, I am now attempting to read, or reread. The fact is I'm dealing with a realm of masturbation, of personal arcana. Stan Lee's rhetoric of community was a weird vibrant lie: every single *true believer*, every single member of the Make Mine Marvel society or whatever the fuck we were meant to be called, received the comics as a private communion with our own obscure and shameful yearnings, and it was miraculous and pornographic to so much as breathe of it to another boy, let alone be initiated by one more knowing. *We* and *you* don't know a thing about what *I* felt back then, anymore than *I* know a thing about what *you* felt.

The fact is that we do know what he felt back then, and he knows what we felt, and so do you. It's obvious, blatant, standardized, like "the generic reality" of the futuristic Oakland detective in his first novel, *Gun, With Occasional Music*—which is what pop culture does to our obscure and shameful yearnings, which is why it's helpful to feather your nest and prime your pump by branching out into Bible stories, Greek myths, Grimm fairy tales, Romantic poetry, grand opera, anthropology, psychoanalysis, and maybe even what Lethem calls "the violently solitary and elitist necessities of High Art." But because he has been at it for a while, because *The Disappointment Artist* is already his tenth book, he has a surprise sleight-of-mind in store. In an essay on Edward Dahlberg, prince of churls, he tips this hand. Dahlberg's memoir of his Kansas City childhood, *Because I Was Flesh*, is "a great book" in "the saddest and simplest way, for Dahlberg has arrayed an armor of rhetoric to fend off his pain, and everywhere the armor proves inadequate."

And what, exactly, was *Flesh* saying? *Flesh* was saying, Lethem explains: "I want my mama." So does Lethem want his mama, the one who called him "kiddo," sent him to public school in Brooklyn, steered him toward Isaac Asimov and Ray Bradbury, took him to *Star Wars* screenings, and worried maybe he was gay; the young woman who, before she gave birth to Jonathan, was a Queens College dropout, a barefoot Jewish folksinger, an ear-piercing Greenwich Village beatnik, a draft-counseling campus wife of an avant-garde artist/SDS professor, a pot-smoking hippie matron in favor of open marriage and day-care centers, opposed to war, grapes, nuclear power, and Robert Moses; the thirty-six-year-old mother who died from a brain tumor in 1978, after giving her son a typewriter for his fourteenth birthday, on which the next summer he wrote his first book. Confined by her countercultural parameters, "I both bloomed within, like the windows of a greenhouse, and rattled against, like the jaws of a trap." Canvassing his pop culture enthusiasms and obsessions, his furious fandom, he finds evasions, surrogates, anodynes, screens, beards, and a parental figure in the carpet bombing. On the one hand, as a mother-less boy,

> Growing up in an artist's family, I seized on comic books and science fiction as a solution to the need to disappoint my father's expectation that I become an artist like himself. These tastes encompassed my real passions: for art that embraced the vernacular vibrancy of pop music and film, and for fusions of imaginative material with the mundane. But they also served as a beard on my own ambition, a cloak on my reverence for the esteemed artifacts of my parents' universe.

On the other, he asked too much:

> Attempting to burrow and disappear into the admiration of certain works of art. I tried to make such deep and pure iden-tification that my integrity as a human self would become optional, a vestige of my relationship to the art.

Works of art can be better than the real world, and maybe even redeem it, but not even Marvel comics can be "both safer than life and fuller, a better family. That they couldn't give." According to Lethem, the first song John Lennon recorded after the Beatles' breakup was called "My Mummy's Dead." Listening to his own past, he hears something that sounds similar: "Each of my novels, antic as they may sometimes be, is fueled by loss. I find myself speaking about my mother's death everywhere I go."

IF BLACK BOLT EVER UTTERED A SYLLABLE THE WORLD WOULD CRACK IN TWO.

2

Hardboiled bittersweet, that's Conrad Metcalf, the private inquisitor in *Gun, With Occasional Music* (1994), a Philip Marlowe, a Lew Archer, but also a Primal Scream in a Brave New Noir: "The thing I wanted wasn't lost in the past at all, and it never had been. It was lost in the future. A self I should have been, but wasn't." Never mind the Sam Spade case he thinks he's working on, which involves the torture and murder of a sheep. Keep your eye on the kangaroo. (Or the sow, ape, and dachshund, all of whom are "evolved.") We are living in a near future of animal hybrids and designer drugs (Acceptol, Regrettol, Forgettol, Believol, Avoidol); of cash registers that play orchestral music when the drawer's open, trash cans that flourish trumpets, water fountains that spout pop tunes, parking meters that strum Hawaiian bottleneck guitar, and tape-deck cranial implants of your own memories edited so you can safely answer any question; where "spoken-word news" and the printed word are against the law, and psychology students go door-to-door ringing your bell to read out loud from Sigmund Freud's *Civilization and Its Discontents*.

Already you are smiling. What amazed about Lethem from the start was this amiability, this ramshackle styling, this loose-limbed ambling through the genres. To each pulpy occasion, instead of masks or capes, he wore sneakers, sweats, leather, shades. He licked the language as if it were a lollipop. "I'll have my lips removed as soon as I learn a way to whistle out my asshole." But also from the beginning he was bereft. In *Gun, With Occasional Music*, see the Babyheads. The near future has decided that it takes too long to grow a kid, during which they are too noisy and ask too many questions, anyway. So, using the same "evolution therapy" that got kangaroos up and talking, scientists fiddled with the human growth process and managed to speed it up so much that you now see toddlers at "babybars" with little yellow fish on their red jumpers and cigarettes tucked behind their ears.

In *Amnesia Moon* (1995), where Jack Kerouac and Philip K. Dick will meet Mel Gibson's Road Warrior and Vladimir Nabokov's Humbert Humbert after the bombs have fallen on America, the sky is purple with radiation poisoning, the mountains are full of biochemical amnesiac fog and mutants from the "rupture" think they can talk to dolphins, almost everybody is bereft: Chaos, for instance, personified here as if Lethem were Milton or Hobbes, who lives in the projection booth of a multiplex in Hatfork, Wyoming, and is forever dreaming someone else's dreams. And Melinda, the fur-covered adolescent girlchild, some kind of selkie out of Celtic folklore, hitching a ride with Chaos to Emerald City and the Wizard of Oz. And Edie, who seeks to improve her Finite Subjective Reality but keeps on flunking her bad-luck test. Not to mention Case Hotchkiss, Everett Moon, Vance Escrow, and Dawn Crash in the Submission District of San Francisco, where, after the fragmentation, they long for "a sort of viral coherence"; they wait for Godot and gestalt.

If *Amnesia Moon* is Pynchon Lite, like *Vineland*, it is also the Philip K. Dickiest of Lethem's novels. Except that Dick was a paranoid pillhead—genuinely convinced, according to his most recent biographer, that telepathic Soviet scientists tried to jam his neural frequencies by bombarding him with abstract splatters of Kandinsky and Picasso from the Hermitage—whereas Lethem is known to hang out at McSweeney's, where the writers want to make a community; and the coherence he longs for throughout his books, the gestalt, is family.

Family, about which *Girl in Landscape* (1998) is especially eloquent, a prose riff on John Ford's *The Searchers* but also Lethem's *Passage to India*, as well as a wonderment in which a Catcher in the Rye reads the Martian Chronicies in a Little House on the Prairie. Pella is thirteen years old, living beneath a poisoned earth with her younger brothers, when their father, Clement, loses an election and their mother, Caitlin, dies of a brain tumor. So it's off by freezer ship to the Planet of the Archbuilders and a frontier settlement on a "landscape of remembrance," a dream terrain of eroded spires and ancient tombs, with black sand and mourning sculptures, fish potatoes and lynch mobs, indigenes with evocative names like Hiding Kneel and Truth Renowned and miniature deer so quicksilver swift they might very well be ghosts.

On this "Planet of Withheld Explanations," the adolescent Pella experiences the terrors of adult sexuality ("The girl's body was *pretentious* with womanhood"), Lethem finds his first fully fledged character, the reader emerges from a sci-fi western more complicated than when he was going in, and we glimpse the homesteading to come in Brooklyn of Rachel, Abraham, and Dylan. Once upon a time, the mother Caitlin told her strong, smart daughter Pella: "Don't you think arms are brave? They just go on, they never get tired or give up or complain." So when Pella, the pioneer woman, raises a new town on an old planet, she already has not only a name for it, Caitlin, of course, but also a motto worthy of a Vonnegut: "Be brave like an arm."

Motherless Brooklyn (1999) is the novel favored by readers of Lethem who'd rather he hadn't entered the mainstream, a peculiar resentment indeed on the part of people who otherwise complain that the mainstream unfairly disdains their populist subversions, their pulp-proud underground, their monastic cells and hermetic texts. About the mainstream: love it or leave it. To want to eat the flowers and sleep in the Hide-a-Bed of the very same rectal-thermometer establishment whose walls you have pledged to "tag" seems to me to be uncool. But *Motherless,* in which Lionel Essrog is only one of many orphans in the hired-muscle and private-eye service of a small-time hood, is way cool, as if Tony Shaloub's Monk, the obsessive-compulsive TV detective, and Philip Roth's Mickey Sabbath had teamed up to solve an Oedipal crime. Lionel, moreover, speaks in tongues. Like Mozart and Malraux, he is afflicted with Tourette's syndrome. He can't help turning everything he hears into a linguistic freak show, "spirit or animal possession, verbal; epileptic seizure, whatever," with "a flapping, inane mouth that covered the world in names and descriptions," and "no control in my personal experience of self."

What happens as Lionel, determined to avenge the murder of the mafioso who got him out of St. Vincent's Home for Boys, follows a deadly trail from a Yorkville zendo with some very odd monks to a Sushi Oceanfood Emporium on the rocky coast of Maine, past Marlon Brando, Ross MacDonald, Daffy Duck, and the Green Hornet, is a brilliant game of verbal tags. ("Ducky fucking Bent!" should appeal to baseball fans who will never forgive the Yankee shortstop for his playoff home run against the Red Sox.) Not only is the narrator unreliable; he has run amok: "I'm a tightly wound loose cannon." He could be Benjy in *The Sound and the Fury,* or Oskar in *The Tin Drum,* or the Hunchback of Notre Dame, a Greek who can only talk in vehement dithyrambs, an Elizabethan stuck in iambic pentameter, a waterbug in Kafka, an elephant in *Aida*, or Gogol's nose. And, as usual with Lethem, he blames himself for what he's lost:

> Is guilt a species of Tourette's? Maybe. It has a touchy quality, I think, a hint of sweaty fingers. Guilt wants to cover all the bases, be everywhere at once, reach into the past to tweak,

neaten, and repair. Guilt like Tourettic utterance flows use-
lessly, inelegantly from one helpless human to another, contemptuous of perimeters, doomed to be mistaken or refused on
delivery.

Nevertheless, remember what your mother told you. BE BRAVE
LIKE AN ARM.

3

So we arrive at last at *The Fortress of Solitude* (2003), and the 1970s Brooklyn boyhood of Dylan and Mingus—salt and pepper, race and music,
yoking and graffiti, levitation and transparency. Just how resonant can a
decade be? What if nothing else for the rest of your life will ever be as
meaningful as how you felt in the seventh grade, being beaten up on your
way home from school? *Play That Funky Music, White Boy.* Is it possible
to grow up at all, much less up, up, and away, in a novel named for Superman's polar hideout, a hope chest and a memory bank with its own lab
and its own zoo, where the Man of Steel from Action Comics went
whenever his nerves were frayed—a novel that is itself a nest of cellars and
attics, of batcaves in which Dylan with his secret identities may be downstairs practicing sarcasm as if it were karate, while his artist-father Abraham is upstairs painting jackets for sci-fi paperbacks and killing time with
blobs of light, even as Mingus's singer-father, Barrett Rude, Jr., on the
next block over, has drawn the shades to darken the room where he burns
freebase cocaine in a glass pipe?
By now you have heard that nerdy Dylan's bohemian parents,
avant-garde Abraham and radical hippie Rachel, move to Boerum Hill in
Brooklyn just when the neighborhood is deciding whether to decay some
more or gentrify, because they believe in community. And send Dylan to
public school, rather than St. Ann's or Packer, because their liberal principles say they should. And Dylan, naturally, is victimized, headlocked
every day by black boys from the projects, one of whom steals his bike,
for which theft his sorry ass will then be kicked by earth-mother Rachel
herself, earning Dylan an enemy for life. And he will be naked before this
enemy when his feckless parent, the Red Queen, "Rachel, the Symbio-
nese soccer mom," suddenly deserts him, disappearing into the sexual and

social revolutions with a grown man as serious about comics as Dylan himself. She will never see her son again, although, signing herself "Running Crab," she does send back the occasional, cryptic postcard. ("Brooklyn was simple compared to his mother.")

And then, miraculously, Dylan is befriended by supercool Mingus Rude, equally motherless but effortlessly gifted, the mulatto son of a celebrated soul singer: "an exploding bomb of possibilities." As if they are characters in the comics they consume like oyxgen, Mingus and Dylan transcend their streets. Games of stickball and skully, movies starring the dead Bruce Lee, comics featuring a Human Torch, an Invisible Girl, and Mole Men, weed-smoking, break dancing, Motown, hip-hop, and funk, Yoo-hoo, Etch A Sketch, Spirograph, and Pixy Stix, all seem staged for these brave two, a private safari into the continent of being boys. They will fly high over stoops and bodegas, the public school, the House of Detention, and the Brooklyn Bridge. At first the purpose of their upward mobility is to tag walls that can't contain them, paint their names on every page in Brooklyn's book: "Under oblivious eyes, the invisible autographed the world." Later, though, Dylan and Mingus turn into crime-stopping vigilantes. And we are asked to believe they actually *fly*. From a homeless superhero who fell off a roof, they inherit a ring that lets them drape a cape and levitate.

A magic ring conferring the ability to fly would seem to belong more to one of Lethem's earlier novels than this masterly, lyrical scan of the warp and weft of childhood, the ligature of fellowship and blood ties. Before everything goes wrong about two-thirds of the way through, *Solitude* has been perfectly poised between sense and stress, aura and object, a man who remembers and the boy who was there. So saturated is its phrasing, so tactile with the first charged feeling of each sight, sound, smell, and sinew, that it seems popular culture might really be the solvent in which contradictions of class and race dissolve. Even after Dylan and Mingus are discovered in a homoerotic scrum—as if they had been choreographed by the Freudian critic Leslie Fiedler in a Huck and Jim, or Ishmael and Queequeg, or Natty Bumppo and Chingachgook, pas de deux—when white Dylan goes off to Stuyvesant High School, Camden College, Berkeley, California, and a vile career in rock criticism, while black Mingus goes to crack cocaine and prison, both passages are, if perhaps perfunctory, nevertheless plausible. But then that magic ring shows up again, behind bars, where instead of letting anybody fly away, it renders them invisible.

Only in a comic book, and not very often there, will a magic trick harmonize the races or bring back your missing mother. *Solitude*, copping out, didn't so much cheat the reader as it threw up its hands and shrugged us off. I give up. Irony hasn't done the job, nor nostalgia, either, so why not try wishful thinking? In this, we seem not to have advanced an inch in at least four decades. Perhaps you recall the essay Norman Podhoretz wrote for *Commentary* in 1963, "My Negro Problem—And Ours." As Dylan was "yoked" in Brooklyn in the 1970s, so Podhoretz, in his very own version of "Play That Funky Music, White Boy," reported "being repeatedly beaten up, robbed, and in general hated, terrorized, and humiliated" in Brooklyn in the 1930s. And as Podhoretz concluded that America's race problem could only be solved by "miscegenation," by making color "disappear," so Lethem helpfully bequeaths Dylan an African American girlfriend in Third World Berkeley.

But Podhoretz is busy these days slandering ex-friends and invading Middle Eastern countries. And how come Berkeley in these pages seems so much more educational than Bennington College? Lethem, who went to Bennington for a bit, calls it Camden in *The Fortress of Solitude*. So did Bret Easton Ellis call it Camden in *Rules of Attraction*, and Jill Eisenstadt, too, in her novel *Far Rockaway*, where Ellis had a walk-on. But Donna Tartt called it Hampden, even though *The Secret History* was dedicated to Ellis and some of us wondered about Tartt's student dope dealer with the Mob connections. A dope deal likewise figures in Dylan's stay at Camden. But unlike either Ellis or Tartt, Lethem failed to notice any incest, gang rape, or murder. And Bennington probably wonders if any of these stoned, horny, ungrateful, and uncomprehending pimples ever went to class or read a book or had a thought or mustered a fierce feeling about anything other than Devo or Marvel.

Which brings us full circle back around to comic books and popular culture. I'm glad to learn from *The Disappointment Artist* that Lethem's father is more interesting than Dylan's was, that his mother, unlike Dylan's, didn't abandon her boy because of narcissism; that Jonathan, unlike Dylan, has siblings. And I am sorry that none of us can fly, besides which we're opaque. But it is time this gifted writer closed his comic books for good. Superpowers are not what magic realism was about in Bulgakov, Kobo Abe, Salman Rushdie, or the Latin America flying carpets. That Michael Chabon and Paul Auster have gone graphic, that one Jonathan, Lethem, writes on and on about John Ford, while another

Jonathan, Franzen, writes on and on about *Peanuts*, even as Rick Moody confides to the *Times Book Review* that "comics are currently better at the sociology of the intimate gesture than literary fiction is," may just mean that the slick magazines with the scratch and sniff ads for vodka and opium are willing to pay a bundle for bombast about ephemera.

But all of it makes me itch. Welcome to New Dork! We have been airpopped and multimediated unto inanity and pastiche. Philip K. Dick and Stan Lee get Hollywood movies. Alienation and sexual terror have their own sitcoms, fashion statements, and marketing niches. The middle finger and the Bronx cheer are required courses in cultural studies. Boomers have made sure that their every febrile enthusiasm since Pampers will last longer than radioactive waste, on digital cable or DVD. Gen Xers are just as solipsistic; anything that ever mattered to them must have been profound, even, say, Debbie Harry of the punk group Blondie talking to MTV while a sirocco blows in one of her ears and out the other and neurons die like flies.

BITE MY CRANK, SUPER GOAT MAN!

Citizen Doctorow

THE LAST TIME I introduced E. L. Doctorow at the Y, on maybe this very same stage, was twenty or so years ago. What we did every month was show a movie, after which I would interview whoever wrote the novel that the movie messed up. If I remember correctly, Timothy Hutton, one of the stars of *Daniel*, joined us on stage. If I'd known then what I do now about Doctorow and film, about the screenplay he wrote for a ten-hour Robert Altman *Ragtime* television series, I'd have asked more interesting questions. Now I know everything, but I've decided not to tell you because life is short.

But let me mention a couple of things about this great novelist. He is also simultaneously a radical historian, a cultural anthropologist, a troubadour, a cost-benefit analyst of assimilation and upward mobility in the great American multiculture, a chronicler of the death of fathers, of the romance of money, and of the higher "latitudes and longitudes of gangsterdom." He is a skinwalker, shape-shifter, stormbird, sherlock, magus, Ancient Mariner, Joe Hill, and Sam Spade. He has put on every imaginable variety of narrative glad rag and jet-propelled pulp-fiction sneaker, and spoken in every syllable of inspired tongue, from western, sci-fi, gothic, and ghost story to fairy tale, fable, and philosophical romance. He is the public intellectual who insists on social justice, and the pilgrim artist who is heartsick, awestruck, ecstatic, scornful, and possessed.

From a nonobservant father he inherited a humanism "that has no patience for a religious imagination that asks me to abandon my intellect." But from his mother's side he received "a spontaneously felt sense of the sacred" that "engages the whole human being as the intellect alone cannot."

To which add the Yiddish accent of his Bronx boyhood with Tolstoy, jazz, and L. Frank Baum, the Bronx High School of Science where Kafka encouraged him to write a story called "The Beetle," the big surprise of Kenyon College in Ohio, where he read Matthew Arnold, and mastered the New Criticism at the neat feet of John Crowe Ransom, Randall Jarrell, and Robert Lowell; his stint in the Army, occupying Germany, and his stretch as a reader for a film company where he parsed far too many westerns, resulting at last in that first novel, after which we could count on his sonar readings for dark signs, frigid depths, evil devices, raven droppings, tiny golems, counterterrorists, cuneiform, and hieroglyphs.

In *The Book of Daniel*, Daniel and Susan are attacked by a "giant eye machine" with insect legs, and dive with open arms into shock therapy and revolutionary space, as if to die "on a parabolic curve." In *Ragtime*, in Sarajevo, Houdini fails to warn the Archduke Franz Ferdinand, and so the green feathers of his plumed helmet turn black with blood. Whereas in Egypt, on a camel, J. P. Morgan is surprised to find the pennant-winning New York Giants swarming "like vermin" over the Great Sphinx, sitting "in the holes of the face." While in Mexico, in the great desert "of barrel cactus and Spanish bayonet," the bomb-making Younger Brother will find Zapata. In *Loon Lake*, a carny worker contemplates the plutocrat he intends to become: "he was a killer of poets and explorers, a killer of boys and girls and he killed with as little thought as he gave to breathing, he killed by breathing he killed by existing he was an emperor, a maniac force in pantaloons and silk slippers and lacquered headdress dispensing like treasure pieces of his stool, making us throw ourselves on our faces to be beheaded one by one with gratitude." In *Billy Bathgate*, Dutch Schultz "lived as a gangster and spoke as a gangster and when he died bleeding from the sutured holes in his chest he died of the gangsterdom of his mind as it flowed from him, he died dispensing himself in utterance, as if death is chattered-out being, or as if all we are made of is words and when we die the soul of speech decants itself into the universe." In *Lives of the Poets*, "a dire desolation will erupt from the sky, drift like a fire-filled fog over the World Trade Center, glut the streets of SoHo with its sulfurous effulgence, shriek through every cracked window, stop the ringing voice of every living soul, and make of your diversified investment portfolio a useless thing."

The Waterworks is both a Gothic and a detective story, about science, religion, and capitalism, but also journalism, politics, and New York. We are reminded of Melville, Poe, Crane, and Edith Wharton, but also Joseph

Conrad. In 1871, as today, the spendthrift city, with its temples raised to savage cults, its gaudy display and blind selection, its humming wires and orphaned children, is a Darwinian jungle, a heart of darkness, and a necropolis. In this new industrial park, after a bloody Civil War, imagine a white stagecoach full of old men in black top hats. A freelance book reviewer for one of the city's many newspapers thinks he sees his dead father in this coach. When this critic disappears, his editor and the only honest cop in Boss Tweed's corrupt New York will seek him from Printing House Square to Buffalo Tavern to the Black Horse. Meanwhile children who have vanished from the streets or drowned in the reservoir turn up in coffins not their own. We move through the mosaics of daily journalism and routine police procedure toward what Doctorow calls "the limbo of science and money." There, in an orphanage and a conservatory, in a laboratory and a ballroom, we will be asked questions about sanity and virtue, vampire capitalism and the morality of medicine, historical truth and natural selection—as, from the blood, bone marrow, and spinal fluid of nameless missing children, the Very Rich and Living Dead are rendered "biomotive" and seen to waltz, with deaf-mute caretaker women, under the shameless water, vaulted heavens, and God-stunned stars.

City of God is about, well . . . everything: both World Wars, the Holocaust, and Vietnam. But also, again, science and religion, reason and faith, prophecy and sacrifice, tellers of stories and watchers of birds. Einstein, Wittgenstein, and Frank Sinatra are characters. And a novelist, looking for his next book in the bare ruined choirs of modern Manhattan. And an Episcopal priest, Thomas Pemberton, who will fall in love with a reform rabbi, Sarah Blumenthal, when the cross that has been stolen from the altar of his Lower East Side church mysteriously reappears on the roof of her Upper West Side synagogue. Popular music and Hollywood movies are characters, too, glorious and ominous. Except one can't imagine *City of God* on any big screen. How do you *adapt* a book as messy as the Bible itself, a hodgepodge of chronicles, verses, songs, and sins, a brilliant scissors-and-pasting of Hebrew gospel, Greek myth, Yiddish diaries, quantum physics, surreal screenplays, prose poems about trench warfare and aerial bombing, and an archive of every scrap of witness to the Nazi occupation of Lithuania? Or *film* the Midrash Jazz Quartet, a rap group of Talmudic interpreters of such pop standard secular hymns as "Me and My Shadow," "Dancing in the Dark," and "Someone Who'll Watch Over Me"? What does gravity look like? Or "unmediated awe"? Or "moral consequence"? Or what Einstein calls the "first sacrament, the bending of starlight"? How, finally, do we *picture* an Episcopal priest who is so fed up with Christianity, and so in love with Sarah, that converting to Judaism is the only way he can think of to redeem himself from knowledge of the death camps?

In *The March*, that's what General Sherman does, humming "The Ride of the Valkyries," from Milledgeville to Savannah to Columbia with sixty thousand Union cavalry and infantry, surgeons and drummer boys, drovers and mules, cattle and cooks, not even counting twenty-five thousand freed slaves following behind, nor the Confederate prisoners needed to troll for landmines, nor the genteel Southern ladies, refugees from ruined planta- tions, with their buggies, their servants, their needlepoint—everything needed for an "infestation" or a plague, except maybe locusts and a frog. And in this train of go-carts, tumbrels, memory, and death, "as if the sky was being pushed in on itself," "as if the armies were strung from the floating clouds," an uprooted civilization is on the hoof. Think not only of the all-devouring armies of Alexander and Genghis Khan, but also of Exodus.

Doctorow has dreamed himself backward from *Daniel* to *Ragtime* to *Waterworks* to Civil War, into the creation myth of the Republic itself, as if to assume the prophetic role of the nineteenth-century writers he admires so much, for whom the Constitution was our sacred text and secular humanism our civil religion. In *The March*, the American identity of a dozen characters is as fluid as the blood they spill. We spend enough time in the ambulances and medical wards, among army nurses and sev- ered heads, to be reminded of Whitman. And enough in the trenches and swamps to think of Stephen Crane. Matthew Brady comes to mind, stil- ling life with photographs. And so does William Faulkner, when a corpse needs a hole. And Flannery O'Connor, whose papers and bones are bur- ied in Milledgeville, under peacock feathers. Toni Morrison might have imagined the white-chocolate Pearl child herself, Emancipation's natural aristocrat. How pomo/meta to meet Coalhouse Walker, Sr., whose son will show up in *Ragtime* to disquiet J. P. Morgan. And for foreign flavor, see Arly and Will, the cross-dressing Confederates who are waiting for Godot or Stoppard. After such a scrub of blood, this bone-scan and immersion therapy, what's left in our heads of *Gone With the Wind* looks more like Edmund Wilson's *Patriotic Gore*.

So many avatars! He is channeling our history and literature, even as he creates it. Ladies and gentlemen, I give you Citizen Doctorow and the Prophet Edgar.

Sgt. Pepper's Lonely Hearts Club Band
(on Václav Havel)

Y OU MAY HAVE missed a headline the other day, in one of the sections of the *New York Times* that wasn't about nesting or e-mail:
STREET CRIME HITS PRAGUE DAILY LIFE, it told us. Nothing really surprising
there. But the subhead to the same story was indeed remarkable: Czech
Capital Discovers One Drawback of Democracy.

Democracy! Not, mind you, rampant inflation, staggering unemployment, runaway greed, corrupt politicians, or anything else to do with
their new free-market Tinkertoy economy. It was because Czechs could
now vote that Japanese tourists and Vietnamese "guest workers" were no
longer safe on the baroque streets of the capital of Kafka, and neo-Nazi
skinheads were suddenly bashing gypsies. It was because their speech at
last was free that they cried for "lustration"—a purge of anyone who ever
had a cup of coffee or a Pilsner with a Party apparatchik in the bad old
days before Frank Zappa. It was because of self-determination that Slo-
vaks were licensed to hate Czechs, while Václav Havel, the reluctant politician, had to run for another term as president of his very own Republic
of Dreams—roughly the size, with roughly the same population, as the
state of Pennsylvania—on a platform of "Not So Fast."

We went to Prague for the first time, in the first place, because of
Havel, having discovered in ourselves in the summer of 1990, after years
of knowing better, a surprising capacity and an unseemly need to
hero-worship. If not a Beckett, he was at least an Ionesco. It had been
possible in New York to see *Largo Desolato* before the Velvet Revolution,
and *Audience* almost immediately afterward, and even allowing for the
rose-colored glasses we wore to these performances (the kaleidoscope

eyes!), they were thrilling. An intellectual suspicious of his own intellections was at work, while all around him the world wrote another, more surprising narrative.

There is obviously a Czech style, ironic, self-deprecating, and sometimes vulgar, that shows up in Hašek, Čapek, Hrabal, and Vaculík, as well as Tom Stoppard's plays and even Milan Kundera's pre-Parisian novels. The wonderful thing about Havel was that he had proved to be braver than his own alter egos, that he'd shrugged off ambivalence like a smoking jacket, pointed himself toward a magnetic pole of decencies, and look what happened.

And when we weren't going to see Havel at a theater, we were reading him in magazines and books—in *Letters to Olga* (from prison), *Disturbing the Peace* (a long interview that would be much revised by events) and the *New York Review* (his correspondence to the world, later published in the volume *Open Letters*). After writing plays about the breakdown of continuity and identity in the modern world; after starting a human-rights watchdog committee, Charter 77, in Prague; after seeing the magazine he edited censored into silence; after thinking subversive thoughts in front of an observation post, a sort of grandstand on stilts, that the security police built directly across the street from his apartment, after a pair of dress-rehearsal arrests . . . he was finally sent away for four years of hard labor. His weekly letters to his wife were all he was allowed to write. They began, as you'd expect, asking for cigarettes and socks. They ended as difficult essays on freedom, responsibility, and community. "Whether all is really lost or not," he said, "depends on whether or not I am lost." His nation found him.

All right, maybe he wasn't perfect. From *Disturbing the Peace* and *Open Letters*, we gather that he had problems with feminists, though they made him feel guilty. And he misconstrued the peace movements in the West, which had a livelier sense of the possibility of change in Eastern Europe than did many dissidents. But compared to any other successful pol in the modern era, not counting Nelson Mandela, of course, he was downright heroic, an intellectual Ferdinand the Bull. As far back as 1965, he had seceded from what he calls the "post-totalitarian panorama" of "pseudo-history" and "automatism," the spider web of secret police, anonymous informers, and faceless flunkies. Even when his plays were banned, he chose to behave as if he were free, in a brewery or in jail. He never contemplated leaving his country, although, typically, he wouldn't hold it against anybody who did choose to emigrate: "What kind of human rights activists would we be if we were to deny people the right that every swallow has!"

His letters, to colleagues in movements like Solidarity and readers of Western magazines, were themselves public examples of "living within the truth," vivid evidence of the existence of what he called a "second culture" of "free thought" and "alternative values," a "parallel structure" of underground theaters, shadow universities, and samizdat publishing, that would eventually undermine the police-state "world of appearances," of "ritual, façades and excuses." (If the State won't wither away, Michael Walzer once suggested, we have to "hollow it out.") By behaving as if we are free—at student protests, on strike, by refusing to vote in the farcical elections, or even by going to a rock concert—we rehabilitate "values like trust, openness, responsibility, solidarity, love." We renew relations with a vanished world where "categories like justice, honor, treason, friendship, fidelity, courage or empathy have a wholly tangible content." We reconstitute "the natural world as the true terrain of politics," "personal experience [as] the initial measure of things," and "human community as the focus of all social action, the autonomous, integral, and dignified human 'I.'"

No wonder the last thing Sam Beckett did before dying was autograph a book for Václav. All writers ought to feel better when one of them makes it really big. In his first speech to the new Republic as its new president, in December 1989, Havel struck a characteristic note: "I assume you did not propose me for this office so that I, too, would lie to you."

Now just look at us in July 1990, on the brilliant cloudless morning of our first full day in Prague, footloose on the Charles Bridge over the swan-strewn Ultava, in the shadow of a gothic tower, swarmed upon by baroque saints, lapped at by Dixieland jazz, levitating to the Castle. Maybe I was full, like Kundera, of too much lightness of being. "Levitating" is an odd word to use when history is so heavy, from the Holy Roman Empire to Stalin's squat, with time out for Jan Hus to be the first Protestant, for which they burned him at the stake. And it was an uphill hike, as if you had to earn the right to be there, from the Inn of the Three Ostriches and the Leningrad paintpots of the Malá Strana to the ramparts of Hradčany and the spires of the Jesuit cathedral of St. Vitus. But Prague exalted. It felt like Mozart.

There was also a fragility I feared for, as Ray Bradbury feared for the fairy towers in *The Martian Chronicles*, as if the façades were sculpted of smoke. We were traveling through Eastern Europe in a kind of caravan—French journalists with four children, a Washington, D.C., science editor, a delegation of noisy New York opinionizers—that fiddled at each new site with our logarithmic scales, like slide rules. Not all of us loved "Praha" as haplessly as I did. There was too little to eat—no bread after nine at night, no ice cream after ten, no open cafés past midnight—and too much silence, except in our hotel, the Forum, where the Japanese tourists fought it out with the Spaniards for the occasional slice of rare roast beef. But Kafka was everywhere, like Kilroy or McDonald's. And it seemed to me that in that silence, everyone was thinking, and what I feared for was the dreamscape delicacy of that thought.

Our maps didn't work. They'd changed the names of subway stops to get rid of "Gottwoldova" and "Cosmonauti." You probably think the "Defenestration of Prague" was a massacre. What happened was that they tossed a couple of Roman Catholics out of a Castle window onto a dung heap. In one engraving, we saw a pair of feet making their exit, a sideways Assumption. The playwright/president himself has spoken of "the fatal frivolity with which history is made here."

The night before our levitation to the Castle, we'd gone for a stroll down Wenceslas Square, where three hundred thousand people had taken the keys out of their pockets and rattled them like wind chimes, "like massed Chinese bells," past the good king's statue and candles burning for the martyred students, to Staroměstké náměsti (Old Town Square), just in time for the changing of the apostles on the famous clock with the bell-ringing skeleton. If Wenceslas Square was a depressing mall of thumping discos and listless moneychangers, Old Town Square was the loveliest urban prospect I have seen in decades of goatlike globe-trudge. We had a front-row seat on the Jan Hus statue to listen to some mop-headed Beatle mimics sing "She Loves You (Yeah Yeah Yeah)."

More than Mozart, the Beatles were what counted in 1990. We met them again on the Castle ramparts, singing "Penny Lane." On radios in taxis, in elevators at the Forum, in courtyards, wine bars, beer halls, and on the Royal Procession from Tyn Church to the Ultava, we heard "Eleanor Rigby" and "Help!" We chased the shadow of a young artist who was building a Yellow Submarine to sail under the Charles Bridge that September. At Vyšehrad, where Princess Libuse took unto her a hardy yeoman, and so spawned the kings of Bohemia, we also listened to Led Zeppelin and the Fine Young Cannibals.

What did this mean? Havel, that leprechaun, wrote in *Disturbing the Peace* of his feelings in prison on hearing of the murder of John Lennon. He seemed to care more about Lennon than he did about Kundera, although, typically, he was kinder to Milan than he needed to be. (Kundera has had nothing to say about the Velvet Revolution. Isn't this strange? Maybe he is too busy thinking about Stockholm. But if V. S. Naipaul was silent on the subject of Salman Rushdie, and John Le Carré craven, maybe writers aren't any better than the rest of us, after all.) Havel first became a dissident while defending a censored Czech rock group. Not only had Frank Zappa beaten us to Prague, but, on the eve of our departure, Havel made it a point to show up in Spartakiadni Stadion for a Rolling Stones concert. And opening for the Stones was to be a Czech rock musician who had been elected to the new parliament. So: the world's first rock 'n' roll president. After which, Sgt. Pepper's Lonely Hearts Club Band.

We did what tourists in Prague were expected to do—sleep in a luxury hotel, eat duck for breakfast, visit the Castle, look at graveyards. At Vyšehrad, the well-born were nicely planted (Dvořák, for example). In Josefov, it was a different story. Though our guidebook described the Old Jewish Cemetery as "picturesque," these tombstones cried out of the earth, like teeth around a scream. (And the next-door art of the death-camp children was what they must have seen.) Or we cooled our feet in the Wallenstein Gardens (a labyrinth, a grotto, peacocks). Visited the Smetana (a chambered nautilus of Art Nouveau). Went to movies on the Revolution (student heroism). Ate ice cream at the Slavia (where Sorrow-steeped young Werthers killed themselves isometrically). Snuffled cappuccino at the Europa, next door to a restaurant that was a replica of the dining room on the *Titanic* (more Czech humor). Bought a ticket to the Magic Lantern (I had to go to the theater where they wrote this script) for a performance of the Kouzelný Cirkus, with horses, clowns, and ballerinas, as if Monty Python's *Life of Brian* had met Ingmar Bergman's *Seventh Seal*. (I'm afraid it's typical that we should have gone to the Magic Lantern for a circus, late as usual, while Timothy Garton Ash, always on time, had been there for a revolution: "swift, almost entirely nonviolent, joyful and funny.") And looked for Agnes of Bohemia . . .

Only to find instead a ten-foot sculpture of a Trabi, the East German People's Car, on four huge naked human legs, with a license plate that said in Czech: "QUO VADIS?" This whimsical cyborg, symbolizing the artist's ambivalent feelings about German reunification, had shown up mysteriously in Old Town Square two months before we did. It was allowed to remain during the "cucumber season" only because the mayor of Prague, Jaroslav Koran, was a friend of Kurt Vonnegut's, a translator of his fiction, and could be counted on to sympathize with hijinks.

I knew of the artist who sculpted the cyborg, David Černý, though I'd never met him. He was a friend of my stepdaughter's, from before the Fall. And also the pilot of the Yellow Submarine scheduled to ship out at the end of cucumber season. He'd created, as well, a Student Slot Machine: You drop in a coin, and the Student, shooting up an arm, shouts: "Freedom! Freedom!" And, since statues in Czechoslovakia are always going up and then toppling down again because of various revolting developments, David had also invented an all-purpose Headless Dignitary, a windmill with mugshots of various Important People stuck on each of its blades, so that, no matter which way the ideological wind was blowing in whatever political weather, there was always someone to salute. Barely born in 1968, entirely innocent of Prague Spring, David and his tribe had lived by their outlaw wits in ironic opposition, in transit underground on discarded Metro tickets to sly conceptual jokes. They didn't know whether to believe that Havel was real. Nor would they even meet with us, their plutocratic elders, credit-card utopiaheads. Like Peter Pan, they ran away. Like the Mystery Cat in T. S. Eliot, Macavity's not there.

But David did show up in the world news before our next visit to Prague. Perhaps you recall the briefly famous pinking of the Prague tank in 1991. Some artists who weren't named in the first small story in the *Los Angeles Times* were arrested for having painted, a shocking pink, the Soviet tank that sat as a monument to the Red Army's liberation of Prague in 1945. One of the artists claimed to have a permit for painting the tank pink, but it proved to be a forgery. This sounded to some of us, in New York, a lot like one of David Černý's subversive jokes. But the story disappeared, and so did David, who was supposed to visit the United States that month.

There followed a couple of unsigned postcards from places like Switzerland and then a copy of the English-language expat journal *Prognosis*, from which we gathered that the pinking of the tank, on April 28, 1991, took forty-six minutes and forty liters of paint, and it looked "like a child's toy or a newborn child." Czech soldiers took twice as long to repaint the tank its primary color, on April 30, so that it looked again like James Joyce's "snotgreen scrotum-tightening sea." On May 15, twenty members of the Czech Parliament slipped out at night to paint it pink again. And Václav Havel, that Captain Kangaroo, lost his temper. David Černý and his friends were suddenly on trial. With the surprising connivance of Vonnegut's buddy, the mayor of Prague, they were accused of "criminal hooliganism" under Paragraph 202 of the Czech penal code—the same notorious statute that had been invoked to arrest Václav Havel in the Evil Empire days. If convicted, they faced two years in prison.

After the second pinking of the tank, Havel wasn't the only dignitary to stamp his foot. "A vile act!" raged Soviet foreign minister Vitaly Churkin. Poor Alexander Dubček, whose personal experience of Red Army tanks went back to 1968, was dragged out of retirement and hustled off to Moscow to apologize, on television, to the Russians. "Where will it end?" asked the president of Brigadoon, missing the point. "Will we have the St. Wenceslas statue painted red, St. Vitus Cathedral in blue, all the paintings in the galleries spray-painted?" He seemed to forget his own defense, in 1976, of the Plastic People of the Universe, at whose trial he demanded to know—I quote from *Open Letters*—why "no one present could do the one thing that was appropriate in this situation: stand up and shout: 'Enough of this comedy! Case dismissed!'"

A pro-Černý "Pink Coalition" of artists, students, and members of KAN—the Club of Non-Aligned Party Members—then clashed with right-wing shock troops from the Movement for Civic Freedom and the Communist Party of Bohemia and Moravia. A dozen rock bands gathered on June 1 in Wenceslas Square for a designated Pink Day. Two separate bank accounts were established in Prague to pay Černý's fines. And by signing a petition that was Pro-Pinking, some sixty deputies to the Federal Assembly and another thousand assorted luminaries violated yet another statute, Law 165, which prohibits "the approval of a proven crime." Meanwhile, the Soviet tank itself had disappeared from its Smichov pedestal, and was said to be hidden away behind armed guards in an unnamed Prague museum. Perhaps the *New York Times* would blame this, too, on democracy.

The Last Innocent White Man

"I USED TO BE funny," Kurt Vonnegut informs us in *A Man Without a Country*, "and perhaps I'm not anymore." This last bit is untrue, of course. In these essays from the pages of the radical biweekly *In These Times*, he is very funny as often as he wants to be. For instance: "My wife is by far the oldest person I ever slept with." And if you don't smile for at least a week at the friendly notion of the corner mailbox as a "giant blue bullfrog," you ought to have your license revoked.

But like Mark Twain and Abraham Lincoln, even when he's funny, he's depressed. His has always been a weird jujitsu that throws us for a brilliant loop. As much as he would like to chat about semicolons, paper clips, giraffes, Vesuvius, and the Sermon on the Mount—"if Christ hadn't delivered the Sermon on the Mount, with its message of mercy and pity, I wouldn't want to be a human being. I'd just as soon be a rattlesnake"— his own country has driven him to furious despair with its globocop belligerence, its contempt for civil liberties, and its holy war on the poor: "Mobilize the reserves! Privatize the public schools! Attack Iraq! Cut health care! Tap everybody's telephone! Cut taxes on the rich! Build a trillion-dollar missile shield! Fuck habeas corpus and the Sierra Club . . . and kiss my ass!" The novelist/pacifist/socialist/humanist who has smoked unfiltered Pall Malls since he was twelve is suing the tobacco company that makes them because, "for many years now, right on the package, Brown and Williamson have promised to kill me. But I am now eighty-two. Thanks a lot, you dirty rats. The last thing I ever wanted was to be alive when the three most powerful people on the whole planet would be named Bush, Dick, and Colon."

So, although he does mention Jerry Garcia, Madame Blavatsky, Rush Limbaugh, and Saul Steinberg ("who, like everybody else I know, is dead now"), besides wonderfully observing that "Hamlet's situation is the same as Cinderella's, except that the sexes are reversed," he can't help but notice that "human beings, past and present, have trashed the joint," and that we are stuck in "a really scary reality show" called "C-Students from Yale." Thus he reiterates what Abraham Lincoln said about American imperialism in Mexico, what Mark Twain said about American imperialism in the Philippines, and what a visiting Martian anthropologist said about American culture in general in a novel Vonnegut hasn't finished writing yet: "What can it possibly be about blow jobs and golf?"

When they were inducted into the National Institute of Arts and Letters in 1973, Kurt Vonnegut said of Allen Ginsberg: "I like 'Howl' a lot. Who wouldn't? It just doesn't have much to do with me or what happened to my friends. For one thing, I believe that the best minds of my generation were probably musicians and physicists and mathematicians and biologists and archaeologists and chess masters and so on, and Ginsberg's closest friends, if I'm not mistaken, were undergraduates in the English department of Columbia University. No offense intended, but it would never occur to me to look for the best minds in any generation in an undergraduate English department anywhere. I would certainly try the physics department or the music department first—and after that biochemistry. Everybody knows that the dumbest people in any American university are in the education department, and English after that."

Well when you say things like this you do not ingratiate yourself with the sort of people whose racket it is to nominate you for things like Nobel Prizes. You may get to eat at the Swedish consulate here in New York, but not at Town Hall in Stockholm with your face on a postage stamp. Once upon a very long time ago I asked him to review a Joe Heller novel for the *New York Times*. This is how he concluded his essay on *Something Happened*: "I say that this is the most memorable, and therefore the most permanent variation on a familiar theme, and that it says baldly what the other variations only implied, what the other variations tried with desperate sentimentality not to imply: That many lives, judged by the standards of the people who live them, are simply not worth living."

Some of those variations are his own. A character in *Slaughterhouse-Five* tells a psychiatrist: "I think you guys are going to have to come up with a lot of wonderful new lies, or people just aren't going to want to go on living." The novelist himself tells us in *Palm Sunday* about seeing a Marcel Ophüls film that included pictures from the Dresden firebombing Vonnegut had lived through as a POW: "The Dresden atrocity," he then decides, "tremendously expensive and meticulously planned, was so meaningless, finally, that only one person on the entire planet got any benefit from it. I am that person. I wrote this book, which earned a lot of money for me and made my reputation, such as it is. One way or another, I got two or three dollars for every person killed. Some business I'm in." In the same open vein, he wonders aloud in *Hocus Pocus*: "How is this for a definition of high art? . . . Making the most of the raw materials of futility."

Indeed. So it goes. Imagine that. And yet there isn't a person in this room who hasn't experienced a personal Kurt kindness, or been kissed with grace by something in one of his novels, or both. The way he goes about his business has helped most of us to go on living, if only to find out what happens next. In *Slapstick* he insisted that even if we aren't "really very good at life," we must nonetheless, like Laurel and Hardy, "bargain in good faith" with our destinies. And he recommended instruction books on such bargaining: Robert's Rules of Order, the Bill of Rights, and the Twelve Steps of Alcoholics Anonymous. To these, *Jailbird* added two more how-to manuals: Lincoln's Second Inaugural, "with malice toward none," and the Sermon on the Mount. *Bluebeard* suggested Goethe's *Faust*, Picasso's *Guernica*, *Gulliver's Travels*, *Alice in Wonderland*, and *Don Quixote*. Elsewhere, at the dedication of a library, he mentioned such "mantras" as *War and Peace*, *Origin of Species*, *Critique of Pure Reason*, *Madame Bovary*, and *The Red Badge of Courage*; and in a speech to mental health professionals, such civilizing "fixtures" as Shakespeare's *Hamlet*, Beethoven's Fifth, Leonardo's *Mona Lisa*, Twain's Huck Finn, the Great Wall of China, the Leaning Tower of Pisa, and the Sphinx.

What are these fixtures, mantras, and manuals but attempts to articulate standards according to which life is worth living? We read him as the woman in *Jailbird* read the books of Starbuck, "the way a young cannibal might eat the hearts of brave old enemies. Their magic would become hers." Add to these his autumnal novel, *Hocus Pocus*, so prematurely valedictory, where the Civil War is far from over, the race war still rages, and a class war between the dyslexic rich and the illiterate poor has just begun; where Eugene Debs Hartke, like Howard Campbell in *Mother Night* and Kilgore Trout in *Jailbird,* will go on trial for treason; where the novelist seems to say good-bye to American history and literature, to Moby-Dick and Walt Whitman, as if covering so much territory—from evolution to outer space, from Abstract Expressionism to Watergate, from Holocaust to Hirsohima—had worn him out. But he came back to us, over the ice and through the fire.

That scary fire: Remembering how he looked in the hospital after he almost burned his house down, Billy Pilgrim this time smoked instead of smoking, and seeing him now in these bright lights, the black humorist in black tie, I think we are blessed. It's as if he had returned, in reverse, from Dresden, like those bombers of his in one of the loveliest passages in our literature: "American planes, full of holes and wounded men and corpses, took off backward from an air field in England. Over France, a few German fighters flew at them backward, sucked bullets and shell fragments from some of the planes and crewmen. . . . The formation flew backward over a German city that was in flames."

> The bombers opened their bomb bay doors, exerted a miraculous magnetism which shrunk the flames, gathered them into cylindrical steel containers, and lifted the containers into the bellies of the planes. . . . When the bombers got back to base, the steel cylinders were taken from the racks and shipped back to the United States of America, where factories were operating day and night, dismantling the cylinders, separating the dangerous contents into minerals. Touchingly, it was mainly women who did this work. The minerals were then shipped to specialists in remote areas. It was their business to put them into the ground, to hide them cleverly, so they would never hurt anybody ever again.

My wish is for Kurt to enjoy his birthday as much as we have. Because then maybe he'd be happy.

Michael Chabon's *The Yiddish Policeman's Union*

The magician seemed to promise that something torn to bits might be mended without a seam, that what had vanished might reappear, that a scattered handful of doves or dust might be reunited by a word, that a paper rose consumed by fire could be made to bloom from a pile of ash. But everyone knew that it was only an illusion. The true magic of this broken world lay in the ability of the things it contained to vanish, to become so thoroughly lost, that they might never have existed in the first place.
—*The Amazing Adventures of Kavalier & Clay*

CERTAINLY, IN ALMOST every Michael Chabon fiction, there is this vanishing—subtractions, desolations, and abandonments; sinister design and rotten luck. In *The Mysteries of Pittsburgh* (1988), his debonair debut novel, young Art Bechstein suspects that his mother was murdered by mobsters who were really after his father. In *Wonder Boys* (1995), his graduate-school slapstick, Grady Tripp has lost one parent to postpartum complications and another to suicide. In *The Amazing Adventures of Kavalier & Clay* (2000), his magnum opus on art, work, buddies, genocide, and the bloodthirstiness of children, Sammy Clayman's father deserts him (twice!) and Josef Kavalier loses his whole family to the Nazis. In *Summerland* (2002), his stealing-home baseball fantasy for kids, Ethan Feld's mother, a veternarian, dies of cancer, and his father, an inventor, is abducted by wolfboys and mushgoblins. In *The Final Solution: A Story of*

Detection (2004), his sly riff on Sherlock Holmes, a nine-year-old German boy named Linus, an orphan, a mute, and a refugee, wanders the English countryside in 1944 with a parrot that sings strings of numbers referring to the cattle cars of the Holocaust. In *Gentlemen of the Road* (2007), his sword-and-sandals serial published in the *New York Times Magazine,* the vagabond physician Zelikman, variously described as a scarecrow and a ghost, drifts through the Dark Ages with a heart turned to stone after the rape and murder of his mother and sister.

Even in *Werewolves in Their Youth* (1999), a mixed-nut assortment of stories, one boy, fatherless, turns himself into a werewolf; another perishes in a Fourth of July fireworks explosion; a third runs off with his new baby half brother to save him from their sadistic father; an infant dies in his mother's arms on a ferryboat, a divorced family therapist is afraid to take a bath with his own daughter, and we get a flabbergasting amount of domestic violence. And finishing up is a horror tale attributed to the shlockmeister August Van Zorn, whom we first met in *Wonder Boys,* with Yuggog, a cannibal queen in an underground necropolis in bone-pit Pennsylvania, feeding on mill workers and anthropologists. *Werewolves* also told us that

> sex had everything to do with violence, that was true, and marriage was at once a container for the madness between men and women and a fragile hedge against it, as religion was to death, and the law of physics to the immense quantity of utter emptiness of which the universe was made.

This chimes, more or less, with the gloomiest feelings of Meyer Landsman, the brokenhearted alcoholic police detective in Chabon's wonderful new novel, *The Yiddish Policeman's Union*. His father committed suicide, his pilot sister died in a plane crash, and the loss of his son Django—"a braided pair of chromosomes with a mystery flaw"—has "hollowed" him out. The "most decorated shammes in the District of Sitka" has only two moods, "working and dead." He overhears people talking about him "in the hushed tones reserved for madmen, assholes, and unwanted guests." He has practically disappeared into slivovitz, deep-fried pork, and "a slipstream of sorrow." His ex-wife, Bina Gelbfish, is now his boss at the precinct station, and he misses her like an arm or heart: "She is getting old, and he is getting old, right on schedule, and yet as time ruins them, they are not, strangely enough, married to each other." When someone tells him, "You take care," he has to admit, "I don't really know how to do that." When everybody tells him not to investigate the execution-style murder of a chess-playing heroin addict, of course he will end up dodging bullets in the Alaskan snow, wondering just how long "it takes hypothermia to kill a Jewish policeman in his underpants."

But there is much more to any Chabon story than loss and disappointment. By magic, paper roses bloom from piles of ash. He has always played with different ways of telling tales. *The Mysteries of Pittsburgh* was a coming-of-bisexual-age novel, a Gatsby for slackers. *Wonder Boys* was a send-up of the groves-of-academe *roman à clef,* winking at Mary McCarthy, Randall Jarrell, and Bernard Malamud even as it tickled the funny bones of magic realism, shlock horror, and quasi-Faulknerian "Mocknapatawpha." *Kavalier & Clay,* with escape-artist Harry Houdini as the superhero template, was a graphic novel that impudently asked us to imagine all the pictures on our own. *Summerland* was a boys' book of pilgrimage and quest, as if Harry Potter had gone to Wrigley Field to save baseball, summertime, storytelling, and his father. *The Final Solution* married Victorian melodrama to the espionage thriller, plus Goethe and Schiller and Gilbert and Sullivan and honeybees. *Gentlemen of the Road* owes as much to movies like *The Black Rose* (1950), with Tyrone Power as an English scholar and Orson Welles as a warlord looking for Kubla Khan, and *Conan the Barbarian* (1981), with Arnold Schwarzenegger punishing the savage tribes for wasting his parents, as it does to *Don Quixote* and *Dr. Zhivago.* And now, insouciantly, this sci-fi noir, a half-baked Alaska in which everybody insists on speaking Yiddish.

And yet, a closet humanist, Chabon has also always listened to all of his characters with blameless patience, willing to stay up past his bedtime, or sleep over an extra day or two, to entertain extenuations, parse motives, and talk us through our creepy dreams. It is as if his protean way with narrative forms extends to human behaviors. He is as sympathetic as he is nosy. Writing a detective novel set in an imaginary Jewish Alaska licenses him to itemize what they wear up there (skullcaps, galoshes, polar-bear jammies), what they eat (pickled tomatoes, Chinese doughnuts, noodle pudding, moose chili), and what they carry in their purse (Tabasco sauce, corkscrews, opera glasses, fish-oil pills). He doesn't so much digress as he circles around. (In her new biography of Leonard Woolf, Victoria Glendinning observes: "His train of thought always took the scenic route.") And we usually feel better coming out of his revolving doors than we did going in.

What's more, he is as whimsical as he is generous: "I can see that some women do indeed look a little like guitars," Art acknowledges in *Pittsburgh*. *Wonder Boys* is, to the best of my knowledge, the only serious novel in which a tuba has a featured role—as a noise, a muse, an umbrella, a symbol of absurdity, and a body dump. Imagine a comic-book artist, like Josef in *Kavalier & Clay,* immortalizing the love of his life, Rosa Luxemburg Saks, by turning her into the Cimmerian moth goddess from the Book of Lo, at once Druidic and Babylonian, with "immense green wings" and "sensuously furred antennae." *Summerland* may not stack up against Salman Rushdie's *Haroun and the Sea of Stories*, or "The Children of the Heart" adventure series in David Grossman's *See: Under Love*, or "The Chums of Chance" in Thomas Pynchon's *Against the Day*, but you have to enjoy the whole idea of a baseball game as "nothing but a great slow contraption for getting you to pay attention to the cadence of a summer day." And in *The Yiddish Policeman's Union*, we love Bina almost as much as Landsman does when she chooses in the cafeteria not to order "the baked thermometer" because "they only had rectal," and when, a few pages later in her ex-husband's forlorn hotel room, she wants to know: "How do you say 'shit heap' in Esperanto?"

Besides, who knew Chabon was so Jewish?

2

Every generation loses the messiah it has failed to deserve.
—The Yiddish Policeman's Union

It's obvious now how Jewish he has always been, as *Gentlemen of the Road* continues to spool itself out in the *New York Times Magazine* past publication day for *The Yiddish Policeman's Union*. The one text imagines what Khazaria may have been like, between the Caucasus and the Volga, the Black Sea and the Caspian, after the Khazar kagan, court, and military caste all converted inexplicably to Judaism in A.D. 740. The other imagines, as of 2008, a Jewish state in Alaska rather than the Middle East, having trouble with Tlingits instead of Palestinians. But it didn't always seem as if Chabon were looking backward, forward, and sideways at his Jewishness.

Maybe because we spent so much time back in 1988 wondering whether the author of *The Mysteries of Pittsburgh* was or wasn't gay, we didn't pay enough attention to Art's Jewish gangster father, who would have enjoyed shooting the breeze and also the competition with such fellow literary gangsters as Benya, the King of Crime in Isaac Babel's *Odessa Stories*, and Dutch Schultz, who died full of words and holes in E. L. Doctorow's *Billy Bathgate*. Maybe because *Wonder Boys* had so many scandalous things to say about writers and writing programs at a big university, we hurried past that hilarious and horrific sixty-page seder scene that confirmed Grady, "orphaned and an atheist," in his feelings about his in-laws and their faith:

> I liked the way the Jewish religion seemed, on the whole, to have devoted so much energy and art to finding loopholes in its crazy laws; I liked what this seemed to me to imply about its attitude toward God, that dictatorial and arbitrary old fuck with his curses and his fiats and his yen for the smell of burnt shoulder meat. . . .

Maybe because *Kavalier & Clay* was such a rollicking encyclopedia on comic-book art, on the "dislocated and non-Euclidean dream spaces," "the infinitely expandable and contractible interstice of time between the panels of a comic book page," and their "total blending of narration and image"—just like *Citizen Kane!*—we sort of took Hitler for granted. But Josef the émigré didn't, knowing perfectly well that his comic-book superhero, The Escapist, hadn't saved his younger brother; knowing that for the Prague Jews he had left behind, there would be no Fortress of Solitude or Bat Cave; knowing even in the navy in Antarctica, while listening to his grandfather sing Schubert on shortwave radio, that Theresienstadt was a German fairy tale for Czechs, "a witch's house made of candy and gingerbread to lure children and fatten them for the table." And when his old partner Sammy finally does get to look at *The Golem*, the dark graphic novel Josef has been working on secretly for years, his first stunned reaction is: "So. You have an awful lot of Jewish stuff in here." This is the Sammy who has already explained to Josef that comic-book superheroes, like Hollywood and Tin Pan Alley, are a Jewish immigrant invention: "Superman, you don't think he's Jewish? Coming over from the old country, changing his name like that. Clark Kent, only a Jew would pick a name like that for himself."

You have an awful lot of Jewish stuff in here.

Not so much in *Summerland*, perhaps, with its mix of Norse myth and Native American folklore, its golden bough and sacred tree, the Yggdrasil, from which ash Ethan makes a magic baseball bat. But *The Final Solution* resonates. Naturally, the little boy who can't talk will attract the interest of the eighty-nine-year-old former detective who still believes that the essential business of human beings is "the discovery of sense and causality amid the false leads, the noise, the trackless brambles of life." Still, in trying to deduce the crime of the century from numbers squawked by a gray parrot, Holmes finds that the secret history thrust upon him is so irrational, so senseless, that he is denied his deepest pleasure—the assembling of "a delicate, inexorable lattice of inferences . . . catching the light in glints and surmises." We are left with ruined intellect and teary eyes: Sherlock Holmes as Oedipus at Colonus.

Gentlemen of the Road suggests in passing that the Khazars might have decided to be Jewish back in the eighth century so as not to rile their rivalrous Christian and Muslim neighbors. But that's about all it has to say on the subject, being otherwise preoccupied with elephants, slave markets, dung fires, minarets, red hair, horse butter, Persian binoculars, and battlefield surgery. This seems to me a sadness, not only because there really were Khazars, who got in the way of the Bulgars, Magyars, and Vikings nibbling at Byzantium until at least the twelfth century, before they disappeared into a tendentious book by Arthur Koestler, *The Thirteenth Tribe* (1976); but also because a remarkable novel has already been written about them—Milorad Pavič's *Dictionary of the Khazars* (1990)—which should have goaded Chabon into exerting himself more than he has. Surely he would have appreciated what Pavič describes as the Khazar way of praying by weeping—"for tears are a part of God by virtue of always having a bit of salt at the bottom, just as shells hold pearls."

But if *Gentlemen* disappoints, *The Yiddish Policeman's Union*, in which the enduring tropes of the private-eye novel and the science-fiction parallel-universe fantasy are mixed and matched, is triumphant, as if Raymond Chandler and Philip K. Dick had smoked a joint with I. B. Singer. In an alternative twentieth century, Russia has gone through three republics without a revolution. The Holocaust is called, instead, the Destruction.

An atom bomb fell on Berlin in 1946. In 1948, Jews in the Holy Land were defeated and savaged by Arabs, so there is no Israel. Enticed by a settlement act that promised them sixty years of sanctuary before their federal district reverted to Alaska, thousands of Yiddish-speaking Jews arrived by a World War I troop transport at a swamp near the old Russian colony of Sitka, where they were numbered, inoculated, deloused, and tagged like migrant birds, only to discover fifty thousand Tlingit Indians already in possession of most of the flat and usable land. After which, nonetheless, crews of young Jewesses in blue headscarves went immediately to work, "singing Negro spirituals with Yiddish lyrics that paraphrased Lincoln and Marx."

Down South, the American First Lady is Marilyn Monroe Kennedy, the Cuban war has not gone well, and the Jews of Sitka are called "the Frozen Chosen."

Jewish Sitka, population 3.2 million, a couple of months shy of the 2008 "Reversion," is one of the novel's finest characters, an imaginary city, a Calvino Despina, as palpable as Tel Aviv, as ghostly as Warsaw, as liverish as Buenos Aires, with newspapers, cigarettes, tunnels, and secrets—everything but public transportation. We visit the Hotel Zamenhof on Max Nordau Street for dead bodies, the Hotel Einstein on Adler for nostalgia, the Ringelblum Avenue Baths for conspiracy, Bronfman University for a joke, the Polar-Shtern Kafeteria for pickled crab apple and perhaps a kreplach shaped like the head of Maimonides, and Goldblatt's Dairy Restaurant, to remember a Jewish massacre of Tlingits. We meet momzers, shtarkers, schlossers, grifters, boundary mavens, patzer ex-cons, bottom-rung bet runners like Penguin Simkowitz, mouse-eyed shtinkers like Zigmund Landau ("the Heifetz of Informers"), ultra-Orthodox black-hat wiseguys like the Verbover Hasidim, in charge of gunrunning, money-laundering, cigarette smuggling, policy racketeering, and all plots involving a Third Temple, and Landsman's partner in crime-stopping, Berko Shermets, a half Tlingit whose Indian line goes all the way back to the creation-mythic Raven but, at this time in this place, an observant Jew "for his own reasons": "He is a minotaur, and the world of Jews is his labyrinth."

After "half a century of a sense of mistakenness," of a smell on the wind of salmon being canned and what Landsman calls "the Brownian motion of collective woe," there are suddenly in Sitka silly signs and parodic portents: First, a face, bearded with sidelocks, has shown up two nights running in the shimmer of the aurora borealis. Next a chicken in the kosher slaughterhouse has turned on the shochet and announced, in Aramaic, the imminent advent of the Messiah. Finally, more seriously, the body of a man named Mendel Shpilman is found dead in a room in Landsman's Zamenhof. Routine inquiries establish that Mendel was not always "a sockless junkie in a cheap hotel." The disowned son of a big-shot rabbi, he is said to have had an IQ of 170, to have learned to read Hebrew, Aramaic, Latin, and Greek when he was eight years old, to have been, according to the black hats, a "miracle boy" with healing powers and quite possibly the Tzaddik-Ha-Dor, "the righteous man of this genera-tion," maybe even their Messiah. He seems also to have been gay, most likely hustled chess to buy drugs, probably tied off his arm with his tefillin to find a vein for heroin, and was definitely shot dead next to a chessboard on which the pieces were arrayed as a problem called a "zugzwang," which is when you have no good moves but you have to move anyway— sort of like the Jews of Sitka on the eve of the Reversion: "They're like goldfish in a bag, about to be dumped back into the big black lake of Diaspora."

(We might have guessed that Mendel's "zugzwang" first appeared in the pages of another fabulist, Vladimir Nabokov, in whose imaginary Zembla the language they spoke was emphatically not Yiddish.)

And not only does nobody care about the dead man, not even Men-del's father, Rebbe Shpilman, the blackest of Verbover hats whose crimi-nality would shame Babel's Benya, but they have ordained that Landsman not care, either.

3

Maybe they're hoping for World War Three. Maybe they want to crank up a new Crusade. Maybe they think if they do this thing, it will make Jesus come back. Or maybe it has nothing to do with any of that, and it's all really about oil, you know, securing their supply of the stuff once and for all. I don't know.

—The Yiddish Policeman's Union

In design, the proposed Third Temple is a restrained display of stonema-son might, cubes and pillars and sweeping plazas. Here and there a carved

Sumerian monster lends a touch of the barbaric. This is the paper that God left the Jews holding, Landsman thinks, the promise that we have been banging Him a kettle about ever since. The rook that attends the king at the endgame of the world.

—*The Yiddish Policeman's Union*

He doesn't know how one proceeds under the circumstances, except with the certainty, pressed to the heart like a keepsake of love, that in the end nothing really matters.

—*The Yiddish Policeman's Union*

Nobody can tell Landsman not to care about a crime. Crime is all he can bring himself to care about. He is otherwise "a disbeliever by inclination." His personal life and the history of the Jews have persuaded him that "heaven is kitsch, God a word, and the soul, at most, the charge on your battery." But responsibility is another matter, and accountability, too, and vulgar curiosity as well. Take away his badge and gun and he'll nose around for answers, anyway, flashing his Hands of Esau Yiddish policemen's union card as a credential. Somehow, the death of his sister and the murder of Mendel are connected. Something weird is going on at the Beth Tikkun Retreat Center, which is less like an honor ranch rehab for rich Jewish addicts than a paramilitary facility for Zionist revanchists. Some ulterior meaning nags at him from Mendel's zugzwang. And why are people talking behind his back in Hebrew? To Bina, the boss who used to be a wife, he tries to explain himself:

> Bina, I did not know this man. He was put in my way. I was given the opportunity to know him, I suppose, but I declined it. If this man and I had gotten to know each other, possibly we would have become pals. Maybe not. He had his thing with heroin, and that was probably enough for him. It usually is. But whether I knew him or not, and whether we could have grown old together holding hands in the lobby, is neither here nor there. Somebody came into this hotel, my hotel, and shot that man in the back of his head while he was off in dreamland. And that bothers me. . . . All these hard-lucks paying rent on a pull-down bed and a sheet of steel bolted to the bath-

room wall, for better or worse, they're my people now. I can't
honestly say I like them very much. Some of them are all right.
Most of them are pretty bad. But I'll be damned if I'm going
to let somebody walk in here and put a bullet in their heads.

This is classic Sam Spade/Philip Marlowe/Lew Archer stuff—the
American private eye, not a declassed aristocrat like Poe's Dupin, nor a
coke-addled scientist fiddler like Conan Doyle's Holmes, nor a titled-
gentry Wimsey, a nosy-genteel Miss Marple, or a world-weary European
bureaucrat cop like Maigret, Van der Valk, or Martin Beck, but a hardboiled, soft-hearted, smart-mouth gumshoe, the last romantic in a corrupt
world—an omelet of St. George, St. Francis of Assisi, and sweet-and-
sour Parsifal, a mixed grill of Galahad and Robin Hood, a submarine
sandwich of stormbird and psychotherapist. The private eye weeps for
you, even a sockless junkie. He evens the odds of the poor and weak
against the rich and violent, the organized criminals, neighborhood bullies, corporate goons, ministries of fear, drug cartels, death squads, and
global conspiracies, usually with a jazz score. To these savories, Chabon
has added the Flying Dutchman and the Wandering Jew, and it works so
well we want it to go on forever, every sorrowful secret just another reason to feel lousy about life.

Except that there's also Bina. She is under instructions to bury the
Mendel Shpilman case, but Bina is one of those biblical matriarchs, like
Rachel or Sarah, "who carry their homes in an old cowhide bag, on the
back of a camel, in the bubble of air at the center of their brains." Ambitious as she is to keep her job after the Reversion, there is a reason she
married Landsman in the first place, before they lost their child. And who
is it that has issued these instructions from above? How come they want
the lid on? Why are the Federal District pols, the Verbover black hats, and
the Washington, D.C., globocops so suddenly in cahoots? What's the
meaning of the counterfeit red heifer spotted by Landsman grazing in the
Indian outback? Who cut a deal with the Tlingits, in exchange for what?
And why, oh why, kill Mendel, who had surely fallen so far out of the
world as not to be in anybody's way?

As in any gratifying mystery, the answers to these questions are often,
although not always, a surprise. It is not surprising, for instance, to find
that zealots are still playing what the Israeli novelist David Grossman has
called the game of "Blow Up the Dome of the Rock and Wait One Turn

for the Arab World's Reaction." Nor is it surprising that, with Bina covering Landsman's back, the red heifer has a harder time fooling anybody. But the red heifer didn't kill Mendel, and neither did the usual suspects. You will have to keep on reading the delicious prose. Everything fits inside with a satisfying snap, like the hasp on a jewel box or the folding of a fan, and left in the air, like smoke, are ghosts and grace notes. As much as Chabon coaxes us to think about warriors and farmers, Hebrew and Yiddish, "Yids" and Tlingits, Israelis and Palestinians, or, for that matter, Boers, Zulus, Puritans, Iroquois, homelands, land grabs, checkpoints, transit camps, penal colonies, 9/11, and Iraq, he also fishes in the deepest waters. Landsman must eventually defend himself to the puppetmasters and gauleiters and petit-Guignol inquisitors. He is not in the least apologetic for having smudged their papyrus blueprints:

> All at once he feels weary of ganefs and prophets, guns and sacrifices and the infinite gangster weight of God. He's tired of hearing about the promised land and the inevitable bloodshed required for its redemption. "I don't care what is written. I don't care what supposedly got promised to some sandal-wearing idiot whose claim to fame is that he was ready to cut his own son's throat for the sake of a hare-brained idea. I don't care about red heifers and patriarchs and locusts. A bunch of old bones in the sand. My homeland is in my hat. It's in my ex-wife's tote bag."

Here *The Yiddish Policeman's Union* reminds me of the only other north-of-the-border Jewish novel in its major league, Mordecai Richler's *Solomon Gursky Was Here* (1989). In Richler's razzle-dazzle, where the Gurskys bore a startling resemblance to the Bronfmans from whom all Seagrams flows, we got 150 years of arctic sky, black ravens, caribou bones, Old Testament loonytunes, Levi-Strauss creation myths, Karl Marxist confabulations, and Gimpel the Fool on permafrost. Everything that wasn't Oedipal would prove to be cannibalistic. And Solomon Gursky himself seems to have agreed with Landsman, in his last words in 1978—IN CAPITAL LETTERS, NO LESS!—to an increasingly dubious biographer: "THE WORLD CONTINUES TO PAY A PUNISHING TOLL FOR OUR JEWISH DREAMERS."

And what are these Jewish dreamers waiting for, if not the Sermon on the Mount or the *Communist Manifesto*? They are waiting, we are told here, "for the time to be right, or the world to be right, or, some people say, for the time to be wrong and the world to be as wrong as it can be." For whom are they waiting? The "despised and rejected of men"; "a man of sorrows and acquainted with grief"; "A bum. A scholar. A junkie. Even a shammes." Have we met such a one? Well, yes. To the private eye as Wandering Jew, it seems to me that Chabon has added the superheroics of Kafka and Freud, the ethics of Maimonides and Spinoza, the politics of Emma Goldman and Grace Paley, the mysticisms of Martin Buber and Simone Weil, a paper rose and a magic bat. Landsman himself, abused as much as Jim Rockford and Jesus Christ, is the righteous man of his generation, the *Northern Exposure* Tzaddik-Ha-Dor.

Joan Didion's *The Year of Magical Thinking*

I

The most terrifying verse I know: merrily merrily merrily life is but a dream.
—Joan Didion, *The Last Thing He Wanted*

THREE TIMES THE mother had to repeat herself, telling the daughter her father was dead. The daughter, Quintana Roo, kept forgetting because she was in and out of comas, septic shock, extubation, or neurosurgery, in one or another intensive care unit on the West Coast or the East. Halfway through this black album—Joan Didion's *Life Studies* and her *Kaddish*, her Robert Lowell and Allen Ginsberg—the daughter is medevacked from the UCLA Medical Center in Los Angeles to the Rusk Institute in New York, but the transfer is complicated. Through a guerrilla action by wildcat truckers who have jackknifed a semitrailer on the interstate, the ambulance must feel its way to an airport that could be in Burbank, Santa Monica, or Van Nuys, nobody seems to know for sure, where a Cessna waits with just enough room for two pilots, two paramedics, the stretcher to which Quintana is strapped, and the bench on which her mother sits, on top of oxygen canisters. And they will have to make a heartland stop.

> Later we landed in a cornfield in Kansas to refuel. The pilots struck a deal with the two teenagers who managed the airstrip:

during the refueling they would take their pickup to a McDonald's and bring back hamburgers. While we waited the paramedics suggested that we take turns getting some exercise.
When my turn came I stood frozen on the tarmac for a
moment, ashamed to be free and outside when Quintana could
not be, then walked to where the runway ended and the corn
started. There was a little rain and unstable air and I imagined
a tornado coming. Quintana and I were Dorothy. We were
both free. In fact we were out of here.

If Didion is reminded of Oz, I am reminded of Didion. We've met this
runway woman more than once before. In *Democracy* her name was Inez
Victor, and after the death of her lover, Jack Lovett, in the shallow end of a
hotel swimming pool in Jakarta, she moved to Kuala Lumpur: "A woman
who had once thought of living in the White House was flicking termites
from her teacup and telling me about landing on a series of atolls in a
seven-passenger plane with a man in a body bag." In *The Last Thing He
Wanted*, her name was Elena McMahon, a journalist who quit reporting on
a presidential campaign to wash up on the wet grass of a runway on one of
those Caribbean islands we only pay attention to when they pop up on the
Bad Weather Channel, after which she disappeared into the lost clusters and
corrupted data of Iran/Contra. The narrator/novelist wonders "what made
her think a black shift bought off a rack sale at Bergdorf Goodman during
the New York primary was the appropriate thing to wear on an unsched-
uled flight at one-thirty in the morning out of Fort Lauderdale–Hollywood
International Airport, destination San Jose Costa Rica but not quite."

There is actually another Cessna in *Last Thing*, single-engined, flying
low, "dropping a roll of toilet paper over a mangrove clearing, the paper
streaming and looping as it catches on the treetops, the Cessna gaining
altitude as it banks to retrace its flight path." Inside the cardboard roll,
whose ends are closed with masking tape, is a message about November 22,
1963. Inside the novel is a message from the novelist, who has become
impatient with "the romance of solitude" and lost interest in such conven-
tions of her craft as the revelation of character:

> I realized that I was increasingly interested only in the techni-
> cal, in how to lay down the AM-2 aluminum matting for the

runway, in whether or not parallel taxiways and high-speed turnoffs must be provided, in whether an eight-thousand-foot runway requires sixty thousand square yards of operational apron or only forty thousand. If the AM-2 is laid directly over laterite instead of over plastic membrane seal, how long would we have before base failure results?

The Year of Magical Thinking requires her to be more personal, even cracked. In one dream, she will be "left alone on the tarmac at Santa Monica Airport watching the planes take off one by one," after her dead husband has boarded without her. In another, a nightmare rescue fantasy, she imagines a rough flight with Quintana between Honolulu and Los Angeles: "The plane would go down. Miraculously, she and I would survive the crash, adrift in the Pacific, clinging to the debris. The dilemma was this: I would need, because I was menstruating and the blood would attract sharks, to abandon her, swim away, leave her alone."

Didion has always juxtaposed the hardware and the soft: humming-birds and the FBI; nightmares of infant death and the light at dawn for a Pacific bomb test; disposable needles in a Snoopy wastebasket and the cost of a visa to leave Phnom Penh; four-year-olds in burning cars, rattle-snakes in playpens, lizards in a crèche; earthquakes, tidal waves, Patty Hearst. Against the "hydraulic imagery" of the clandestine world, its conduits, pipelines, and diversions, she opposes a gravitational imagery of black holes and weightlessness. Against dummy corporations, phantom payrolls, rocket launchers, and fragmentation mines, she opposes wild orchids washed by rain into a milky ditch of waste. Half of her last novel was depositions, cable traffic, brokered accounts, and classified secrets. The other half was jasmine, jacaranda petals, twilight, vertigo.

In *The Year of Magical Thinking*, these conjunctions and abutments—scraps of poetry, cramps of memory, medical terms, body parts, bad dreams, readouts, breakdowns—amount to a kind of liturgical sing-song, a whistling in the dark against a "vortex" that would otherwise swallow her whole with a hum. This then is how she passes the evil hours of an evil year, with spells and amulets. Her seventy-year-old husband, John Gregory Dunne, has dropped dead of a massive heart attack in their living room in New York City, one month short of their fortieth wedding anni-versary. She can't erase his voice from the answering machine, and refuses to get rid of his shoes. Her thirty-eight-year-old daughter, Quintana Roo Dunne Michael, has only been married five months before she is out of one hospital into another, a flu that somehow "morphed" into pneumonia and was followed by a stroke. One morning in the ICU Didion is startled to see that the monitor above her daughter's head is dark, "that her brain waves were gone." Without telling Quintana's mother, the doctors have turned off her EEG. But "I had grown used to watching her brain waves. It was a way of hearing her talk."

So we watch her listen—to the obscene susurrus of electrodes, syringes, catheter lines, breathing tubes, ultrasound, white cell counts, anticoagulants, ventricular fibbing, tracheostomies, thallium scans, fixed pupils, and brain death, not to neglect such euphemisms as "leave the table," which means to survive surgery, and "subacute rehab facility," which means a nursing home. But she also consults texts by Shakespeare, Philippe Aries, William Styron, Gerard Manley Hopkins, Sigmund Freud, W. H. Auden, E. E. Cummings, Melanie Klein, Walter Savage Landor, C. S. Lewis, Matthew Arnold, D. H. Lawrence, Delmore Schwartz, Dylan Thomas, Emily Post, and Euripides. And, simultaneously, she is watching and listening to herself. How does she measure up to the stalwart grieving behaviors of dolphins and geese?

> We have no way of knowing that the funeral itself will be anodyne, a kind of narcotic regression in which we are wrapped in the care of others and the gravity and meaning of the occasion. Nor can we know ahead of the fact (and here lies the heart of the difference between grief as we imagine it and grief as it is) the unending absence that follows, the void, the very opposite of meaning, the relentless succession of moments during which we will confront the experience of meaninglessness itself.

Nor did this book have any way of knowing that Quintana would die this August, twenty months after her father. At New York–Presbyterian Hospital where John Dunne is pronounced dead, a social worker says to a doctor about the brand-new widow: "It's okay. She's a pretty cool customer." Little did they know. What she was really thinking was, "I needed to be alone so that he could come back."

2

*I realized that my impression of myself had been of someone who could
look for, and find, the upside in any situation. I had believed in the logic
of popular songs. I had looked for the silver lining. I had walked on
through the storm. It occurs to me now that these were not even the songs
of my generation.*

—Joan Didion, *The Year of Magical Thinking*

In a 1997 appreciation, practically a CAT scan, of Joan Didion's novels
and essays, Elizabeth Hardwick spoke of "a carefully designed frieze of
the fracture and splinter in her characters' comprehension of the world,"
"a structure for the fadings and erasures of experience," and, to accommodate "the extreme fluidity of the fictional landscape," a narrative
method of "peculiar restlessness and unease." She cited bereaved mothers,
damaged daughters, "percussive dialogue," and "sleepwalking players"; a
martyred "facticity" and revelations "of incapacity, doubt, irresolution,
and inattention"; "a sort of cocoon of melancholy," "a sort of computer
lyricism," and "a sort of muscular assurance and confidence"; a "witch-
ery" of "uncompromising imagination" and "an obsessive attraction to
the disjunctive and paradoxical in American national policy and to the
somnolent, careless decisions made in private life."

All quite true, but Hardwick missed that finding "the upside in any
situation." Me, too. Didion and I were neophytes in Manhattan during
the late-fifties Ike Snooze, both published by William F. Buckley, Jr., in
National Review alongside such equally unlikely beginning writers as
Garry Wills, Renata Adler, and Arlene Croce, back when Buckley hired
the unknown young just because he liked our zippy lip and figured he'd
take care of our politics with the charismatic science of his own personality. Later, ruefully, he called us "the apostates." So I've been reading
Didion ever since she started doing it for money, have known her well
enough to nod at for almost as long, have reviewed most of her books
since *Play It As It Lays,* and cannot pretend to objectivity. Even when I
take furious exception to something she says—about Joan Baez, for
instance: "So now the girl whose life is a crystal teardrop has her own
place, a place where the sun shines and the ambiguities can be set aside a

little while longer"; or such condescension as "the kind of jazz people used to have on their record players when everyone who believed in the Family of Man bought Scandinavian stainless-steel flatware and voted for Adlai Stevenson"—I remain a partisan, in part because she's a fellow westerner, like Pauline Kael, and we must stick together against the provincialism of the East. And in part because I've been trying for four decades to figure out why her sentences are better than mine or yours . . . something about cadence. They come at you, if not from ambush, then in gnomic haikus, ice-pick laser beams, or waves. Even the space on the page around these sentences is more interesting than could be expected, as if to square a sandbox for the Sphinx.

Still, I wouldn't have thought looking for the upside was a big part of her repertoire. She's an Episcopalian, not a von Trapp—a declared agnostic about history, narrative, and reasons why, a devout *disbeliever* in social action, moral imperatives, abstract thought, American exemptions, and the primacy of personal conscience. Inside this agnosticism, in both novels and essays, there is a neurasthenic beating herself up about bad sexual conduct, nameless derelictions, and well-deserved punishments— a human being who drinks bourbon to cure herself of "bad attitudes, unpleasant tempers, wrongthink"; who endures "the usual intimations of erratic cell multiplication, dust and dry wind, sexual dyaesthesia, sloth, flatulence, root canal"; who has discovered "that not all of the promises would be kept, that some things are in fact irrevocable and that it had counted after all, every evasion and every procrastination, every mistake, every word, all of it"; who has misplaced "whatever slight faith she ever had in the social contract, in the meliorative principle, in the whole grand pattern of human endeavor"; who still believes that "the heart of darkness lay not in some error of social organization but in man's own blood"; who got married instead of seeing a psychiatrist; who puts her head in a paper bag to keep from crying; who has not been the witness she wanted to be; whose nights are troubled by peacocks screaming in the olive trees—an Alcestis back from the tunnel and half in love with death. *You know me, or think you do.*

Although this Alcestis may have sometimes fudged the difference between fatalism and lassitude, what she *does* believe in, besides "tropism[s] towards disorder" and the dark troika of dislocation, dread, and dreams, is Original Sin. She tells stories in self-defense: "The princess is caged in the consulate. The man with the candy will lead the children into the sea."

Over and over again in these stories, wounded women make strange choices in hot places with calamitous consequences. This, admit it, is Didion the closet romantic, who actually rooted for the journalist Elena McMahon and the American diplomat Treat Morrison to make it in *The Last Thing He Wanted*: "I want those two to have been together all their lives."

But it's personal—intuition and anxiety, frazzled nerves and love gone wrong: nothing to do with the rest of us or the world's mean work. As she explained in *The White Album*, "I am not the society in microcosm. I am a thirty-four-year-old woman with long straight hair and an old bikini bathing suit and bad nerves sitting on an island in the middle of the Pacific waiting for a tidal wave that will not come." To which she added in *A Book of Common Prayer*: "Fear of the dark can be synthesized in the laboratory. Fear of the dark is an arrangement of fifteen amino acids. Fear of the dark is a protein."

Thus she'd seem the unlikeliest of writers to turn into a disenchanted legionnaire "on the far frontiers of the Monroe Doctrine," at the porous borders of the American imperium. Somehow, though, she went left and went south, to discover in the Latin latitudes more than her own unbearable whiteness of being. In El Salvador between "grimgrams," body dumps, and midnight screenings on video cassettes of *Apocalypse Now* and *Bananas*, Didion decided that Gabriel García Márquez was in fact "a social realist."

> In El Salvador one learns that vultures go first for the soft tissue, for the eyes, the exposed genitalia, the open mouth. One learns that an open mouth can be used to make a specific point, can be stuffed with something emblematic; stuffed, say, with a penis, or, if the point has to do with land title, stuffed with some of the dirt in question. One learns that hair deteriorates less rapidly than flesh, and that a skull surrounded by a perfect corona of hair is not an uncommon sight in the body dumps.

So the essayist who in *Slouching Towards Bethlehem* liked Howard Hughes and John Wayne more than Joan Baez and the flower children, who in *The White Album* found more fault with Doris Lessing, Hollywood liberals, and feminism than with mall culture and Manson groupies, ends up in *Salvador*, *Miami*, and *After Henry* savagely disdainful of Ronald Reagan and the "dreamwork" of American foreign policy—"a dreamwork devised to obscure any intelligence that might trouble the dreamer." The daughter of conservative Republicans who's told us that she voted "ardently" for Barry Goldwater in 1964 will describe in *Political Fictions* the abduction of American democracy by a permanent political class, an oligarchy consisting not only of the best candidates big money can buy, their focus groups, advance teams, donor bases, and consultants, but also the journalists who cover the prefab story, the pundit caste of smogball sermonizers, the spayed creatures of the talk-show ether, and the apparatchiks in it for career advancement, agenda enhancement, a book contract, or a coup d'état. And the writer of fiction who started out with *Play It As It Lays*, a scary manual on narcissism, leaves town for Panama instead of Hawaii, for Costa Rica and "Boca Grande," and other tropics of "morbidity and paranoia," where, as if she had graduated overnight from the middle school of Raymond Chandler and Nathanael West to a doctoral program with Graham Greene, Octavio Paz, Nadine Gordimer, and André Malraux, she writes postcolonial NAFTA novels.

It's not just that the momentum she worries so much about has taken Didion in surprising directions. It's that we should not perhaps have been surprised. How lazy to have labeled her the poster girl for anomie, wearing a migraine and a bikini to every volcanic eruption of the postwar zeitgeist; a desert lioness of the style pages, part sybilline icon and part Stanford seismograph, alert on the fault lines of the culture to every tremble of tectonic fashion plate. Yes, the sixties seemed so much to hurt her feelings that her prose at times suggested Valéry's *frémissements d'une feuille effacée*—shiverings of an effaced leaf—as if her next trick might be evaporation. But as early as *Bethlehem*, for every syllable on rattlesnakes and mesquite there was also an inquiry into Alcatraz and body bags from Vietnam. *The White Album*, an almanac of nameless blue-eyed willies, had nonetheless a lot to say about Huey Newton and the Panthers, Bogotá and Hoover Dam, and the storage of nerve gas in an Oregon army arsenal. In *After Henry*, on a December morning in 1979, she visited the Caritas transit camp for Vietnamese refugees near Kai Tak airport, Kowloon, Hong Kong, where "a woman of indeterminate age was crouched on the pavement near the washing pumps bleeding out a live chicken." She also just happened to stop in on the Berkeley nuclear reactor, flashing back to her fifties grammar-school days of atom bomb drills and fifties nightmares of deathly light while chatting up the engineer and inspecting the core, the radiation around the fuel rods, and the blue shimmer of the shock wave under twenty feet of water, water "the exact blue of the glass at Chartres."

Sensitive, to be sure, like a photo plate, a litmus paper, or an inner ear. But writers ought to bruise easily, and obviously the brute world—from California, with its stealth bombers, lemon groves, biker boys, Taco Bells, poker parlors, cyclotrons, and snipers, where horses catch fire and are shot on the beach, to the rest of the revolting world, with its bird racket, salt mines, banana palms, anaconda skins, casinos, tanks, and Elliott Abrams— has left fingerprints and stigmata. Cynthia Ozick described Isaac Babel as "an irritable membrane, subject to every creaturely vibration." Although Didion never rode with the Red Cavalry, she has certainly slummed enough with filmmakers, intelligence agents, and social scientists to be very irritable indeed, and, like the anthropologist in *A Book of Common Prayer*, she has come close to losing faith in her own method and powers of description:

> I studied under Kroeber at California and worked with Levi-Strauss at São Paulo, classified several societies, catalogued their rites and attitudes on occasions of birth, copulation, initiation and death; did extensive and well-regarded studies on the rearing of female children in the Mato Grosso and along certain tributaries of the Rio Xingu, and still I did not know why any one of these female children did or did not do anything at all.
>
> Let me go further.
>
> I did not know why I did or did not do anything at all.

3

It's undeniable, isn't it, said Kate on the phone to Stephen, the fascination of the dying. It makes me ashamed. We're learning how to die, said Hilda. I'm not ready to learn, said Aileen; and Lewis, who was coming straight from the other hospital, the hospital where Max was still being kept on in ICU, met Tanya getting out of the elevator on the tenth floor, and as they walked together down the shiny corridor past the open doors, averting their eyes from the other patients sunk in their beds, with tubes in their noses, irradiated by the bluish light from the television sets, the thing I can't bear to think about, Tanya said to Lewis, is someone dying with the TV on.

—Susan Sontag, "The Way We Live Now"

Somewhere in the nod we were dropping cargo. Somewhere in the nod we were losing infrastructure, losing redundant systems, losing specific gravity. Weightlessness seemed at the time the safer mode. Weightlessness seemed at the time the mode in which we could beat both the clock and affect itself, but I see now that it was not.

—Joan Didion, *The Last Thing He Wanted*

In *Harp* (1989), his single stab at autobiography, almost a slasher attack on who he was and how he came to be that way, John Gregory Dunne thought out loud about his mother and his brothers and being Irish Americans in Hartford, Connecticut; about Princeton and the army and murder and suicide; about Henry James, Truman Capote, George Eliot, and Lillian Hellman; about television talk shows, Frankfurt whorehouses, Palestinian refugee camps, cardiac surgery, and why he wrote. He would rather not have thought about why he wrote, but heart trouble had turned him introspective. He seemed to decide that he wrote novels like *True Confessions*, *Dutch Shea, Jr.*, and *The Red White and Blue*, and nonfiction like *The Studio*, *Vegas*, and *Harp*, in order to even the psychic score. In general he was full of class hatred. Specifically he was possessed by an Irish American animus toward WASPs, plus some contempt for his own posturing in this resentment as he re-created the four stages of his "steerage to suburbia" saga: "immigrant, outcast, assimilated, deracinated." The army may have helped, too: "If I had not gone into the army as an enlisted man, if I had not experienced what it was like to be a have-not, I doubt I ever would have been so professionally drawn to outsiders." On the other hand, he wasn't much for wallowing in the Old Sod, had never been deeply stirred by the Troubles, had no allegiance at all to the IRA, "nor even any particular enthusiasm for Yeats or O'Casey." Being *outside* was all right by him, a source of energy, a gift of material, a blackjack, and some body heat. Truman Capote's mistake, he said, was "to believe himself a citizen of the world of fashion when in fact he only had a green card."

Stylistically, Dunne was inclined to ridicule. The Irish voice, he informed us, "gets a kick out of frailty and misfortune; its comedy is the comedy of

the small mind and the mean spirit. Nothing lifts the heart of the Irish car-
oler more than the small vice, the tiny lapse, the exposed vanity. . . ." And
so he ridiculed himself. This is one of the things a writer does when, suddenly, he is afraid of dying. Dunne said he traveled "easier without the baggage of history, and all of history's social and genetic freight," but if that
freight is one of the things that kills us, it is also one of the reasons why we
travel at all.

When he found out from the doctors that he was getting a pacemaker
instead of a coffin, he told his wife, "I think I know how to end this book
now." He didn't really. His wife said "Terrific" but he just stopped. After
he stopped, I remember thinking that spouses are another sort of history
and a different kind of religion, and wondering whether it was easier to
be Irish if you are married to someone who wasn't. I liked the hostility of
Harp. It wasn't just that after reaching out with Gatsby for the green light
at the end of Daisy's dock, he then swatted it like a mosquito. It was more
that, hard as he was on everybody else, he was harder on lyric afflatus,
performance blarney, and himself. He seemed to have been born to write
his savage novels and nurse his bloody grudges.

When they asked his wife at the hospital whether to fetch a priest, she
said yes. Never mind that Dunne, although a Catholic, hadn't believed in
the resurrection of the body. Nor does his Episcopalian wife. What she
finds impossible isn't deciding on priests and autopsies and cremation, on
marble plates and Gregorian chants and "a single soaring trumpet" at the
funeral, or whether, because she is spending so much time in intensive
care with Quintana, to buy several sets of blue cotton scrubs, or when she
ought to start working again, but if she should stick a preposition into a
sentence of the galleys of the novel John didn't live to see published: "Any
choice I made could carry the potential for abandonment, even betrayal."

They had been married for forty years. Except for the first five months,
when John still worked at *Time*, they both stayed home and wrote in an
amazing intimacy. "We were together twenty-four hours a day." Even
during the occasional week apart, if she were teaching in Berkeley or he
had gone to Las Vegas, they talked on the telephone several times a day.
When, in the second paragraph of her first column for *Life* magazine, she
dropped a rhetorical grenade—"We are here on this island in the middle
of the Pacific in lieu of filing for divorce"—upset readers simply weren't
aware that John had edited the column, as he edited everything she wrote,
and then drove her to Western Union so she could file it. If this seems not

to have done their books any harm, nor did it do their screenplays any good.

You'd think they needed each other to breathe. But you'd also think that Didion, the tarmac woman, has been rehearsing death for many years on many runways. It's her preferred tropic, as skepticism is her preferred meridian. Maria in *Play It As It Lays* not only expects to die soon but also believes that planes crash if she boards them in "bad spirit," that loveless marriages cause cancer, and that fatal accidents happen to the children of adulterers. Charlotte in *A Book of Common Prayer* dreams only of "sexual surrender and infant death," and came to Boca Grande in the first place because it's "at the very cervix of the world, the place through which a child lost to history must eventually pass." The body count in *Democracy* is remarkable, not even including the AID analyst and the Reuters correspondent who are poisoned in Saigon in 1970 by oleander leaves, "a chiffonade of hemotoxins." In *The Last Thing He Wanted*, everybody we care about will die, leaving only Arthur Schlesinger, Jr., to eat by candlelight and Ted Sorensen to swim with the dolphins.

> We might expect if death is sudden to feel shock. We do not expect this shock to be obliterative, dislocating to both body and mind. We might expect that we will be prostrate, inconsolable, crazy with loss. We do not expect to be literally crazy, cool customers who believe that their husband is about to return and need his shoes.

She picks up the EKG electrodes and the syringes the paramedics left on her living room floor, but the blood is more than she can handle. To the social worker at the hospital, as if he were the emissary of the army at your door in dress greens with bad news from the battlefield, she wants to say, "I'm sorry, but you can't come in." She puts John's cell phone in its charger. She puts his silver money clip in the box where they keep passports and proof of jury service. She calls a friend at the *Los Angeles Times* so they won't feel scooped by the *New York Times*. She will not authorize an organ harvest: "How could he come back if they took away his organs, how could he come back if he had no shoes?" Besides: "His blue eyes. His blue imperfect eyes." She is meticulous about ritual, up through and including St. John the Divine, "and it still didn't bring him back." She can't bring herself to throw away a wafer-thin alarm clock he gave her that stopped working the year before he died; she can't even remove it from the table by her bed. She can't eat, can't sleep, can't think without remembering, can't remember without hurting, and for six long months can't even dream. She rereads John's books, finding them darker. She understands, for the first time, "the power in the image of the rivers, the Styx, the Lethe, the cloaked ferryman with his pole," the burning raft of grief. No matter where she hides, the vortex finds her.

"Marriage is not only time," she says; "it is also, paradoxically, the denial of time. For forty years I saw myself through John's eyes. I did not age." She tells us that in the rituals of domestic life—setting the table, lighting the candles, building the fire, clean towels, hurricane lamps, "all those souffles, all that crème caramel, all those daubes and albondigas and gumbos"—she found an equal, countervailing meaning to her childhood apprehensions of the mushroom cloud. She quotes Eliot from *The Waste Land*: "These fragments I have shored against my ruins." And we are encouraged to think that, just maybe, *The Year of Magical Thinking* is another such stock of rubbled remnants against the worst of nights. But it seems to me as well a habitation of brave hearts and brilliant intellect: a library, an aquarium, a greenhouse, an ice palace, a hall of mirrors, a museum of sacred monsters, a coliseum, and a memory dump. We are surrounded by her fragments. We can shuffle our own magic:

John was talking, then he wasn't.

You sit down to dinner and life as you know it ends.

On takeoff he held my hand until the plane began leveling. He always did. Where did that go?

I was thinking as small children think, as if my thoughts or wishes had the power to reverse the narrative, change the outcome.

I had to believe he was dead all along. If I did not believe he was dead all along I would have thought I should have been able to save him.

No eye was on the sparrow.

When someone dies, I was taught growing up in California, you bake a ham.

In the sense that it happens one night and not another, the mechanism of a typical cardiac arrest could be construed as essentially accidental: a sudden spasm ruptures a deposit of plaque in a coronary artery, ischemia follows, and the heart, deprived of oxygen, enters ventricular fibrillation.

After that instant at the dinner table he was never not dead. Shine, Little Glow Worm.

The votive candles on the sills of the big windows in the living room. The *te de limon* grass and aloe that grew by the kitchen door. The rats that ate the avocados.

I had allowed other people to think he was dead. I had allowed him to be buried alive.

The craziness is receding but no clarity is taking its place.

We are imperfect mortal beings, aware of that mortality even as we push it away, failed by our very complication, so wired that when we mourn our losses we also mourn, for better or worse, ourselves. As we were. As we are no longer. As we will one day not be at all.

Let them become the photograph on the table. Let them become the name on the trust accounts. Let go of them in the water.

If Joan Didion went crazy, what are the chances for the rest of us? Not so good, except that we have her example to instruct us and sentences we can almost sing. Look, no one wants to hear about it, your death, mine, or his. What, as they listen, are they supposed to do with their feet, eyes, hands, and tongue, not to mention their panic? If they do want to hear about it—the grief performers, the exhibitionists of bathetic wallow, the prurient ghouls—you don't want to know them. And maybe craziness is the only appropriate behavior in front of a fact to which we can't ascribe a meaning. But since William Blake's Nobodaddy will come after all of us, I can't think of a book we need more than hers—those of us for whom this life is it, these moments all the more precious because they are numbered, after which a blinking out as the black accident rolls on in particles or waves; those of us who have spent our own time in the metropolitan hospital Death Care precincts, wondering why they make it so hard to follow the blue stripe to the PET scan, especially since we would really prefer never to arrive, to remain undisclosed; those of us who sit there with Didion in our laps at the oncologist's cheery office, waiting for our fix of docetaxel, irinotecan, and dexamethasone, wanting more Bach and sunsets.

I can't imagine dying without this book.

Writing for His Life

JOHN WAS A teller of stories. They popped up in articles and speeches, at the dinner table, outside on the deck in the sun. He had favorites he polished and told so often his family knew them by heart. He was proud of that family—proud of the children (daughter, Amy; son, Andrew; step-daughter, Jen) and grandchildren (Tiana, Eli, and Oscar) and spoke often of their exploits, another piece of his storytelling. How he loved new ones, which was why he traveled so often, even though he was otherwise a man of routine who went no farther than his front stoop or back garden. And why he was such a good listener.

John hated all holidays, including his birthday—except Thanksgiving, when he wanted his family and friends around *his* kitchen table as he carved the turkey and sneaked a bite of skin, having insisted on my cooking extra legs and thighs so there would be enough dark meat. But he had a sense of ceremony and he taught me to celebrate milestones, whether a third-grade Prize Day or college graduations or the awarding of a Ph.D. Of course he was there within moments to exult in the birth of all three of his grandchildren.

The only possession he cared about was his house—a thirteen-and-a-half-foot-wide funky brownstone filled, naturally, with books.

He was a man of many passions: New York way up on the list. Moving around, he preferred subways to buses—he could tell you the best route to anywhere and where to stand on the platform to be closest to the exit at the other end of the trip—and preferred both to taxis. Although he grew up in southern California, John hated to drive, so failed to renew his license sometime in the seventies. He walked with hands in his pockets, even down stairs—I was always afraid he would trip and not be able to catch himself.

Sports—he would have loved to have been the new Red Smith. The *Times* gave him a sports column for a while, until he brought the CIA into a piece on a strike by the NFL (which they wouldn't print) or the time he planned to cover a baseball game and a tennis tournament on the same afternoon but couldn't find his limo at Forest Hills when he was ready to go over to Shea Stadium (not sure if they ran that story).

Actresses with smoky voices—Blythe Danner, Susan Saint James, Dana Delany, Lauren Bacall. And a very few heroes: Adlai Stevenson, Murray Kempton, Joan Baez, and Bobby Kennedy are the only ones that come to mind.

As anyone who knew him will attest, his tastes were catholic—Mozart, to *Candide*, to *Evita*, to Fats Domino, to Springsteen, to "Suds in a Bucket." He knew everything and forgot nothing from Sufi lapwings to parodies of Swinburne; he was a living database.

John worked in many venues, saying yes to every publication that asked him to write (including *Penthouse* and *Playboy*, although not *Hustler*), but, with the exception of *First Edition* (WGBH) and his sixteen-year stint on *CBS Sunday Morning*, resisted invitations to speak on television—to the consternation of program coordinators.

He was loyal and forgiving of his friends although he never called or wrote. He refused to write e-mails, let alone letters, to his mother, whom he dearly loved. As I loved him; John was one of *my* passions.

Okay, he wasn't perfect: He loved gossip (reading Page Six and Liz Smith every morning) and could not be trusted with secrets; John was a blurter. He was stubborn and he ignored his health. He consumed nothing but coffee until dinnertime and smoked at least a pack and a half of cigarettes until the day they cut away 40 percent of his lung. It took three times in rehab and the destruction of more than one marriage to end his drinking. And he wouldn't share the remote.

But he was a man of deep integrity and faithful his entire life to his one true religion: Never cross a picket line.

John is no longer here to tell his stories, so we must tell them for him. Let us begin.

—Sue Leonard
New York City, 2011

Andrew Leonard

A computer analysis of my father's collected works reveals: 97.4 percent of everything he wrote can be safely ignored. All that verbiage is utilitarian scaffolding, employed to hold up just ten critical words. They are:

Tantrum
Cathedral
Linoleum
Moxie
Thug
Dialectic
Splendid
Brood
Libidinal
and Qualm

Those familiar with my father's tendencies might quibble: Where are the mystagogues and omophagous worms? He was famous for his erudition. You give us "moxie" and "thug"?

But as exciting as the fancy-pants words may be, they are not essential to understanding the John Leonard Project. They are baroque ornamentation.

I also excised all words my father delighted in simply because they pleased his ear. Words such as "kayak" and "rutabaga." It would be a mistake to hope for revelatory insight into the essence of my father from these words. Quite the opposite: I am unaware of any physical evidence proving John Leonard was ever within fifty yards of a kayak, and I am skeptical about whether he could have told the difference between a rutabaga and a Brussels sprout.

Freud, I'm sure, would caution against the perils involved in posthumously editing one's father, but in one of my father's columns, the word "rutabaga" appears five times. That is excessive.

Even more problematic is a third category I have chosen to skip: recurring compound phrases of two or more words that do hint at murkier depths. Categorical imperatives, imperialist lackeys, internal contradictions, and unindicted co-conspirators, all of which have a habit of showing up in the unlikeliest of places, such as snuggling up next to Blythe Danner in a Lifetime TV movie review.

But what self-respecting critic does *not* seize the chance to weave Hegel, Kant, Mao, and Watergate into an appreciation of *CSI Miami*? My father was more industrious than most in his high-culture infiltrations, but this does not, I think, fundamentally distinguish his cathedrals from those built by others.

So on with it!

My father cherished tantrums and hated thugs. Cathedrals he built, admired, and sang the praises of. But he was suspicious of linoleum. Moxie, he adored. The dialectic, always present. Brooding, whenever possible. "Splendid," a word of highest praise, although easy to confuse with "dazzling," the last word in his review of *One Hundred Years of Solitude*—or "triumph," the last word in his review of *Song of Solomon*.

Which brings us to "libidinal."

In my interpretation of the lexicon I have relied heavily on *Private Lives*, the columns he wrote for the *New York Times* in the late 1970s. There's a lot of libido in *Private Lives*. More than I counted on. In two consecutive columns, my father dropped the smart bombs "libidinal *cathexis*" and "libidinal compost heap."

Talk about excessive! In the latter case, the children are playing downstairs, in the libidinal compost heap. We'll just leave that alone. But, in the case of the former—after some research—I learned that *cathexis* is a Greek word, employed to translate the German word *bestzung*, which was itself used by Sigmund Freud to refer to the "concentration of psychic energy on some particular person, thing, idea, or aspect of the self." An expert in Freudian psychotherapy could probably provide more nuance, but I choose to define libidinal *cathexis* as the concentration of psychic energy on some person, thing, idea, or aspect of the self, for the purpose of gaining great pleasure.

That is the John Leonard Project—both his means and his ends. He did not like to pan books or movies or TV shows or children, except when absolutely necessary. Instead, he lived to exalt, to spread the dazzle, and in the process of doing so, make of his own words a libidinal tsunami. When my father was *on*, and he was almost always *on*, even to the last, his words incited passion, got the heart racing, stirred the blood and the mind and the soul. In the midst of it all, one unself-consciously gasps. Afterward, even those of us who don't smoke reach for a cigarette.

This was true from the beginning. After generating my list, and poring over *Private Lives*, I opened up my father's gin-soaked debut novel, *The Naked Martini*. I was comforted to discover, like old friends, the word "brood" on the first page and "libido" on the second.

Finally, I will concede that there is one last group of words that transcend the automatically generated lexicon. In one column, my father, who did not particularly care for cats, told of watching a kitten named Gulliver convert an inadvertent fall off a window sill into a perfectly executed double back flip. My father was charmed, despite himself. The kitten imperative cannot be denied. "If there is a chord in us that kittens strike," he wrote, "maybe there's one for justice, and for mercy, for sacrifice and reciprocity, kindness and respect."

My father believed in all those words and lived up to all those words. And he loved every last one of his words, the fancy and the salt of the earth, the scaffolding and the ornamentation and the raw bones. I have no qualms in suggesting that all of us, in this regard, are his willing and eager, even if unindicted, co-conspirators.

Amy Leonard

I inherited many things from my father, some more beneficial than others. On the positive side, there is my love of the life of the mind and a deep passion for liberal politics. Of more dubious benefit, my fondness for alcohol and anything fried and salty. But there is one gift from Dad that has truly helped define me: a crazy love of sports. My father was a fan, with an emphasis on "fanatic." As such, my father passed on his Rules of Rooting, based on the premise that one can *always* find a reason to cheer on a team.

Rule 1: You support your own team. This may seem obvious, but being a true supporter is not for the faint of heart. Your team represents you and your philosophy. Sure, you root for the hometown team, or where you went to college, but if you have a choice in that, you should pick the team that needs you most (i.e., the losers). Not the perennial winners who are easy to love, but rather the scrappy also-rans. And when your team loses, over and over again, you wear those losses with a badge of honor and a certain amount of pride. Part of rooting for your team entails never giving up on them. You never leave a game early. Dad did not care if it was 20–0 in the bottom of the ninth, you did not leave. Some will say this is because you don't want to miss that rare but amazing come-from-behind victory, but that is not the reason. You don't leave because *this is your team.* They are playing for you and it is dishonorable to give up on them. If you do leave early, you run the risk of the ultimate insult: You are just like those Dodger fans, who leave early to avoid traffic. (Shudder.) If by some stroke of good fortune your team wins it all, you revel in it, but with a certain sense of embarrassment. We are not supposed to win—obviously there has been some mistake.

Rule 2: You can always root for the underdog. The lowest seed, the poorest team, the ones with no business being there. And if they win, you have the sweet feeling of scoring one for the little guy.

Rule 3 (and most sacrosanct): You always root against the Yankees. This rule may be modified, depending on season and sport, to substitute the Dallas Cowboys, Notre Dame, or Duke. The sad irony now is that my favorite team, the Florida Gators, has joined the pantheon of winning teams people love to hate. But that is the cross the true fan must bear.

After these rules there is a complicated calculus of rooting that could involve when the team integrated, does it have a black coach, is it owned communally (one can always support the Green Bay Packers). All part of his theory of "sports socialism."

Having set up the parameters of fandom, I want to share three sports memories of my father. The first is from my sophomore year in college. This was not a great year for Dad, the last before he stopped drinking. But he was thrilled I was in NYC, and though my college (Barnard) did not have a football team, he was excited to support Columbia's, so off we went each weekend to watch the Lions play. If you know anything about the years 1984–88 (my college years), you'll know that Columbia lost every single game it played. In fact, it broke the record for most consecutive losses in college football. *This* was my dad's kind of team!

The second memory is from when he had lung surgery and was recovering in the hospital. It was during the Super Bowl, so Dad and I watched the game together. We ate salty snacks and rooted for the New England Patriots, complete underdogs and supposedly totally outmatched against the powerful St. Louis Rams. New England won, thus beginning a football dynasty we now root against—sports is very complicated.

The last memory is the Saturday before he died. The big bash for my stepmother's seventieth birthday was winding down and we were sitting downstairs. I knew he must have been incredibly tired, but he turned to me and said, somewhat imperiously, "Now we will watch the game." He had taped the Florida-Georgia football game (a huge rivalry) and wanted to share it with me, even though he knew who had won. So I watched the game, and my dad watched me, in my crazy sports-fanatic mode, whoopin' and hollerin', as my beloved Gators crushed the Dogs. I left the next day before he woke up; he died three days later.

So I think of my father now, as I root for the woefully inept Washington Nationals (my new home team), and bask in the glow of the underdog candidate becoming president, and I know he would be exceedingly proud that his legacy continues in me.

Jen Nessel

When he wasn't reading a book, marking it up with exclamation points and dogearing every page while watching a basketball game and eating potato chips, John could be found either in his garden, a hungry solar panel, sun worshipper, urban Druid, Aztec sacrifice of a napping cat, or crouched over his desk, inside a bunker of books, the fastest two-finger typist in the West.

John had many moving parts, exploding in as many directions as one of his sentences, but he was, above all, an Enthusiast.

He was, of course, a passionate book booster and consummate stylist, the world's foremost proponent of the semicolon. He counseled friends; championed young writers and traveled hungrily; feasted on ideas and subsisted on red meat, French fries, and ice cream; and he loved my mother more than I've ever seen anyone love another human being in real life.

John was deeply principled. He was fiercely loyal, never let go of a grudge (he once refused to shake Henry Kissinger's hand at a party), treated everyone as though they were entitled to dignity and respect, never fawned, never sucked up.

I always thought of John as a giant head, a benign version of the great and powerful Oz before the curtain's pulled back. John could barely change a light bulb and once insisted impatiently that he couldn't fax me a document I needed because the machine was out of paper.

I knew John my whole life; he became my second father when I was nine years old. He never talked down to us as kids; our opinions and stories mattered in their own right. Of course he had a drink in his hand or a bottle hidden in a closet through much of my childhood, which took its own toll on each of us in different ways, but there was a richness to life in that house on Seventy-eighth Street.

We read favorite poems to each other in the living room or watched *M★A★S★H* and *Hill Street Blues* together as though the characters were important people in our lives. We saved up stories from our days to eat for dinner. My classmates marveled at the range of topics that came up at our dinner table that somehow always, annoyingly, connected to something we were discussing in class: history, politics, literature.

In the late seventies, our lives were always on the record. Everyone in the family was fodder for his *Private Lives* columns. He never named anyone, so it seemed people would always attribute to whichever daughter they knew whatever mortifying moment he had revealed in the service of an elegant point. For the record, I was the girl with the galaxy of freckles, and Amy did all the embarrassing things.

John named his alter ego in *Private Lives* Dmitri, after the brother Karamazov.

It always puzzled people, who thought of him surely as an Ivan, the serious intellectual. But Dmitri was the one besotted with love and drink, as John was besotted with my mother and scotch.

The novel's central act is patricide, and John thought a lot about fatherhood, about being a father and a stepfather, about the fathers who disappoint and destroy. When he taught criticism at Columbia, his first assignment was to trash a classic, and his last assignment was always for the students to review their fathers. And then they would all go out and get drunk.

John had his stock stories that we all knew—the time they made him kill a rattlesnake and make it into a belt at a logging camp, turning him into a pacifist forever after, or the time he was a young sophomore putting an issue of the *Harvard Crimson* to bed in the wee hours of the morning and heard the voice of a young Joan Baez lifting transcendent into the Cambridge night. Right before he dropped out.

But the story he told more than any other was his Kobo Abe story. Every time he found a fresh audience, he would launch into his Kobo Abe story, and we would get up to clear the dishes. It was a wonderful story: On a trip to Japan in 1982, John met the novelist Kobo Abe. Abe had fallen into a deep depression and writer's block after reading *One Hundred Years of Solitude*, certain that he could never hope to write anything as great. Several days later, Gabriel García Márquez was awarded the Nobel Prize, and John, drawing on his limited knowledge of Japanese culture, honor, and hara-kiri, feared the worst. He raced to Abe's house, where his wife greeted John at the door and told him that Kobo was happily writing away upstairs. "García Márquez has won the Nobel Prize," she explained. "Since he is now among the immortals, there is no longer any question of competition."

John was in a lot of pain his last year, his lungs being drained and filling up with fluid every day, an infinitely renewable resource no one wanted, but he was never late with his copy. The first regular deadline he missed—I'm fairly certain in his life—was the *Harper's* column due two days after he died.

How do we make sense of the deaths of our loved ones, of their physical absence? Where does that intelligence, that amassing of knowledge, and the thirteen thousand books he famously read, go? We're a mixed family, both atheists and agnostics, but I know that John has joined the immortals.

Jane O'Reilly, writer

I remember meeting John. He and I were walking from separate directions down Plympton Street in Cambridge when we ran into a mutual friend who was an editor at the *Harvard Crimson*. My friend had once casually remarked that "you can always tell when a woman has written a story," a remark that pretty much put me off trying out for the *Crimson*, even though I remained a groupie. It was 1957. John was a freshman and had just successfully gone through a *Crimson* competition. (Hard to have guessed he would become the only man on the entire staff of the *New York Times* to join with the women's suit in 1974.) He was sunny, taller than he looked, slightly owlish, and given to chuckling. He was marked for stardom, in that small *Crimson* firmament. But then, unaccountably, he never returned after the following summer. Gone back to California. Mysterious.

I spent many, many happy evenings at what became John's house on the Upper East Side. Christmas Eve we usually spent at my apartment, for a party that now seems to have been astonishingly lavish and delightful, topped off by gathering around my old pump organ while someone who could actually play it led us in a carol sing. John's favorite was "We Three Kings." He would begin chuckling with anticipation as we approached the fourth verse and dolefully belt out

> *Myrrh is mine its bitter perfume*
> *Breathes a life of gathering gloom*
> *Sorrowing sighing bleeding dying*
> *Sealed in the stone cold tomb.*

And then, one Christmas in the early eighties, John fell over the piano stool, landed on his back on the floor, and I realized he was almost too drunk to stand up. We both stopped drinking not too long after that, although I think I might have been a year earlier. Sometimes we spoke about going to meetings, having a sponsor, thinking about stupid slogans that worked. But not very much. We were on separate trains, going to the same destination. Oddly, I think his writing flourished in sobriety; he cast his wonderfully intelligent net even wider, and chuckled more. Although, perhaps, he became something more of a hermit, barricaded in his small study behind a wall of new books. My writing career, on the other hand, seemed to dissolve. What interests me at this moment is remembering, with brand-new astonishment, what incredible buoyancy John gave to my life, my career, and our friendship.

He didn't give off that distinctly New York odor, slightly electrical and slightly rancid, of ambition. Perhaps I am fooling myself about his confidence, but in my memory, he managed to allow me to take my own talent for granted, for a while, and how I wish he were here right now so we could talk about how remarkable it all, in fact, was.

Victor Navasky, *The Nation*

I first met John in the summer of 1958. I was editing and publishing a tall, thin journal of political satire named *Monocle*. One day I saw in the *Harvard Crimson* a 750-word take-no-prisoners assault on our magazine. The byline: John Leonard, who turned out to be a Harvard sophomore. The review, which was packed with the dazzling literary-political-cultural-sociological allusions that in later years came to be recognized as Leonard's signature, attacked *Monocle* for its provenance (Yale), its shape (phallic), its style (insufficiently funny), and its content. (McCarthyism was yesterday's target—enough already.) Other than that . . .

I have now had a chance to refresh my recollection and pulled the original review from the *Crimson*'s archive. I realize I did not begin to do it justice. Here is Leonard's lede:

> In this somber age of Nixon, Nikes, and Maidenform bras, we make very few demands on anyone with the courage to be funny. But even within this abysmal temperance, we look at the latest issue of *Monocle* (a magazine of political satire) much like the young man watching his mother-in-law plunge over a cliff in his brand new Cadillac—with mixed emotions.

Naturally I sent Leonard a note, congratulating him on his parody of a book review and inviting him to write for us, and *mirabile dictu*, as William F. Buckley, Jr., his subsequent employer, might have said, five years later, he finally got around to it—in the form of a brilliant parody of a letter from Whittaker Chambers to his grandchildren.

And what with one thing and another, when in 1967 Christopher Lehman-Haupt called to say that the *New York Times Book Review* was looking to hire a young editor and I threw Leonard's name into the pot, all I knew was that he was hired and fifteen minutes later he had risen from subeditor to books columnist, to editor in chief. Among his references for the job, one William F. Buckley, Jr., had submitted to the powers that be at the *Times* the definitive proof that Leonard was not a secret *National Review* conservative—his *Monocle* essay parodying Buckley and Co.

Gloria Steinem, feminist

John entered my life in 1967. We were a few writers and editors who met in each other's living rooms to plot what we were sure was a daring action: refusing to pay the part of our income tax that went to the Vietnam War. Eventually, four hundred people signed the Writers and Editors War Tax Protest, thus tempting the ire of the IRS.

John had much better ideas for a title than such a lumpy and literal one. As it turned out, we could have risked one of John's catchier titles. Not only did the *New York Times* refuse to publish this ad, but our radical action turned out to be like punching a pillow. The IRS took no legal measures against us, just took the money out of our bank accounts.

It's hard to feel rebellious if no one notices. John came to our rescue. He pointed out that going through a long legal process to attach each of our bank accounts had cost the government more than it collected, and also that we had invented a new way of voting.

This is what I remember most: John's kindness. His intelligence and enthusiasm and sense of humor and sense of justice are all super-clear from his writing, but it's possible that, to know the depth of his kindness, you had to be there.

No matter what grandiose or smartass or scared thing one of us came up with in those months of meetings, John somehow managed to appreciate it and also transform it into something better. He made us feel smarter than we were. Because he was also fearless in attacking any person or event that was unkind, we knew he had high standards, yet he also helped us believe we could meet them.

It is not easy to be outraged and to be kind at the same time, but John was. He had the courage to go out on a limb, to care, to praise, to fall in love with creations and minds not his own.

The Japanese novelist Haruki Murakami, when he accepted the Jerusalem Prize, and was worried that he might seem to be on one side or the other, said, "Between a high, solid wall and an egg that breaks against it, I will always stand on the side of the egg."

John, too, was always on the side of the egg.

Esther Broner, writer

It was 1977, winter in Peterborough, New Hampshire. We had to walk the icy grounds of the MacDowell Colony with cleats clipped onto our shoes. A group of us colonists were seated together over dinner each night discussing John Leonard's *Private Lives* in the *New York Times*. We had a right to the column for we were the John Leonard Fan Club.

Leonard, our mentor, was in love: in love with literature, his children, the teacher—"the woman in the house"—with community, friendship, baseball. He spoke of friends, some "halfway through the novels of their lives and worried about the next couple of chapters." Or friends "who burn holes in your patience." He wrote of what he dared not tell his son: "that sacrifice was reciprocity; grace and mercy, love and justice are more than just ideas."

"We need T-shirts to formalize this loose group," said the printmaker Judith Plotnick. She had to go to the city on business and promised to stop off at the *Times* for a photograph. "What's it for?" asked the picture editor. "T-shirts." No one at the *Times* ever had T-shirts made for them.

We did not have a means of transferring photo to T-shirt in Peterborough, so Judith painstakingly drew the picture by hand for each club member; the lines became indistinct with repetition. His features began to vanish; he had the vagueness, the aura of a choirboy.

We didn't know in life if he was ever a choirboy, but to us his words were holy writ.

Jill Krementz, photographer

My husband, Kurt Vonnegut, and I joined Sue and John for regular Sunday dinners throughout the many years of our friendship. Sometimes we would meet up in their neighborhood, sometimes in ours. It was always more about conversation than food, though we all liked Italian the best. John loved to have a medium-rare pork chop, Kurt went with the linguini and clam sauce . . . and a Manhattan, which I would share. Sue was mostly vegetarian and I liked the veal piccata. Sometimes John's mother would join us and when she did, she and Kurt could find themselves conspiratorially aligned in making periodic breaks for the bar where they could have a cigarette. Mostly we talked about politics and books. Kurt thought John was the smartest man he knew. We all did.

Eden Ross Lipson,
The New York Times Book Review

What is remarkable about the golden era of the *Times Book Review*, from the time John took charge at the end of 1970, until well after he left it to become a cultural critic in 1975, is that there was only one new person on the staff, me. The change—and it was immediate, explosive, and thrilling— was made by the same staff of veteran editors that had put out the polite and predictable *Book Review* before.

John was the conductor, the ringmaster, the soloist leading an increasingly professionally merry, daring band. As before, the books poured in; previewing editors went through stacks of galleys. The oldest convention prevailed: You can tell great books and terrible books pretty quickly, so you spend most of your time trying to be fair and supportive to what lies in the middle. The physical *Book Review*—a big, high-ceilinged room with large steel desks, grimy linoleum floors, pigeons on the windowsills, clacking typewriters—belonged to a once-upon-a-time era of newspapers. The work, making sense of never-ending stacks of books, was familiar. It was the permission, John's encouragement, that made it new and fun.

No review could or can stop a big commercial title, but it was giddying to see how an intelligent, enthusiastic review could start a national conversation about a book. Dig, look, see what you can find. Have fun.

"John, I found a book at the bottom of the stack. Just a quarter page in the back of the publisher's catalogue, but not like anything I've ever read. Take a look, we should do something with it." *The Woman Warrior.*

The *Book Review* was a kind of catbird seat, spotting issues forming on the horizon of the nation's consciousness, calling attention to what was coming, not just what was past.

It was thrilling. And it was fun. Oh, but it was fun.

Letty Cottin Pogrebin, writer

In an Either/Or world, John Leonard lived a Both/And life.

He was *both* a fair-minded journalist *and* an unreconstructed leftie, a formidable intellect *and* a regular guy, a deeply contemplative man *and* a person who, when pleased, absolutely twinkled. His voice was distinctive and engaging, consistent and true, both in print *and* broadcast media, highbrow periodicals *and* pop culture venues, editorial meetings *and* his friends' living rooms.

Most people remember John for his Brobdingagian literary talents, the copious Leonardian essays whose spiraling sentences, coruscating images, and stunning metaphors dazzled as they edified and whose criticism managed to be both trenchant and generous.

I remember him for all of that but also for the way he treated women. At a time when most men boxed us into simplistic bifurcated stereotypes— *either* we were smart *or* pretty, pussycats *or* ball-breakers, Eve Harrington *or* June Cleaver—John saw us in full. He never prejudged or pigeonholed us, our prose, our minds. He took women seriously.

I met him in 1967 when he first joined the *New York Times Book Review.* At the time, I was the director of publicity for Bernard Geis Associates, a small publishing house that specialized in what used to be called "nonbooks"—tomes by boldfaced names like TV host Art Linkletter or heavyweight champion Floyd Patterson.

Though it was obvious that few of the titles on Geis's lists merited notice in the *TBR,* John always let me do my job, which was to pitch my company's books with the strongest arguments I could muster. Once that pro forma exercise was out of the way, however, John and I would talk about real books and real writers, about radical politics, the Vietnam War, how much we loathed Lyndon Johnson and Richard Nixon.

Doubleday published my own first book, *How To Make It in a Man's World*, in 1970. I didn't pitch it to John, who by then was a powerful daily book critic for the *Times*, but somehow he took notice of it and gave me a rave review. Instantly, astonishingly, his review brought assignments to my doorstep, and within weeks of its publication, I was able to quit my job at Geis and write full-time.

From 1971 to 1975, when he was editor of the Sunday *Times Book Review*, I wrote reviews for him after receiving his standard advice: Don't pan a book unless absolutely necessary. Don't flex your writerly muscles, show off your superior knowledge, or trot out your bitingly clever ripostes at the expense of another writer's dignity. Be true to your critical assessment of the book but never forget that behind the author's name on the title page stands a person who is feeling exposed and vulnerable right now and who may have spent years of his or her life trying to make that book the best it could be. Don't cut your career teeth on the flesh of a fellow or sister writer.

I've known dozens of editors over the last forty-odd years but never one quite like John Leonard who was both a brilliant cultural arbiter *and* a spectacularly decent human being.

Celia McGee, critic

At the summit of summonses I haven't been able to refuse, I would put the offer of a job in the mideighties editing four of *New York* magazine's cultural critics, John Leonard included.

But John wasn't someone you just included. Certainly not I. He was the Zeus of the Mt. Olympus of writing I aspired someday to climb—and also, since John had long been washed in the waters of feminism, its Hera and Athena.

Assigned to edit John's weekly television column, that's exactly not what I did. Oh, sure, I might fine-tune the punctuation in some of his gorgeously concatenatious sentences, or make sure he didn't repeat a phrase from columns gone by. Occasionally one of his pitch-perfect historical references would draw us down lanes of intellectual memories, or make us laughingly speculate about which political firecracker he had planted in his prose might incense the magazine's higher-ups. He avoided those in authority like a plague of neocons—his old habit had been to sneak in early and drop off his copy while the office was still empty—but with me he was a softie, and would actually come in late enough for a chat.

One of my proudest moments came in 2006, when the National Book Critics Circle board, of which I was a member, took my suggestion (and Linda Wolfe's and Art Winslow's) that John receive its Ivan Sandrof Lifetime Achievement Award.

John already had the most brilliant daughter, son, and stepdaughter, yet he made room for the acolyte I had wanted to be since I first read his essays in college, a place where he was mythic as the genius who had had the good sense (and sense of humor) there to drop out. He used to tell me stories about how he headed back home to California, and UC Berkeley, and Pacifica Radio, where he brought on Pauline Kael. That staffing account always conjured for me a vision of John and the tiny, pugnacious, bescarved Kael drifting offshore on a broadcast schooner, yucking it up about Godard, Elizabeth Taylor, and Marx.

John taught me, above all, how to *be*: to stick to my love of a particular kind of writing and thinking, to my principles, to my ideals, to my moral guns. He was a sharpshooter at that, John Leonard, a pacifist straight-shooter if ever there was one.

Maureen Corrigan, critic

I always tell people who ask how I became the book critic on *Fresh Air* that I owe my job to two lucky breaks—one of them being John Leonard.

Back in 1988, *Fresh Air* contacted me and asked if I would whittle down and record a first-person exposé I'd written for the *Village Voice* about the loony way AP English exams were being graded. Of course, I jumped at the chance. I eventually recorded the commentary, and, since the folks at *Fresh Air* liked it, they asked if I would be interested in doing occasional book reviews. But, first, they had to check with John Leonard, the show's weekly book reviewer. His response was: "Sure, bring her on. There are plenty of good books to go around."

Think about that response and ask yourself how many people you know (including yourself) would be so generous.

I only met John once—on a picket line (of course!) for striking *Daily News* writers. But I owe my over-twenty-year career in what has to be one of the best jobs in literary journalism to him. I took over as weekly book reviewer after John left *Fresh Air*, but he has never been replaced.

That's because—as I always make sure to tell those people who ask how I got my job at *Fresh Air*—John Leonard was the best all-round culture critic of our time.

Gene Seymour, New York *Newsday*

The late New York *Newsday* fused broadsheet intelligence with tabloid sass—a combination that worked well enough for the paper's Long Island parent company, but drew the dismissive "tabloid-in-a-tutu" tagline, mostly from proprietors of competing metropolitan dailies. Nevertheless, those of us lucky to have worked there loitered long enough in higher and lower precincts of the profession to know a noble experiment when we saw one.

Certainly John did. To tease at one of his favorite analogies, he liked to imagine himself as an itinerant honky-tonk singer roaming the back roads and lower-profile interstates in search of any venue where he could sing his songs as he wished. And when *Newsday* gave John his own column to rhapsodize about all things cultural and/or political, he made himself comfortable enough to tell his readers why S. J. Perlman looked less silly in retrospect than Hunter S. Thompson or what Michael Dukakis should have said in the 1988 presidential debate when asked whether he'd change his mind about capital punishment if his wife were raped and murdered. John hand-delivered these glittering missives to *Newsday*'s Manhattan newsroom each week and, because he was our emissary to the upper reaches of the literary world, some of us idling between our own daily assignments would try to catch him on the way in (or out) in search of anecdotes, quips, and bon mots about books and the people who wrote them.

He seemed, however, far less interested in lit-chat than in whatever we reporters, reviewers, and editors happened to be working on or talking about. What did we think about last night's candidates' debate or Knicks game? What about Al Sharpton's latest rhetorical heave into the power structure's end zone? These discussions would veer seamlessly and blithely into other, less lofty areas of mutual concern; for instance, the TV series *La Femme Nikita*. He pledged allegiance to the title character while I confessed to an unhealthy fascination with her darkly enigmatic boss, Madeleine. I knew he was gathering intelligence for future installments of his weekly reports from the cultural fronts. But who wouldn't be honored to have one's brain picked by John Leonard, for whom no genre, no endeavor, no person was alien or bereft of interest?

Ramon Parkins, *CBS Sunday Morning*

Many, many years ago I read a John Leonard review, in the *New York Review of Books*—it took a month. It sent me running to the nearest bookstore for material evidence and supporting tools, collections of short stories, photocopied pages of obscure long-lost periodicals, and a pound of coffee. Lord, I decided . . . life is too short. I don't know why I didn't put it together—that the guy who made me question the very worth of my college degree was the same guy now on my television set on *Sunday Morning*, talking about television, and movies, and yes, books.

When did this guy get out—when did he have fun? Fun is what happens to you while you are busy reading other book reviews.

Years later I would have the honor of being the last in a line of John's television producers, hoping to match picture to the well-structured language John put on the page. My job, as I quickly learned, was to keep the gatekeepers from screwing with the copy. Simple enough. I failed miserably. I gained a friend and a mentor.

John smoked Tareytons—the same brand as my father. I would share hours in his office waiting for our piece to be screened and we would talk, about family, Dennis Potter, Cold War dreams, twelve steps, the long march to freedom, and Dana Delaney. And the seven words you cannot say on television: "Complicated," "Scruple," "Grace," "Wit," "Truth," and "Primo Levi."

John was a small-d democrat—and television long before the Internet was our public square, a place where we could see ourselves, imagine our better selves, our hopes and our dreams. We who labor in this medium on our best days still believe that.

Jennifer Szalai, *Harper's*

I remember little about my first encounter with John, though it would mark the start of an almost continuous correspondence over the sixty-nine months that we would work together on his New Books column for *Harper's* magazine. What I do remember is having an acute awareness of who John Leonard was and trying to mask my nervousness with a timorous kind of high-handedness. I was clinging to the young, inexperienced editor's fixed idea of her job description. I was an editor, and an editor is supposed to edit, right?

So I would send memos back to John in which I worried over every other sentence, with queries that were sometimes helpful and sometimes not, and I soon learned what was least helpful was the long-winded interrogation into whether he *really* meant X, when one might also say Y, but if he did mean X it was okay, as long as he *really* meant it. John would usually respond to such an inquiry with a terse "YES. STET," a phrase that I will always associate with him. He was the only writer I worked with every single month, and it was from him—with him—that I learned the importance of directness and the art of what another *Harper's* editor called "the judo move": the small change that has a big effect. As an editor he had worked with so many writers, and as a writer he had worked with so many editors, that he would sometimes make reference to the "bullying" that he believed was characteristic of the business, but then I also got the sense that John, who cared so deeply about reading and writing that it was as much a moral and existential activity as it was an intellectual one, wouldn't have had it any other way.

Mary Gordon, writer

I want to speak to a particular contribution John Leonard made to the world of letters, and that is the unparalleled support he gave to women writers. In this, he did a great deal to create a new breed of critic. If you look at the landscape of American letters before the 1970s when John first made his mark, it is a landscape remarkably short on women. But John Leonard always went out of his way to anoint the women writers who excited his admiration. Among his harem were Toni Morrison, Maxine Hong Kingston, Cynthia Ozick, and Louise Erdrich, to name only a few.

I'll never forget the day, nearly thirty years ago, when I was read over the phone John's review of my first novel, *Final Payments*. John's was my first national review. I felt like a ship that had been launched by a fragrant spiced breeze gently but forcefully introducing me into the larger sea. And this is what John did for so many of us: He made us believe that the reader of our dreams is out there, waiting for us, listening, supporting, understanding, seeing, hoping always for our best, never relishing our missteps but cheering us on in this ridiculous enterprise in which we are all involved.

John (paraphrasing Virginia Woolf), we thank you for giving us the courage to hold on to our vision, for refusing the headmaster's job, the measuring rod, the highly ornamental pot in favor of the spiced breeze upon which our visions test their tentative and fragile wings.

Toni Morrison, writer

John,

You were the first—I suspect only—critic/reviewer to read and judge my work without condescension or patronage. You stood out as being a man who cherished books, and whose disappointment was never animosity toward or contempt for an author—but simply your documented yearning for the best the text could have been. You avoided the blatant but easy pride some critics take in verbal toxin.

But more than that, much more, you were, as one of my characters says, "a friend of my mind."

How did I know? I saw and shared your raucous joy at a party at my house; the delight you took in the goings-on in Stockholm in 1993—its seriousness, its drama, and its fun. And always there were your eager eyes, curiosity, keen intelligence, and laughter.

Big love,
Toni

Maureen Howard, writer

In the kindest way, not a touch of condescension, John Leonard instructed me on bloggers. That would have been 2003. He had edited *These United States*, a collection of essays. I had conjured the history of my beloved Connecticut from "Sinners in the Hands of an Angry God" to the show-manship of P. T. Barnum, the Colt repeating rifle, and Clare Boothe Luce, but I was clearly behind the Internet times. John, with energy, and often urgency, connected us to the current scene of where we were, the then and now in our U.S.A., the unsocial network of the homeless and privi-leged, the idiot box running on empty, the many things we may not need yet buy at discount including, lest we forget, a war in Vietnam.

There was that heartrending apologia to many of his complaints, the hope that turning back for an instant might alleviate his painful view of the moral scene. The other side of his despair was the joy that John gave his readers, his pleasure in pop culture; and then again his admiration for that comic spirit from on high, Beckett. He was, don't you know, very smart and ever so learned. Dante to Derrida with only a touch of the professorial when he wished to step up to the podium. Performative yes, Leonard's side glance and/or exuberant display at "gaudy false bottom narratives and its dreamy disinformation, spooking has been postmodern long before there ever was a Jaguar, a Jacuzzi, or a Sorbonne. *Counterintelligent!*"

That night when we were about to drive home after celebrating the mapping of Alaska to Wisconsin, Sue Leonard; my husband, Mark Probst; Richard Lingeman; and John were stuffed in our Subaru Legend. I tried, but could not get my seat belt hitched. Leaning from the backseat John tugged until, safe at last, we took off for uptown. Seat belt frayed but still sturdy. It was then that I asked about blogs and don't I wish I had said: Please just keep the pages coming, hard copy your lifeline of words—wise, witty, deeply spelled out—thrown out to us, to me if you will, a girl from a factory town in Connecticut come to the Imperial City. Blog from the beyond if you will. We are in need of a reality check in *These United States,* of your honesty, anger, and wit to tell us who we are, who we may be.

Eduardo Galeano,
on learning of John's death

i am drunk, or trying to be,
i am crying, like a baby would be,
i knew it would happen
but it doesn't help,
and i ask why,
why,
why,
and i perfectly know why
but it doesn't help.

Grateful acknowledgment is made for permission to reprint the following selections (some of which have been edited for this book):

Fresh Air, National Public Radio: "Peggy Noonan's *What I Saw at the Revolution*" (1990); "*No Turning Back*, Barbara Ferraro and Patricia Hussey, with Jane O'Reilly" (1990); "Philip Roth's *Patrimony*" (1991). *Fresh Air with Terry Gross* is produced by WHYY in Philadelphia, and distributed by NPR.

Harper's Magazine: "Richard Powers's *The Time of Our Singing*." Copyright © 2003 by *Harper's Magazine*. All rights reserved. Reproduced from the January issue by special permission.

The Harvard Crimson: "The Cambridge Scene" (1958); "Pasternak's Hero: Man Against the Monoliths" (1959). © 2012 The Harvard Crimson, Inc. All rights reserved. Reprinted with permission.

The Nation: "Tom Wolfe's *The Bonfires of the Vanities* and Jim Sleeper's *In Search of New York*" (issue of November 28, 1987); "Don DeLillo's *Libra*" (September 19, 1988); "Salman Rushdie's *The Satanic Verses*" (March 13, 1989); "Thomas Pynchon's *Vineland*" (February 26, 1990); "Günter Grass: Bad Boys and Fairy Tales" (December 24, 1990); "Milan Kundera's *Immortality*" (June 10, 1991); "Norman Mailer's *Harlot's Ghost*" (November 18, 1991); "Dear Bill" (November 18, 1991); "Meeting David Grossman" (October 17, 1994); "Eduardo Galeano Walks Some Words" (June 26, 1995); "Amos Oz in the Desert" (November 11, 1996); "Morrison's Paradise Lost" (January 26, 1998); "Ralph Ellison, Sort Of (Plus Hemingway and Salinger)" (June 14, 1999); "Bill Ayers's *Fugitive Days*" (October 15, 2001); "Jacobo Timerman, Renaissance Troublemaker" (December 6, 1999; revised 2004). Reprinted with permission from *The Nation* magazine.

The New Press: "When Studs Listens, Everyone Else Talks" and "The Last Innocent White Man" from *The Last Innocent White Man in America* by John Leonard (1993); "Ed Sullivan Died for Our Sins" (originally published in *A Really Big Show*, text by John Leonard, edited by Claudia Falkenburg and Andrew Solt, Viking Studio) and "Family Values, Like the House of Atreus" from *Smoke and Mirrors* by John Leonard (1997); "Amazing Grace" (speech at the Arts Club) from *When the Kissing Had to Stop* by John Leonard (1999); and "Why Socialism Never Happened Here" (originally published in *Salon*) from *Lonesome Rangers* by John Leonard (2002). Grateful acknowledgment is made to The New Press for permission to reprint these works. Certain pieces appeared under different titles.

The New York Review of Books: "Blowing His Nose in the Wind" (under the title "Liaisons Dangereuses," issue of July 19, 2001); "Jonathan Lethem's *Men and Cartoons*, *The Disappointment Artist*, and *The Fortress of Solitude*" (April 7, 2005); "Joan Didion's *The Year of Magical Thinking*" (October 20, 2005); "Michael Chabon's *The Yiddish Policeman's Union*" (June 14, 2007). © *The New York Review of Books*.

The New York Times: "Nabokov's *Ada*" (Books of The Times; The Nobel-est Writer of Them All, issue of May 1, 1969); "Doris Lessing's *The Four-Gated City*" (Books of The Times; Another List, December 4, 1969); "Gabriel García Márquez's *One Hundred Years of Solitude*" (Books of The Times; Myth Is Alive in Latin America, March 3, 1970); "Supergirl Meets the Sociologist" (Books of The Times; Supergirl Meets the Sociologist, April 15, 1970); "Arthur Koestler's *Arrow in the Blue* and *The Invisible Writing*" (Books of The Times; Teaching the 20th Century, June 23, 1970); "Maxine Hong Kingston's *The Woman Warrior*" (In Defiance of 2 Worlds, September 17, 1976); "Edward Said's *Orientalism*" (Books of The Times; Reviewing the Specialists Eden and Babylon, December 1, 1978); "Robert Stone's *A Flag for Sunrise*" (Books of The Times; October 16, 1981); "Maureen Howard, *Big as Life*" (Up From Bridgeport, July 1, 2001). © 1969, 1970, 1976, 1978, 2001 The New York Times. All rights reserved. Used by permission and protected by the copyright laws of the United States. The printing, copying, redistribution, or retransmission of this content without express written permission is prohibited.

Newsday: "Nan Robertson's *Getting Better*." From *Newsday* © 1988. All rights reserved. Used by permission and protected by the copyright laws of the United States. The printing, copying, redistribution, or retransmission of the material without express written permission is prohibited.

Pacifica KPFA: "Richard Nixon's *Six Crises*," © 1962 courtesy of the Pacifica Radio Archives

Playboy: Gay Talese's "Thy Neighbor's Wife," *Playboy* magazine (May 1980). Copyright © 1980 by *Playboy*. Reprinted with permission. All rights reserved.

"A Dance to John" © 2009 by Jules Feiffer. From the collection of Sue Leonard. Reprinted by artist's permission.

The following works, some in differet form, were previously published:

Ms. Magazine: "AIDS Is Everywhere" (1988); "On the Beat at *Ms.*" (1988)

The National Review: "The Demise of Greenwich Village" (1958); "The Ivory Tower" (1959)

The following selections, some under different titles, also appeared in John Leonard anthologies published by The New Press:

"Doris Lessing's *The Four-Gated City*"; "Don DeLillo's *Libra*"; "Salman Rushdie's *The Satanic Verses*"; "Milan Kundera's *Immortality*"; "Günter Grass: Bad Boys and Fairy Tales"; and "Norman Mailer's *Harlot's Ghost*" in *The Last Innocent White Man in America* (1993); "Edward Said's *Orientalism*"; "Meeting David Grossman"; "Eduardo Galeano Walks Some Words"; "Amos Oz in the Desert"; "Morrison's Paradise Lost" in *When the Kissing Had to Stop* (1999); "Ralph Ellison, Sort of (Plus Hemingway and Salinger)"; and "Blowing His Nose in the Wind" in *Lonesome Rangers* (2002).

The following pieces are published for the first time in this collection:

Speech at Brearley School, New York: "Reading for My Life," 1996
Speech at the 92nd Street Y, New York: "Citizen Doctorow," 2006
Speech at the Swedish Embassy of the United Nations: "The Last Innocent White Man," 2007
"Sgt. Pepper's Lonely Hearts Club Band (on Václav Havel)," 2007